Fodor's 2001

New Orleans

Fodor's Travel Publications • New York, Toronto, London, Sydney, Auckland
www.fodors.com

CONTENTS

MAPS

Circled letters in text correspond to letters on the photographs. For more information on the sights pictured, turn to the indicated page number ⒶⳆ on each photograph.

DESTINATION NEW ORLEANS

Day in and day out, New Orleans may be the most festive city in the world. Many destinations have a single celebratory season—Rio its Carnival, Edinburgh its Festival—but when the party's over, life reverts to a workday pace. In New Orleans the party is never quite over. Official celebrations fill up the calendar, from the most famous, Mardi Gras, to the less so— try the Great French Market Tomato Festival. And even when there's no official fete in the works, New Orleans parties on, to the beat of some of the best traditional jazz in the world. Down here when they say, *"Laissez les bons temps rouler!"* they're not kidding. When you visit New Orleans, be ready to let the good times roll.

Daytime, before *les bons temps* get seriously rolling, is perfect for appreciating the distinctive look of New Orleans—part Deep South, part

Ⓐ 54

Caribbean French Colonial, with a dash of local quirkiness thrown in. This architectural brew can be seen in all its splendor in the French Quarter. The Creole-style Ⓓ**LaBranche Houses** stand out with their filigreed cast-iron balconies. Just down the block at the Ⓔ**Cabildo,** the colonial style is Span-

ARCHITECTURE

Ⓑ 164

ish (they, too, had a brief run here), and the history is thick. Move on to the Garden District, where showbiz meets Spanish moss. More than a few celebrities call the District home, at least part-time. Novelist Anne Rice was born here and uses familiar landmarks as settings in her books. A walking tour of the area will lead you to Ⓐ**Robinson House,** the loveliest of all the area's elegant antebellum homes, and will whet your appetite for a day trip along the Great River Road. The Deep South gets no deeper than this. Majestic plantation homes such as Destrehan, Oak Alley, Laura, and Houmas House dot the landscape. You can spend the night in Ⓑ**Nottoway** plantation, the grandest and indisputably the largest, which has more columns than most dwellings have windows. Back in town at

Ⓒ 34

the historic ©**St. Louis Cemetery #1,** guided tours weave through the maze of crypts. The young Peter Fonda and Dennis Hopper tripped out here in *Easy Rider*—demonstrating, at least on film, that in New Orleans any place is a potential party zone.

Ⓔ 24

Ⓐ 80

DINING

Ⓑ 75

Ⓒ 90

This is a city that revels in the pleasures of the palate, so it's no wonder that some visitors come to New Orleans primarily for the food. The unique cuisine blends elements of French, Caribbean, African, and Spanish cookery. Crawfish is one star ingredient that can be served boiled, fried, and garnished in distinctive ways. The delicious sauces at handsome Ⓐ**Galatoire's,** perfected since 1905, set the standard. Arnaud's, Brennan's, and Broussard's are esteemed as well. Contemporary cuisine also flourishes, sometimes updating traditional fare. As in France, chefs here achieve a measure of fame.

Some, like Frank Brigsten of Brigsten's and Ⓕ**Susan Spicer** of Bayona, have followers among the most passionate food lovers. Cajun maestro Ⓑ**Paul Prudhomme** of K-Paul's Louisiana Kitchen—seen on TV and on your supermarket's spice shelf—is a real celebrity. So is Emeril Lagasse, of Ⓒ**Emeril's,** among other dining establishments. But sometimes it's the setting, not the food, that's the draw. Both locals and visitors make their way to the Ⓓ**Napoleon House Bar and Cafe,** a study in faded grandeur under murmuring ceiling fans. And everyone loves the simple, congenial Ⓔ**Praline Connection,** as much

for the tidy dining room as the yummy southern-Creole cooking. More casual still is the Central Grocery, the much celebrated purveyor of the *muffuletta* sandwich, made with cold cuts, cheese, and chopped olives. Seemingly it's nothing special, but the taste will leave you questing to re-create it back home.

A⟩ 124

MUSIC

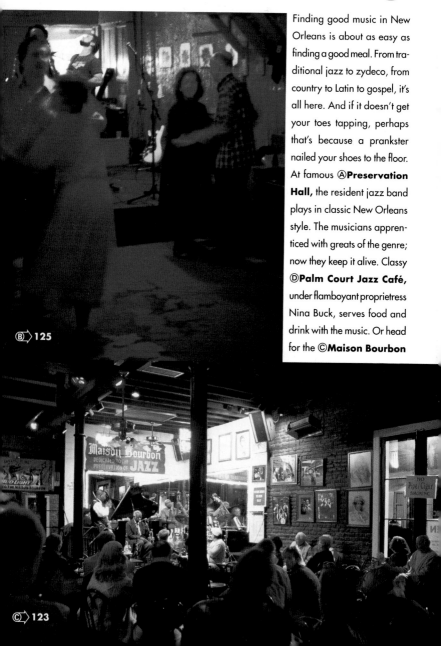

Finding good music in New Orleans is about as easy as finding a good meal. From traditional jazz to zydeco, from country to Latin to gospel, it's all here. And if it doesn't get your toes tapping, perhaps that's because a prankster nailed your shoes to the floor. At famous Ⓐ**Preservation Hall,** the resident jazz band plays in classic New Orleans style. The musicians apprenticed with greats of the genre; now they keep it alive. Classy Ⓓ**Palm Court Jazz Café,** under flamboyant proprietress Nina Buck, serves food and drink with the music. Or head for the ©**Maison Bourbon**

Ⓑ⟩ 125

©⟩ 123

Ⓓ⟩124

for live jazz or the Ⓑ**Maple Leaf,** where you can dance to an eclectic range of funk bands. Seeing no reason why the party should end at a set hour, the city issues 24-hour liquor licenses. Seeing no reason why the music should end at sun-up, New Orleans musicians also work the day shift, like the lone sax player you might see on the Ⓕ**Riverwalk.** Note that in New Orleans, street music sometimes beats club music. And you can still have "big fun on the bayou" at dance halls in Cajun Country and see local musicians in their element in Ⓔ**St. Martinville** and environs.

Ⓕ⟩43

Ⓔ⟩177

Ⓐ 128

As if the music festival New Orleans offers nightly weren't enough, once a year, in late April and early May, the city pulls out all the stops. Thousands of performers—and hundreds of thousands of fans—converge on Fair Grounds Race Track and other venues around town for the annual ⒶⒷ©**New Orleans Jazz & Heritage Festival.** Great jazz can be heard, but so can just about every other kind of music known in America, on no fewer than a dozen stages. Big names are everywhere at "Jazz Fest," but an even greater treat is hearing a talented headliner-to-be, or just enjoying a small-town band. Crafts and food stalls round out the festival, so you can eat well and do a bit of shopping between sets.

JAZZ FEST

Ⓑ 128

© 128

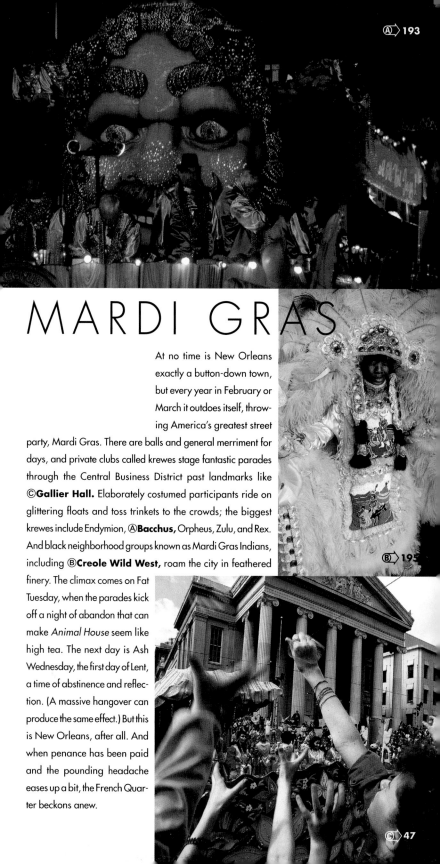

MARDI GRAS

At no time is New Orleans exactly a button-down town, but every year in February or March it outdoes itself, throwing America's greatest street party, Mardi Gras. There are balls and general merriment for days, and private clubs called krewes stage fantastic parades through the Central Business District past landmarks like ©**Gallier Hall.** Elaborately costumed participants ride on glittering floats and toss trinkets to the crowds; the biggest krewes include Endymion, Ⓐ**Bacchus,** Orpheus, Zulu, and Rex. And black neighborhood groups known as Mardi Gras Indians, including Ⓑ**Creole Wild West,** roam the city in feathered finery. The climax comes on Fat Tuesday, when the parades kick off a night of abandon that can make *Animal House* seem like high tea. The next day is Ash Wednesday, the first day of Lent, a time of abstinence and reflection. (A massive hangover can produce the same effect.) But this is New Orleans, after all. And when penance has been paid and the pounding headache eases up a bit, the French Quarter beckons anew.

GREAT ITINERARIES

New Orleans in 5 Days

New Orleans is a city to savor at a leisurely pace, mostly on foot and with an eye for the unusual and even outrageous. Children find it as fascinating as their parents do. Five days is time enough to capture the essence of the city and its environs.
☺ So that you don't show up somewhere and find the doors locked, shuffle the itinerary segments with closing days in mind.

DAY 1

Think Ⓑ French Quarter, the heart of the old city since its founding in 1718. The traditional breakfast of café au lait and beignets at Café du Monde on Jackson Square is a must. Walk along the riverfront and peek into intimate courtyards, galleries, and antiques shops on Chartres and Royal streets. Tour one of the house museums or the Cabildo. For lunch

Ⓑ▷ 20

have a po'boy sandwich or muffuletta, both classics. A carriage ride through the narrow streets gives you a bird's-eye view and a colorful local guide. Bourbon Street is jumping at night. Try a spicy seafood dish to the hot sounds of jazz or blues, and of course a Hurricane drink at Pat O'Brien's is de rigueur.
☺ This is fine any day but Monday, when many of the historic buildings are closed.

Ⓐ▷ 43

DAY 2

The streetcar is your ticket to Uptown and the Garden District with its antebellum mansions and ancient live oak trees. Take the St. Charles Avenue streetcar from the Central Business District, getting off at Washington Avenue for the Garden District houses. Lunch at Commander's Palace is straight out of an Anne Rice novel (her house is nearby). After you eat, take the streetcar to Audubon Park. A six-block walk on the pedestrian path brings you to Ⓒ Audubon Zoo, one of the country's best. After dinner at a bistro on Magazine Street, take in some live music at the legendary clubs uptown like Tipitina's or the Maple Leaf Bar.
☺ Don't do this on Sunday if you are interested along the route in Lafayette Cemetery or the Memorial Hall Confederate Museum. The House of Broel's Victorian Mansion and Doll House Museum are closed Monday.

DAY 3

It's back to nature in bayou country. Schedule a bus tour that takes you to a plantation upriver in the morning and on a swamp tour in the afternoon. Lunch is included. The plantation homes are beautifully restored to give you that Gone With the Wind feeling. From the boat in the swamp you'll learn about the birds, fish, and fauna—watch out for those alligators! Back in town extend the rural feel with lively Cajun and zydeco

music into the early morning hours downtown at Mulate's or Michaul's; you can grab a late dinner at either.
☺ This won't work on Sunday if you're exploring on your own, with a view toward stopping at one of the restaurants we list in Cajun Country, because many of them are closed then. If you are taking an escorted tour of the plantations and swamps, food will be provided, so any day will do.

DAY 4

Spend the day on the riverfront of the mighty Mississippi. Check out the Aquarium of the Americas and its IMAX theater. Then ride the ferry across the Mississippi for lunch on the other side in Algiers Point. The narrow streets of Victorian houses, most lovingly restored, invite an after-lunch stroll. A tour of Blaine Kern's Mardi Gras World lets you see how Carnival is done. A photo of you inside an elaborate costume is a great souvenir. Take the ferry back across the river for a front-seat view of the sunset and have dinner at the Ⓐ Riverwalk Marketplace. The evening can be capped with a run on the slot machines at Harrah's New Orleans casino or a return to Bourbon Street in the French Quarter nearby.
☺ These suggestions are good for any day of the week.

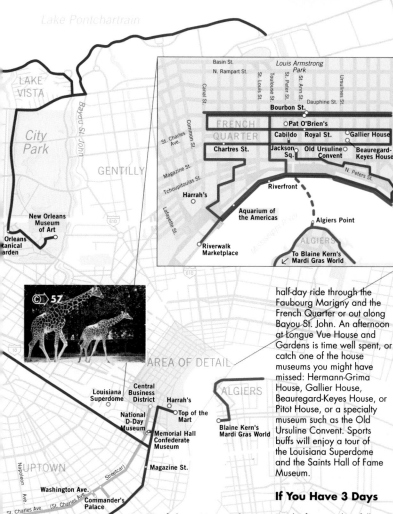

DAY 5

Art and Lake Pontchartrain beckon. Start the day with a tour of the New Orleans Museum of Art and the Botanical Garden, both in City Park. Hire a taxi to drive out along Lake Pontchartrain. You can pack a picnic lunch to eat on the lakeshore or try one of the seafood restaurants in West End. For the afternoon return to uptown and Magazine Street; you'll find lots of collectibles in the shops and galleries along this 5-mi "Street of Dreams," as it is dubbed. A tour of the National D-Day Museum (or of the Memorial Hall

Confederate Museum, for history buffs) on Lee Circle rounds out the day. Several five-star restaurants in the area are open for dinner. A nightcap in the Top of the Mart revolving lounge lets you toast high above the city's lights to your quick return to New Orleans.
🕑 *Never on Monday, when the New Orleans Museum of Art and the Botanical Garden are closed. The drive along Lake Pontchartrain is easier on weekdays, when two-way travel is allowed along Lakeshore Drive.*

If You Have More Time

There is always another famous restaurant or music venue to try. For daytime fun rent a bicycle from Bicycle Michael's and take a leisurely half-day ride through the Faubourg Marigny and the French Quarter or out along Bayou St. John. An afternoon at Longue Vue House and Gardens is time well spent, or catch one of the house museums you might have missed: Hermann-Grima House, Gallier House, Beauregard-Keyes House, or Pitot House, or a specialty museum such as the Old Ursuline Convent. Sports buffs will enjoy a tour of the Louisiana Superdome and the Saints Hall of Fame Museum.

If You Have 3 Days

For the first two days follow Day 1 and Day 2 above for major highlights of the city: the French Quarter, the Cabildo, a view of the Mississippi, Bourbon Street, the Garden District, and a streetcar ride. Trade a visit to the Audubon Zoo for one to the Aquarium of the Americas if fish are more your thing, or work in a ferry ride across the river. Recommended for the third day is a tour of a plantation home upriver for regional and historic flavor. Back in the city, take in one of the outstanding museums from Day 5 and save some time for browsing and shopping in the Warehouse District and on Magazine Street. Don't miss some Cajun or zydeco music.

1 EXPLORING NEW ORLEANS

Sure, there are sites of historical importance here, but to get the most out of your visit, sit on a levee along Old Man River and watch the boats roll along. Stroll through the French Quarter and note plant-filled balconies with their wrought iron dripping Mardi Gras beads. Wander down Bourbon Street and stop every few feet to catch a riff through a club's open door. Ride the St. Charles Avenue streetcar past pillared homes shrouded with live oaks. Type A personalities: wind down. This is the Big Easy.

T HERE'S AN OLD SONG, SO POPULAR IN THIS CITY, with the oft-quoted line, "Do you know what it means to miss New Orleans?" Each person might miss something different—barges and paddle wheelers on the mighty Mississippi, the unforgettable and inimitable cuisine, the lively and accomplished music, the rollicking nightlife, the languorous pace—but you will, inevitably, know.

By Mary
Gehman

Despite its sprawling size, to its residents New Orleans is intimate and small-town, made up of dozens of neighborhoods where families have lived within the same blocks for generations. Red beans and rice are served throughout the city on Monday, people visit the tombs of their departed on All Saints' Day, and from the smartest office to the most down-home local bar, folks are ready to celebrate anything at the drop of a hat. As they say in New Orleans, *laissez les bons temps rouler*— let the good times roll!

To experience this fun-filled city, you can begin with the usual tourist attractions, but you must go beyond them to linger in a corner grocery store, sip a cold drink in a local joint, or chat with a stoop-sitter. Orleanians love their city—most of them wouldn't live anywhere else. They treasure custom and tradition, take in stride the heat and humidity of a semitropical climate, and look at life with a laid-back attitude that makes New Orleans a close cousin to her Caribbean neighbors.

Getting Your Bearings

The city radiates from an 8-mi stretch between the Mississippi River and Lake Pontchartrain, covering roughly 365 square mi of flat, swamp-drained land. The heart of the city, downtown, includes the famous old French area called the Vieux Carré (Old Square), or the French Quarter; the Central Business District (CBD); and the riverfront. Across the river from downtown is an extension of New Orleans known as Westbank, which includes the areas of Algiers and Gretna.

The rest of the city of New Orleans is composed of four sections that spread out from Downtown: Uptown to the southwest, Mid-City to the north, and Faubourg Marigny and Gentilly to the east. Large suburban areas, such as Metairie and Kenner to the west and New Orleans East to the east, have developed in the past 30 years and today make up what is called Greater New Orleans.

Directions in a city that bases its compass on the curve of the river can be hopelessly confusing. Canal Street, a long avenue that runs from the river to the lake, divides the city roughly into uptown and downtown sections. Streets to the north of Canal are named North and run downtown; those to the south of Canal are named South and run uptown. Only the French Quarter is laid out in a grid pattern. Ask an Orleanian for directions and you are likely to hear about so many blocks downriver or upriver on the lake or river side. The best advice is to keep a map handy at all times.

New Orleans's housing patterns are very mixed. It is not uncommon to find mansions on one block and run-down tenements on the next, or nearby. Visitors should be alert to conditions around them, taking precautions not to wander alone on deserted streets or in questionable areas. New Orleans has a high crime rate. If in doubt about the safety of sites to visit, ask hotel personnel for advice, tour areas in groups when possible, and take a cab at night. (Areas requiring special precautions are noted throughout this chapter.)

The downtown and Algiers sections are best explored on foot because sites are near each other and should be experienced at a slow pace. For other areas, biking, driving, or riding the streetcar is recommended because of the long distances covered. Finding the unexpected is what makes New Orleans fun: the tours that follow are designed with that sense of adventure in mind.

The heart of New Orleans is the French Quarter, or Vieux Carré, a 6-by-12-block rectangle along the Mississippi River where the city was originally settled by the French in 1718. Here the Creoles (children born in the colony to French and Spanish settlers) built their stately town houses, cathedral, marketplace, opera houses, and theaters. And here, served by African slaves, they developed one of the most sophisticated styles of living in North America.

Much of this old-world influence began to fade when, in 1803, the Louisiana Purchase was signed and the Americans, who were predominantly Anglo-Saxon, moved into power. The Civil War in the 1860s put an end to the Golden Age of antebellum New Orleans, and the French Quarter went through years of decline and neglect. Only since the mid-20th century have the buildings been restored.

The Quarter is conventionally divided into Upper and Lower sections, with Jackson Square at the midpoint. The Upper French Quarter includes Jackson Square, the riverfront, and several immediate blocks toward Canal Street, containing the most frequented and photographed sites. If you have more time and stamina for walking, the Lower French Quarter, which includes the French Market, encompasses some exciting fringe places not as well known but well worth the effort. Beyond the Lower French Quarter, up Frenchmen Street, is Faubourg Marigny, an area developed in the early 1800s. This neighborhood is now home to a mélange of eateries, cafés, music clubs, and collectibles shops.

The Mississippi River dominates New Orleans, even passing through one corner of it. The corner on the west bank is called Algiers, which was settled in the late 1800s and remained isolated until a modern bridge and regularly scheduled ferries connected it with the east bank in the 1960s. Algiers continues to maintain a small-town flavor with pocket parks surrounded by Victorian cottages and oak-canopied streets.

The Foot of Canal Street is also along the river, joining the French Quarter and the CBD. It contains major visitor attractions such as the Aquarium of the Americas, Woldenberg Riverfront Park, Harrah's New Orleans casino, and the Riverwalk shopping and entertainment complex. Upriver is the Warehouse District, formerly part of the extensive wharf system but in more recent years a burgeoning arts and cultural area with posh galleries, music clubs, restaurants, and condos fashioned from old commercial buildings.

The St. Charles Avenue streetcar follows the Mississippi River on a route several blocks inland along St. Charles Avenue, home to antebellum mansions, the Garden District, and the university section uptown. It's easy to get off the streetcar en route to visit the Superdome, take in the art and history museums around Lee Circle, or stroll around the lush Garden District, but you will have to pay the fare again when you reboard.

City Park and the Lakefront are accessible primarily by automobile. The park covers a vast area that includes the New Orleans Museum of Art, the Botanical Garden, and Storyland, an entertainment area for children, not to mention miles of lagoons, golf courses, and recreation areas. Along the lakefront there is a seawall with steps that invites sitters and provides lots of open spaces for relaxation.

Visitors with more time can explore outlying attractions such as the Chalmette Battlefield and National Cemetery, lying some 5 mi south of New Orleans; or Kenner, a suburb 15 mi to the west that includes the New Orleans International Airport, with a cluster of museums detailing such aspects of local history as the railroads, the Saints football team, Mardi Gras, and space exploration.

Fodor's Choice

Favorite Sights

★ **Audubon Zoo.** One of the best natural-habitat animal parks in the country provides hours of amusement, with sea lions, a white tiger, a flamingo pond, a tropical-bird house, and the Louisiana Swamp, featuring large alligators.

★ **City Park.** Encompassing 1,500 acres, this enchanting park contains the New Orleans Museum of Art, which specializes in pre-Columbian, African, and local creations; the lovely Botanical Garden; and artificial lagoons.

★ **French Market.** This bustling complex of renovated centuries-old buildings, extending several blocks along Decatur and North Peters streets, encompasses shops, restaurants, cafés, and a flea market.

★ **Hermann-Grima House.** One of the largest and best preserved examples of American architecture in the Quarter, this house has the best docents in the biz.

Special Moments

★ **Canal Street ferry ride.** The most romantic view of the city and its skyline can be seen from the deck of the ferry that crosses the Mississippi River to Algiers Point every 20 minutes from the Canal Street terminal.

★ **City Park Carousel.** Adults and children alike love riding the exquisitely refurbished 1906 Last Carousel, replete with authentic wooden flying horses, giraffes, zebras, and other exotic creatures.

★ **Riverfront stroll.** The ever-changing Mississippi is easily watched from pedestrian walks along Woldenberg Riverfront Park. You may catch a local musician or the calliope from the steamboats.

★ **St. Charles Avenue streetcar.** The most fun way to explore the CBD, the Garden District, and Uptown is to take a ride on one of the historic city streetcars that run along St. Charles Avenue.

UPPER FRENCH QUARTER

Unlike historic downtown areas of many other American cities, the French Quarter is largely a residential district, sharing streets with shops, restaurants, and offices. It is alive with the sights, sounds, and odors of a major port city and entertainment hub. Yet, behind the wrought-iron gates of its buildings are tranquil, intimate courtyards hidden from view. This intertwining of the public and private in the Quarter gives it a charm rarely matched in other U.S. cities. The Vieux Carré Commission, formed in 1936 to preserve the historic integrity of the Quarter, controls all renovation and rebuilding with strict codes. Notice that, with the exception of Bourbon Street, there are very few neon signs or garish flashing lights, and that buildings throughout the Quarter conform to the architectural style of the late 1700s to mid-1800s. Although the commission enforces building codes that preserve the authenticity of the exterior of buildings, modernization is allowed inside.

There are always a number of mule-drawn carriages giving half-hour tours around the narrow streets while drivers recite a mixture of folklore and fact about the old city. Mules have replaced horses because mules are more tolerant of high temperatures and can go longer without water.

As local directions often refer to the number block that a site is on (as in the 500 block of Royal Street), block numbers are included in the French Quarter blocks of the French Quarter and CBD map. The numbers across the top of the map are applicable to all the streets parallel to North Rampart Street. Those streets in the French Quarter that are perpendicular to North Rampart Street all start at 500 at Decatur Street and progress at increments of 100 at each block in the direction of North Rampart.

Numbers in the text correspond to numbers in the margin and on the French Quarter and CBD map.

A Good Walk

Tours of this historic area usually begin in **Jackson Square** ①, the heart of the French Quarter. This square, like those found in most French towns, has a church, a seat of government, and major shops. **St. Louis Cathedral** ②, where Pope John Paul II has given a service, dominates the square. Two Spanish colonial–style buildings, now museums, flank the cathedral: to the left, the **Cabildo** ③, the seat of the Spanish government in the 1700s; and to the right, the **Presbytère** ④, which has exhibits on Mardi Gras. The handsome rows of brick apartments on either side of the square are the **Pontalba Buildings** ⑤, built in 1850. The row on the right (as you face the cathedral), the **1850 House** ⑥, is open for tours. A few doors away in that row of houses is the **Louisiana Office of Tourism** ⑦, a good place to stop for information.

After noting the **Werlein House** ⑧ (just off the square), the former home of Elizabeth Werlein, who helped save many of the historic buildings we enjoy today, stroll along Royal Street with its lace ironwork balconies, antiques shops, galleries, and restaurants. Turning right onto Royal from behind the cathedral, you'll pass St. Anthony's Garden (☞ St. Louis Cathedral, *below*) between two alleyways, Pirate's Alley and Père Antoine Alley. **Faulkner House** ⑨, where the young William Faulkner lived, is up Pirate's Alley, and down Orleans Street in a hotel on the right is the former **Quadroon Ballroom** ⑩, where it is said that up until Civil War times dashing French and Creole men chose mistresses from among the lovely free women of color who danced with them there. Off Royal Street, down Dumaine Street, is the **New Orleans Historic Voodoo Museum** ⑪, which houses artifacts used in rituals. Back across Royal Street on Dumaine stands **Madame John's Legacy** ⑫, a West Indies–style house (now a state museum) named for a fictitious free woman of color.

The **Miltenberger Houses** ⑬ on Royal Street are historic homes of the 1830s. The cornstalk and morning glory design of an iron fence across the street shows the intricacy of cast-iron work in the late 1800s. The **Spring Fiesta Historic Town House** ⑭ is two blocks down St. Ann Street.

At this point you can choose to venture off the beaten path to a number of places. Several blocks lakeside is Louis Armstrong Park, a large park with several sights, including Congo Square, a former location of voodoo rituals. Across Rampart Street from the park is the site of the former J&M Music Shop, where rock 'n' roll greats recorded. A few blocks past the park is the historic St. Louis Cemetery #1, which should be visited with a tour. Storyville, to the left of the cemetery, was a red-light district at the turn of the century and no longer exists as such; today it's a housing project.

SPEAKING LIKE A LOCAL

NEW ORLEANS, LIKE MANY cities, has its own peculiarities in terms of speech. Because it was founded by the French, the city has many street names that a visitor might be inclined to pronounce true to the French. In fact, local pronunciation is quite different. There are also some local terms that can be confusing if you're not aware of them. For vocabulary specifically referring to local cuisine, see Chapter 2.

Various theories claim that the similar accents found in such places as Boston, New York, and New Orleans evolved because people from countries like Ireland, Germany, and Italy settled early on in these port towns. In New Orleans, you will not hear natives with thick, Georgia-peach drawls. But you might hear some "dese, dem, dat," and "dose," as in "Who dat say gonna beat dem Saints?!"

One thing that always sets visitors apart is their reference to the trolley. It's a streetcar in New Orleans, not a trolley. And many locals say New-ah-e-yons, not New Or-lenz, N'aw-lins, or New Or-leenz. Still, you'll probably fit in fine with the easier-to-pronounce New Or-lenz; the key things to avoid are placing the emphasis on "new" rather than "Or" and using a long "e" sound in "leans." But—here's a curveball—it is Or-leenz Street.

You need to forget any French you've studied when pronouncing street names. This is where the Texan in the back of class whom everybody snickered at gets his revenge. If you ask what direction Freret (Frer-ay, in French) Street is, you will be met by a blank stare. (The correct pronunciation is Fer-et.) Burgundy Street is Bur-*gun*-dee; Carondelet is Cahr-on-duh-let; Chartres is Chart-ers; Conti is Con-tie; Iberville is Eye-berville; and Tchoupitoulas is Chop-a-tool-us. And if someone asks you, "Where y'at?," he's saying howdy, not asking where you are.

Bayou (by-you). Creek.

Banquette (ban-ket). Sidewalk.

Cold drink. Soda with ice.

Doubloons (dub-loons). Aluminum coins, often colored, which Mardi Gras krewes emboss with the theme and date of their parades and throw out to crowds.

Fais-do-do (fay-doh-doh). Country dance. A Cajun expression derived from the French verbs *faire* (to make or do) and *dormir* (to sleep): mothers wanted children to go to sleep so they could dance.

Gallery. Porch or balcony.

Gris-gris (gree-gree). Voodoo charm; often a small bag filled with several ingredients.

Krewe (crew). A private club that parades at Mardi Gras.

Lagniappe (lan-yap). A little something extra at no extra cost.

Levee (leh-vee). Embankment.

Metairie (Met-a-ree or Met-tree). Suburb of New Orleans.

Neutral ground. Median in a large thoroughfare, such as the land on which the St. Charles Avenue streetcar runs. It is so named because tensions between the Americans, who lived Uptown, and the Creoles, who lived in the French Quarter, were so keen in the early years of the colony that the land separating the two rival neighborhoods was considered a neutral area.

Parish. County.

Shotgun house. Common architectural style: a long narrow house so-called because a bullet could pass from the front to the back door without hitting a wall.

Ward. Division of the city, as in Sixth Ward.

Where y'at? How are you doing? Correct response is "Hey, where y'at?"

Vieux Carré (View kah-ray). French Quarter; translated directly as Old Square.

Now you'll probably want to head back toward the river for some refreshment. Café du Monde, on Decatur Street across from Jackson Square, serves up great café au lait and beignets (four-corner French doughnuts). A raised area overlooking Jackson Square, **Washington Artillery Park** ⑮ is a favorite spot for photographing the famous postcard panorama of New Orleans. Behind this park and across the railroad tracks is the Moon Walk, a raised promenade that is part of **Woldenberg Riverfront Park** ⑯. This is a great stretch of open space where you can stroll along the river and watch the ships pass. If you are lucky, the steamboat *Natchez* will be readying to leave its dock along the park, and you can catch the strains of the calliope played on its steam engine.

The tall complex of buildings to the right of the overview on Decatur Street is **Jackson Brewery** ⑰, a former brewery that now houses a shopping center and bars and eateries such as Planet Hollywood and the Hard Rock Cafe. Down Decatur Street another block is **Bienville Place** ⑱, with its massive statue of the founder of New Orleans, Sieur de Bienville, and to the statue's right on Decatur Street is the **Folklife and Visitor Center of the Jean Lafitte National Park** ⑲.

A block to the right is Chartres Street, and a left turn here leads back to Jackson Square, where **Le Petit Théâtre** ⑳ commands the corner of Chartres and St. Peter streets. Several doors down at 636 St. Peter Street, Tennessee Williams wrote his most famous play, *A Streetcar Named Desire*.

The **LaBranche Houses** ㉑, a series of Creole town houses across St. Peter Street, date to the 1830s. The heavily balconied one at the corner of Royal Street is the most decorative building in the French Quarter. A reminder of the residential nature of the area is the A&P supermarket on the opposite corner, small and antiquated by today's standards but the only true grocery store in the French Quarter.

If you walk up St. Peter Street to Bourbon Street you will pass two city landmarks (☞ Chapter 4), Preservation Hall, known for its authentic jazz performers, and Pat O'Brien's, home of the Hurricane cocktail. Raucous and crowded **Bourbon Street** ㉒ is filled with bars, restaurants, music clubs, and novelty shops. If you'd like to wait till later in the day to explore Bourbon Street, your next stop after the LaBranche Houses should be the **Historic New Orleans Collection** ㉓, a museum that has exhibits on local history. Continue your step back into history with a tour through the lovely **Hermann-Grima House** ㉔, just off Bourbon Street on St. Louis Street, or the **Musée Conti Wax Museum** ㉕, around the block on Conti Street.

This is also an area known for its venerable, old restaurants: Antoine's, Brennan's, Galatoire's, and Arnaud's are within blocks of each other, as are such new but no-less revered eateries as Broussard's, Bayona, Nola, K-Paul's Louisiana Kitchen, Louis XVI, and Mr. B's. Arnaud's houses the **Germaine Wells Mardi Gras Museum** ㉖, with Mardi Gras costumes and artifacts from the owner's family.

A few blocks toward the river and across St. Louis Street from the Napoleon House Bar & Café is **Maspero's Exchange** ㉗, an eatery today but formerly the location of a slave auction, as were several other buildings in this area. The imposing Victorian building that takes up the whole next block between St. Louis and Conti streets is the Old New Orleans Court House, which is being restored as the elegant home of the **Louisiana Supreme Court** ㉘. A block toward the river and one block toward Canal Street, on Chartres Street, is the **New Orleans Pharmacy Museum** ㉙, where the leech jars in the window make one grateful for modern medicine. From the museum, the river is only a block away to the right and Jackson Square is straight ahead.

TIMING

To take in most of these sights you should plan a full day, allowing for leisure time to browse in shops, tour museums, snack at cafés, and listen to a street musician or watch a portrait artist at work. A tour of a home or museum is usually an hour in length.

Sights to See

18 **Bienville Place.** This small, European-style park has three oak trees and a large marble-base statue of the city's founder, French Canadian Jean-Baptiste le Moyne, sieur de Bienville. In the bronze tableau by local artist Angela Gregory, Bienville is flanked by the French priest Father Athanase, who accompanied him on his landing, and a Native American chief who reportedly welcomed them. The park is a few blocks from the site where Bienville landed in 1717, claiming the area for the capital city of the French colony of Louisiana. ⊠ *N. Peters and Decatur Sts.*

22 **Bourbon Street.** Tacky and touristy it may be, but you'll probably at least want to take a stroll here. This famous street takes you past some of the typical bars, restaurants, music clubs, and novelty shops that have given this strip its reputation as the playground of the South. The noise, raucous crowds, and bawdy sights are not family fare; if you go with children, do so before sundown. Although the street is usually well patrolled, it is wise to stay alert to your surroundings. The street is blocked to make a pedestrian mall at night; often the area is shoulder-to-shoulder, especially during major sports events and Mardi Gras.

At Toulouse Street is the former site of the **French Opera House,** one of New Orleans's most opulent public buildings, which burned down in 1919. There is probably a Lucky Dog vendor nearby, with a vending cart shaped like a hot dog. These carts were immortalized by John Kennedy Toole in his Pulitzer Prize–winning novel about New Orleans, *A Confederacy of Dunces.* St. Ann Street marks the beginning of a strip of gay bars.

3 **The Cabildo.** Dating from 1799, this Spanish colonial–style building is named for the Spanish council—or *cabildo*—that met there. The transfer of Louisiana to the United States was made in 1803 in the front room on the second floor overlooking the square. The Cabildo later served as the city hall and then the supreme court. There are three floors of multicultural exhibits recounting Louisiana history—from the colonial period through Reconstruction—with countless artifacts, including the death mask of Napoléon Bonaparte. In 1988 the building suffered terrible damage from a four-alarm fire. Most of the historic pieces inside were saved, but the top floor, roof, and cupola had to be replaced. The Cabildo is almost a twin to the **Presbytère** (☞ *below*) on the other side of the cathedral. ⊠ *Jackson Sq.,* ☎ *504/568–6968.* ☞ *$5; 20% discount on tickets to 2 or more of the following museums if purchased together: Presbytère, Cabildo, 1850 House, Old Mint, and Madame John's Legacy.* ☉ *Tues.–Sun. 9–5.*

NEED A
BREAK?   Open 24 hours, **Café du Monde** (⊠ 813 Decatur St., ☎ 504/581–2914) serves up café au lait and beignets (and not much else) in a style that has not varied for more than a century. Don't miss it.

6 **1850 House.** A docent leads you through this well-preserved town house and courtyard, part of the **Pontalba Buildings** (☞ *below*). Notice the lovely ironwork on the balconies of the apartments: The former owner,

Baroness Micaela Pontalba, introduced cast (or molded) iron with these buildings, and it eventually replaced much of the old hand-wrought ironwork in the French Quarter. The initials for her families, A and P—Almonester and Pontalba—are worked into the design. A gift shop and bookstore run by Friends of the Cabildo is downstairs. ⊠ *523 St. Ann St.,* ☎ *504/568–6968.* ▣ *$3; 20% discount on tickets to 2 or more of the following museums if purchased together: Presbytère, Cabildo, 1850 House, Old Mint, and Madame John's Legacy.* ☉ *Tues.–Sun. 9–5.*

❾ Faulkner House. The young novelist William Faulkner lived and wrote his first book, *Soldier's Pay,* here in the 1920s. He later returned to his native Oxford, Mississippi, and became a Pulitzer Prize–winning writer. The house now is not open to visitors but is the site of **Faulkner House Books** (☞ French Quarter *in* Chapter 6) and the literary group **Pirate's Alley Faulkner Society,** which promotes local and Southern writers. ⊠ *624 Pirate's Alley,* ☎ *504/524–2940.*

❿ Folklife and Visitor Center of the Jean Lafitte National Park. A good stop for visitors new to Louisiana and the area, this center has free visual and sound exhibits on the customs of various ethnic groups in the state, as well as free daily history tours of the French Quarter. The daily history walking tour is at 10:30. Tickets are handed out one per person (you must be present to get a ticket), beginning 9 AM. The office also supervises and provides information on Jean Lafitte National Park Barataria Unit across the river from New Orleans, and the Chalmette Battlefield, where the Battle of New Orleans was fought in the War of 1812. ⊠ *419 Decatur St.,* ☎ *504/589–2636.* ☉ *Daily 9–5.*

㉖ Germaine Wells Mardi Gras Museum. During a 31-year period (1937–68), Germaine Cazenave Wells, daughter of Arnaud's restaurant founder Arnaud Cazenave, was queen of carnival balls a record 22 times for 17 different krewes, or organizations. Many of her ball gowns, in addition to costumes worn by other family members, are on display. ⊠ *Arnaud's Restaurant, 813 Bienville St., 2nd floor (enter through restaurant),* ☎ *504/523–5433.* ▣ *Free.* ☉ *Daily 10–2 and 6–10.*

NEED A BREAK?   **Napoleon House Bar and Cafe** (⊠ 500 Chartres St., ☎ 504/524–9752) is a favorite gathering place for local characters. The bar is renowned for drinks such as the Pimm's Cup and the Sazerac. Snack on a muffuletta sandwich (ham, salami, mozzarella, and olive salad on seeded bread) or a cheese plate, and enjoy the atmosphere. Napoléon never made it to Louisiana, but he would have felt right at home here in the building intended for him in exile.

★ ✿ ㉔ Hermann-Grima House. One of the largest and best-preserved examples of American architecture in the Quarter, this Georgian-style house has the only restored private stable and the only working 1830s Creole kitchen in the Quarter. American architect William Brand built the house in 1831. Cooking demonstrations on the open hearth are held here all day Thursday from October through May. You'll want to check the gift shop, which has many local crafts and books. ⊠ *820 St. Louis St.,* ☎ *504/525–5661.* ▣ *$6; $10 combination ticket with the Gallier House.* ☉ *Tours weekdays 10–3:30.*

㉓ Historic New Orleans Collection. This private archive and exhibit complex, with thousands of historic photos, documents, and books, is one of the finest research centers in the South. It occupies the 19th-century town house of General Kemper Williams and the 1792 Merrieult House. Changing exhibits on local history and tours of the houses, grounds, and archives are scheduled. Children under 12 are not ad-

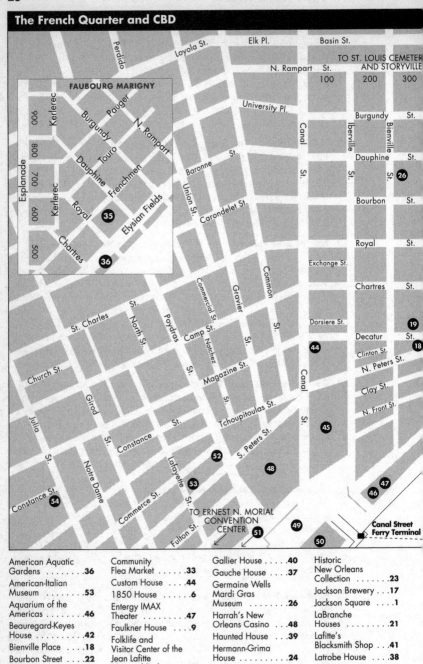

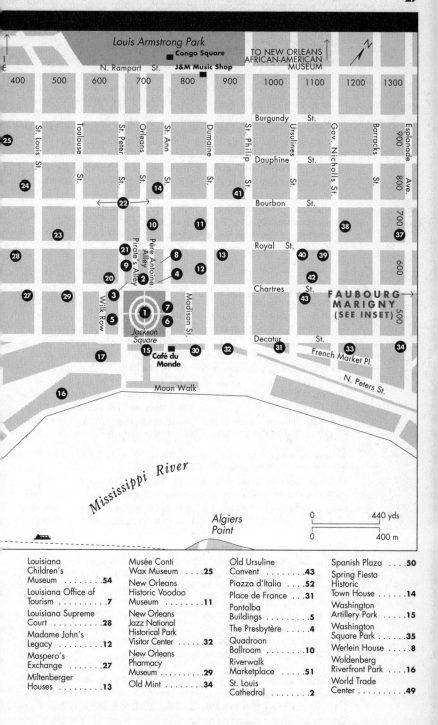

mitted. ⊠ *533 Royal St.,* ☎ *504/523–4662.* ⊠ *Exhibit at 533 Royal St. and use of research library at 410 Chartres St. free; tour of houses or archive galleries $4.* ⊙ *Tues.–Sat. 10–4:30.*

🔟 Jackson Brewery. Also called Jax Brewery, this is a former brewery remodeled to house a three-section shopping and entertainment complex. Outside are multilevel terraces facing the river, and inside are more than 50 shops (including the monumental Virgin Megastore) and galleries plus a food court and restaurants. Live music can often be heard from various areas. The **Planet Hollywood** restaurant is on the first two floors of the brewery, and the **Hard Rock Cafe** is in a separate building. Those interested in Creole and Cajun cooking might wish to visit the **New Orleans School of Cooking,** in the first section, near Planet Hollywood, which features local chefs. ⊠ *620 Decatur St.,* ☎ *504/566–7245.*

NEED A BREAK?   For the taste of French New Orleans, try the croissants and French breads at **La Madeleine** (⊠ 547 St. Ann St., ☎ 504/568–9950) on Jackson Square, on the corner of Chartres and St. Ann streets. Soups, salads, and entrées are available, and a cup of café au lait is the crowning touch.

★ **❶ Jackson Square.** Surrounded by historic buildings and filled with plenty of the city's atmospheric street life, the heart of the French Quarter is today a beautifully landscaped park. Jackson Square was founded in 1718, but until the 1850s, the square was called the Place d'Armes and was a military marching ground. It was also the site of public executions carried out in various styles, including burning at the stake, beheading, breaking on the wheel, and hanging. A **statue of Andrew Jackson,** victorious leader of the Battle of New Orleans in the War of 1812, commands the center of the square. The words carved in the base on the cathedral side of the statue—"The Union must and shall be preserved"—are a lasting reminder of the federal troops who occupied New Orleans during the Civil War and who inscribed them.

Among the notable buildings around the square is **St. Louis Cathedral** (☞ *below*). Two Spanish colonial–style buildings, the **Cabildo** (☞ *above*) and the **Presbytère** (☞ *below*), flank the cathedral. The handsome rows of brick apartments on either side of the square are the **Pontalba Buildings** (☞ *below*). The park is landscaped in a sun pattern, with walkways set like rays streaming out from the center, a popular garden design in the royal court of King Louis XIV, the Sun King. People are forbidden to feed the pigeons in the park, a law necessary to control the pigeon population. In the daytime, dozens of artists hang their paintings on the park fence and set up outdoor studios where they work on canvases or offer to draw portraits of passersby. These artists are easy to engage in conversation and are knowledgeable about many aspects of the Quarter and New Orleans. You can also be entertained by a variety of musicians, dancers, tarot-card readers, and magicians who perform on the flagstone pedestrian mall surrounding the square. ⊙ *Daily 8–6, excluding special events.*

OFF THE BEATEN PATH   **J&M MUSIC SHOP –** A plaque on this 1835 building marks it as the former site of the recording studio that launched the rock 'n' roll careers of such greats as Fats Domino, Jerry Lee Lewis, Little Richard, and Ray Charles. It's one of the most significant musical landmarks in New Orleans. Owned by Cossimo Matassa, the studio spanned a decade from 1945 to 1955. ⊠ 838 N. Rampart St.

㉑ LaBranche Houses. This complex of lovely town houses, built in the 1830s by widow LaBranche, fills the half block between Pirate's Alley and Royal and St. Peter streets behind the **Cabildo** (☞ *above*). The house on the corner of Royal and St. Peter streets, with its rounded cast-iron balconies bedecked with flowering plants, is the most photographed residence in the French Quarter. All are privately owned. The apartments are upstairs and there are shops on the ground floor.

⑳ Le Petit Théâtre. Since 1916 this building has been home to a community-based theater group (☞ The Arts *in* Chapter 4) that produces seven plays each season in addition to several children's plays. It was erected in 1789 and underwent considerable reconstruction in 1960. As home to the Tennessee Williams Festival every spring, Le Petit Théâtre attracts national attention. The flagstone patio with its fountain is postcard-perfect. ⊠ *616 St. Peter St.,* ☎ *504/522–9958.* ◳ *Admission by ticket during theater season, Sept.–June.*

OFF THE
BEATEN PATH

LOUIS ARMSTRONG PARK – This large park with its grassy knolls and lagoons is named for native son and world-famous musician Louis Armstrong (1900–71), whose statue by Elizabeth Catlett is near the brightly lit entrance on the outer boundary of the French Quarter. It is ironic that Armstrong was not welcome to play most of the well-known clubs of his home city during much of his illustrious career because of segregation; in his later years, when he could have, he refused to do so. To the left inside the park is **Congo Square,** an inlaid-stone space, where African slaves and free persons of color gathered during the 18th and early 19th centuries on Sunday to socialize, speak their native African tongues, and dance to their own forms of music. The drums can still be heard at times when neighborhood musicians congregate. Marie Laveau, the greatly feared and respected voodoo queen of antebellum New Orleans, had her home a block away on St. Ann Street and is reported to have held voodoo rituals here regularly.

Behind Congo Square is a large gray building, the **Morris F. X. Jeff Municipal Auditorium,** and to the right behind the auditorium is the **Mahalia Jackson Center for the Performing Arts.** The **New Orleans Jazz National Historical Park,** with exhibits and live performances, is planned for a complex of smaller buildings near the center of the park. This complex is home to WWOZ, an FM radio station that broadcasts only New Orleans music. The park is patrolled by a security detail, but be very careful when wandering. ⊠ *N. Rampart St., between St. Philip and St. Peter Sts.,* ☎ *504/589–4806.* ◔ *Auditorium and performing arts center open by event; check local newspapers for listings. National park visitors center, daily 9–5.*

❼ Louisiana Office of Tourism. In addition to maps and hundreds of brochures about sights in the city and its environs, this information center has guides who can answer questions. At press time the office was under renovation and had moved to a small temporary space in the Presbytère (☞ *below*); call before you go. ⊠ *529 St. Ann St.,* ☎ *504/568–5661.* ◔ *Daily 9–5.*

㉘ Louisiana Supreme Court. The imposing Victorian building that takes up the whole block of Royal Street, between St. Louis and Conti streets, is the Old New Orleans Court, erected in 1908. After years of vacancy and neglect, this magnificent edifice is being partially restored as the elegant home of the Louisiana Supreme Court. Part of the movie *JFK* was filmed here in 1991.

⑫ Madame John's Legacy. Now a state museum, this is the only example in the French Quarter of West Indian architecture and early Creole–colonial home design, with the first floor built high off the ground and a porch (called a gallery) running along the front and back of the house. The original building at 632 Dumaine Street dated to 1726, but the building you see is an exact replica that was built in the late 1700s, after the original structure was destroyed by fire. The house has undergone some renovation through the years and has a colorful past. The first owner, Jean Pascal, a French sea captain, was killed by Natchez Indians. The name "Madame John's Legacy" was adopted in the late 1800s from a short story by New Orleans writer George Washington Cable. The popular tale was about Madame John, a "free woman of color" (a localism for free African-Americans), who, like many other women of her race at that time, became the mistress of a Frenchman. Having never married, her master, John (Jean), bequeathed his house and estate to her on his deathbed. The museum showcases exhibits of the architecture, restoration, and archeological finds of the house on the ground floor and a rotating art exhibit on the second floor. ✉ *632 Dumaine St.,* ☎ *504/568–6968.* 🎟 *$3; 20% discount on tickets to 2 or more of the following museums if purchased together: Presbytère, Cabildo, 1850 House, Old Mint, and Madame John's Legacy.* ◷ *Tues.–Sun. 9–5.*

㉗ Maspero's Exchange. This restaurant once was a slave auction house and for many years thereafter the Exchange Coffeehouse, where the city's notable Creoles gathered. An interesting feature of the building is that it seems from the outside to have only two floors, whereas inside there is a middle floor, called an entresol, in the section above the window arch at the top of what appears to be the first floor. This narrow middle floor was used for storage. Only a few buildings in the Quarter have an entresol. ✉ *440 Chartres St.*

⓭ Miltenberger Houses. The widow Miltenberger built this row of three brick town houses in the 1830s for her three sons. Two generations later, Alice Heine, born here in 1910, became famous for wedding Prince Albert of Monaco. Although the marriage ended childless and in divorce, Princess Alice was a sensation in New Orleans. ✉ *900, 906, and 910 Royal St.*

Mississippi River. When facing the river, you see to the right the **Crescent City Connection,** a twin-span bridge between New Orleans and the west bank, and a ferry that crosses the river every 20 minutes. The river flows to the left downstream for another 100 mi until it merges with the Gulf of Mexico. Directly across the river is the ferry landing and a ship-repair dry dock in a neighborhood called **Algiers Point** (☞ *below*). The river is always active with steamboats carrying tour groups, tugboats pushing enormous barges, and oceangoing ships plying its waters. Sometimes a dredge boat is visible, dredging the river's bottom of silt to keep the channel open for large ships.

✋ ㉕ Musée Conti Wax Museum. More than 100 wax figures of past and present Louisiana celebrities are arranged in tableaux with written and audio explanations; the gift shop stocks local memorabilia. ✉ *917 Conti St.,* ☎ *504/525–2605.* 🎟 *$6.75.* ◷ *Daily 10–5:30.*

⓫ New Orleans Historic Voodoo Museum. A large collection of artifacts and information on voodoo as it was—and still is—practiced in New Orleans is here at the only such museum in the world. The gift shop sells gris-gris potions and voodoo dolls. Readings, lectures, and voodoo, vampire, and cemetery tours are available through the museum. ✉ *724 Dumaine St.,* ☎ *504/523–7685.* 🎟 *$7.* ◷ *Daily 10–8.*

㉙ New Orleans Pharmacy Museum. This building was the apothecary shop and residence of Louis J. Dufilho, America's first licensed pharmacist with his own shop, in the 1820s. His botanical and herbal gardens are still cultivated in the courtyard. To tour the museum is to step

VAMPIRES AROUND NEW ORLEANS

NEW ORLEANS'S ECCENTRIC charm and mystique have inspired many great fiction writers, but none have even approached the colossal commercial success enjoyed by Anne Rice. Rice's occult classics have spawned a cottage industry within New Orleans's tourist trade as devoted readers from around the globe seek to retrace the steps of her characters, especially in the French Quarter and the Garden District. Diehards hang out in front of Rice's house waiting for a glimpse of their idol and comparing notes with fellow aficionados. Whether you're in that deep or merely an avid reader, the following tips may enhance your visit to the land of red beans and rice. Addresses are given for sites not covered elsewhere in this book.

In the French Quarter, **Gallier House,** a mid-19th-century mansion, is perhaps the model for the fictional home of the vampires Lestat, Louis, and Claudia. Three nearby blocks of Royal Street (700–900) were covered with dirt and used in the film *Interview with the Vampire,* as was the house at 632 Dumaine. In **Jackson Square,** Lestat had his first encounter with Raglan James in *The Tale of the Body Thief,* and Lasher first appeared here in *The Witching Hour.* In *Interview with the Vampire,* Lestat drank the blood of a priest at **St. Louis Cathedral.** Various characters dine at **Galatoire's** and **Desire Oyster Bar** (300 Bourbon St.). Just outside the French Quarter are the historic and labyrinthine **St. Louis Cemeteries #1 and #2,** mentioned in both *Interview with the Vampire* and *Queen of the Damned.*

Anne Rice's house is in the Garden District: the Greek Revival–Italianate mansion at **1239 1st Street.** Members of the fictional Mayfair clan are buried in the quite real **Lafayette Cemetery 1.** Across the street from the cemetery is **Commander's Palace,** the site of various Mayfair family dinners, especially after

funerals. The minimall the **Rink** (✉ 2727 Prytania St.) is the home of the **Anne Rice Collection** (☎ 504/899–5996). The **Garden District Book Shop** (☎ 504/895–2266) specializes in Rice's books. Anne Rice owns the house at 2523 Prytania Street. A massive white house at 1415 3rd Street was greatly admired by Michael Curry. Rice keeps her extensive doll collection at 19th-century **St. Elizabeth's Home** (✉ 1314 Napoleon Ave., ☎ 504/899–6450) in Uptown New Orleans, a mile upriver from the Garden District. She owns the former orphanage, which is open for tours by appointment.

Just behind Magazine Street from the Garden District are two churches with some of the most beautiful frescoes and stained glass in the city, dating to the 1850s. The German Baroque **St. Mary's Assumption** (✉ 2030 Constance St.) is the site of Michael Curry and Rowan Mayfair's wedding in *The Witching Hour.* Anne Rice's real-life parents were married in the Italianate **St. Alphonsus** (✉ 2045 Constance St.). Take a taxi to the churches, which are in a high-crime area. Tours are organized by the **Friends of St. Alphonsus** (☎ 504/456–5315).

The swamps and bayous that surround New Orleans have a distinct aura of mystery, making them ideal backdrops for such scenes as Claudia and Louis's dumping the body of Lestat. The **Pitot House** inspired Louis's Pointe du Lac in *Interview with the Vampire.* **Destrehan Plantation** and **Oak Alley** served as locations in the film. **Madewood Plantation** is the prototype for the Mayfair family's country home, Fontrevault (☞ The Great River Road *in* Chapter 7).

Anne Rice has two ways to keep her fans updated on her busy life: Her Web site is www.annerice.com, and her phone line, on which she keeps a recorded message that she changes periodically, is 504/522–8634.

back into 19th-century medicine. Even the window display, with its enormous leech jar and other antiquated paraphernalia, is fascinating. ⊠ *514 Chartres St.,* ☎ *504/565–8027.* ☜ *$2.* ☉ *Tues.–Sun. 10–5.*

❺ Pontalba Buildings. Baroness Micaela Pontalba built these twin sets of town houses, one on each side of Jackson Square, in the late 1840s; they are known for their ornate cast-iron balcony railings. The daughter of a wealthy Spaniard, Don Almonester y Rojas, she inherited the prime real estate around the square and had these apartment buildings constructed to leave a permanent European imprint on the heart of the old city. She also helped fund the landscaping of the square and the erection of the Andrew Jackson statue in its center. The strong-willed baroness married her cousin Baron Celestin de Pontalba in France. She caused a scandal on both sides of the Atlantic when she had a near-fatal fight with her father-in-law, left her husband, and returned to Louisiana in the 1840s to build the apartments. She later returned to Paris, where she is buried. The Pontalba Buildings are publicly owned; the side to the right of the cathedral, on St. Ann Street, is owned by the state, and the other side, on St. Peter Street, by the city. In the state-owned side is the **1850 House** (☞ *above*) and at 540-B St. Peter Street on the city-owned side is a plaque marking this apartment as that of Sherwood Anderson, literary figure and mentor to William Faulkner. Anderson lived here in the 1920s.

★ ❹ The Presbytère. One of twin Spanish colonial–style buildings flanking St. Louis Cathedral, this one, on the right, now holds outstanding exhibits about Mardi Gras. It was originally designed to house the priests of the cathedral; instead, it served as a courthouse under the Spanish and later under the Americans. The Mardi Gras exhibits fill the first two floors with hundreds of pieces of Carnival memorabilia, including elaborate costumes and jewelry. Interactive displays and videos illustrate the history of Mardi Gras in New Orleans and other parts of the state. ⊠ *Jackson Sq.,* ☎ *504/568–6968.* ☜ *$5; 20% discount on tickets to 2 or more of the following museums if purchased together: Presbytère, Cabildo, 1850 House, Old Mint, and Madame John's Legacy.* ☉ *Tues.–Sun. 9–5.*

❿ Quadroon Ballroom. In the early 1800s the wooden-rail balcony was a ballroom where, it is believed, free women of color met their French suitors, as Madame John of **Madame John's Legacy** (☞ *above*) is said to have done. The quadroons (people whose racial makeup is one-quarter African) who met here were young, unmarried women. The girls' mothers traditionally accompanied them to the balls to make sure that any man who took a serious interest in their daughters had the means to support both a mistress and the several children who would be born to the relationship. If the Frenchman married a woman of his own race and had a legitimate second family, he often continued to support his first family. If you read the plaque at the entrance to the building, you'll learn that the ballroom later became part of a convent and school for the Sisters of the Holy Family, a religious order founded in New Orleans in 1842 by the daughter of a quadroon. The nuns moved in 1964 to a suburb in eastern New Orleans. ⊠ *Bourbon Orleans Hotel, 717 Orleans St., 2nd floor.*

❷ St. Louis Cathedral. The oldest active cathedral in the United States, this church at the heart of the old city is named for the 13th-century French king who led two crusades. The current building, which replaced two former structures destroyed by fire, dates from 1794, although it was remodeled and enlarged in 1851. In 1964 the cathedral was elevated to the status of minor basilica, one of only 15 such churches in the United States. Pope John Paul II held a prayer service for clergy

MAKING THE MOST OF MARDI GRAS

MARDI GRAS HAPPENS TO BE the most vibrant, colorful moment of the year in the Crescent City, and some advance planning can make a visit at this time an even better experience. Navigating the mammoth crowds and sheer size of the event can be daunting to even the most seasoned travelers, but there are things you can do. You can meet the first challenge by finding a place to stay early in the game; making reservations a year ahead would not be too soon.

Remember that Mardi Gras is always a work in progress. As well-planned as events may be, there are always surprises. You don't need to schedule your day down to the hour. Allow yourself to go with the momentum and enjoy the spontaneity. This being said, you can still have fun preparing for the action. For background information and a list of publications about Mardi Gras, *see* "Carnival" *in* Chapter 8. It's helpful to review the dates and routes of parades you want to check out. Chapter 6 lists places to buy masks and costumes.

A number of things can make life easier during your Mardi Gras adventure. First, remember that no matter how chaotic things appear, New Orleans is a leader in crowd management and has been handling this event for many years. The city's 1,700 police officers are well trained to manage crises as well as the routine day-to-day glitches that occur anytime a million human beings gather to celebrate. If you travel to New Orleans for Mardi Gras weekend, remember the revelry has been going on already for a couple of months and the city has settled into a pattern of partying.

For your part, use common sense, dress comfortably, and leave your valuables safely locked up at home or in safe deposit boxes at your hotel. Although there are several hundred portable rest rooms throughout the city during Mardi Gras, if you are in the French Quarter you'll have a hard time finding facilities, so plan accordingly. And although celebrants aboard parade floats will throw much-coveted beads and keepsakes to you, remember that it is illegal to throw anything at them. It is also illegal to carry metal or glass containers.

Be aware of pickpockets. Don't carry excessive amounts of cash and don't wear jewelry that could tempt the wrong person. Travel with one or more other person rather than alone if possible, and set a permanent meeting spot where your family or group will convene at pre-set times throughout the day.

Children are especially vulnerable during Mardi Gras and must be carefully watched. Getting lost is easy in the midst of the ever-swelling crowds. Caught up in the excitement, unsupervised children may be likely to run too close to a float and risk being injured.

As for where to be, and when, it depends on your interests. If you yearn to be in the middle of the madness, Royal Street and Bourbon Street in the French Quarter may be for you. The scene will be wall-to-wall people, many adorned in the most outrageous attire of the season. If you'd rather be in a family atmosphere, consider St. Charles Avenue, Uptown, or Veterans Memorial Boulevard in Metairie, where families gather and spend the entire day and night. Those are both main parade routes and the action is lively and festive, yet a bit more orderly than in the French Quarter.

And if you just happen to be in town at the right time, you can witness one of the most unique attractions of the season—the Mystic Krewe of Barkus parade, featuring more than 1,000 dogs (yes, dogs), costumed and marching through the streets of the French Quarter with their similarly adorned owners. Only then will you realize the full and unique meaning of some of the locals' favorite words: *only in New Orleans.*

— By Paul A. Greenberg

here during his New Orleans visit in 1987; to honor the occasion, the pedestrian mall in front of the cathedral was renamed Place Jean Paul Deux. The statue of the Sacred Heart of Jesus dominates **St. Anthony's Garden,** which extends behind the rectory to Royal Street. From Royal Street can be seen a monument to 30 members of a French ship who died in a yellow fever epidemic in 1857. ⊠ *615 Père Antoine Alley,* ☎ *504/525–9585.* ▱ *Free.* ☉ *Tours Mon.–Sat. 9–4:30, Sun. 1–4:30.*

OFF THE
BEATEN PATH

ST. LOUIS CEMETERY #1 – New Orleans's "cities of the dead," with rows of crypts like little houses, are one of the city's most enduring images. The oldest cemetery in the city, on the boundary of the French Quarter, is an example of the unique, aboveground burial practices of the French and Spanish. Because of the high water level, it was difficult to bury bodies underground without having the coffin float to the surface after the first hard rain. Modern-day burial methods permit underground interment, but many people prefer these ornate family tombs and vaults, which have figured in several movies, among them *Easy Rider.*

Buried here are such notables as Etienne Boré, father of the sugar industry; Homer Plessy of the *Plessy v. Ferguson* 1892 U.S. Supreme Court decision establishing the separate but equal Jim Crow laws for African-Americans and whites in the South; and most notably, Marie Laveau, voodoo queen. Her tomb is marked with Xs freshly chalked by those who still believe in her supernatural powers.

A second Marie Laveau, believed to be her daughter, is buried in **St. Louis Cemetery #2,** four blocks beyond this cemetery, on Claiborne Avenue. **St. Louis Cemetery #3** is at the end of Esplanade Avenue, a good drive from here. Although these cemeteries are open to the public, it is dangerous to enter them alone because of frequent muggings inside; group tours are a rational option (☞ Sightseeing *in* Smart Travel Tips A to Z). ⊠ *#1: Basin and Conti Sts.* ☉ *Daily 9–3.*

⓮ Spring Fiesta Historic Town House. This lovely 19th-century home has been restored by the same people who sponsor the annual Spring Fiesta, a celebration of the Quarter's beautiful homes and genteel lifestyle of days gone by. ⊠ *826 St. Ann St.,* ☎ *504/581–1367.* ☉ *Only open for group tours, which must be arranged in advance.*

OFF THE
BEATEN PATH

STORYVILLE – The legitimatized red-light district that lasted from 1897 to 1917 has been destroyed, and in its place today is a government housing complex. Storyville spawned splendid Victorian homes that served as brothels, and brought uptown and downtown jazz players together for the first time to create what became known as New Orleans jazz. This area has been the subject of many novels, songs, and films; the Louis Malle film *Pretty Baby,* starring a very young Brooke Shields, was inspired by the Storyville photographer E. J. Bellocq. When the district was shut down in 1917, some buildings were razed almost overnight; the housing project was built in the 1930s. Only a historical marker on the "neutral ground" (median) of Basin Street remains to mark alderman Sidney Story's experiment attempting to legalize prostitution and other vice. ⊠ *Basin St. next to St. Louis Cemetery #1.*

⓯ Washington Artillery Park. This raised concrete area on the river side of Decatur Street, directly across from Jackson Square, is a great spot to relax and photograph the square and the barges and paddle wheelers on the Mississippi. The cannon mounted in the center and pointing toward the river is a model 1861 Parrot Rifle used in the Civil War. This monument honors the local 141st Field Artillery of the Louisiana National Guard that saw action from the Civil War through World War

II. Marble tablets at the base give the history of the group, represented today by the Washington Artillery Association. ✉ *Decatur St., between St. Peter and St. Ann Sts.*

❽ Werlein House. Elizabeth Werlein, the woman who led a movement to save the French Quarter from demolition in the early 20th century, lived here. There is a plaque (tucked behind the shutter if the shop on the bottom floor is open) recognizing Werlein's role. A preservationist award in Werlein's honor is given every year to a property owner in the French Quarter who has upgraded the value of a building and its grounds. The house is not open for tours. ✉ *630 St. Ann St.*

★ ❽ **Woldenberg Riverfront Park.** One of the most accessible riverfront areas in the country, this stretch of green from Canal Street to Esplanade Avenue has a breathtaking view of the Mississippi River as it curves around New Orleans, giving the city the name the Crescent City. The wooden promenade section in front of the French Quarter is called **Moon Walk,** named for Mayor Moon Landrieu, under whose administration in the 1970s the riverfront beyond the flood wall was first opened to public view. Woldenberg Park is named for its benefactor, local businessman Malcolm Woldenberg, whose statue is in the park. *Ocean Song,* a large kinetic sculpture near the statue of Woldenberg, was created by local artist John T. Scott. ☽ *Weekdays 6 AM–10 PM, weekends 6 AM–midnight.*

LOWER FRENCH QUARTER AND FAUBOURG MARIGNY

The area of the French Quarter nearer to Esplanade Avenue, called by locals the Lower Quarter, makes an exciting tour for anyone interested in places that locals are more likely to frequent. The tour includes Frenchmen Street beyond the French Quarter, which in recent years has become known for its music clubs and eating places. There are generally fewer police officers in these areas than around Jackson Square, so be aware of your surroundings, and take a cab at night.

Numbers in the text correspond to numbers in the margin and on the French Quarter and CBD map.

A Good Walk

Decatur Street east of Jackson Square runs along the historic **French Market** ㉚, a four-block stretch of stalls, shops, and restaurants. Grab a cold drink (local jargon for soft drink with lots of ice in a "go cup") where Decatur and North Peters streets meet. Stop for a moment while getting your drink to salute the dazzling gold-leaf statue of Joan of Arc on her horse at **Place de France** ㉛. The temporary **New Orleans Jazz National Historical Park Visitor Center** ㉜ behind the statue to the left at 916 North Peters Street (which is a walkway and not a street) offers a good introduction to the local music scene. Then head up toward Esplanade Avenue.

The small, triangular Latrobe Park, beyond the Market Café, often has live music and an endless stream of passersby. Back on Decatur and in the alley behind the market there are lots of places to browse. An array of products and people fill the **Community Flea Market** ㉝. Local vendors are likely to speak in the distinctive New Orleans accent, a linguistic cousin of the Brooklyn accent. You'll pass the Palm Court Jazz Café (✉ 1204 Decatur St.), which serves up hot jazz with its Creole dishes (☞ French Quarter *in* Chapter 4).

The **Old Mint** ㉞, an imposing brick building at Esplanade Avenue, minted Confederate coins during the Civil War but today houses the New Orleans Jazz Collection and rotating history and art exhibitions.

Across Esplanade Avenue (*es*-plan-aid) lies the Faubourg Marigny (*foe*-borg *mah*-rih-nee), whose narrow streets—especially Frenchmen Street—have coffeehouses, bookstores, restaurants, and music clubs; a good way to enjoy this unassuming neighborhood is by bicycle. **Washington Square Park** ㉟, between Royal and Dauphine streets, is a good place to rest, play Frisbee, or listen to an open-air concert. The far side of the park borders on Elysian Fields, a major thoroughfare. A block down on the right is the **American Aquatic Gardens** ㊱, a commercial nursery that creates a restful oasis filled with water lilies, and fountains. Return back along the park on Dauphine Street two blocks to Touro Street. Architecture here covers a wide range from classic Creole cottage to Victorian mansion, all in various stages of rehabilitation.

Go one block down Royal Street and cross Esplanade Avenue and you're back into the French Quarter. The privately owned **Gauche House** ㊲ is an 1856 Creole estate in the grand style. At Barracks Street you can look to the right at John James Audubon's first studio (⊠ 721 Barracks Street), where the famous artist and ornithologist began his career. Architecture enthusiasts will thrill at the simplicity of line and composition of the **Latrobe House** ㊳, built in 1814, which is, as the sign claims, probably the oldest example of Greek Revival architecture in New Orleans. At Governor Nicholls Street is the **Haunted House** ㊴ of local ghost-lore fame.

Continuing down Royal Street, you pass **Gallier House** ㊵, the former home of architect James Gallier, built in 1857 and now a museum. Stop at the corner of Ursulines Street and look back up Royal to the roof of the Haunted House to see a widow's walk, a small room on the roof from which you can see the river. Women would watch for their husbands' ships to return from dangerous voyages.

Two blocks away on Bourbon is **Lafitte's Blacksmith Shop** ㊶, today a popular bar. If its walls could speak, they would tell about the notorious pirate Jean Lafitte, who reportedly fronted his vast buccaneer empire with a legitimate business here. This part of Bourbon Street begins the raucous nightclub-filled area that is the center of the gay community. In the surrounding blocks is a cluster of lesbian and gay bars.

Down Ursulines Street to the left at Chartres Street is a lovely brick-wall garden that belongs to the **Beauregard-Keyes House** ㊷ next door. Docents proudly recount the house's long history and show off its fine furniture and courtyard. Across Chartres Street is the **Old Ursuline Convent** ㊸, the oldest surviving building in the Mississippi Valley, now a museum. The street behind the convent is Decatur Street and will bring you back to the French Market.

TIMING

To walk the whole tour, plan on a half day. If you stop to eat or relax along the way or tour museums (tours last about an hour), count on spending a full day for this tour. Frenchmen Street clubs come alive at night around 9 if you're planning to club hop with the locals.

Sights to See

㊱ **American Aquatic Gardens.** A commercial nursery a short hike from the French Quarter in the **Faubourg Marigny** (☞ *below*), this is a wonderfully relaxing place in which to observe a variety of grasses, reeds, and water lilies. Dozens of artistic fountains add pleasant water sounds. You're not pressured to buy anything. ⊠ *621 Elysian Fields,* ☎ *504/944–0410.* ⊙ *Daily 9–5.*

★ ㊷ **Beauregard-Keyes House.** This stately 19th-century mansion with period furnishings was the temporary home of Confederate General P.

G. T. Beauregard. The house and grounds had severely deteriorated in the 1940s when the well-known novelist Frances Parkinson Keyes moved in and helped restore it. Her studio at the back of the large courtyard remains intact. Keyes wrote 40 novels in this studio, all in longhand, among them the local favorite, *Dinner at Antoine's*. If you do not have time to tour the house, be sure to take a peek through the gates at the beautiful walled garden at the corner of Chartres and Ursulines streets. Landscaped in the same sun pattern as Jackson Square, the garden is in bloom throughout the year. ⊠ *1113 Chartres St.,* ☎ *504/523–7257.* ⊿ *$4.* ⊙ *Mon.–Sat. 10–3, tours on the hr.*

㉝ **Community Flea Market.** At this child of the 1960s near the end of the French Market, dozens of merchants rent tables to sell a variety of goods. The sharp-eyed shopper can find bargains here, especially among the collectibles and local memorabilia, jewelry, ceramics, old magazines, and records. ⊠ *Decatur St., near Governor Nicholls St.* ⊿ *Free.* ⊙ *Daily 7–7, hrs may vary depending on weather.*

NEED A BREAK?
At **Croissant d'Or/Patisserie** (⊠ 617 Ursulines St., ☎ 504/524–4663), French pastries are baked on the premises. This was an Italian ice cream parlor, and the interior has ornate Italian decorations.

Faubourg Marigny. Faubourg means suburb, and this one was developed in the early 1800s by Bernard Marigny, a wealthy planter. Faubourg Marigny lies across Esplanade Avenue from the French Quarter. Coffeehouses, bookstores, restaurants, and music clubs line Frenchmen Street. All the streets are narrow and intersect at odd angles; look for street names in inlaid tiles at crosswalks. This neighborhood, and Frenchmen Street in particular, is where some of the city's best musicians play. Music venues of note include **Checkpoint Charlie's, the Dragon's Den, Café Brasil,** and **Snug Harbor** (☞ French Quarter *in* Chapter 4).

A good way to enjoy this unassuming neighborhood is by bicycle; you can rent one at **Bicycle Michael's** (☞ Participant Sports and Fitness *in* Chapter 5). If biking poops you out, relax in **Washington Square Park** (☞ *below*). ⊠ *Bordered by Esplanade, Franklin, and St. Claude Aves., and the Mississippi River.*

NEED A BREAK?
P. J.'s Coffee and Teas (⊠ 634 Frenchmen St., ☎ 504/949–2292) is a neighborhood hangout that serves hot and iced coffee or tea and pastries. Part of a local chain, this is a good place to people-watch and catch some music from sidewalk tables.

★ ㉚ **French Market.** The sounds, colors, and smells here are alluring: street performers, ships' horns on the river, pralines, muffulettas, sugarcane, and Creole tomatoes. Originally a Native American trading post, later a bustling open-air market under the French and Spanish, the French Market now contains shops, offices, and eating places. This stretch of renovated buildings with graceful arches, some areas open-air and some enclosed, extends several blocks along Decatur and North Peters streets. The market has always figured strongly in the life of the city. You'll enjoy exploring not only from the street but also from the flagstone areas alongside and behind the buildings. On weekends street performers and musicians usually enliven the market's outdoor areas.

Although the **Farmer's Market** section of the French Market blends in well with the ensemble, the two open-air sheds that comprise it and the **Community Flea Market** (☞ *above*) were built more recently, in 1936, as part of a Works Progress Administration project. Since then, farmers from the New Orleans area have pulled their trucks up to the loading bays here and offered their produce for sale. If you arrive very early in the morning, you are likely to see some of the better-known chefs in the city culling through the baskets and cartons of fresh fruits, vegetables, seafood, and seasonings and ordering for their restaurants.

Latrobe Park, a small recreational area within the French Market, honors Benjamin Latrobe, designer of the city's first waterworks. A modern fountain evoking a waterworks marks the spot where Latrobe's invention once stood. Sunken seating, fountains, and greenery make this a lovely spot to relax with a drink served from a kiosk nearby. ⊠ *Decatur St.*

④ **Gallier House.** Famous New Orleans architect James Gallier designed this as his family home in 1857. Today it contains an excellent collection of early Victorian furnishings. The tour includes the house, servants' quarters, grounds, and a gift shop. Take a moment to look through the carriageway; it is the only one in the city with a carriage parked in it. ⊠ *1132 Royal St.,* ☎ *504/525–5661.* ☑ *$6; $10 combination ticket with the Hermann-Grima House.* ◷ *Tours weekdays 10–3:30.*

㉟ **Gauche House.** One of the most distinctive houses in the French Quarter, this mansion and its service buildings date to 1856. The cherub design of the effusive ironwork is the only one of its kind. It was once the estate of businessman John Gauche and is still privately owned. This house is not open to the public. ⊠ *704 Esplanade Ave.*

㊴ **Haunted House.** Within this splendid mansion, Delphine Macarty Lalaurie, wealthy mistress of the house, reportedly tortured her slaves in the 1830s. When a fire broke out in the attic in 1834, firefighters found slaves shackled to the walls and in horrible condition. An outraged community is said to have run Madame Lalaurie from the house. Although much of this story was later put in doubt, rumors persist that the house is haunted by the screams of the unfortunate slaves. This house is not open to the public. ⊠ *1140 Royal St.*

④ **Lafitte's Blacksmith Shop.** The striking anvil no longer sounds in this ancient, weathered building. You'll hear only the clinking of glasses at this favorite local bar (☞ Bars and Lounges *in* Chapter 4) for patrons from all walks of life. Legend has it that the pirate Jean Lafitte and his cronies operated a blacksmith shop here as a front for their vast, illicit trade in contraband, though no historic records have been found to support this legend. The building, dating from 1772, is interesting as one of the few surviving examples of soft bricks reinforced with timber, a construction form used by early settlers. ⊠ *941 Bourbon St.,* ☎ *504/523–0066*

㊳ **Latrobe House.** The young New Orleans architect Henry Latrobe designed this modest house with Arsene Latour in 1814. Its smooth lines and porticoes started a passion for Greek Revival architecture in Louisiana, evidenced later in many plantation houses upriver as well as in a significant number of buildings in New Orleans. This house, believed to be the earliest example of Greek Revival in the city, is not open to the public. ⊠ *721 Governor Nicholls St.*

OFF THE
BEATEN PATH

NEW ORLEANS AFRICAN-AMERICAN MUSEUM – Set in a historic villa surrounded by lush greenery, this modest collection of local black art, history, and artifacts has a strong Caribbean feel. Tremé, the area of the museum, is the oldest black neighborhood in America. Originally a plantation owned by Claude Tremé, it was subdivided into residential lots in 1812. Many free people of color lived here, in houses that still stand. Because the museum is four blocks outside the French Quarter in an economically depressed area, you should take a cab. ⊠ *1418 Governor Nicholls St.,* ☎ *504/527–0989.* ☑ *$4.* ◷ *Tues.–Sat. 10–5.*

32 **New Orleans Jazz National Historical Park Visitor Center.** Information and exhibits on the city's great jazz musicians are presented in this temporary location while the park readies its permanent buildings in Armstrong Park. You can listen to the various forms of jazz and learn about their evolution and the musicians who gave the world this unique music. Lectures, demonstrations, and other educational live programs are featured. ⊠ *916–918 N. Peters St., French Market,* ☎ *504/589–4841.* ☞ *Free.* ☉ *Daily 9–5, but call for possibly shorter seasonal hrs.*

34 **Old Mint.** Today the Old Mint is used mainly for rotating exhibitions on southern history and as the home of the **New Orleans Jazz Collection,** which includes Louis Armstrong's first trumpet. Sheet music, artifacts, and photos of jazz players trace the history of the American music form. The **Louisiana Historical Center,** which holds the French and Spanish Louisiana archives, is open free to researchers by appointment. The building dates to 1835 and is where the Confederacy minted its money during the Civil War; later, Confederate soldiers were imprisoned in the thick-walled mint while Union troops occupied New Orleans. After the war, legal tender again was printed here until 1909. In the late 1970s the state restored the mint and turned it into a landmark in the Louisiana State Museum system. At the Barracks Street entrance, notice the one remaining sample of the mint's old walls—it'll give you an idea of the building's deterioration before its restoration. ⊠ *Esplanade Ave. and Decatur St.,* ☎ *504/568–6968.* ☞ *$5; 20% discount on tickets to 2 or more of the following museums if purchased together: Presbytère, Cabildo, 1850 House, Old Mint, and Madame John's Legacy.* ☉ *Tues.–Sun. 9–5.*

43 **Old Ursuline Convent.** The Ursulines were the first of many orders of religious women who came to New Orleans and founded schools, orphanages, and asylums and ministered to the needs of the poor. Their original convent was built in 1734 and is now the oldest French colonial building in the Mississippi valley. **St. Mary's Church,** adjoining the convent, was added in 1845. The original tract of land for a convent, school, and gardens covered several French Quarter blocks. The sisters were attended by slaves who occupied a small, narrow building still visible from the side facing Ursulines Street. Now an archive for the archdiocese, the convent was used by the Ursulines for 90 years. The formal gardens, church, and first floor of the old convent are open for guided tours. You'll want to see the herb gardens, which inspired one of the nuns to become the first pharmacist in the United States: she was never licensed, but she published a list of herbs that cured various maladies. The Ursuline Academy, the convent's girls' school founded in 1727, is now uptown on State Street, where the newer convent and chapel were built. The academy is the oldest girls' school in the country. ⊠ *1100 Chartres St.,* ☎ *504/529–3040.* ☞ *$5.* ☉ *Tours Tues.–Fri. at 10, 11, 1, 2, and 3, weekends at 11:15, 1, and 2.*

31 **Place de France.** A wedge-shape pocket park in the French Market holds a dazzling gold-leaf statue of Joan of Arc on her steed. The statue was a gift from France in 1972 to celebrate the historic ties between Louisiana and France. Two antique cannons guard the park and the four flags raised behind the statue: those of France, the United States, Louisiana, and New Orleans. The statue stood at the foot of Canal Street but was moved here in 1999 to make way for Harrah's New Orleans Casino. ⊠ *Decatur and N. Peters Sts.*

35 **Washington Square Park.** This park in the **Faubourg Marigny** (☞ *above*) provides a large green space in which to play Frisbee, listen to an open-air concert, or catch some sun. The park is closed at night; there is no security during the day, so be cautious. The far side of the park borders Elysian Fields, once a grand boulevard that city officials hoped would equal Paris's Champs-Elysées, for which it was named. It never achieved that grandeur, but it is a major thoroughfare. Weindorf, a German wine festival, is held here every September. ✉ *Bordered by Royal, Dauphine, and Frenchmen Sts. and Elysian Fields.*

FOOT OF CANAL STREET AND ALGIERS POINT

Foot of Canal Street

Canal Street, 170 ft wide, is said to be the widest main street in any city in the United States and one of the most active. It was once scheduled to be made into a canal; plans changed, but the name remains. One of the fastest-growing and most exciting areas of New Orleans is where Canal Street meets the river. Referred to by locals as the foot of Canal Street, it is within walking distance of the French Quarter (about 10 minutes) and most downtown hotels. The riverfront has been developed in recent years, and the former riverfront site of the 1984 World's Fair has been incorporated into the CBD. The RTA (Regional Transit Authority) has a streetcar that rolls through the bustling riverfront area and along Canal Street. You can use it to visit some of the sites covered in the following tour. This streetcar line is being extended along Canal Street through Mid-City and will eventually connect with the New Orleans Museum of Modern Art in City Park.

A word about the wide median strip in Canal Street, called the neutral ground by locals: In the early 1800s, after the Louisiana Purchase, the French Creoles residing in the French Quarter were segregated from the Americans who settled on the upriver side of Canal Street. The communities had separate governments and police systems, and what is now Canal Street was neutral ground between them. Today, animosities between these two groups are history, but the term neutral ground has survived as the name for all medians throughout the city.

Numbers in the text correspond to numbers in the margin and on the French Quarter and CBD map.

A Good Walk

Begin a few blocks from the river at the **Custom House** ㊹, where 200 years ago the river met the land. Look down the four blocks to the left that lead to the Mississippi River and note how much alluvial soil has been deposited by the river over the years—land that today has some of the main attractions in the city.

Down Canal Street on the left is **Canal Place** ㊺, a fashionable shopping complex. At the end of Canal Street on the left are the **Aquarium of the Americas** ㊻ and the **Entergy IMAX Theater** ㊼, with Woldenberg Riverfront Park (☞ Upper French Quarter, *above*) around and behind them, forming a major educational and entertainment attraction.

Canal Street ends another block down at the Mississippi River with the Canal Street Ferry Terminal (☞ Algiers Point, *below*). **Harrah's New Orleans Casino** ㊽, a turreted brick complex, dominates on the right. The **World Trade Center** ㊾ across from the casino is surrounded by statues and plazas. Behind the World Trade Center is the **Spanish Plaza** ㊿, a large, sunken plateau with lovely tiles and a fountain. To the right, down several steps, is the entrance into **Riverwalk Marketplace** (51), an old warehouse strip that has been transformed into a ½-mi market holding more than 200 shops, cafés, and restaurants.

Exiting from the third level of the Riverwalk, you can see how the marketplace complex conveniently ties the New Orleans Hilton Riverside and Spanish Plaza at its lower end to the **Ernest N. Morial Convention Center** at its upper end. This stretch of land held the 1984 Louisiana World Exposition (World's Fair).

Three short blocks away from the water on Poydras Street is **Piazza d'Italia** ㉒, a postmodern Roman-inspired ruin. The **American-Italian Museum** ㉝ is on the edge of the piazza and chronicles Italian contributions to the city. You'll find that the hodgepodge of shops, music clubs, and restaurants in this area provides interesting browsing. However, it can be deserted late at night, so use caution.

On Julia Street, three blocks up Commerce Street from the great arch of the piazza, lies the **Warehouse District,** the location of art galleries, glass-blowing studios, furniture-making shops, bars, and eateries. This area has become a new neighborhood with a number of the old warehouses converted to upscale condos. It also is home to the **Louisiana Children's Museum** ㉞. To get back to Canal Street, catch the St. Charles Avenue streetcar two blocks past Camp Street where it travels downtown on Carondelet Street.

TIMING

It will take about a half day for a leisurely stroll among the shops and galleries and a walk along the riverfront. The aquarium takes at least two hours, and the IMAX theater is one hour. Shopping or browsing in the Riverwalk Marketplace can take one to two hours. For a pleasant all-day trip, you can combine this walk with the Algiers Point tour (☞ *below*) or check out the shopping chapter for places to reach by bus or cab on Magazine Street. Sights along the New Orleans riverfront are open in the evening and are patrolled; other places, if you are on foot, should be visited only during daylight hours.

Sights to See

㉝ **American-Italian Museum.** Italian–New Orleanian customs are explained and artifacts exhibited in this carefully curated museum. The research library includes records of the large local Italian immigrant community. ✉ *537 S. Peters St.,* ☎ *504/522–7294.* ☞ *Free.* ☉ *Wed.–Sat. 10–2.*

㊻ **Aquarium of the Americas.** In this major family attraction, more than 7,000 aquatic creatures swim in 60 displays ranging from 500 to 500,000 gallons of water. Each of the four major exhibit areas—the Amazon River Basin, the Caribbean Reef, the Mississippi River, and the Gulf Coast—has fish and animals native to that environment. The spectacular design allows you to feel part of the watery world by offering close-up encounters with the inhabitants. A gift shop and café are on the premises.

Woldenberg Riverfront Park (☞ Upper French Quarter, *above*), which surrounds the aquarium, is a tranquil spot with a view of the Mississippi. Package tickets for the aquarium and a river cruise are available outside the aquarium. You can also combine tickets for the aquarium and the **Entergy IMAX Theater** (☞ *below*) or for the aquarium, a river cruise, and the Audubon Zoo in a package; you can take the river cruise by itself. ✉ *Foot of Canal St.,* ☎ *504/581–4629.* ☞ *Aquarium $13; combination ticket with IMAX $17.25.* ☉ *Sun.–Thurs. 9:30–6 (last ticket sold at 5), Fri.–Sat. 9:30–7 (last ticket sold at 6).*

㊺ **Canal Place.** In addition to such tony stores as Saks Fifth Avenue, Brooks Brothers, and Ralph Lauren Polo, this upscale shopping and office complex contains **Canal Place Cinema,** the only location in this area that screens first-run movies. The four theaters and the concession stand have artwork based on local novelist Walker Percy's *The Moviegoer.* The **Wyndham New Orleans at Canal Place** (☞ Chapter 3) tops the complex; its dining rooms and lobby have a fantastic view of the river. ✉ *333 Canal St.,* ☏ *504/587–0739.*

44 **Custom House.** Government offices now fill this massive building, which has been home to many, including General Butler, commanding officer of the Union troops during the Civil War occupation of New Orleans. Built in 1849, it occupies the whole block and replaces what had been Fort St. Louis, which guarded the old French city. The building has identical entrances on all four sides, because at the time it was completed no decision had been made as to which side would be the main entrance. You are welcome to look around, but there are no tours of the building. Future plans call for an insectarium to be built by the Audobon Institute. ✉ *423 Canal St.*

47 **Entergy IMAX Theater.** This cinema along the river and adjacent to the **Aquarium of the Americas** (☞ *above*) has an 11,500-watt digital sound system and a screen 5½ stories tall. The theater shows classic IMAX fare—high-quality nature films related to the sea, Earth, and outer space that are suitable for everyone in the family. ✉ *Foot of Canal St.,* ☏ *504/581–4629.* ▣ *Theater $7.75, combination ticket with aquarium $17.25.* ☉ *Shows daily on the hr 10–6 (last film at 6; arrive 30 mins before any show time).*

Ernest N. Morial Convention Center. One of the largest and most modern convention facilities in the country, the center is 1.1 million square ft and is named for the mayor who oversaw the construction of the center's first phase. New Orleans depends on its extensive convention business; here it hosts conferences that draw hundreds of thousands of conventioneers and events that exhibit large industrial equipment, airplanes, trucks, and more. Two on-site kitchens are capable of preparing 20,000 meals a day. It's not open for tours. A fourth phase of expansion is planned for sometime during the decade. ✉ *900 Convention Blvd.,* ☏ *504/582–3000.*

48 **Harrah's New Orleans Casino.** The only land-based casino in Louisiana, the new Harrah's contains 175,000 square ft of space divided into five areas, each with a New Orleans theme: Jazz Court, Court of Good Fortune, Smugglers Court, Mardi Gras Court, and Court of the Mansion (☞ Gambling *in* Chapter 4). ✉ *512 S. Peters St.,* ☏ *504/533–6000 or 800/427–7247.* ☉ *Daily 24 hrs.*

54 **Louisiana Children's Museum.** One of the best learning facilities of its type in the country has lots of hands-on activities, a special playscape for infants and toddlers, a theater with spectacular science shows, math and physics labs, a waterworks, and a miniature grocery store. ✉ *420 Julia St.,* ☏ *504/523–1357.* ▣ *$5.* ☉ *Late Aug.–early June, Tues.–Sat. 9:30–4:30, Sun. noon–4:30; early June–late Aug., Mon.–Sat. 9:30–4:30, Sun. noon–4:30. Last ticket sold at 4.*

52 **Piazza d'Italia.** This modern, award-winning plaza by local architect Charles Moore is a gathering place for the large Italian community on St. Joseph's Day and Columbus Day. Its postmodern style, reminiscent of a Roman ruin, has been featured in several movies, most prominently in the opening scene of *The Big Easy.* On the South Peters Street side of the piazza is the **American-Italian Museum** (☞ *above*).

....

NEED A
BREAK?

Mulate's Cajun Restaurant (✉ 734 Convention Center Blvd., ☏ 504/522–1492), is a lively place. You can listen to live Cajun music while tasting the famous dishes of southwestern Louisiana. **The Praline Connection** (✉ 907 S. Peters St., ☏ 504/523–3973) serves the soul food version of Creole cuisine in a fun atmosphere that often includes live jazz.

....

⑤ Riverwalk Marketplace. This three-block-long shopping and entertainment center with 140 shops and eateries is laid out in three tiers and connected by a promenade that stretches along the river's edge. Plaques along the walkway relate bits of the Mississippi River's history and folklore. Nearby at the Poydras Street streetcar stop is a grand splash of color, a 200-ft-long Mexican mural on the flood wall. The tropical motifs are creations of Julio Quintanilla, and the mural is a gift to New Orleans from Mérida, Mexico, the artist's native city. Various cruise ships leave from the Julia Street Wharf slightly upriver and can often be seen from the front of the Riverwalk. ⊠ *1 Poydras St.,* ☎ *504/592–0526.* ☉ *Daily 10–9.*

⑤ Spanish Plaza. For a terrific view of the river and a place to relax, go behind the **World Trade Center** (☞ *below*) at 2 Canal Street to Spanish Plaza, a large, sunken plateau with beautiful inlaid tiles and a magnificent fountain. The plaza was a gift from Spain in the mid-1970s; live music is often played here, and a loading area and ticket offices for riverboat cruises face the river.

Warehouse District. It draws artists and other creative types today, but this area that runs parallel to the river from Poydras Street to Howard Avenue and Tchoupitoulas Street to St. Charles Avenue was originally developed in the late 1800s to service the port. Warehouse buildings and factories here were abandoned by the mid-1900s when much of the port's trade moved upriver or to the Gulf Coast. In the 1980s, influenced by the World's Fair nearby on the river, developers began renovating the sturdy old buildings into condos, shops, and studios. The loft space attracted some of the city's best-known artists and craftspeople. This district, referred to as the SoHo of the South, is home to some of the city's finest art galleries (☞ Chapter 6), as well as the **Louisiana Children's Museum** (☞ *above*). Julia Street and the blocks off it in this stretch are fun to explore for their glass-blowing studios, furniture-making shops, bars, and eateries.

⑭ World Trade Center. Dozens of foreign consulates and many international trade offices are housed in this 33-floor building facing the river. **Top of the Mart** (☞ Bars and Lounges *in* Chapter 4), on the top floor, is a revolving bar that has dancing and gives a great view of the city and river. The building is surrounded by statues and plazas; Winston Churchill is memorialized in a bronze statue in **British Park Place,** also known as Winston's Circle, where the stone-inlaid street curves in front of the Riverfront Hilton to the right; and a bronze equestrian statue of Bernardo de Galvez, Spanish governor of Louisiana in the 1780s, guards the entrance of the **Spanish Plaza** (☞ *above*) behind the World Trade Center. ⊠ *2 Canal St.,* ☎ *504/581–4888.*

Algiers Point

Directly across the Mississippi River from the French Quarter and Canal Street is the Westbank (as the west bank is known) neighborhood of Algiers, which is a part of New Orleans. Extending out into the curve of the river is the 25-block area known as Algiers Point, which is accessible by ferry from the Canal Street Ferry Terminal (☞ Boat & Ferry Travel *in* Smart Travel Tips A to Z). Settled at the turn of the century, Algiers Point is an extension of New Orleans but a world apart from the city. Its quiet, tree-lined streets, quaint shops, and renovated Victorian houses are aspects of a community that has managed to remain somewhat isolated. In the early days of New Orleans, Algiers was a holding area for the African slaves from the many ships that made their way into the port. The slaves were ferried across the river to the French Quarter, where they were auctioned. It is speculated that Algiers is named for the North African slave port.

Algiers Point is best experienced by walking along its quiet streets, admiring the architecture, and savoring its small-town feel. However, because it is primarily residential and is separated from the main part of the city by the river, it is isolated; you should take the usual precautions for personal safety. The big attraction here is Blaine Kern's Mardi Gras World, where Mardi Gras floats are made. A one-man Algiers Point welcoming and information service is offered by Russell Templet (pronounced TOM-play) at his **Hair and Style Shop** (✉ 143 Delaronde St., ☎ 504/368–9417) a half block on the right from the ferry landing. Feel free to drop in and say hello.

Numbers in the text correspond to numbers in the margin and on the Algiers Point map.

A Good Walk

Blaine Kern's Mardi Gras World (55), the main attraction on this side of the river, lies a five-minute drive downriver. You can take a free shuttle there or stroll the **Jazz Walk of Fame,** a pedestrian path that leads from the ferry terminal to Mardi Gras World, and then catch the shuttle that runs daily from 9:30 to 4 back to the ferry. The ferry terminal is also the start of the neighborhood walk.

The following walk takes you around the historic renovation district that is bordered by Morgan Street, Patterson Road, Verret Street, Opelousas Avenue, and Powder Street. Note the various sizes and styles of houses, from ornate mansions to modest shotgun houses (in which all the doors open one behind another in a straight line, so you could fire a gun from the front step to a backyard wall without hitting a wall in between), a popular style of working-class architecture in New Orleans. Since these homes were all built around the early 1900s, they reflect the Victorian influence in vogue at that time.

From the ferry terminal, walk down on the left to Morgan Street. The Moorish-inspired Algiers Courthouse, built in 1896 and still in use, is on Morgan Street facing the levee. Its distinctive clock tower can be seen from the French Quarter. Bermuda Street at the next corner is lined with typical Victorian cottages, as are Pelican Avenue and Lavergne and Verret streets. No houses here are open to the public, but homeowners are flattered when strollers stop to admire the many fine examples of historic preservation and restoration. Walk down Bermuda Street, take a left on Pelican Avenue and follow it to Verret Street. At this corner is a vintage gas station (no longer in use) with its unique Gulf sign intact.

Confetti Park, a triangular playground, will be on your right a block down Verret Street. It has a whimsical iron fence and walkways inlaid with marbles, doubloons, and shards of pottery. Across the street is a town square dominated by **Holy Name of Mary Church** (56), a fine example of 1920s Gothic architecture. Within the square, McDonogh Memorial Park has a provincial French atmosphere, with small houses and shops lining its sides. An obelisk in the center honors local residents who died in various wars.

Two blocks beyond the park lies Opelousas Avenue, once as grand as St. Charles Avenue. This wide street with a canopy of oaks has since fallen on hard times, and you should be careful when walking here. As an alternative, wander along Seguin, Alix, and Eliza streets on your way back to the ferry terminal, taking time to study the ornate houses with lush gardens.

Back on the ferry, you will notice Bollinger Algiers, Inc., on your right. Oceangoing vessels are put into dry dock here for repairs and refur-

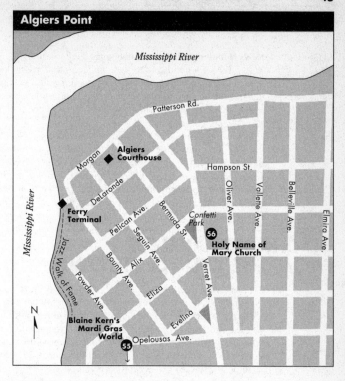

Algiers Point

bishing, a reminder that New Orleans is a world-class port. Some work areas are visible from the ferry and levee.

TIMING

Allot two to three hours for the ferry rides and the neighborhood walk. The ferry takes a half hour each way, and you'll want at least an hour to wander along the streets of this small-town neighborhood. Count on another two hours if you take in the Jazz Walk of Fame and Mardi Gras World. The ferry ride is fine at night, but caution is advised if you do any walking on the Algiers side after dark.

Sights to See

🐾 following the text of a review is your signal that the property has a Web site, where you will find details and, usually, images; for a link, visit www.fodors.com/urls.

🖐 **55** **Blaine Kern's Mardi Gras World.** Mardi Gras is born here each year, where many of the city's most elaborate parade floats are born. You can watch the artists and builders at work, view a film about Mardi Gras, and buy Carnival memorabilia in the gift shop. A photo of yourself with one of the giant figures used on the floats makes a terrific souvenir. There's a chest full of costumes that children are welcome to try on. Blaine Kern has for many years been the best-known artist and creator of Mardi Gras floats; he often personally conducts tours through this one-of-a-kind facility. A free shuttle van meets the ferry to take visitors to Mardi Gras World (and it's a good idea to use it; the blocks before you get there are often deserted). ✉ *233 Newton St.,* ☎ *504/ 361–7821.* 🖼 *$11.50 includes cake and coffee.* ⊙ *Daily 9:30–4:30 (hrs vary around Mardi Gras).* 🐾

56 **Holy Name of Mary Church.** The largest church in Algiers, this red-brick building was constructed in 1929 to replace a former church from

1871. It is designed in English Gothic style and dominates the 400 block of Verret Street. ⊠ *500 Eliza St.,* ☎ *504/362–5511.*

NEED A
BREAK? **News N Brews at the Point Coffeehouse** (⊠ 347 Verret St., ☎ 504/ 367–2326) is a good spot to meet the locals and get the latest political scoop. There are tables and chairs on the sidewalk and a good selection of coffees, teas, salads, sandwiches, and pastries. It's owned by councilman Troy Carter, who drops in fairly regularly.

Jazz Walk of Fame. The many famous musicians in New Orleans who invented jazz and have kept it dynamically alive are honored in this 3,300-ft walk along the levee. The lampposts here have buttons that, when pushed, give a brief biography and a sampling of the musician's work. Photos and plaques also contain information. Benches overlooking the Mississippi River make this a pleasant place to relax and catch some river breezes. ⊠ *Algiers Levee at the Algiers Ferry Terminal.*

ST. CHARLES AVENUE FROM THE CBD TO UPTOWN

The best way to explore the CBD, the Garden District, and Uptown New Orleans is to ride the historic St. Charles Avenue streetcar. In the CBD are hotels, office buildings, and government buildings. You can exit the streetcar at Poydras Street for a side trip to the Superdome, or you could walk from Canal Street to the Superdome and back to the Poydras Street streetcar stop and start the tour there. Lee Circle, with its imposing statue of General Robert E. Lee, marks the end of the CBD; several museums and art centers can be accessed from this streetcar stop. The Garden District is full of gracious homes; you may view many pillared mansions from the streetcar or exit at Washington Street and follow the walking tour. New Orleans's Uptown area takes in many more homes, churches, schools, and universities. Audubon Park and Zoo are here; you may exit at the streetcar stop at the park to explore these attractions.

In the early 1900s streetcars were the most prominent mode of public transit and ran on many streets, but today they operate only along the riverfront, Canal Street, and St. Charles Avenue. The streetcars are well maintained by the Regional Transit Authority, which also operates the city buses. Avoid rush hours—from 7 to 9 and 3 to 6—or you may have to stand much of the way and will not be able to enjoy the scenery or sights.

Numbers in the text correspond to numbers in the margin and on the St. Charles Avenue from the CBD to Uptown map.

CBD and Lee Circle

A Good Ride and Walk

To begin the tour, board the streetcar at the **St. Charles–Common Street stop** ①, marked by a small yellow sign. The first four blocks up St. Charles Avenue are not remarkable; they include office buildings and banks typical of any business district. At the third stop, Poydras Street, the skyscrapers on either side are among the most impressive in the city— the 27-story Pan American Life Insurance building on the left and the 50-story One Shell Square on the right. If you wish, exit at Poydras Street for the Louisiana Superdome.

After Poydras Street, the next three stops along St. Charles Avenue pass through the seat of the American government during New Orleans's antebellum years. Lafayette Square, a small park with a bronze fountain in the center and statues of Henry Clay, Benjamin Franklin, and John McDonogh (benefactor of public education in New Orleans), is on the left at the first stop. On the far side of Lafayette Square is the Federal Court of Appeals, Fifth Circuit.

On the right at the first stop is Gallier Hall, a former city hall. It is considered the finest example of Greek Revival architecture in New Orleans, with Grecian Ionic touches and a portico of white marble. Built in 1850, it was designed by local architect James Gallier and is now used for city offices and as a reception facility and theater.

In two stops is Julia Street; the block on the left, Julia Row, has the Thirteen Sisters—13 redbrick row houses from 1833 that line the entire right side of the 600 block. The Warehouse District—the center of which is the 400 and 500 blocks of Julia Street—is the hub of the city's art community (☞ Foot of Canal Street and Algiers Point, *above*, and Warehouse District *in* Chapter 6).

The intersection up ahead is **Lee Circle** ②; bend down and look up to the left to see the statue of Robert E. Lee. You can exit at this stop to explore a number of museums. Upon exiting just beyond Lee Circle, face the statue in the circle and walk to your right. Beyond Howard Avenue is the new **Ogden Museum of Southern Art** ③, with its major regional collection. Walk back to Howard Avenue, turn left, and then turn left again on Camp Street. The **Memorial Hall Confederate Museum** ④, with its Civil War artifacts, is on the left, and the **Contemporary Arts Center** ⑤, with art exhibits, a cybercafé, and performance spaces, is on the right. Back on Howard Avenue, one block farther down is the **National D-Day Museum** ⑥, two warehouse-size buildings that house tanks and other vehicles from World War II. When you are done touring the area, reboard the streetcar at Lee Circle.

The Jerusalem Temple, on the corner on the right after Lee Circle, where the U.S. 90 expressway crosses St. Charles Avenue, is home to the city's large Shriner community. Built in 1916, the temple has intricate mosaic tile scenes on its facade.

Two stops after Lee Circle is Martin Luther King Jr. Boulevard. This streetcar stop is your chance to see the Martin Luther King Jr. statue, which is 15 blocks to your right.

The Red Room restaurant and nightclub (☞ Music Venues *in* Chapter 4), one of the more novel buildings in the city, is on the left at the intersection of Josephine Street and St. Charles Avenue, after three more stops. Each piece of the original restaurant inside the Eiffel Tower in Paris was shipped here and carefully reassembled in 1986. The Pontchartrain Hotel, a venerable, old-style grand hotel (☞ Garden District/Uptown *in* Chapter 3), is on the right as you approach the next stop, at Josephine Street.

The Garden District starts at the next stop, the wide intersection at Jackson Avenue. The next five blocks on the left contain most of the district. Some homes on the next three blocks of St. Charles Avenue date to the 1850s and display classic Greek Revival features in the simple, graceful lines of their columns, doorways, and window frames. Exit at Jackson Avenue to visit the **House of Broel's Victorian Mansion and Doll House Museum** ⑦—the name says it all. Washington Avenue, intersecting at the next stop, is in the heart of the Garden District. Exit here for the Garden District walking tour.

TIMING

This first segment of the streetcar tour, from the CBD to the Garden District, takes approximately 25 minutes if you do not leave the street

car. The Louisiana Superdome is about a half-hour walk from the streetcar; the Superdome tour takes another hour and a half. Add one to
two hours for seeing the museums and art centers around Lee Circle.
Julia Street and the Warehouse District, with many art galleries and a
children's museum, are within easy walking distance toward the river.
You could make a day of sightseeing by visiting Lee Circle and Julia
Street. The streetcar is available and generally safe well into the night;
however, you should not take the side trip to the Superdome on foot
after business hours.

Sights to See

⑤ Contemporary Arts Center. The center, in a warehouse that has won
prizes for its restoration, serves as an anchor in the arts district. Works
by local artists and traveling special exhibits are showcased. The center also hosts concerts, films, theatrical and dance performances, and
art-related workshops and seminars. ⊠ *900 Camp St.,* ☎ *504/523–
1216.* ▭ *Varies with event.* ☉ *Daily; sometimes closed when preparing new exhibits, so call ahead.*

NEED A   In the Contemporary Arts Center, the modernistic cybercafé **N.O. Net**
BREAK?   **Cafe** (⊠ 900 Camp St., ☎ 504/523–0990) mixes lunch and cocktails
           with the usual coffee fare. Free access to the Internet keeps patrons in
           touch with the outside world.

⑦ House of Broel's Victorian Mansion and Doll House Museum. Antique
furnishings fill this restored antebellum home. The dollhouse collection of owner Bonnie Broel includes beautiful miniatures of Victorian,
Tudor, and plantation-style houses. ⊠ *2220 St. Charles Ave.,* ☎ *504/
522–2220.* ▭ *Mansion and museum $5.* ☉ *Mon.–Sat. 10–4.*

② Lee Circle. A bronze statue of Civil War general Robert E. Lee stands
high above the city on a white marble column in this traffic circle; Lee
faces due north, as he has since 1884. Recent extensive renovation and
new construction have greatly improved the riverside area of the circle. The **Contemporary Arts Center** (☞ *above*), the new **Ogden Museum of Southern Art,** the **National D-Day Museum,** and the **Memorial
Hall Confederate Museum** (☞ *below* for all) are a worthwhile group
of art and history museums.

OFF THE   **LOUISIANA SUPERDOME –** A national sports facility, the site of many
BEATEN PATH   Sugar Bowls and a number of Super Bowls, and home to the New Or-
                 leans Saints football team, the Superdome seats up to 100,000 people
                 and is one of the largest buildings of its kind in the world. Built in 1975,
                 it has a 166,000-square-ft playing field and a roof that covers almost 8
                 acres at a height of 27 stories. The bronze statue on the Poydras Street
                 side is the Vietnam Veterans Memorial. The New Orleans Sports Arena,
                 behind the Superdome, is home to the New Orleans Brass hockey team
                 and Tulane University's basketball team. Across from the Superdome on
                 Poydras Street is a large abstract sculpture called the *Krewe of Poydras.*
                 The sculptor, Ida Kohlmeyer, meant to evoke the frivolity and zany spirit
                 of Mardi Gras. A good walk (about eight long blocks) down Poydras
                 Street to the right off St. Charles Avenue brings you to the Superdome.
                 Along the way you will pass the Bloch Cancer Survivors Monument, a
                 block-long walkway of whimsical columns, figures, and a triumphal
                 arch, in the median of Loyola Avenue at its intersection with Poydras
                 Street. The streets around the Superdome and Civic Center are usually
                 busy during business hours, but at night and on weekends, except dur-
                 ing a game, this area generally is deserted and should not be explored

alone. ⊠ *1 Sugar Bowl Dr.,* ☎ *504/587-3810.* ☜ *Tour $6.* ☉ *Tours weekdays 10:30, noon, and 1:30 except during some events.*

MARTIN LUTHER KING JR. STATUE – Mounted on a marble pillar, this bronze bust of King is in the median of Claiborne Avenue near the boulevard named for the famous civil rights leader. The pillar, engraved with excerpts from King's "I have a dream" speech, is the site of an annual rally and wreath-laying ceremony on the Martin Luther King Jr. national holiday. King, who often visited New Orleans, helped found the Southern Christian Leadership Conference (SCLC) at the New Zion Baptist Church (⊠ 2319 3rd St.) in this area. ⊠ *2 streetcar stops after Lee Circle, on the right off St. Charles Ave. Walk 15 blocks up Martin Luther King Jr. Blvd. to Claiborne Ave.*

❹ Memorial Hall Confederate Museum. This museum in an ivy-covered stone building at Lee Circle has an extensive collection of artifacts from the Civil War, including uniforms, flags, and personal items from soldiers. There are also effects from generals and officials such as Jefferson Davis. Opened in 1891, it's the oldest museum in Louisiana. ⊠ *929 Camp St.,* ☎ *504/523-4522.* ☜ *$5.* ☉ *Mon.–Sat. 10–4.*

NEED A BREAK?   The **Hummingbird Grill** (⊠ 804 St. Charles Ave., ☎ 504/523-9165) is an aging greasy spoon fictionalized by New Orleans novelists and dear to many New Orleanians of all social strata. It's open around the clock.

★ ❻ National D-Day Museum. The brainchild of historian and writer Dr. Stephen Ambrose, retired professor at the University of New Orleans, this massive two-warehouse facility is the only museum dedicated to the 1944 D-Day invasion of Normandy and 18 other beach invasions during World War II. Exhibits include a replica of the Higgins boat troop-landing craft, which were made in New Orleans; a British Spitfire and an American Avenger fighter planes; a tank; and many other artifacts presented in excellent themed displays that interpret the events of the era. The Louisiana Memorial Pavilion building has a theater that plays war footage and documentaries. ⊠ *925 Magazine St.,* ☎ *504/527-6012.* ☜ *$6.* ☉ *Daily 9–5.*

❸ Ogden Museum of Southern Art. At press time, the former landmark Howard Memorial Library on Lee Circle was set to open as a fine new regional art museum in fall 2001. Until then, selected works can be seen at 603 Julia Street on weekdays from 10 to 5; call the number below for more information. More than 500 works collected since the 1960s by local developer Robert Houston Ogden form the center of an eclectic collection. A walkway leads to a second building. ⊠ *615 Howard Ave.,* ☎ *504/539-9600.*

❶ St. Charles-Common Street car stop. In the French Quarter, Royal Street changes its name to St. Charles Avenue upon crossing Canal Street. If you miss one streetcar, duck into **Pearl Restaurant**'s oyster bar at 119 St. Charles and have some fresh, salty raw oysters while awaiting the next one.

Garden District

With its beautifully landscaped gardens surrounding elegant antebellum homes, the Garden District lives up to its name. None of the private homes is open to the public on a regular basis, but the occupants do not mind visitors enjoying the sights from outside the wrought-iron fences that surround their magnificent estates. What cannot be ap-

St. Charles Avenue from the CBD to Uptown

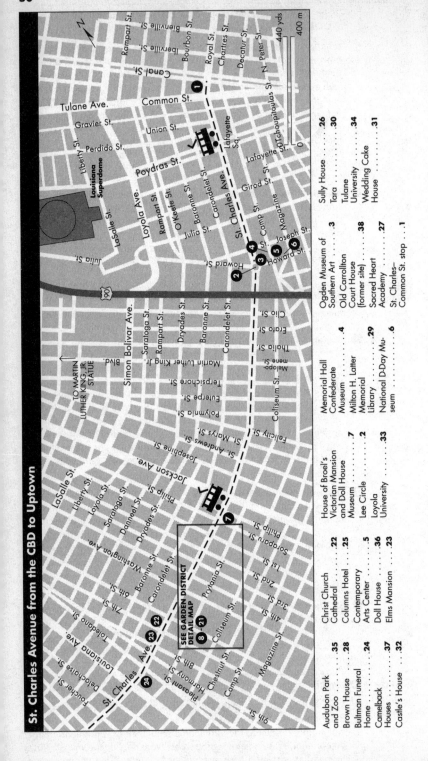

Audubon Park and Zoo **35**
Brown House **28**
Bultman Funeral Home **24**
Camelback Houses **37**
Castle's House **32**

Christ Church Cathedral **22**
Columns Hotel **25**
Contemporary Arts Center **5**
Doll House **36**
Elms Mansion **23**

House of Broel's Victorian Mansion and Doll House Museum **7**
Lee Circle **2**
Loyola University **33**

Memorial Hall Confederate Museum **4**
Milton H. Latter Memorial Library **29**
National D-Day Museum **6**

Ogden Museum of Southern Art **3**
Old Carrollton Court House (former site) **38**
Sacred Heart Academy **27**
St. Charles– Common St. stop ...**1**

Sully House **26**
Tara **30**
Tulane University **34**
Wedding Cake House **31**

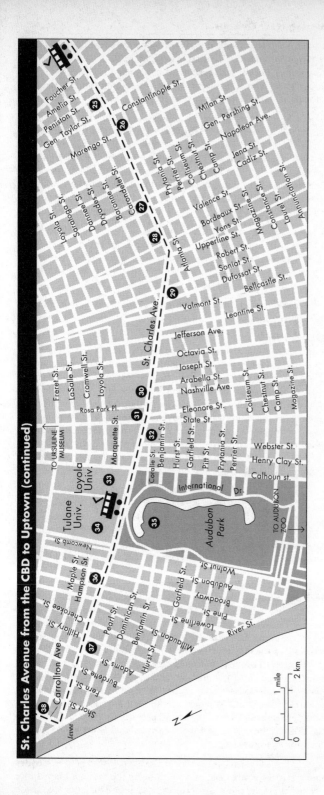

St. Charles Avenue from the CBD to Uptown (continued)

preciated from the outside of these mansions are the sumptuous, carefully preserved interiors: ceilings as high as 22 ft, crystal chandeliers, hand-painted murals, Italianate marble mantels and fireplaces, pine floors, spiral staircases, mahogany window and door frames, handmade windowpanes, and elaborate carved moldings.

The area, originally the vast Livaudais Plantation, was laid out in streets and blocks in the late 1820s. It attracted wealthy Americans who were not welcome in the Creole sections of the city. Here they constructed Greek Revival mansions with beautifully landscaped English gardens in front and on both sides of the main house. The Garden District, developed in the antebellum Golden Age when cotton was king, was part of a separate city called Lafayette until 1852, when it was incorporated into New Orleans.

In recent years celebrities such as author Anne Rice, actors Delta Burke and Gerald McRaney, and musician Trent Reznor of Nine Inch Nails have bought homes in this area. Hollywood actors often stay in the Garden District while filming locally. Group tours of this area are available (☞ Sightseeing *in* Smart Travel Tips A to Z).

Numbers in the text correspond to numbers in the margin and on the Garden District map.

A Good Walk

One block from the streetcar stop at the intersection of Washington Avenue and Prytania Street is **The Rink** ⑧, a small shopping complex that was once a roller-skating rink. Across Washington Avenue is the impressive facade of the **Behrman Gym** ⑨. Continuing down Washington Avenue toward Coliseum Street, notice that the 1600 block, on the right, is taken up by the white-walled **Lafayette Cemetery 1** ⑩. Although the gates are generally open during working hours, it is not advisable to wander among the unguarded tombs. One of the grandest restaurants in New Orleans is Commander's Palace (☞ Garden District/Uptown *in* Chapter 2), across from the cemetery.

If you stroll down Coliseum Street three blocks to 2nd Street and turn left, you will be in an area with some of the most beautiful and historic homes in the South. The **Schlesinger House** ⑪ is a classic Greek Revival; continue down 2nd Street and turn right on Prytania to the **Toby-Westfeldt House** ⑫, which has a large garden. Across Prytania Street on the opposite corner is the regal **Louise S. McGehee School for Girls** ⑬. Walk back up Prytania Street to the **Adams House** ⑭, which has a curved gallery, and continue on to the **Women's Guild of the New Orleans Opera Association House** ⑮, which you will recognize by its distinctive octagonal turret. Across Prytania Street is the **Brennan House** ⑯, with its Ionic and Corinthian columns; a few doors down in the middle of the block is the **Anne Rice House** ⑰, a house with extravagant cast-iron work that is owned by the novelist. Cross Prytania Street at 3rd Street and walk up 3rd to the **Robinson House** ⑱, one of the most elegant in the district. Return to Prytania Street and cross to the other side for the **Briggs-Staub House** ⑲, one of the few Gothic Revival houses in the city. Farther down on this block, on the same side of the street, is the **Villere-Carr House** ⑳, blending several architectural styles. Cross Prytania Street at the corner of 4th Street to **Colonel Short's Villa** ㉑, best known for its iron fence.

To conclude the Garden District tour, walk down 4th Street to St. Charles Avenue, board the streetcar, and continue up the avenue. Many more mansions along the route are of the same style and magnitude as those of the Garden District, though most gardens along St. Charles Avenue are not as large.

TIMING

There are so many beautiful things to observe along this walk that you should allow plenty of time for strolling and enjoying it all. Plan two hours for the tour and another half hour for a refreshment stop. The streetcar ride from Canal Street takes approximately 25 minutes.

Sights to See

⑭ Adams House. The curved gallery on the left side of this circa-1860 house makes it unusual. The Greek Revival style is evident in the columns and the windows. ⊠ *2423 Prytania St.*

⑰ Anne Rice House. Built in 1856, this house and the one directly behind it facing St. Charles Avenue are two of four houses in the Garden District renovated by Anne Rice in recent years. This one is under renovation. The one behind it on St. Charles is used to house her many guests. Neither house is open to the general public. Notice the detail in the cast-iron work on the galleries and the marble entrance hall of this house. Ms. Rice lives and does her writing in an impressive mansion at 2239 First Street, a few blocks from here. ⊠ *2523 Prytania St.*

⑨ Behrman Gym. This gym had the first indoor pool in the South and was the training site of John L. Sullivan when he fought "Gentleman Jim" Corbett. It dates from the turn of the century, when it was the Southern Athletic Club. Today only the distinctive wooden facade remains. ⊠ *1500 Washington Ave.*

⑯ Brennan House. Built in 1852, this house exemplifies the Greek Revival style—notice the Ionic and Corinthian columns that support the broad galleries. Inside is a magnificent gold ballroom decorated by a Viennese artist for the original owners. ⊠ *2507 Prytania St.*

⑲ Briggs-Staub House. One of the few Gothic Revival houses in the city was built around 1849 and has undergone several restorations. The architecture of spires and angles is reminiscent of European structures. ⊠ *2605 Prytania St.*

㉑ Colonel Short's Villa. In addition to the prevalent Greek Revival style and the unusually abundant ironwork of the gallery, the house is known for its iron fence, with a pattern of morning glories intertwining with cornstalks. Legend has it that Colonel Short purchased the fence for his wife, who was homesick for Kentucky. Another cornstalk fence very much like this one appears in the French Quarter at 915 Royal Street. ⊠ *1448 4th St.*

⑩ Lafayette Cemetery 1. From the gates of the cemetery you can see the lavish aboveground vaults and tombs of the families who built the surrounding mansions. Begun around 1833, this was the first planned cemetery in the city with symmetrical rows and roadways for funeral vehicles. In 1852, 2,000 yellow fever victims were buried here. The cemetery and environs figure in Anne Rice's popular trilogy, *The Vampire Chronicles,* and movies such as *Interview with the Vampire* have used this walled cemetery for its eerie beauty. Although the gates are generally open during working hours, it is not advisable to wander among the unguarded tombs. A guided tour is offered by **Save Our Cemeteries** (☎ 504/525–3377). ⊠ *1400 block of Washington Ave.* 🖾 *Tour $6.* ☉ *Weekdays 7:30–2:30, Sat. 7:30–noon; tours Mon., Wed., Fri. 10:30.*

⑬ Louise S. McGehee School for Girls. A private girls' school since 1929, this regal building served as a residence when it was built in 1872. The Renaissance Revival building has Corinthian columns, classic window design, and a spiral staircase inside. ⊠ *2343 Prytania St.*

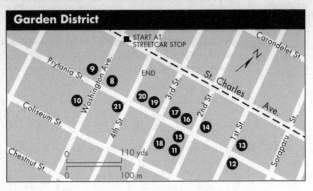

⑧ The Rink. This small collection of specialty shops was once the South's first roller-skating rink, built in the 1880s. Locals can be found here browsing in the **Garden District Book Shop,** which has a good selection of regional, rare, and old books. Sometimes the novelist Anne Rice autographs her books here. ⊠ *Washington Ave. and Prytania St.*

NEED A BREAK?	A pleasant place to relax is outdoors on the deck of **Still Perkin'** (⊠ 2727 Prytania St., ☎ 504/899–0335) at The Rink. Gourmet coffees and teas and baked goods are served.

★ **⑱ Robinson House.** Styled after an Italian villa, this home built in the late 1850s is one of the largest and most elegant in the district. Doric and Corinthian columns support the rounded galleries. It is believed to be the first house in New Orleans with "waterworks," as indoor plumbing was called then. ⊠ *1415 3rd St.*

⑪ Schlesinger House. The columns and the simple lines in the framing of doors and windows are notable features here. This house is a classic example of the Greek Revival style popular in the 1850s, which was used in many plantation homes upriver as well. Its lovely ironwork was added to the front gallery in the 1930s. ⊠ *1427 2nd St.*

⑫ Toby-Westfeldt House. Dating to the 1830s, this unpretentious raised cottage sits amid a large, plantationlike garden, surrounded by a copy of the original white picket fence. Thomas Toby, a Philadelphia businessman, moved to New Orleans and had this house built well above the ground to protect it from flooding. The simple Greek Revival architecture lacks the embellishments that later became popular in homes of that style. This house is thought to be the oldest in this part of the Garden District. ⊠ *2340 Prytania St.*

⑳ Villere-Carr House. Although it has a number of interesting Greek Revival features such as a squared Greek-key doorway and squared window frames, this building borrows freely from several other styles. The eclectic mansion was built around 1870. ⊠ *2621 Prytania St.*

⑮ Women's Guild of the New Orleans Opera Association House. This Greek Revival house, built in 1858, has a distinctive octagonal turret that was added in the late 19th century. The last private owner, Nettie Seebold, willed the estate to the Women's Guild of the New Orleans Opera upon her death in 1955. It is now furnished with period pieces and used for receptions and private parties. This is one of the few houses in the area open to the public, but only for groups of 20 or more with advance reservations. ⊠ *2504 Prytania St.,* ☎ *504/899–1945.*

Uptown

Lying west of the Garden District, Uptown is the area on both sides of St. Charles Avenue along the streetcar route. It includes many mansions similar to those in the Garden District, as well as Loyola and Tulane universities and a large urban park named for John James Audubon.

Numbers in the text correspond to numbers in the margin and on the St. Charles Avenue from the CBD to Uptown map.

A Good Ride

Christ Church Cathedral ㉒, a beautiful Gothic Revival Episcopal church, is on your right on St. Charles Avenue between 6th and 7th streets. The **Elms Mansion** ㉓, down the block from the cathedral, was built around 1869. It has marble fireplaces, stained-glass windows, and original tapestries. The **Bultman Funeral Home** ㉔ is the huge white mansion on your left at the intersection of Louisiana Avenue.

Unity Temple, the circular building on the left, at Peniston Street, was built in 1960 by a student of Frank Lloyd Wright. Its harmonious and simple design reflects Wright's influence. The **Columns Hotel** ㉕, which certainly suits its name, is on the right after Peniston Street. The Rayne Memorial Methodist Church, built in 1875 and notable for its Gothic-style gables and arched windows, is on the next block up from the Columns Hotel, on the left. The 1887 Queen Anne–style Grant House, up the block from the Rayne Memorial Church, has a highly decorative porch and balcony balustrades. Popular local architect Thomas Sully is credited with its design. The **Sully House** ㉖, the family home of the famous architect himself, is in the middle of the next block, before Marengo Street.

The large avenue intersecting at the next stop is Napoleon Avenue, the starting point for the many Mardi Gras parades that wind their way down St. Charles Avenue to Canal Street. Copeland's Restaurant, on the corner to the left, is named for its proprietor, Al Copeland, the former owner of Popeye's Famous Fried Chicken. Dominating the opposite corner, also on the left, is a church built in the early 1900s in Colonial Revival style.

The spectacular **Sacred Heart Academy** ㉗, a private girls' school, is on the right in the next block, past Jena Street. On the left past Cadiz Street, St. George's Episcopal Church, dating from 1900, is in the Romanesque style, with softly curved arches. The oldest house on St. Charles Avenue (circa 1850s) is the 4621 St. Charles House on the right, before Valence Street; renovations have added details that are obviously not part of the original building. The **Brown House** ㉘, on the right before Bordeaux Street, is the largest mansion on St. Charles Avenue. The Hernandez House, in the next block past the Brown House, to the right, is a showcase home illustrating the Second Empire style. Its mansard roof is relatively rare in New Orleans.

Several houses in the next block past the Hernandez House are turn-of-the-century buildings, though they artfully re-create an antebellum style. The Tudor style, with its steep gables, Gothic arches, and half timbering, was popular when banana magnate Joseph Vaccaro built the Vaccaro House, on the left, in 1910. The **Milton H. Latter Memorial Library** ㉙, a Beaux Arts mansion that is now a public library, is on the left at Soniat Street.

The Benjamin House, between Octavia and Joseph streets, is a stunning mansion (circa 1916) that is made of limestone, an expensive and unusual building material for New Orleans. In the next block, past Joseph Street on the right, is the McCarthy House, a typical Greek Revival home, with ornate columns and flat-top doors and windows. Tara, the plantation home used in the film *Gone With the Wind,* was a set, but the New Orleans **Tara** ㉚, coming up on the right side of the avenue in the next block, is real.

Look carefully or you'll miss the Georgian Colonial Revival **Wedding Cake House** ㉛, in the block past Tara, on the right. Exit here if you want to visit the Ursuline Museum. As you enter the university district, dominating the next block on the left is the Gothic St. Charles Avenue Presbyterian Church.

Castle's House ㉜, on the left after State Street, is another Georgian Colonial Revival similar to the Wedding Cake House. The St. Charles Avenue Christian Church, two blocks from Castle's House, on the left, is 1923 Colonial Revival. On the right, across from the St. Charles Avenue Christian Church, is Temple Sinai, the first Reform Jewish congregation in New Orleans. This building dates to 1928; the annex on the corner was built in 1970.

Loyola University ㉝, on the right, takes up the next block past Temple Sinai. The Jesuit institution is well-known for its communication and law faculties. **Tulane University** ㉞, founded in 1884, is directly beside Loyola. Campuses for both universities extend back several blocks off the avenue. The streetcar makes three stops in this stretch, but there is so much to see that you must watch carefully. On the left, across the avenue from the two universities, is Audubon Park, and behind it, Audubon Zoo. Exit here to visit **Audubon Park and Zoo** ㉟.

Back on the St. Charles Avenue streetcar again, the heavy stone archway on the right just after Tulane University is the entrance to Audubon Place, referred to locally as Millionaire's Row. A security guard checks people entering the two-block-long private drive, which has some of the most elegant mansions in the city. Zemurray House, the columned white mansion facing the archway, was built in 1907 by Sam Zemurray, president of the United Fruit Company. It is now the residence of the president of Tulane University.

Notice the **Doll House** ㊱, the miniature house in the corner yard on the right at Broadway, the next major intersection. At Broadway, to the left, is the Loyola University School of Law. It's in an Italianate building that was the main house of the Dominican Sisters, who operated Mary's Dominican College for Women here until the 1980s.

St. Charles Avenue continues for two more stops past Broadway until it turns, just short of the levee. Some of the houses in this stretch, originally part of the small town of Carrollton, are modest. Especially interesting are two houses on the left, between Hillary and Adams streets, called the **Camelback Houses** ㊲.

As the streetcar makes the bend after Short Street, St. Charles turns into Carrollton Avenue. To the left in the distance is the grassy knoll of the levee, an artificial earthen wall built for both flood protection and to keep the Mississippi River flowing in its original course. When you get around the turn you'll be in the Riverbend neighborhood, where you'll have to look behind the shopping strip on the left facing Carrollton Avenue for a town square surrounded by Victorian cottages—most of which are now specialty shops and restaurants (☞ Maple Street/Riverbend *in* Chapter 6). The tour ends at the next stop, so prepare to leave the streetcar, unless you wish to stay aboard another 20 minutes to ride to the end of the line.

As you exit, the large, stately columned building on your right that today is an elementary school was built in 1855 as the **Old Carrollton Court**

House ㊳. You can cross the tracks, spend some time browsing in the shops and eateries in Riverbend (Camellia Grill, ☞ Garden District/Uptown *in* Chapter 2, is especially recommended), or you could continue on the streetcar to the line's end at Claiborne Avenue for another 20 minutes. Whether you exit the streetcar at Riverbend or Claiborne Avenue, you can return to Canal Street and the French Quarter by a reverse ride; you will, however, have to pay a new fare.

TIMING

The ride on the streetcar from Canal Street to Riverbend takes about 45 minutes (considerably more during rush hour). From Washington Avenue in the Garden District, the ride is about 20 minutes. Plan a half day minimum for visiting the Audubon Zoo and enjoying the park that surrounds it.

Sights to See

Amistad Research Center. This important archive of primary source materials on the history of America's ethnic minorities, race relations, and the civil rights movement is at **Tulane University** (☞ *below*). It is the only such archive in the deep South and is the largest collection of primary documents on African-Americans in the United States. ⊠ *Tilton Hall,* ☎ *504/865–5535.* ▣ *Free.* ☉ *Mon.–Sat. 9–4:30.*

★ ☕ ㉟   **Audubon Park and Zoo.** Formerly the plantation of Etienne de Boré, the father of the granulated sugar industry in Louisiana, **Audubon Park** is one of the largest (340 acres) and most acclaimed metropolitan parks in the United States. Designed by Frederick Law Olmsted (who also laid out New York City's Central Park), it has the world-class **Audubon Zoo** (☞ *below*), picnic and play areas, a golf course, a miniature train, riding stables, a tennis court, and a river view. There are also miles of winding lagoons and trails for biking, hiking, and jogging. The park and zoo were named for the famous ornithologist and painter John James Audubon, who spent many years working in and around New Orleans. None of the original buildings from its former plantation days remains; in fact, none of the buildings that housed the 1884–85 World's Industrial and Cotton Centennial Exposition, which was held on these acres and gave New Orleans its first international publicity after the Civil War, has survived.

As you exit the streetcar at Walnut Street and pass through the dramatic columned entrance to Audubon Park, the Audubon Zoo lies directly ahead, about 12 city blocks in the distance. You can walk there by taking the macadam path to the right across the park (approximately a 25-minute walk). This route takes you through the golf course and down Oak Alley, a stretch of aged moss-hung oak trees that form a canopy over the path. Emerging from Oak Alley, you will cross Magazine Street, a busy thoroughfare; from there signs will direct you to the zoo entrance, another two blocks ahead.

You can also walk to your left from the St. Charles Avenue entrance along a lagoon for a more picturesque stroll and then return to the entrance to catch the free shuttle van to the zoo, which operates every 15 minutes daily 9:30–5. Walkers can also continue along the route to the left, across the park to the zoo; although scenic, this is a considerably longer walk.

To return to the streetcar on St. Charles Avenue, board the free shuttle van outside the zoo. To go directly back downtown, the Magazine Street bus passes the zoo entrance regularly and goes to Canal Street. You can also take a boat to Canal Street, as explained below.

If time permits, you may want to take the road to the left as you exit the zoo, cross the railroad tracks, and stroll along **Riverview Drive,** a long stretch of land behind the zoo that is part of Audubon Park, on the levee overlooking the Mississippi River. The river lookout includes Audubon Landing, a large open area for picnics, kite flying, and sports, where the *John James Audubon* cruise boat docks. There is a landscaped walkway along the river on the left. ⊠ *6500 Magazine St.,* ☎ *504/581–4629, cruise 504/586–8777.* 🖼 *Park free. Combination admission to Aquarium of the Americas downriver and cruise available; prices vary.* ☉ *Cruises daily 11, 1, 3, and 5 for 7-mi river ride to French Quarter and Canal St.* ✆

Audubon Zoo. This first-class zoo in **Audubon Park** (☞ *above* for shuttle information) uses natural-habitat settings to display and breed animals. It is home to a family of extremely rare white (albino) alligators and also holds the Louisiana Swamp, the tropical-bird house, the butterfly exhibit, the flamingo pond, and the sea lions. Directions are clearly marked; there are concession stands and an unusual gift shop. ⊠ *6500 Magazine St.,* ☎ *504/581–4629.* 🖼 *$9, combination ticket for zoo and Aquarium of the Americas $17.50.* ☉ *Daily 9:30–5, summer weekends till 6; last ticket sold 1 hr before closing.*

28 **Brown House.** Completed in 1902, the Brown House is the largest mansion on St. Charles Avenue—it took five years and a quarter of a million dollars to build. Its solid, monumental look, Syrian arches, and steep gables make it a choice example of Romanesque Revival style. ⊠ *4717 St. Charles Ave.*

24 **Bultman Funeral Home.** This huge, white mansion with an enclosed garden is a working funeral home. Tennessee Williams set his play *Suddenly Last Summer* here in the solarium, which is now open for occasional Sunday afternoon concerts. ⊠ *3338 St. Charles Ave.,* ☎ *504/895–7766.*

37 **Camelback Houses.** When these were built in the late 1800s, houses were taxed by the width and height of their facades: working-class homes were usually narrow and long. Sometimes a second floor was added to the back half of the house, giving it the architectural designation of "camelback." The camelback and the gingerbread-type decoration on porches were very popular features at the turn of the century. ⊠ *7628–7630, 7632–7634, and 7820–7822 St. Charles Ave.*

32 **Castle's House.** Noted local architect Thomas Sully designed this 1896 Georgian Revival house after the Longfellow House in Cambridge, Massachusetts. The interior has often appeared in the pages of design magazines. ⊠ *6000 St. Charles Ave.*

22 **Christ Church Cathedral.** This beautiful Gothic Revival Episcopal church completed in 1887 has arched windows and steeply pitched gables, architectural features that were precursors to the New Orleans Victorian style. The cathedral is the oldest non–Roman Catholic church in the Louisiana Purchase: the congregation was established in 1805, and this is the third building erected on the same site. It is the diocesan headquarters of the Episcopal Church. ⊠ *2919 St. Charles Ave.*

25 **Columns Hotel.** In recent years this elegant white hotel, built in 1884 as a private home, has been the scene of TV ads and movies. The interior scenes of Louis Malle's *Pretty Baby* were filmed here. The hotel (☞ Garden District/Uptown *in* Chapter 3) has a popular bar and a grand veranda for sipping cocktails; there's live music some nights and during Sunday brunch. ⊠ *3811 St. Charles Ave.,* ☎ *504/899–9308 or 800/445–9308.*

36 **Doll House.** Designed in the same Tudor style as the main house beside it for the daughter of a former owner, this is the smallest house in New Orleans to have its own postal address. ⊠ *7209 St. Charles Ave.*

㉓ Elms Mansion. Built in 1869, this elegant home with marble fireplaces and stained-glass windows had the Confederate president Jefferson Davis as a frequent guest. The house, which has been carefully restored and furnished with period pieces, is the site of many receptions. ⊠ *3029 St. Charles Ave.,* ☎ *504/895–5493. Open for group tours only, but call in case this changes.*

㉝ Loyola University. The Jesuits built this complex facing the avenue in 1914. The modernistic Gothic-style building on the corner is the **Louis J. Roussel Building,** which houses the communications department. The campus, with its dorms, recreational center, and library, extends for two blocks behind the **Church of the Holy Name of Jesus,** a masterfully constructed Gothic and Tudor edifice. ⊠ *6363 St. Charles Ave.*

Middle American Research Institute. This research and reference library at **Tulane University** (☞ *below*) has exhibits of pre-Columbian and Central and South American culture. Established in 1924, the institute has an extensive collection of pre-Columbian Mayan artifacts and the largest collection of Guatemalan textiles in the nation, as well as a large library on Central America. ⊠ *Dinwiddie Hall, 4th floor,* ☎ *504/865–5110.* ▣ *Free.* ⊙ *Weekdays 8:30–4:30.*

㉙ Milton H. Latter Memorial Library. A former private home now serves as the most elegant public library in New Orleans or anywhere else. Built in 1907 and ornamenting its own beautifully landscaped block, this Beaux Arts mansion was once the home of silent-screen star Marguerite Clark, who lived here in the 1940s. It was then purchased by the Latter family and given to the city as a library in 1948 in memory of their son, who was killed in World War II. You can sit a spell and leaf through a copy of Walker Percy's *The Moviegoer* or Anne Rice's *The Vampire Lestat* (two popular novels set in New Orleans), or just relax in a wicker chair on the glass-enclosed porch. This is one of the few mansions on St. Charles Avenue that is open to the public. ⊠ *5120 St. Charles Ave.,* ☎ *504/596–2625.* ⊙ *Mon.–Thurs. 11–6, Sat. 11–5; hrs may vary, so call ahead.*

㊳ Old Carrollton Court House. This large, stately columned building that today is an elementary school was built in 1855 as a courthouse serving the city of Carrollton before it was merged into New Orleans in 1874. An imposing structure of stucco and stone, it is typical of southern courthouses in antebellum days. ⊠ *719 S. Carrollton Ave.*

㉗ Sacred Heart Academy. Unique aspects of this building, a Catholic girls' school built in 1899, include wide, wraparound balconies (or galleries) and colonnades that face a large garden. ⊠ *4521 St. Charles Ave.*

㉖ Sully House. This was the family home of local architect Thomas Sully, who designed it around 1890. Sully was known for his use of deep shades of color and varied textures. Similar gables, towers, and gingerbread appear on many other homes in the vicinity. ⊠ *4010 St. Charles Ave.*

㉚ Tara. A replica built from the plans of the movie set of *Gone With the Wind,* Tara seems almost dwarfed here by far more sumptuous houses. ⊠ *5705 St. Charles Ave.*

㉞ Tulane University. The venerable university, next to Loyola University on St. Charles Avenue, has been called by some the Harvard of the South. Three original buildings face the avenue: **Tilton Hall** (1901) on the left, **Gibson Hall** (1894) in the middle, and **Dinwiddie Hall** (1936) on the right. The Romanesque style, with its massive stone look and arched windows and doors, is repeated in the several buildings around a large quad behind these. Modern campus buildings extend another three blocks to the rear. Tulane is well known for its medical school, law school, and fine main library. The **Sophie H. Newcomb College for Women**

shares part of the Tulane campus but has a separate dean and faculty. It is known for the **Newcomb College Center for Research on Women,** a fine women's resource center that brings in speakers, writers, and academics throughout the school year. Also here are the **Amistad Research Center** and **Middle American Research Institute** (☞ *above* for both). ⊠ *6823 St. Charles Ave.*

OFF THE
BEATEN PATH
URSULINE MUSEUM – This is a collection of memorabilia and documents tracing the history of the Ursuline nuns from France to New Orleans in 1727. You'll need to walk about eight blocks to the right on State Street till you get to Claiborne Avenue. The Wedding Cake House (☞ *below*) is the closest sight on the streetcar tour to this museum. ⊠ *2635 State St.,* ☎ *504/866–1472.* ☜ *Free.* ☉ *By appointment only.*

③① **Wedding Cake House.** A portico and decorative balconies help this house outshine most other mansions on the avenue. Its key beauty is the beveled lead glass on its front door, one of the most beautiful entryways in the city. ⊠ *5809 St. Charles Ave.*

BAYOU ST. JOHN–LAKEFRONT

A drive is a good way to get a scenic view of the environs of the city, which is spread out for 8 mi between the Mississippi River and Lake Pontchartrain. City Park, a massive urban green space, runs the length of much of this stretch and has languid lagoons and moss-draped ancient oaks. Lake Pontchartrain, 25 mi across, has a very nautical atmosphere, with sailboats and fishing part of the scene.

Numbers in the text correspond to numbers in the margin and on the Bayou St. John–Lakefront map.

A Good Drive

Begin on Canal Street, the main avenue of downtown New Orleans, which connects the Mississippi River with Lake Pontchartrain. Heading away from the river, take a right at South Jefferson Davis Parkway, approximately 3 mi from where Canal Street begins at the river. Follow the parkway four blocks and over the railroad tracks. Directly ahead on the left begins a natural inlet of slow-moving water called **Bayou St. John** ①, which leads into **Lake Pontchartrain** about 5 mi out.

Take a left immediately after the railroad tracks and just before the end of the bayou; turn right after a half block to follow the bayou to Moss Street. Pass the traffic light at the Orleans Avenue Bridge and continue for one more long block to the Dumaine Street Bridge; take a right, cross over the bridge, and turn left at the end onto Moss Street. Bayou St. John will now be on your left.

Turn right on Orleans Avenue and left on North Broad Street for the **Zulu Social Aid and Pleasure Club** ②, the headquarters of this famous African-American Mardi Gras krewe. Retrace the route back to Orleans Avenue and turn right on Moss Street to the **Pitot House** ③, a structure dating from the late 1700s that you can tour. Follow Moss Street for another few blocks as it curves with the bayou until it intersects with Esplanade Avenue. Turn left and cross the Esplanade Avenue Bridge; **City Park** lies directly ahead. Go halfway around Beauregard Circle, with the statue of General P. G. T. Beauregard in its center. The Civil War hero, mounted on his horse, is in full uniform and looks ready to charge down Esplanade Avenue.

As you enter the park, the **New Orleans Museum of Art** ④ comes into view directly ahead on Lelong Avenue. Follow the half circle behind the museum, take a right onto Roosevelt Mall, cross the bridge, and take an immediate left onto Victory Avenue; the **New Orleans Botanical Garden** ⑤ is on the right. Past the garden is **Storyland** ⑥, a children's fantasy play area; next door in the **Carousel Gardens** ⑦ are several amusement rides, including a beautifully refurbished 1906 carousel.

As you drive away from the Carousel Gardens, on the left are tennis courts. Make a left at the end of the courts, and left again onto Dreyfous Drive. The peristyle on the right, with its tall columns and cement lions overlooking the lagoon, is a favorite spot for picnics and parties. Farther along this avenue is the **Timken Center** ⑧, a restaurant with public rest rooms, a playground, and a nearby bandstand. Cross the narrow bridge; in the curve on the left are two large gnarled oaks known as the Dueling Oaks because of the frequent duels held under them in the late 1700s to early 1800s. The one-way road forks to the right along the lagoon. Turn left near the end of this road and right onto Lelong Drive to the front of the park where you entered.

Take a left halfway around Beauregard Circle onto Wisner Boulevard, along Bayou St. John (now to your right). Continue on Wisner Boulevard for another 3½ mi to the lakefront; City Park will be on the left most of the way. At Harrison Avenue look to the right for Park Island, with its beautiful modern homes and gardens facing the bayou. Farther up on the left is the driving range for the City Park golf club. Cross Robert E. Lee Boulevard, and then go straight a few blocks until the road follows a semicircle under an overpass; make a right turn on to Lakeshore Drive. The lake—not yet visible from behind the levee—is on the right. Keep right on Lakeshore Drive, along Lake Pontchartrain, for about 2 mi. If you can't follow this route on a weekend, when Lakeshore Drive has been made one-way, west to east, see the alternate route described below.

The sight of the lake is impressive: it measures 24 mi across and stretches as far as the eye can see. The University of New Orleans lies about a mile to the right and beyond that the Lakefront Airport (for small aircraft); neither is visible from here. To the left, farther out, is the marina, and beyond that the suburb of Metairie.

Along Lakeshore Drive you will notice several shelters with rest rooms and telephones. Soon after you pass Marconi Drive, on the left are the **Mardi Gras Fountains** ⑨, built to honor the many clubs that parade during the Mardi Gras season.

Lakeshore Drive has two-way traffic along its entire length from Monday through Friday; on weekends, it becomes one-way east to west from West End toward Canal Boulevard. If you are traveling this route on a weekday, follow Lakeshore Drive until it turns left into West End Boulevard. The first street on the right leads to the Orleans Marina on Breakwater Drive. On weekends, as you come out toward the lake on Wisner Boulevard, turn left onto Robert E. Lee Boulevard and go a mile to the intersection with West End Boulevard, where you will turn right at the traffic light onto Lakeshore Drive and left a block later onto Lake marina Avenue. This becomes Breakwater Drive, and the Orleans Marina will be on the right.

Once on Breakwater Drive, take the very first right and make a long, horseshoe curve around West End Park, which is actually a very wide median. Notice the rows of boat houses that line the route. Some are elegant weekend getaways for boat owners who keep their boat below and an apartment above, with a deck out over the water behind.

Enter the Orleans Marina parking lot to the right, almost at the end of the horseshoe curve. When you walk down the pier of the marina, the Southern Yacht Club will be to the right. This is one of the most refreshing scenes in New Orleans, far from downtown, with soft breezes blowing, gulls calling, and the rhythmic patter of sailboat halyards slapping the masts. The lighthouse that marks the harbor is visible across the channel on the right. As you leave the marina, take a right to the end of the curve, and then turn left back onto Breakwater Drive; a collection of restaurants and night spots surrounds the parking lot to the right.

To return downtown, continue on Breakwater Drive, turn right onto West End Boulevard, and take another right onto Lakeshore Drive. At the traffic light a block later, turn right and circle gradually to the left onto Pontchartrain Boulevard. A large civil defense air-raid shelter, a relic from the 1950s, is on the left, partially underground. Just past the shelter stands a large Celtic cross on a landscaped mound, which commemorates the thousands of Irish immigrants who built a canal— long since covered over—through this area in the 1830s. The boulevard eventually becomes I–10.

Travel west on I–10 to reach the **Linear Parkway** ⑩, a path along the lake that's good for walking and biking. The path is on both sides of the Causeway bridge, where bird lovers will want to gather for the **Bird-Watcher's Delight** ⑪.

Back on I–10 going south, exit at the METAIRIE ROAD–CITY PARK sign. On the right is Metairie Cemetery, which you can drive through to observe a variety of lavish aboveground tombs and vaults. To reach the cemetery, continue to Metairie Road at the traffic light, turn left under the overpass, and left again to drive along the other side of the expressway. A sign will indicate where you should turn to enter the cemetery. If you are interested in a particular tomb or aspect of the cemetery, inquire at the office, in the back to the right.

Leaving Metairie Cemetery, return on the feeder road beside the expressway, turning right at the traffic light onto Metairie Road. On the left are the grounds of the New Orleans Country Club. Turn left farther on at the sign for **Longue Vue House and Gardens** ⑫, an English-style country estate. After the tour of Longue Vue, return to Metairie Road, turn right, and go under the expressway overpass. At the next traffic light, turn right onto Canal Street, which will take you downtown and to the French Quarter.

The lakefront is patrolled by the levee police, but it is a vast area and can be isolated in spots. Although locals may be fishing and crabbing at night, it is not advisable to linger along the seawall or at the marina after sunset.

TIMING

The drive, with a brief stop or two, takes approximately an hour. You will probably want to spend some time relaxing along the lakefront or in the marina. Count another two hours each to tour the New Orleans Museum of Art and Longue Vue House and Gardens.

Sights to See

❶ **Bayou St. John.** A bayou is a creek, a narrow waterway that normally joins a larger body of water. This bayou—the only remaining bayou in New Orleans—borders City Park on the east and runs about 7 mi from Lake Pontchartrain to just past Orleans Avenue. It is named for John the Baptist, whose nativity (St. John's Eve, June 23), the most important day in the year for voodoo practitioners, was notoriously celebrated on the bayou's banks in the 1800s.

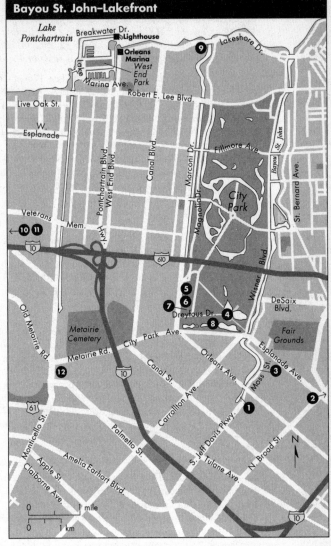

❶ Bird-Watcher's Delight. Every evening at dusk from April through August, massive flocks of purple martin swallows gather near the Causeway bridge that spans Lake Pontchartrain. For 20 to 25 minutes the sky around the entrance to the Causeway in Metairie (a 15-minute drive from downtown New Orleans on I–10) blackens with fluttering wings and resounds with swallow calls. Gradually the swirling clouds of birds swoop under the bridge and find roosts for the night. There's a viewing area and there are plans to build a large bird sanctuary near the bridge. On either side of the causeway is a hiking path (☞ Linear Parkway, *below*).

★ ✋ **❼ Carousel Gardens.** This amusement park has a New Orleans treasure as its centerpiece—a carousel from 1906 that is on the National Register of Historic Places. The horses on one of the few remaining authentic carved wooden carousels in the country are periodically restored by artisans in Connecticut. Surrounding it are a roller coaster, tilt-a-whirl, Ferris wheel, bumper cars, and other rides. A miniature train takes adults and children throughout the area on its own track, and there is a wading pool with bronze statuary. ⊠ *Victory Ave., City Park,* ☎ *504/483–9356.* ⊑ *General admission $1; unlimited ride ticket $8.* ☉ *Hrs vary by season; closed in winter except for last 3 wks of Dec. and the 1st wk of Jan., and when park is rented out for parties.* ⊛

★ **City Park.** A sugar plantation during the late 1700s, City Park is one of the largest urban recreation areas in the country, a great place to picnic, walk or jog, fish, feed the ducks, or just relax. The 1,500-acre park has the largest number of mature live oak trees in the world; more than 250 are registered with the Live Oak Society. Included within City Park's boundaries are the **Timken Center, New Orleans Botanical Garden, Storyland, Carousel Gardens, New Orleans Museum of Art** (☞ *above and below*), tennis courts, and a golf course. The artificial lagoons meandering through the park are home to wild geese, ducks, and swans, and native flora and fauna thrive among the ancient moss-draped oaks. Art Deco benches, fountains, bridges, and ironwork in the park are a remnant of the 1930s refurbishment by the Works Progress Administration. Around Christmas every year, the main area of the park dons thousands of Christmas lights and decorations for the annual Celebration in the Oaks. In good weather, paddle boats can be rented; the boat concession was moving in 2000, so call for an update. ⊠ *Bordered by City Park Ave., Robert E. Lee Blvd., Marconi Dr., and Bayou St. John,* ☎ *504/482–4888.* ⊛

OFF THE BEATEN PATH

JAZZLAND – This new 140-acre amusement park, which opened in spring 2000, has more than 30 attractions, including a wide variety of kiddie and adult thrill rides and (to suit the musical theme) a music pavilion. Some highlights are the Boomerang, a 12-story-high steel roller coaster, one of the largest in the country; a simulated rocket ride; and a water-ski show. Jazzland is in eastern New Orleans, about 12 mi from downtown. ⊠ *12301 Lake Forest Blvd., junction of I–10 and I–510,* ☎ *504/253–8000.* ⊑ *$31.* ☉ *Late May–late Oct., daily 10–10. Hrs may be limited in Sept. and Oct; call in advance.*

Lake Pontchartrain. This is a popular spot for fishing and boating: in good weather you can see lots of sailboats and windsurfers. Swimming, though once very common, is not advisable now because the lake is heavily polluted; intense clean-up efforts are under way. Lakeshore Drive, a road along Lake Pontchartrain, has many park and picnic areas that are generally filled on warm weekends and holidays. There also are many parking bays that encourage you to stop and take a walk or sit on the seawall, the cement steps bordering the lake. The wall is a 5½-mi levee and seawall protection system, built by the Orleans Levee Board in the 1930s and leased to the U.S. government for a hospital and for army and navy installations during and after World War II. There was also a navy air station at Elysian Fields and Lakeshore Drive—the present site of the University of New Orleans. The land around the seawall area (Lake Vista) was turned into private residential districts in the 1930s. Lakefront real estate has since been among the most expensive in the city. This area is relatively safe during the day because of frequent police patrols. Visitors are advised not to linger after sunset. ☉ *Lakefront recreational area daily 8 AM–10 PM.*

❿ **Linear Parkway.** Along the south shore of Lake Pontchartrain is the Linear Parkway, a 7½-mi path for biking and hiking. This is a great place to see and hear local birds, watch the sun set over the lake, or chat with other walkers. You can plan a picnic for one of the informal rest stops along the way, but be well prepared because there are no rest rooms, water fountains, or concession stands anywhere nearby. Free parking is provided at both ends of the trail: in Bucktown and at the Williams Boulevard Boat Launch. Depending on the season, you can combine walking here with the Bird-Watcher's Delight (☞ *above*).

⑫ Longue Vue House and Gardens. Eight acres of beautiful gardens embellished with fountains surround this city estate fashioned after the great country houses of England. The Greek Revival mansion is decorated with its original furnishings of English and American antiques, priceless tapestries, modern art, porcelain, and pottery. The gardens have various themes; the formal Spanish court is modeled after a 14th-century Spanish garden. The Discovery Garden is designed for children, with whimsical oversize tools, dig-and-discover programs for young gardeners, and a corner for storytelling. ⊠ *7 Bamboo Rd., ☎ 504/488–5488. ☜ $7, Discovery Garden $3. ☉ Mon.–Sat. 10–4:30, Sun. 1–4:30; last tour at 4.*

⑨ Mardi Gras Fountains. These circular, 60-ft fountains along the lakefront rise and fall in varying heights with changing Mardi Gras colors—gold, purple, and green. They operate erratically, however, and often need repair. Along the walk from the parking area to the fountains, a series of ceramic tiles bear the names, symbols, and colors of the different Mardi Gras krewes (clubs). The fountains and plaques were installed in 1962. ⊠ *Lakeshore Dr. near Marconi Dr. ☉ Daily 8 AM–10 PM.*

NEED A BREAK?	**Bruning's Restaurant** (⊠ 1922 West End Park, ☎ 504/282–9395), overlooking Lake Pontchartrain, was a real local institution, serving traditional New Orleans cuisine (with whole fried flounder a specialty) in a casual family setting. Bruning's was destroyed in Hurricane George and the owners hope to rebuild. Meanwhile, they are running a smaller, but similar, restaurant next door.

⑤ New Orleans Botanical Garden. A must-see for anyone interested in the flora and fauna of the South and a good place to relax, this 10-acre garden has a tropical conservatory, a water-lily pond, a formal rose garden, azalea and camellia gardens, and horticultural gardens, all decorated with fountains and sculptures by world-renowned local artist Enrique Alferez. You can take a guided tour (call ahead for times) or browse through the Pavilion of Two Sisters, a European-style orangery that houses a small horticultural library and a gift shop. ⊠ *Victory Ave., City Park, ☎ 504/483–9386. ☜ $3. ☉ Tues.–Sun. 10–4:30; hrs may vary by season.*

★ ④ New Orleans Museum of Art (NOMA). Gracing the main entrance to City Park is this well-regarded art museum. The jeweled treasures, particularly some of the famous eggs by Peter Carl Fabergé, are a favorite exhibit, along with European and American painting, sculpture, drawings, prints, and photography. The museum holds one of the largest glass collections in the country and a large collection of Latin American colonial art. The comprehensive Asian art wing includes a good selection of Japanese painting of the Edo period; African, Oceanic, Pre-Columbian, and Native American art are also represented. The Courtyard Café in the museum looks out on a lovely sculpture garden. ⊠ *1 Collins Diboll Circle, City Park, ☎ 504/488–2631. ☜ $6, free Thurs. 10–noon for Louisiana residents. ☉ Tues.–Sun. 10–5.* ✎

③ Pitot House. One of the few surviving houses that lined the bayou in the late 1700s, Pitot House was bought by James Pitot in 1810 and used as a country home for his family. Pitot built one of the first cotton presses in New Orleans and served as the city's mayor from 1804 to 1805, and later as parish court judge. The Pitot House was restored and moved a block to its current location in the 1960s to mark the 1708 site of the first French settlement in the New Orleans area. The house is noteworthy for its stucco-covered brick-between-post construction. The galleries across the front and right side are typical of the West Indies style brought to Louisiana by early planters. American antiques of the early 1800s furnish the house. ⊠ *1440 Moss St.,* ☎ *504/482–0312.* ☞ *$5.* ⊘ *Wed.–Sat. 10–3, last tour at 2.*

☾ ➏ **Storyland.** This is a whimsical and entertaining theme park for children, with 26 storybook exhibits built around fairy-tale characters. Children can climb, slide, and pretend to be Pinocchio, Captain Hook, or the Little Mermaid. There are regular performances in the Puppet Castle. ⊠ *Victory Ave., City Park,* ☎ *504/483–9381.* ☞ *$2.* ⊘ *Hrs vary by season; call ahead.*

➑ **Timken Center.** Built in 1913 as a casino, this Spanish mission–style building has long served as a restaurant, with public rest rooms for park visitors. Po'boy sandwiches are standard fare, along with plate lunches; a Ben & Jerry's Ice Cream counter dishes up dessert. This is a favorite stop for tour buses. There is a large playground for small children, and the Popp Bandstand, a copper-dome performance stage that often provides live music, is nearby. Timken Center is a new name; the sign may still say Casino Building. ⊠ *Dreyfous Dr., City Park,* ☎ *504/483–9446.*

➋ **Zulu Social Aid and Pleasure Club.** Few other institutions embody the local African-American heritage as well as this venerable club, home to the Mardi Gras krewe of the Zulus. Activities here usually are open only to members, but the lounge has an exuberant clientele that welcomes visitors, and the souvenir shop is open to anyone wishing to take home a bit of authentic New Orleans black history. The club is located in Mid-City, away from the area frequented by tourists; we recommend you drive or take a taxi here. ⊠ *Lounge, 732 N. Broad St.; souvenir shop, 722 N. Broad St.,* ☎ *lounge 504/822–9850, souvenir shop 504/ 822–1559.* ⊘ *Lounge daily 1 PM–1 AM, souvenir shop Mon.–Tues., Wed.– Sat. 11–5:30; hrs of both may vary during Mardi Gras.*

ELSEWHERE AROUND NEW ORLEANS

St. Claude Avenue

Leading away from the French Quarter, North Rampart Street extends into St. Claude Avenue (State Highway 46). After passing through the Ninth Ward, one of the city's most colorful areas, and ending at Chalmette Battlefield, it turns into St. Bernard Highway.

Jackson Barracks Military Museum. This is an indoor-outdoor display of aircraft and tanks used by Louisiana's Army National Guard and Air National Guard. Housed in the original Jackson Barracks powder magazine, which was built in 1857, the museum exhibits memorabilia, weaponry, and artifacts from all major U.S. wars including Desert Storm. ⊠ *Jackson Barracks, St. Claude Ave. at Orleans Parish line,* ☎ *504/ 278–8242.* ☞ *Free.* ⊘ *Weekdays 8–4, Sat. 9–3, or by appointment.*

Chalmette National Cemetery. Hundreds of Louisiana soldiers from various wars have been buried here since 1864. You can drive through and view the war monument and thousands of graves. **Chalmette National Historic Park** includes the site of the Battle of New Orleans, fought in 1815 by the United States under General Andrew Jackson against the British under General Sir Edward Packenham. The **Beauregard Plan-**

tation House, constructed in 1840, serves as a visitor center, with historical exhibits, a diorama, and films about the battle. ⊠ *St. Bernard Hwy. (Rte. 46), 6 mi from downtown New Orleans,* ☎ *504/589–4430.* 🎫 *Free.* ⊙ *Daily 9–5.*

Kenner

Kenner is a close-in suburb, home to New Orleans International Airport and also a historic district, Rivertown. A statue marks the spot in Rivertown where the explorer La Salle first set foot in the region in 1682. For information about a pass for the various museums here, *see* Rivertown, U.S.A., *below.*

🔄 **Children's Castle.** Kids can get involved in music, magic, mime, puppets, and storytelling at this facility. There are workshops and activities such as puppet making. ⊠ *501 Williams Blvd.,* ☎ *504/468–7231.* 🎫 *$3.* ⊙ *Tues.–Sat. 9–5. Shows at 11:30 and 1.*

🔄 **Freeport–McMoRan Daily Living Science Center, Planetarium, and Space Station.** This hands-on learning center focuses on science, health, and environmental issues. The planetarium in the Science Center has a high-powered telescope used to point out seasonal wonders in the heavens. The Space Station includes a prototype of a NASA space station with a rocket booster and a space-travel simulation. ⊠ *409A Williams Blvd.,* ☎ *504/468–7229.* 🎫 *$5; planetarium shows $1 extra; observatory $1 extra, not included in general pass.* ⊙ *Tues.–Sat. 9–5; last ticket for the Space Station 3:30 planetarium shows Tues.–Fri. at 2, Sat. at 11 and 2; observatory Fri.–Sat. dark–10:30 PM.*

🔄 **Louisiana Toy Train Museum.** Housed appropriately in a former train depot, the museum depicts railroad history through a display of photos, model trains, films, and slide shows. It also has model steam locomotives. Children love the hands-on displays. ⊠ *519 Williams Blvd.,* ☎ *504/468–7231.* 🎫 *$3.* ⊙ *Tues.–Sat. 9–5.*

🔄 **Louisiana Wildlife and Fisheries Museum.** The museum displays 700 species of animals, some in their natural habitat, and has a 2,500-gallon aquarium. An outdoor living exhibition behind the museum, the **Canne Brulé Native American Center of the Gulf South,** has Native Americans in traditional dress demonstrating pirogue making, palmetto-hut building, dancing, beading, and storytelling. ⊠ *303 Williams Blvd.,* ☎ *504/468–7231.* 🎫 *$3.* ⊙ *Tues.–Sat. 9–5.*

Mardi Gras Museum. A visit here may be the next best thing to being in New Orleans during Mardi Gras. Carnival is simulated in a participatory experience with live music, moving floats, and revelers tossing throws. There are also king cakes, historic exhibits, and a theater showing footage of Mardi Gras parades and celebrations. ⊠ *421 Williams Blvd.,* ☎ *504/468–7231.* 🎫 *$3.* ⊙ *Tues.–Sat. 9–5.*

Rivertown, U.S.A. A collection of turn-of-the-century Victorian cottages have been refurbished to house antiques shops, offices, and restaurants. Along the main stretch are a variety of museums; a $13 pass is available for all except the Children's Castle and the Space Station. There's a beautiful overview of the Mississippi River at La Salle's Landing along the river. ⊠ *15 mi from New Orleans at end of Williams Blvd., off I–10,* ☎ *504/468–7231.*

Saints Hall of Fame Museum. This is a must-see for sports fans. There are busts and memorabilia of the popular home pro football team. Highlights of all past seasons are shown on video. The museum also has a playing-field room. ⊠ *409 Williams Blvd., Kenner,* ☎ *504/468–7231.* 🎫 *$3.* ⊙ *Tues.–Sat. 9–5.*

2 DINING

So you've never heard of a mirliton? Wouldn't go near dirty rice? We have a glossary just for you. The flavors of New Orleans will stay with you long after you're back to your spaghetti-filled life. But be prepared: you'll never again be able to eat with relish in a Cajun restaurant anywhere outside Louisiana. It's difficult to get a bad meal in this town—whether in an elegant old-world dining room or in a tiny mom-and-pop storefront—so read up on your cuisine options, and savor every bite.

By Gene
Bourg

A DISTINCTIVE COOKING STYLE is as deeply embedded in New Orleans's psyche as its distinctive architecture and music are. Each reflects in its own way an exuberance of spirit that has made the city a favorite destination of world travelers. Classifying the city's cooking styles can be frustrating, however. The two major divisions of the cuisine—the urban Creole and the more rustic Acadian (or "Cajun")—often merge in a single dish. Mainstream South Louisiana cuisine is fraught with a network of subcuisines drawn from a polyglot of cultures.

Today menus in New Orleans's restaurants reflect nearly 300 years of ethnic overlap. The major influences have come from France (both before and after the revolution of 1789), Africa, Spain, the region's Native Americans, the Caribbean, and, more recently, southern Italy, Germany, and the former Yugoslavia. During the 1980s, Asian chefs joined the culinary melting pot with brand-new treatments of seafood drawn from Louisiana's bountiful coastal wetlands and the Gulf of Mexico.

Despite the increasingly blurred lines separating all these styles, there are some distinguishing characteristics in Creole and Cajun, the two mother cuisines. Creole cooking carries an urban gloss, whether it's a proletarian dish of semiliquid red beans atop steaming white rice or a supremely elegant sauce of wine and cream on delicate-flesh fish.

Cajun food, on the other hand, is decidedly more rough-hewn and rural. The first waves of Acadian settlers found their way to the Louisiana bayous and marshes in the middle of the 18th century. Most had already been farmers and fishermen in Canada and France. Lard was the tie that bound much of the Cajuns' early cooking. For the more sophisticated Creole cooks, it was butter and cream.

To present-day New Orleanians, much of the so-called Cajun food popularized in the 1980s is as exotic as it is to New Yorkers or San Franciscans. One reason is that traditional Cajun gastronomy does not rely heavily on jalapeño peppers, cream sauces, and pasta. Another is that the rest of America discovered chef Paul Prudhomme's blackened fish before Louisiana did. The result is that the number of highly visible New Orleans restaurants serving food that even approaches the lusty spirit of Acadian cooking does not exceed five.

The free-wheeling menus (as well as the decor and prices) at celebrity chef Emeril Lagasse's three New Orleans restaurants—Emeril's, Nola, and Delmonico—vary considerably from one place to the other. Other newer dining spots in the city rarely follow Creole-Cajun culinary traditions. Their menus are more likely to be aimed at contemporary tastes for lighter, eclectic dishes. An example is Cuvée, unveiled in the Central Business District at press time, where chef Richard Starr redefines legendary dishes like shrimp rémoulade.

Restaurants serving virtually every variation on the city's culinary style—from po'boys and red beans and rice to old-line dishes lavished with butter or cream—fill the French Quarter. But most ethnic restaurants, from Italian to Vietnamese, are more likely to be found in other parts of New Orleans and its environs.

The cost of a meal in the city's more upscale restaurants—with their smart decor, expensive ingredients, and carefully selected wines—is about what you'd expect to pay in other U.S. cities. The bargains are found in the more casual full-service restaurants, where a simple lunch or dinner can frequently be had for much less than $20. However, even the more expensive restaurants offer fixed-price menus of three or four courses for substantially less than what an à la carte meal costs, and coffee or tea is usually included. As a rule, serving sizes are more than generous—some would say unmanageable for the average eater—so many diners order two appetizers rather than a starter and a main course, which can make ordering dessert more practical.

For information on mealtimes, reservations, attire, and tipping, *see* Dining *in* Smart Travel Tips A to Z.

Cuisine Categories

New Orleans's restaurants that specialize in local cuisines have been grouped into the following five categories:

Avant-Garde. The innovative cooking is sometimes lighter than true Creole or Cajun, although many of the dishes still have ties to South Louisiana.

Cajun-Inspired. Kitchens in these restaurants show direct and recognizable influences from the hearty and rustic cuisine of the Southwest Louisiana Acadians. Seasonings are often more intense than in Creole cooking, and pork and game are prominent ingredients.

Contemporary Creole. The food usually includes some traditional Creole dishes, but there's more creativity. Local ingredients are used in novel ways, but the basic flavors adhere to the Creole standards of richness and depth. Trout with pecans and bread pudding soufflé are typical.

Creole with Soul. This food reflects both the robust style of Southern black cooks and the spicier aspects of early New Orleans cuisine.

Traditional Creole. These restaurants specialize in rather complex dishes that have been familiar to generations of New Orleans restaurant goers. Shrimp rémoulade, gumbo, trout meunière, and bread pudding are some examples.

Glossary

The following terms appear frequently in this section:

Andouille (ahn-*dooey*). A mildly spiced Acadian sausage of lean pork, it often flavors gumbos, red beans and rice, and jambalayas.

Barbecue shrimp. The shrimp are not barbecued but baked in their shells in a blend of olive oil, butter, or margarine and usually seasoned with bay leaf, garlic, and other herbs and spices.

Béarnaise (bay-ar-*nayz*). This rich sauce of egg yolk and butter flavored with tarragon is used on meats and fish.

Beignet (ben-*yay*). Originally a rectangular puff of fried dough sprinkled with powdered sugar, beignet now can also refer to fritters or crullers containing fish or seafood.

Bisque. A thick, heartily seasoned soup, bisque is most often made with crawfish, crab, or shrimp. Cream appears in the French versions.

Bouillabaisse (*booey*-yah-base). A Creole bouillabaisse is a stew of various fish and shellfish in a broth seasoned with saffron and often more assertive spices.

Boulette (*boo*-let). This is minced, chopped, or pureed meat or fish shaped into balls and fried.

Bread pudding. In the traditional version, stale French bread is soaked in a custard mix, combined with raisins and baked, then served with a hot, sugary sauce flavored with whiskey or rum.

Café au lait. This hot drink is a blend, often half and half, of strong coffee and scalded milk.

Café brûlot (broo-*loh*). Cinnamon, lemon, clove, orange, and sugar are steeped with strong coffee, then flambéed with brandy and served in special pedestaled cups.

Chicory coffee. The ground and roasted root of a European variety of chicory is added to ground coffee in varying proportions. Originally used for reasons of economy, coffee with chicory is now favored by many New Orleanians. It lends an added bitterness to the taste.

Crème brûlée (broo-*lay*). Literally, this means "burned cream." It is a cream custard with a crust of oven-browned sugar.

Dirty rice. In this cousin of jambalaya, bits of meat, such as giblets or sausage, and seasonings are added to white rice before cooking.

Dressed. A po'boy "dressed" contains lettuce, tomato, and mayonnaise or mustard.

Étouffée (ay-too-*fay*). Literally, "smothered," the term is used most often for a thick stew of crawfish tails cooked in a roux-based liquid with crawfish, fat, garlic, and green seasonings.

Gumbo. From an African word for okra, it can refer to any number of stewlike soups made with seafood or meat and flavored with okra or ground sassafras (filé powder) and myriad other seasonings. Frequent main ingredients are combinations of shrimp, oysters, crab, chicken, andouille, duck, and turkey. A definitive gumbo is served over white rice.

Jambalaya (jam-buh-*lie*-uh). Rice is the indispensable ingredient in this relative of Spain's paella. The rice is cooked with a mix of diced meat and seafood in tomato and other seasonings. Shrimp and ham make frequent appearances in it, as do sausage, green pepper, and celery.

Meunière (muhn-*yehr*). This method of preparing fish or soft-shell crab entails dusting it with seasoned flour, sautéing it in brown butter, and using the butter with lemon juice as a sauce. Some restaurants add a dash of Worcestershire sauce.

Mirliton (*merl*-i-*tawn*). A pale green member of the squash family, a mirliton is usually identified as a vegetable pear. The standard preparation is to scrape the pulp from halved mirlitons, fill them with shrimp and seasoned bread crumbs, and bake them.

Muffuletta. The city's southern Italian grocers created this round-loaf sandwich traditionally filled with ham, salami, mozzarella, and a layer of chopped, marinated green olives. Muffulettas are sold whole and in halves or quarters.

Oysters Bienville (byen-*veel*). In this dish, oysters are lightly baked in their shells under a cream sauce flavored with bits of shrimp, mushroom, and green seasonings. Some chefs also use garlic or mustard.

Oysters en brochette (awn-bro-*shet*). Whole oysters and bits of bacon are dusted with seasoned flour, skewered, and deep-fried. Traditionally, they're served on toast with lemon and brown butter.

Oysters Rockefeller. This dish, baked oysters on the half shell in a sauce of pureed aromatic greens laced with anise liqueur, was created at Antoine's, which keeps its recipe a secret. Most other restaurants make do with spinach.

Panéed veal (pan-*aid*). Breaded veal cutlets are sautéed in butter.

Po'boy. A hefty sandwich, the po'boy is made with the local French bread and any number of fillings: roast beef, fried shrimp, oysters, ham, meatballs in tomato sauce, and cheese are common. A po'boy "dressed" contains lettuce, tomato, and mayonnaise or mustard. When shellfish are used and the bread is buttered and heated, it becomes a "loaf."

Ravigote (rah-vee-*gote*). In Creole usage, this is a piquant mayonnaise, usually with capers, used to moisten cold lumps of blue crabmeat.

Rémoulade (ray-moo-*lahd*). The classic Creole rémoulade is a brick-red whipped mixture of olive oil with mustard, scallions, cayenne, lemon, paprika, and parsley. It's served on cold peeled shrimp or lumps of backfin crabmeat.

Souffléed potatoes. These thin, hollow puffs of deep-fried potato are produced by two fryings at different temperatures.

Tasso (*tah*-so). Acadian cooks developed the recipe for this lean, intensely seasoned ham. It's used sparingly to flavor sauces and gumbos.

Fodor's Choice

★ **Galatoire's.** At this old-style French-Creole bistro, you can savor time-tested winners (bouillabaisse, spring lamb chops in béarnaise sauce, seafood-stuffed eggplant) in a perfect setting—a single, narrow dining room lit with glittering brass chandeliers and bordered with white-frame mirrored panels. *$$$–$$$$*

★ **Clancy's.** This minimally decorated bistro appeals to professionals and business types with its sophisticated charm and imaginative treatments of New Orleans favorites. *$$–$$$*

★ **Mandich's.** A local favorite, this place may not look like much, but the food includes ambitious trout and shellfish dishes, as well as straightforward, home-style dishes. *$$–$$$*

★ **Acme Oyster and Seafood Restaurant.** Don't expect coddling at this no-nonsense eatery, where you can get raw oysters on the half shell, red beans and rice, and great shrimp, oyster, and roast-beef po'boys. *$–$$*

★ **West End Café.** Classic New Orleans diner food is the stock in trade at this friendly, efficient eatery near the shore of Lake Pontchartrain. Red beans, po'boys, and boiled or fried seafoods are definitive and delicious. *$–$$*

Brunch

Upscale restaurants on the tourist track often serve very reasonable, fixed-price brunch menus, many of them buffet style. A jazz group often supplies live music. Sunday, from late morning to early afternoon, is the prime time for brunch, although a few restaurants offer brunch on other days, too. Among the more reliable spots for these brunches are Commander's Palace, Palace Café, and Mr. B's Bistro, all for the festive atmosphere and food quality; Begué's in the Royal Sonesta Hotel, for the lavish buffet selections; Arnaud's, for the glittery main dining room; and the Praline Connection in the Warehouse District for the grand gospel brunch, with choirs from local churches.

Prices

Prices reflect the cost of a dinner appetizer, entrée, and dessert.

CATEGORY	COST*
$$$$	over $40
$$$	$25–$39
$$	$15–$24
$	under $15

per person, excluding drinks, service, and 9.5% tax in New Orleans and 9% tax in most other parishes in the metropolitan area

French Quarter

American Casual

$–$$ ✕ **Angeli.** This always-open restaurant on a busy corner of the lower French Quarter is a godsend for night crawlers. The wide glass walls and soft, bright colors can be uplifting enough to draw a sizable clientele at normal mealtimes as well as during the wee hours. Mediterranean concoctions show up all over the menu—bruschetta, hummus, gyros, a Greek salad, and pita rolls with a wide range of fillings. The focus blurs a bit with hamburgers, eggs Benedict, chicken wings with blue-cheese dressing, and meatballs with spaghetti. The salads and burgers offer the safest routes to satisfaction. Old movies are occasionally shown in the large dining room, and the margaritas are deftly mixed. ⊠ *1141 Decatur St.,* ☎ *504/566–0077. AE, MC, V.*

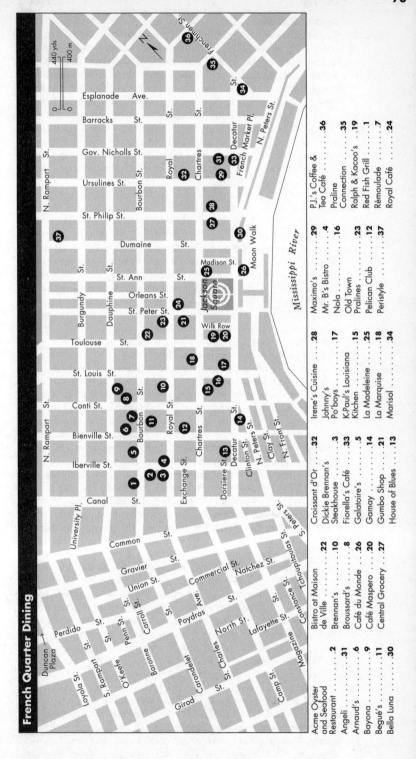

French Quarter Dining

Avant-Garde

$$$–$$$$ ✕ **Peristyle.** Some of the most creative cooking in New Orleans emanates
★ from the kitchen of this smartly turned-out yet very approachable lit-
tle restaurant on the French Quarter's edge. Chef Anne Kearney takes
a thoroughly modern and personal approach to Continental cooking
on a small, ever-changing menu. In either the intimate bar, lined with
tables, or in the dining room proper, regulars dig into Kearney's superb
veal and sweetbreads ravioli, grilled sea bass with pickled lemon vinai-
grette, and veal chop with pickled cabbage. The wine list is small but
nicely matched to the dishes. (At this writing the restaurant was un-
dergoing renovation, which was expected to be completed by summer
2000.) ⊠ *1041 Dumaine St.,* ☎ *504/593–9535. Reservations essential.
MC, V. Closed Sun., Mon. No lunch Tues.–Thurs. or Sat.*

$$$ ✕ **Bayona.** "New World" is the label chef Susan Spicer applies to her
★ cooking style—such dishes as turnovers filled with spicy crawfish tails;
a bisque of corn, leeks, and chicken; or fresh salmon fillet in white-
wine sauce with sauerkraut. Her grilled duck breast with pepper-jelly
glaze and shrimp with coriander sauce are among the creations that
originally made Spicer's reputation. These and other imaginative dishes
are served in an early 19th-century Creole cottage on a quiet French
Quarter street. The chef supervised the renovation of the handsome
building, now fairly glowing with flower arrangements, elegant photographs, and, in one small dining room, trompe l'oeil murals suggesting
Mediterranean landscapes. ⊠ *430 Dauphine St.,* ☎ *504/525–4455.
Reservations essential. AE, DC, MC, V. Closed Sun.*

$$$ ✕ **Bella Luna.** If luxurious surroundings and a knockout view of the
Mississippi River are high on your list of priorities, this elegant restau-
rant in the French Market complex should fill the bill. Handsome French-
style windows line one wall in the plush main dining room, offering
views of the riverbank and the ships and excursion boats gliding by.
The second dining space is enclosed on three sides by even more glass,
exposing the river on one side, the city skyline straight on, and French
Quarter rooftops on the other side. The kitchen takes an eclectic ap-
proach, although the strongest accent is Italian. Good bets are the pas-
tas, especially penne with roasted eggplant, Gorgonzola, peppers, and
fried herbs in Fontina sauce. ⊠ *French Market, near Decatur and Du-
maine Sts.,* ☎ *504/529–1583. AE, DC, MC, V. No lunch.*

$$$ ✕ **Bistro at Maison de Ville.** Small-scale chic has been the cachet of this
sleekly intimate spot, just a few steps from the raucous bawdiness of
Bourbon Street. Its fans certainly don't come in to stretch their limbs.
Only inches separate the tables, with those along the full-length banquette close enough to become, in effect, a table for 20. But lustrous
mahogany and soft light from elegant wall lamps work their magic, along
with Impressionistic oils reflected by the mirrors on the opposing wall.
From the tiny kitchen come stylish, flavorful creations reflecting a modern approach to Creole and American cooking—barbecue shrimp with
New Orleans rice cakes, cleverly composed salads, saffron-sage broth
with quail ravioli, and grilled salmon with a pecan-flavored wild rice.
⊠ *733 Toulouse St.,* ☎ *504/528–9206. AE, DC, MC, V. Closed Sun.*

$$$ ✕ **Marisol.** A lovely shaded garden and frequently superb food are among
★ the assets of this bright, attractive restaurant near the Mississippi
River. A bold floral design animates the soft gold of the dining room's
walls. Owner-chef Peter Vazquez is a self-taught cook with a fertile imag-
ination and a gift for matching flavors in his frequently changing
menus. Mussels are steeped to succulence in basil, scallions, and wine.
A peppery Thai-style soup of crab and coconut is a marvelous mar-
riage of elegance and fire. Roasted red snapper's freshness is under-
lined by a light application of tomato and pureed eggplant. Desserts
are often strikingly original, as in a crème brûlée flanked by lemon

madeleine cookies. Wines are carefully chosen to pair well with the kitchen's creations. ⊠ *437 Esplanade Ave.,* ☎ *504/943–1912. AE, DC, MC, V. Closed Mon. No lunch Tues.–Thurs. and Sat.*

$$$ ✕ **Pelican Club.** Sassy New York flourishes are found throughout the menu
★ of this smartly decorated but eminently comfortable place in the heart of the French Quarter. Still, evidence of chef Richard Hughes's South Louisiana origins also keeps popping up. In three handsome dining rooms inside a balconied old town house, he turns out a stew of shell-fish that's a clever improvisation on both San Francisco's cioppino and Louisiana's bouillabaisse. A touch of saffron in his jambalaya of chicken, sausage, and shellfish makes it a cousin of Spain's paella. Closer to home are red snapper stuffed with crabmeat; a bisque of bourbon, crab, and corn; and a crème brûlée in the grandest French-Creole tradition. ⊠ *615 Bienville St.,* ☎ *504/523–1504. AE, D, DC, MC, V. No lunch.*

Cafés and Coffeehouses

$ ✕ **Café du Monde.** For most visitors, no trip to New Orleans would
★ be complete without a cup of chicory-laced café au lait and a few sugar-dusted beignets in this venerable Creole institution. The dozens of tables, inside or out in the open air, are jammed at almost any hour with locals and tourists feasting on the views of Jackson Square and the hub-bub on Decatur Street. The magical time to go is just before dawn, when the bustle subsides and you can almost hear the birds in the crepe myr-tles across the way. Satellite locations in four malls (the New Orleans Centre and Riverwalk Marketplace in the CBD, Lakeside Shopping Center in Metairie, and Esplanade Mall in Kenner) are convenient but lack the character of the original. ⊠ *French Market, Decatur and St. Ann Sts.,* ☎ *504/525–4544. No credit cards.*

Cajun-Inspired

$$$–$$$$ ✕ **K-Paul's Louisiana Kitchen.** In this rustic French Quarter café, chef
★ Paul Prudhomme started the blackening craze and added "Cajun" to America's culinary vocabulary. Two decades later, thousands still consider a visit to New Orleans partly wasted without a visit to K-Paul's for his inventive gumbos, fried crawfish tails, blackened tuna, roast duck with rice dressing, and sweet-potato–pecan pie. Prices are steep at din-ner but moderate at lunch; servings are generous. There's a second-floor balcony on Chartres Street and an upstairs room where diners can pass the time with cocktails before being seated. Reservations for dinner are also accepted (a recent change of policy). ⊠ *416 Chartres St.,* ☎ *504/524–7394. AE, DC, MC, V. Closed Sun.*

Contemporary Creole

$$$–$$$$ ✕ **Gamay.** Don't be fooled by the soft pastels and dainty touches in the
★ modest-size dining room: much of the food is as boldly seasoned and as lavishly dished out as any in town, thanks to owner-chef Greg Son-nier's celebrated South Louisiana style. You can start with something as simple as an avocado soup with a dash of cream and a fillip of hon-eydew or as challenging as a super-rich barbecue shrimp pie. Slow-roasted duck (also served at Gamay's sister restaurant, Gabrielle; ☞ Mid-City, *below*) is lean and luscious. Shrimp, crab, and oysters often enrich the sauces on the expertly cooked fish. Desserts, especially the strawberry and blueberry shortcakes, are a dream. The wine list is short but choice, and service is friendly and attentive. ⊠ *Bienville House Hotel, 320 Decatur St.,* ☎ *504/299–8800. AE, DC, MC, V. Closed Sun., Mon. No lunch Sat.–Thurs.*

$$$–$$$$ ✕ **Nola.** Fans of chef Emeril Lagasse who can't get a table at Emeril's
★ in the Warehouse District have this sassy and vibrant French Quar-ter restaurant as an alternative. Lagasse has not lowered his sights with Nola's menu, as lusty and rich as any in town. He stews boudin

(blood sausage) sausage with beer, onions, cane syrup, and Creole mustard before ladling it all onto a sweet-potato crouton. Trout is swathed in a horseradish-citrus crust before it's plank-roasted in a wood oven. Pasta comes laden with sautéed eggplant and a sauce of smoked tomatoes and Parmesan. The combinations seem endless. At dessert time, go for the coconut cream or apple-buttermilk pie with cinnamon ice cream. ⊠ *534 St. Louis St.,* ☏ *504/522–6652. AE, D, DC, MC, V. No lunch Sun.*

$$$ ✕ **House of Blues.** Jazz clubs that serve food are a decidedly mixed bag in New Orleans. The House of Blues, however, challenges the status quo with a casual restaurant that produces respectable po'boys, étouffées, and jambalaya, as well as meat loaf, baby back ribs, and pork chops that only the pickiest southerner might disdain. Salads, sandwiches, and vegetarian dishes are done with considerable imagination. At the Sunday gospel brunch, a huge buffet is set out in the concert area while the stage rocks with the sounds of some of the city's best gospel groups. Seating is available in the open-air Voodoo Lounge as well as the spacious, if rather flashy, booth-lined dining room. The alternative to making reservations is a very long wait in line. ⊠ *225 Decatur St.,* ☏ *504/529–2583. AE, D, DC, MC, V.*

$$$ ✕ **Royal Café.** From the sidewalk at the corner of Royal and St. Peter streets you can almost hear the ceiling fans whirring overhead on the Royal Café's three tiers of balconies, framed in lacy, gray cast iron. From the tables on the second floor, the ornate ironwork also frames fascinating perspectives along the Quarter's "Main Street." In the busily, colorfully decorated downstairs room, the kitchen turns out dishes combining familiar New Orleans ingredients, such as a green salad with fried okra, shrimp-and-crabmeat étouffée, oyster-and-artichoke soup, and a Creole fricassee of duck and andouille sausage. At breakfast and brunch times, fancy sauces and garnishes make the omelets especially tempting. Reservations are accepted for the ground floor only. ⊠ *706 Royal St.,* ☏ *504/528–9086. AE, D, DC, MC, V. Closed Sun.*

$$–$$$ ✕ **Mr. B's Bistro.** The energy never seems to subside in this attractive restaurant, with servers darting between the wood and glass screens that reduce the vastness of the dining room. Diners sitting on the green vinyl banquettes and at other tables choose from a dependable contemporary Creole menu centering on meats and seafood from a grill fueled with hickory and other aromatic woods. Pasta dishes, especially the pasta jambalaya with andouille sausage and shrimp, are fresh and creative. The traditional-style bread pudding with Irish whiskey sauce is excellent, too. Lunchtime finds most of the tables taken up by locals, who like the correctly composed club sandwich, the Creole takeoff on pasta carbonara, and other main attractions from the fixed-price menu. ⊠ *201 Royal St.,* ☏ *504/523–2078. AE, D, DC, MC, V.*

Continental

$$$–$$$$ ✕ **Begué's.** Warmth and color soften the fanciness of the Royal Sonesta Hotel's prestigious restaurant. Wide arched windows have views of a courtyard teeming with greenery and flowers, and the chairs are as body-hugging as you'll find. The menu is a blend of modern French sophistication and Creole-inspired flavors: baked oysters arrive on the half shell under a sauce made with leeks and Parmesan; the tomato-and-tasso bisque is the soul of silky goodness; salmon shows up nestled inside a feathery phyllo crust. Service is a pleasing combination of informality and correctness. The Friday seafood buffet and Sunday jazz brunch buffet are especially good times to sample the comforts and dishes here. ⊠ *Royal Sonesta Hotel, 300 Bourbon St.,* ☏ *504/553–2278. AE, D, DC, MC, V.*

Dessert

$ ✕ **Croissant d'Or.** Locals compete with visitors for a table in this col-
★ orful, pristine pastry shop that serves excellent and authentic French
croissants, pies, tarts, and custards, as well as an imaginative selection
of soups, salads, and sandwiches. Wash them down with real French
breakfast coffee, cappuccino, or espresso. In good weather, the cheer-
ful courtyard, with its quietly gurgling fountain, is the place to sit. A
filling lunch can be had for less than $10. Hours are 7 AM to 5 PM daily.
⊠ *617 Ursulines St.,* ☎ *504/524–4663. MC, V.*

$ ✕ **La Madeleine.** The lines are ever present in this bakery-café, which
is part of a chain. The huge selection of pastries includes napoleons,
cheesecakes, and éclairs, as well as a variety of brioches and breads
from the wood-burning oven. Salads, soups, sandwiches, and light entrées are also available. It closes at 9 PM daily. ⊠ *Jackson Sq., 547 St.
Ann St., French Quarter,* ☎ *504/568–9950;* ⊠ *601 S. Carrollton Ave.,
Uptown,* ☎ *504/861–8661. AE, DC, MC, V.*

$ ✕ **La Marquise.** This tiny little coffee shop just off Jackson Square is
a satellite of the Croissant d'Or (☞ *above*) and offers the same good
coffees, croissants, and pastries. It's a bit cramped but practical and
cozy. ⊠ *625 Chartres St.,* ☎ *504/524–0420. No credit cards.*

$ ✕ **Old Town Pralines.** Among the great delicacies left us by the 19th-
century Creoles are pralines—thin, hardened-sugar-and-pecan patties
that are wonderful for capping off a fine dinner or for a quick munch
(the shop doesn't offer seating). The pralines are cooked so the pecan
flavor permeates the candy and the firm texture is just right. They're
sold individually in wax-paper packets or in boxes holding one to three
dozen. The shop will ship them for you, too. ⊠ *627 Royal St.,* ☎ *504/
525–1413. No credit cards. Closed Sun.*

Italian

$$$–$$$$ ✕ **Maximo's.** This place jumps: it also serves straightforward Italian
fare that's several cuts above the local norm. But don't look for extra
space in the deep, narrow room, which resembles a railroad club car
on especially crowded nights. The most desirable haven is one of the
cozy booths along the left wall, an expanse of exposed brick hung with
photographs of jazz musicians. A great way to begin is with mussels
steeped in a garlicky wine broth. Big nuggets of "fire-roasted" lamb,
beef, and shrimp are marvels of judicious seasoning. Garlic, pepper,
and herbs invigorate the natural juices of thick, tender pork chops. The
house's cheesecake is a winner, too, and the cellar holds the best se-
lection of Italian wines, many modestly priced, in the city. ⊠ *1117 De-
catur St.,* ☎ *504/586–8883. AE, D, DC, MC, V. No lunch.*

$$$ ✕ **Irene's Cuisine.** Its walls are festooned with enough snapshots, olive
jars, garlic braids, and crockery for at least two more restaurants. But
this just adds to the charm of this cozy Italian-Creole eatery on an obscure corner in the French Quarter. From Irene DiPietro's kitchen
comes succulent roasted chicken brushed with olive oil, rosemary, and
garlic; tubes of manicotti bulging with ground veal and mozzarella; and
big, fresh shrimp, aggressively seasoned and grilled before joining lin-
guine glistening with herbed olive oil. End with an Italian-style baked
Alaska, covered with a blue flame of ignited grappa liqueur. If you come
at peak dinner hours, you may have to wait in the convivial little
"holding room" for a table. ⊠ *539 St. Philip St.,* ☎ *504/529–8811.
Reservations not accepted. AE, MC, V. Closed Sun. No lunch.*

Po'boys and Other Sandwiches

$–$$ ✕ **Fiorella's Café.** Scouring the booths at the French Quarter's flea mar-
ket can sharpen any appetite. Just a few steps away from the hubbub
is this very casual and friendly eatery specializing in classic po'boys and
New Orleans–style "plate lunches." Red beans and rice show up on

Monday, meat loaf takes the spotlight on Tuesday, and Thursday is the day for butter beans; hearty breakfasts are an everyday feature. All deliver the rib-sticking goodness of a New Orleans home kitchen. The spaces are tight and rather dark, but that doesn't take the shine off the menu. Prices are easy to swallow, too. The café closes at 5 PM. ⊠ *45 French Market Pl. (another entrance on Chartres St.),* ☎ *504/528–9566. AE, D, DC, MC, V. Closed Sun.*

$ ✕ **Café Maspero.** A half-hour wait in line—usually outside the door—is the norm for a sample of Café Maspero's two-fisted hot and cold sandwiches. The pastrami and corned beef are on the greasy side, and the half-pound hamburger (with cheese or chili or both) is long on bulk and short on taste. But low prices and big portions keep 'em coming. Arched doors and windows give the vast brick dining room a little character. Service is perfunctory. ⊠ *601 Decatur St.,* ☎ *504/523–6250. No credit cards.*

$ ✕ **Central Grocery.** This old-fashioned Italian grocery store in the French Quarter produces authentic *muffulettas,* one of the greatest gastronomic gifts of the city's Italian immigrants. They're good enough to challenge the po'boy as the local sandwich champ and are made by filling soft round loaves of seeded bread with ham, salami, mozzarella, and a salad of marinated chopped green olives. Each sandwich, about 10 inches in diameter, is sold in quarters and halves. You can eat your muffuletta at a counter, but some prefer to take theirs out to a bench on Jackson Square or the Moon Walk along the Mississippi riverfront, both just a few blocks away. The grocery closes at 5:30 PM. ⊠ *923 Decatur St.,* ☎ *504/523–1620. No credit cards.*

$ ✕ **Johnny's Po'boys.** Strangely enough, good po'boys are hard to find in the French Quarter. Johnny's compensates for the scarcity with a cornucopia of them, put together in the time-honored New Orleans manner. Inside the soft-crust French bread come the classic fillings—lean boiled ham, well-done roast beef in a garlicky gravy, crisply fried oysters or shrimp, and a wide variety of others. The chili may not cut it in San Antonio, but the red beans and rice are respectable. The surroundings are rudimentary. ⊠ *511 St. Louis St.,* ☎ *504/523–9071. No credit cards. No dinner Sun.*

Seafood

$$–$$$ ✕ **Red Fish Grill.** A high energy level and a riotous color scheme put this big, bouncy place, owned by Ralph Brennan of the city's premier restaurant clan, right in tune with Bourbon Street's festive atmosphere. Casual is the byword in the large, central dining space, edged on three sides by banquettes, smaller rooms, and a huge oyster bar, all festooned with images reflecting the menu's focus on seafood. The kitchen's handiwork includes a delicious barbecue-shrimp po'boy, a seafood gumbo with nuggets of alligator sausage, and a good selection of grilled fish garnished with such interesting combinations as crabmeat and roasted corn. The signature dessert is a variation on the bananas Foster theme, with banana beignets soaking up vanilla ice cream and a brown-sugar sauce. A bar menu is available after 3 PM. ⊠ *115 Bourbon St.,* ☎ *504/598–1200. AE, DC, MC, V.*

$$ ✕ **Ralph & Kacoo's.** Getting past the door to the vast dining spaces usually means taking a ticket and waiting your turn in a crowded bar decorated in a bayou theme. The motif continues inside with nostalgic clutter and swamp prints. The extensive menu mixes and matches local fish and shellfish, intensely seasoned and cooked the usual ways. Freshness and consistency, trademarks of Ralph & Kacoo's, are found in the raw oysters, shrimp rémoulade, trout meunière, fried seafood platter, and the crawfish dishes, which are served only when they're in season. This restaurant is popular with families. ⊠ *519 Toulouse St.,*

French Quarter, ☎ *504/522–5226;* ✉ *601 Veterans Blvd., Metairie,* ☎ *504/831–3177. Reservations not accepted. AE, D, MC, V.*

$–$$ ✕ **Acme Oyster and Seafood Restaurant.** A rough-edge classic in every
★ way, this no-nonsense eatery at the entrance to the French Quarter is
a prime source of cool and salty raw oysters on the half shell; great
shrimp, oyster, and roast beef po'boys; and state-of-the-art red beans
and rice. Table service, once confined to the main dining room out front,
is now provided in the rear room as well. Expect rather lengthy lines
at the marble-top oyster bar. Crowds are sparser in the late afternoon.
✉ *724 Iberville St.,* ☎ *504/522–5973. Reservations not accepted.
AE, DC, MC, V.*

Steaks

$$$–$$$$ ✕ **Dickie Brennan's Steakhouse.** "Straightforward steaks with a New
Orleans touch" is the axiom at this luxurious, 350-seat addition to the
list of the city's steaks-and-chops specialists, the creation of a younger
member of the Commander's Palace clan. In lavish spaces lined with
dark-cherry walls and a drugstore-tile floor, diners dig into classic cuts
of top-quality beef, veal, and lamb. The standard beefsteak treatment
is a light seasoning and a brush of butter. Other options are a garlic
rub, steak more deeply charred, or a crust of either black peppercorns
or mushroom duxelle, along with five buttery sauces. The menu does-
n't lack for typical New Orleans seafoods and desserts, among them
a fine shrimp rémoulade and bread pudding. The decor and amenities—
from the cigar supply in the bar to the antique-brass sconces—proclaim
clubbiness. ✉ *716 Iberville St.,* ☎ *504/522–2467. AE, DC, MC, V.*

Traditional Creole

$$$$ ✕ **Arnaud's.** This is one of the grandes dames of classic Creole restau-
rants, and it still sparkles. The main dining room's outside wall of or-
nate etched glass reflects light from the charming old chandeliers while
the late founder, Arnaud Cazenave, gazes from an oil portrait near the
extra-high ceiling. When the main room fills up, the overflow spills into
a labyrinth of plush banquet rooms and bars. The big, ambitious menu
includes classic dishes as well as some newer creations in a more con-
temporary style. Always reliable are cold shrimp Arnaud, in a superb
rémoulade, and creamy oyster stew, as well as the fish in crawfish sauce,
beef Wellington, and fine crème brûlée. Expect fairly hurried service on
especially crowded nights, but rely on the reservations desk to perform
efficiently. A jacket is required in the main dining room. ✉ *813 Bienville
St.,* ☎ *504/523–5433. Reservations essential. AE, D, DC, MC, V.*

$$$$ ✕ **Brennan's.** Lavish breakfasts of elaborate poached egg dishes are
what first put Brennan's on the map more than 40 years ago. They're
still a big draw, although the two floors of luxuriously appointed din-
ing rooms, in a gorgeous 19th-century building, often fill up just as
quickly at dinner. The best seats include views of the lush, tropical court-
yard and fountain, which are illuminated at night. Eye-opening cock-
tails flow every morning, followed by the tasty poached eggs sandwiched
between such things as hollandaise, creamed spinach, artichoke bot-
toms, Canadian bacon, and fried fish. Headliners at lunch or dinner
include blue-ribbon, textbook versions of oysters Rockefeller and
seafood gumbo, sautéed fish blanketed in crabmeat, good veal and beef
dishes, and bananas Foster, a dessert that was created here. ✉ *417 Royal
St.,* ☎ *504/525–9711. Reservations essential. AE, D, DC, MC, V.*

$$$$ ✕ **Broussard's.** No French Quarter restaurant surpasses Broussard's
for old-fashioned spectacle. What was once a dowdy Creole bistro is
now a soft-edged, glittery mix of elaborate wall coverings, chandeliers,
porcelain, and polished woods, with a manicured courtyard to boot.
If the menu blazes no trails, it contains respectable renditions of the
fancier Creole standbys further upgraded with Continental touches.

The savory cheesecake of crab and shrimp with dill and roasted sweet peppers is a star among the appetizers, along with lumps of backfin crab in a spicy sauce. Other luxurious sauces crown fillets of fresh pompano, braised quail, and rack of lamb. ⊠ *819 Conti St.,* ☎ *504/581–3866. AE, D, DC, MC, V. No lunch.*

$$$–$$$$ ✕ **Galatoire's.** Galatoire's always has epitomized the old-style French-
   ★   Creole bistro, with a lengthy menu filled with sauces that can be humdrum in lesser restaurants. Many of the recipes date back to 1905. Fried oysters and bacon *en brochette* are worth every calorie, and the brick-red rémoulade sauce sets the standard by which others should be measured. Others on the long list of winners include a Creole bouillabaisse (which must be ordered a couple of hours in advance), meaty veal or spring lamb chops in béarnaise sauce, and seafood-stuffed eggplant. The setting downstairs is a single, narrow dining room lit with glistening brass chandeliers; the bentwood chairs at the white-cloth tables add to the timeless atmosphere. The quality of service varies from waiter to waiter. A recent renovation has produced second-floor dining rooms and a bar for those awaiting tables. The changes have brought an end to the lines out on the sidewalk, except during major holidays and the most popular tourist events. Reservations are accepted for the second-floor dining room; they are also taken for downstairs during periods such as midsummer, when business is slower. ⊠ *209 Bourbon St.,* ☎ *504/525–2021. Jacket required. AE, DC, MC, V. Closed Mon.*

$$ ✕ **Gumbo Shop.** Even with a thoroughly modern glass door at the rear entrance, this place evokes a sense of old New Orleans almost as much as does the ancient Cabildo just across St. Peter Street. The menu amounts to a roster of relics: jambalaya, shrimp Creole and rémoulade, red beans, bread pudding, and seafood and chicken-and-sausage gumbos heavily flavored with tradition. None of them will titillate a trend-seeking palate. The patina on the ancient painting covering one wall seems to deepen by the week, and the red-check tablecloths and bentwood chairs are taking on the aspect of museum pieces. But, in all probability, that is what accounts for the long lines that form here every day and night. ⊠ *630 St. Peter St.,* ☎ *504/525–2486. AE, D, DC, MC, V.*

$–$$ ✕ **Rémoulade.** Operated by the owners of the posh Arnaud's (☞
   ★   *above*) just around the corner, Rémoulade is a much more laid-back eatery with minimal frills and easy-to-swallow prices. It offers the same Caesar salad and pecan pie, as well as a few of the starters: shrimp Arnaud in rémoulade sauce, oysters stewed in cream, turtle soup, and shrimp bisque. Just inside the doors are a marble-counter oyster bar and a mahogany cocktail bar dating to the 1870s. Dark-wood walls, tile floors, mirrors, a pressed-tin ceiling, and brass ceiling lights create an environment made for such New Orleans staples as boiled shrimp, crawfish, crabs, barbecue shrimp, and jambalaya. Casual grazers will find po'boys, burgers, pizzas, and lots of seafood dishes with South Louisiana pedigrees. It's open every day till around midnight, making it a handy stopping point during an evening of nightcrawling. ⊠ *309 Bourbon St.,* ☎ *504/523–0377. AE, D, DC, MC, V.*

Central Business District (CBD)

Avant-Garde

$$$$ ✕ **Grill Room.** The British furnishings and paintings span several centuries in these dazzling dining spaces, with ingeniously arranged body-hugging chairs and banquettes and large academic canvases depicting aspects of upper-class England. The breakfast, lunch, and dinner menus change daily and are filled with appropriately exotic and sumptuous ingredients, often flown in from Europe and the Orient. Whether the results always merit the very hefty price tag, however, has become de-

batable. The day's fish might be the epitome of flavor and refinement or an exercise in overkill. A meat course might be a flawless rack of lamb on one visit and a disappointingly sauced veal tenderloin on the next one. Breakfast, with its blend of the familiar (several treatments of poached eggs with meat or seafood in rich sauces) and the unusual (kippers, European cereals, and tropical juices), is an event. The wine cellar and its sterling collection of vintage Bordeaux reds is awesome. ✉ *Windsor Court Hotel, 2nd level, 300 Gravier St.,* ☎ *504/522–1992. Reservations essential. Jacket required. AE, D, DC, MC, V.*

$$–$$$$ ✕ **Gerard's Downtown.** The proprietor-chef at this smartly turned
★ out, and very impressive, newcomer is Gerard Maras, an alumnus of Commander's Palace and Mr. B's Bistro, who puts his own impeccably fresh and elegantly flavored spin on the menu. Paper-thin, freshly made ravioli with bits of lobster float in a luscious saffron broth with leeks. Lumps of backfin crabmeat join asparagus in a textbook-perfect risotto. The herb-crusted lamb chop's ideal companion is a moist cake of "satin" potatoes, baked and layered with cream and Camembert. Mouthwatering desserts include a dreamy chocolate "soup" submerging a thick disk of dark-chocolate cake. Warmth and understatement are among the dining room's assets, reflected in the earthy olive hue of the walls and the lustrous red mahogany of the classically simple bar. The glass walls of the corner location permit soothing views of Lafayette Square's oak trees, the stately columns of Gallier Hall, and the passing streetcars on the St. Charles line. ✉ *500 St. Charles Ave.,* ☎ *504/592–0200. AE, D, DC, MC, V. Closed Sun. No lunch Sat.*

$$–$$$ ✕ **Metro Bistro.** This cushy spot just a block off Canal Street is a standout for its blend of attractiveness and practicality, as well as its good, hearty food. Near the mahogany bar, a huge, stylized mural suggests the New Orleans skyline. Above the burnished-wood chairs and banquette frames, the deep-gold walls rise to billows of sound-absorbing panels just below the 15-ft ceiling. Tiny cobalt blue lamps cast a soft light on the dishes, in which traditional French and contemporary New Orleans styles meet. The *salade niçoise* holds bits of tuna carpaccio. Double-cut pork chops in a natural sauce, Burgundian beef stew, and a garlicky cassoulet are tailor-made for hefty appetites. Grilled fish sit between Creole stewed corn and a frizzle of sweet potato. And desserts are rich in flavor and creativity. ✉ *Pelham Hotel, 200 Magazine St.,* ☎ *504/529–1900. AE, D, DC, MC, V.*

Cajun-Inspired

$$–$$$ ✕ **Bon Ton Café.** The Bon Ton's opening in 1953 marked the first appearance of a significant Cajun restaurant in New Orleans. Its crawfish dishes, gumbo, jambalaya, and oyster omelet have retained their strong following in the decades since. The bustle in the excellently maintained dining room reaches a peak at lunchtime on weekdays, when businesspeople from nearby offices come in droves for the baked eggplant with shrimp, the fried catfish, the turtle soup, and a warm, sugary bread pudding. The veteran waitresses are knowledgeable and fleet-footed. ✉ *401 Magazine St.,* ☎ *504/524–3386. AE, MC, V. Closed weekends.*

Contemporary Creole

$$$ ✕ **Palace Café.** Members of the Commander's Palace branch of the Brennan family operate this big, colorful restaurant on Canal Street just a few blocks from the Mississippi riverfront. Crafted from a multistory building that was the city's oldest music store, the Palace is a convivial spot to try some of the more imaginative contemporary Creole dishes such as crab chops, rabbit ravioli in piquant sauce, grilled shrimp with fettuccine, and seafood Napoleon. Desserts, especially the white-chocolate bread pudding and Mississippi mud pie, are luscious. Drugstore-

82

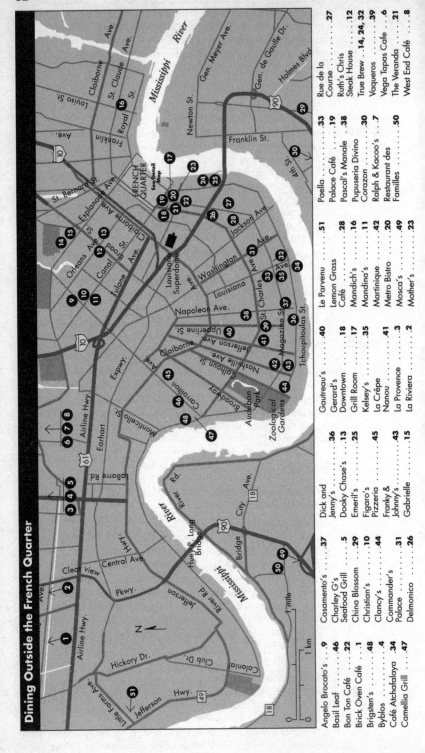

Dining Outside the French Quarter

tile floors, stained-cherry booths, and soothing beige walls set the mood. A handsome curved staircase at the center of the lower floor leads to the wraparound mezzanine lined with a large, brightly colored wall painting populated by the city's famous musicians. ☒ *605 Canal St.,* ☎ *504/523–1661. Reservations essential. AE, DC, MC, V.*

Continental

$$$–$$$$ ✗ **The Veranda.** The elegant Old South meets modern-day luxury in this vast complex of rooms on the Hotel Inter-Continental's lobby level. The most spectacular space is a lofty, glass-enclosed room filled with tropical plants and lacy garden furniture. The other rooms are done in a formal antebellum style. The dinner menu diverts from the familiar fare of luxury hotels with numerous creations of chef Willy Coln, a local favorite. The result is smoked Nova Scotia salmon cheek-by-jowl with shrimp rémoulade and sautéed red snapper with lump crabmeat. The better choices include the crab cakes, marinated shrimp, Wiener schnitzel, and beefsteak in pepper sauce. The extensive pastry buffet is always beckoning. ☒ *Hotel Inter-Continental, 444 St. Charles Ave.,* ☎ *504/525–5566. AE, D, DC, MC, V.*

Po'boys and Other Sandwiches

$$ ✗ **Mother's.** Thousands of tourists leave New Orleans believing that this island of blue-collar sincerity amid glittery hotels and office buildings is the city's ultimate in down-home eats. However, many locals find the place has declined in the dozen or so years since the new owners expanded operating hours and enlarged the menu. Still, Mother's keeps dispensing its delicious baked ham and roast-beef po'boys (ask for "debris" on the beef sandwich and the bread will be slathered with meat juices and shreds of meat), home-style biscuits and jambalaya, and a very good chicken gumbo in a couple of dining rooms. Breakfast eggs and coffee are sometimes cold, and cleanliness is not an obsession, but that doesn't seem to repel the hordes fighting for seats at peak meal-times. Service is cafeteria style, with a counter or two augmenting the tables. ☒ *401 Poydras St.,* ☎ *504/523–9656. No credit cards.*

Vietnamese

$$–$$$ ✗ **Lemon Grass Café.** What draws the regulars here are the aromatic and spicy flavors of Vietnamese cuisine, specifically, that of Saigon, with occasional French influences and lots of eye appeal. The dining room is another visual feast, a soothing, contemporary blend of rice-paper screens, pale walls, and simple, yet striking, patterns. Try crisp spring rolls filled with minced chicken, jicama root, wood-ear mushrooms, carrot, and onion; juicy soft-shelled crab, roasted in a light salt-and-pepper crust; beautifully seared fish, its moistness heightened with a light, pungent sauce; and thin slices of duck breast escorted by sticky rice. Desserts are surprisingly imaginative for an Asian restaurant, with choices in styles from Asian to European, as in a chocolate Bavarian-cream pie and a strawberry napoleon. ☒ *International House, 217 Camp St.,* ☎ *504/523–1200. AE, D, DC, MC, V. No lunch weekends.*

Faubourg Marigny

Creole with Soul

$–$$ ✗ **Praline Connection.** Down-home cooking in the southern-Creole style is the forte of this laid-back, likable restaurant a couple of blocks from the French Quarter, with a branch in the Warehouse District as well. The fried or stewed chicken, smothered pork chops, barbecue ribs, and collard greens are definitively done. And the soulful filé gumbo, bread pudding, and sweet-potato pie are among the best in town. Add to all this some of the lowest prices anywhere, a congenial staff, and a neat-as-a-pin dining room, and the sum is a fine place to spend an hour or two. The adjacent sweetshop holds such delights as sweet-potato cookies and Creole pralines. In the Warehouse District branch the Sunday gospel brunch is rousingly entertaining. ⊠ *542 Frenchmen St., Faubourg Marigny,* ☎ *504/943–3934;* ⊠ *901 S. Peters St., Warehouse District,* ☎ *504/523–3973. Reservations not accepted. AE, D, DC, MC, V.*

Garden District/Uptown

American

$　✕ **Camellia Grill.** Every diner should be as classy as Camellia Grill, a one-of-a-kind eatery that deserves its following. Locals vie until the early morning hours for one of the 29 stools at the gleaming counter, each place supplied with a large, fresh linen napkin. The hamburger—four ounces of excellent beef on a fresh bun with any number of embellishments—is unexcelled in the city. Other blue-ribbon dishes are the chili, the fruit and meringue pies, the garnished omelets, and the "cannibal special"—uncooked hamburger and egg with chopped onion on rye. To wash it down, try an orange or coffee freeze with ice cream. Everything's made on the premises and served by bow-tied, white-waist-coated waiters with the fleetest feet in the business. ⊠ *626 S. Carrollton Ave., Uptown,* ☎ *504/866–9573. No credit cards.*

Avant-Garde

$$$　✕ **Gautreau's.** Modest in size but ambitious in its cooking, this haven
★　of sophistication is half hidden in a quiet, leafy residential neighborhood. Don't look for a sign outside; there is none. The ever-changing menu usually includes fine crab cakes with an herbal tartar sauce, duck confit with truffle oil and dried Mission figs, veal T-bone with a marsala-thyme butter, and filet mignon in robust sauces. At dessert time, try the superb crème brûlée or the caramelized banana split. The 40-seat downstairs dining room, once a neighborhood drugstore, is encased in lustrous oxblood enamel. Along one wall extends the old pharmacy's original polished wood cabinets, now filled with liquors and glassware. The second-floor dining room is less noisy. ⊠ *1728 Soniat St., Uptown,* ☎ *504/899–7397. Reservations essential. AE, D, DC, MC, V. Closed Sun. No lunch.*

Cafés and Coffeehouses

$　✕ **P. J.'s Coffee & Tea Cafés.** Long before coffeehouses became as fashionable as running shoes, the original P. J.'s on Maple Street, near Tulane University, was hissing and fizzing with mochas, lattes, and the like. Today, its franchises, which are open daily from early morning to near midnight, have peppered the city with coffeehouses of different sizes and atmospheres. The New Orleans–style coffee-and-chicory is the real thing, but there's a bounty of other blends and roasts for the seeker of the offbeat. ⊠ *10 locations, including 644 Camp St., CBD,* ☎ *504/529–3658;* ⊠ *634 Frenchmen St., Faubourg Marigny,* ☎ *504/ 949–2292;* ⊠ *5432 Magazine St., Uptown,* ☎ *504/895–0273.*

$　✕ **Rue de la Course.** The charm of this little coffeehouse on a quiet corner of Magazine Street (supplemented by several spin-offs elsewhere in town) lies as much in its lived-in look as in its caffe latte, sturdy espresso, and other coffees flavored with vanilla, hazelnuts, or chocolate almond. No gimmickry intrudes on the atmosphere, which combines the calm of a library with the spontaneity of an old-fashioned general store (one wall is lined with bins of coffee beans). A few tables outside are perfect for relaxing and sipping an Italian cream soda topped with whipped cream. It closes nightly at 11. ⊠ *1500 Magazine St., Lower Garden District,* ☎ *504/529–1455;* ⊠ *3128 Magazine St., Garden District,* ☎ *504/899–0242;* ⊠ *219 N. Peters St., French Quarter,* ☎ *504/523–0206;* ⊠ *401 Carondelet St., CBD,* ☎ *504/525– 5200. No credit cards.*

Caribbean

$$–$$$ ✕ **Martinique.** The French Caribbean meets New Orleans in this mod-
★ est yet charming dining room and its airy, tropical courtyard. Attractive photographs and folksy, brilliantly colored Caribbean scenes perk
up the pale yellow walls of the small dining room. Lighter variations
on Caribbean themes are the chef's style. The dishes, all suffused with
delicate herbal and spicy flavors, range from bracing poached oysters
with lime and cayenne to lamb sausage with minted beans. Good, too,
are the cod fritters, carrot and leek soup, salmon in pineapple-sesame
sauce, and *blaff*, a Martiniquaise bouillabaisse that's perfect for a cool
evening. Sorbets and fresh mango are typical desserts. Reservations are
accepted only for parties of five or more. ⊠ *5908 Magazine St., Uptown,* ☎ *504/891–8495. MC, V. Closed Mon. No lunch.*

Contemporary Creole

$$$–$$$$ ✕ **Commander's Palace.** No restaurant captures New Orleans's gas-
★ tronomic heritage and celebratory spirit as well as this one in a stately
Garden District mansion. The upstairs Garden Room's glass walls
have marvelous views of the giant oak trees on the patio below, and
the other rooms promote conviviality with their bright pastels or del-
icate wall paintings. Chef Jamie Shannon's classics include poached oys-
ters in a seasoned cream sauce with Oregon caviar; a spicy and meaty
turtle soup; terrific crab cakes in an oyster sauce; and a wonderful sautéed
trout coated with crunchy pecans. Among the addictive desserts are
the bread pudding soufflé and chocolate Sheba, a wonderful Bavarian
cream. Several hundred people might dine at Commander's on a given
day, but its size rarely interferes with the quality of the food or ser-
vice. The special weekend brunch menus are less ambitious but also
less costly. ⊠ *1403 Washington Ave., Garden District,* ☎ *504/899–
8221. Reservations essential. Jacket required. AE, D, DC, MC, V.*

$$$ ✕ **Brigsten's.** Chef Frank Brigsten's fusion of Creole refinement and
★ Acadian earthiness reflects his years as a protégé of Paul Prudhomme.
The owner-chef's ever-changing menus add up to some of the best South
Louisiana cooking you'll find anywhere. Everything is fresh and filled
with the deep and complex tastes that characterize Creole-Cajun food.
The cream of oysters Rockefeller soup is a revelation. Rabbit and
chicken dishes, usually presented in rich sauces and gravies, are full of
robust flavor. The roux-based gumbos are thick and intense, and the
fresh banana ice cream is worth every calorie. Fans of blackened food
couldn't do better than with this prime rib, in a spicy charred coating.
Trompe-l'oeil murals add whimsy to the intimate spaces of a turn-of-
the-century frame cottage. ⊠ *723 Dante St., Uptown,* ☎ *504/861–7610.
Reservations essential. AE, MC, V. Closed Sun. and Mon.*

$$$ ✕ **Dick and Jenny's.** Stints at Commander's Palace, Gautreau's, and Up-
perline have given chef Richard Benz a talent for coming up with inno-
vative dishes that meld logically with familiar combinations of typical
New Orleans ingredients. At his and wife Jenny's breezily casual restau-
rant he produces food that should satisfy both local purists and others
looking for new wrinkles. Fried oysters are super fresh and perfectly cooked.
The meaty, judiciously seasoned crab cakes arrive atop fried green tomato
slices and a fiery red-pepper sauce. Beef tournedos is lavished with seared
foie gras and a reduction of port wine and balsamic vinegar. Helping to
enliven the dining room and bar, fashioned from a turn-of-the-century
frame cottage, are large, colorful canvases done by the chef himself. ⊠
4501 Tchoupitoulas St., Uptown ☎ *504/894–9880. Reservations not
accepted. AE, DC, MC, V. Closed Sun., Mon. No lunch.*

$$–$$$ ✕ **Clancy's.** The easy, sophisticated charm and consistently classy
★ menu have made this minimally decorated bistro a favorite with pro-
fessional and business types from nearby neighborhoods. Most of the

dishes are imaginative treatments of New Orleans favorites. Some specialties, like the fresh sautéed fish in cream sauce flavored with crawfish stock and herbs, are exceptional. Other signs of an inventive chef are the expertly fried oysters matched with warm Brie; the grilled chicken breast in lime butter; and a peppermint ice-cream pie. Simpler dishes such as filet mignon in Madeira sauce benefit from careful, knowledgeable preparation. The decor is neutral, with gray walls and a few ceiling fans above bentwood chairs and white linen cloths. The small bar is usually filled with regulars who know each other. ⊠ *6100 Annunciation St., Uptown,* ☎ *504/895–1111. AE, MC, V. Closed Sun. No lunch Mon. and Sat.*

$$–$$$ ✕ **Kelsey's.** Randy Barlow, the owner-chef at this attractive restaurant, spent years working under the celebrated Paul Prudhomme. Although the mentor's influences are obvious in the deep, South Louisiana flavors of Barlow's food, he has forged a style of his own. His spicy jambalaya of chicken, sausage, Cajun ham, and rabbit is one of the best versions anywhere. A home-style gumbo with seafood, chicken, and sausage has just the right balance of spicy and mellow flavors. Shrimp étouffée, in a moderately peppery sauce, is loaded with shrimp flavor. Try the orange–poppy seed cheesecake. Interesting watercolors and oils decorate the three dining rooms and roomy bar, lined in bare-wood lathing. ⊠ *3923 Magazine St., Uptown,* ☎ *504/897–6722. Reservations essential. AE, MC, V. Closed Sun. and Mon. No lunch Sat.*

Creole with Soul

$$ ✕ **Café Atchafalaya.** Homespun cooking with a definitely southern accent is the menu's focus inside this ancient, white-clapboard building near the Uptown riverfront. Fresh vegetables and hearty fruit pies are specialties, as are the fried green tomatoes, stuffed pork chop, boiled beef brisket with potato, and lemon chess pie. Frills are few in the modest dining room, with its bare-top tables, chalkboard of specials, and posters and fish prints. It's a natural for a leisurely weekend breakfast or brunch with neighborhood types stopping in after a jog through the oak-lined streets nearby. ⊠ *901 Louisiana Ave., Uptown,* ☎ *504/ 891–5271. Reservations not accepted. No credit cards. Closed Mon.*

French

$$–$$$ ✕ **La Crêpe Nanou.** French chic for the budget-minded is the style in
★ this welcoming little bistro, where, during peak hours, you may have a half-hour wait at the friendly bar for a table. Left Bank Paris is evoked with woven café chairs out on the sidewalk, a velvet curtain just inside the door, awnings that resemble Metro-station architecture, and a menu loaded with properly earthy pâté maison, hearty lentil soup, french fries that are really French, and lavish dessert crepes. Spaces are a little tight in the oddly configured dining areas, but the whimsical paintings and profuse greenery lighten the spirits. Regulars, mostly young professional types from the nearby frame cottages, give the place a clubby air. ⊠ *1410 Robert St., Uptown,* ☎ *504/899–2670. Reservations not accepted. MC, V. No lunch.*

Italian

$$$ ✕ **Pascal's Manale.** Few restaurants are as closely identified with one dish as this one is with barbecue shrimp. The original version, introduced a half century ago, remains, with jumbo shrimp, still in the shell, cooked in a buttery pool zapped with just the right amount of spice and pepper. The rest of the menu, mostly seafood and Italian-style creations, is uneven, but often done with respect for local traditions. The turtle soup, fried eggplant, and baked or raw oysters in various sauces are good ways to start. Sautéed veal with shrimp, chicken bordelaise, and seafood with pasta are other reliable choices. The restaurant's popularity with out-of-towners usually means a wait for a table, even if it's reserved, and the bar's party atmosphere makes it comfortable only for the gregarious. Space is at a premium in the two dining rooms, too, and the clientele is usually in a partying mood. ⊠ *1828 Napoleon Ave., Uptown,* ☎ *504/895–4877. Reservations essential. AE, MC, V. No lunch weekends.*

$$ ✕ **Figaro's Pizzeria.** Even in Creole-Cajun country, pizza holds considerable sway. Doubters can stop in at Figaro's, the favorite Uptown spot for New Orleanians who can't shake the craving for either American- or Italian-style pizza. In the small interior dining room, or at a table in the connecting tented space, the faithful come not only for the familiar species, but also for such toppings as crawfish étouffée with wild mushrooms and ginger, or yellowfin tuna with a salsa of caramelized onions, roasted sweet peppers, and mangoes. The menu also lists a number of other dishes, such as veal with linguine, roasted duck or chicken, and a corn-and-crab soup spiked with bourbon. ⊠ *7900 Maple St., Uptown,* ☎ *504/866–0100. Reservations not accepted. AE, MC, V.*

Mexican

$$–$$$ ✕ **Vaqueros.** Stretched-leather chairs, a little tortilla-cooking station, and folksy decoration are the first visible clues that Vaqueros looks to Mexico and the American Southwest, especially Texas, for its inspirations. Yet the dishes are rarely conventional. Salsas often convey both peppery and mellow sensations, and chili con carne appears with black beans and venison. Grilled fish might show up in a zesty sauce flavored with chilies and tropical fruit. Still, plenty of tacos, fajitas, enchiladas, and the like are served up in the two spacious dining rooms, which usually buzz with activity. The Southwestern-style Sunday brunch buffet, served on the covered patio, is a special treat. ⊠ *4938 Prytania St., Uptown,* ☎ *504/891–6441. Reservations not accepted. AE, D, DC, MC, V. Closed Mon. No lunch Sat.*

Seafood

$–$$ ✕ **Casamento's.** Encased in gleaming white ceramic tiles, Casamento's has been a haven for Uptown seafood lovers since 1918. Family members still staff the long, marble raw-oyster bar up front and the immaculate kitchen out back. Between them is a small dining room with a similarly diminutive menu. The specialties are oysters lightly poached in seasoned milk, and fried shrimp, trout, and oysters, impeccably fresh and greaseless. They're served with fried potatoes and a good selection of domestic beers. Even the houseplants have a just-polished look. ⊠ *4330 Magazine St., Uptown,* ☎ *504/895–9761. Reservations not accepted. No credit cards. Closed Mon. and early June–late Aug.*

$–$$ ✕ **Franky & Johnny's.** Seekers of the quintessential New Orleans neighborhood restaurant need look no further. Team pennants, posters, and football jerseys vie for space on the paneled walls of the low-ceiling bar and dining room while a jukebox blares beneath them. From the kitchen's steaming cauldrons come freshly boiled shrimp, crabs, and crawfish, piled high and ready to be washed down with ice-cold beer. On the day's po'boy roster might be fried crawfish tails or oysters, meatballs in tomato sauce, or roast beef with gravy. Table service is rudimentary. ⊠ *321 Arabella St., Uptown,* ☎ *504/899–9146. Reservations not accepted. D, MC, V.*

Spanish

$$ ✕ **Paella.** New Orleans restaurants offering traditional Spanish cooking have always been hard to come by. This light-filled and friendly casual restaurant tries to fill the gap with a mostly Spanish menu that has a high success rate. The gazpacho is properly thick and flavorful. Lamb Chilindron, stewed in a reddish sauce, is piquant and fresh-tasting, and shrimp swathed in a lusty garlic sauce has a distinctively

Mediterranean flair. Curiously, the two paellas, one with seafood and the other a valenciana with pork and chicken, are so-so offerings. The wine list has a good, and attractively priced, selection of riojas. ⊠ *3637 Magazine St., Uptown,* ☎ *504/895–0240. AE, DC, MC, V. Closed Sun.*

Thai

$$ ✕ **Basil Leaf.** Familiar Thai standbys—spring rolls, pad thai, chicken and coconut soup, and the like—get a new lease on life in the kitchen of owner-chef Siam Titiparwat. These expertly done traditional dishes are backed up by a slew of thoroughly original creations in the crisp, simple dining room, enlivened with several brilliantly colored paintings. Gently flavored green and red Thai curries, especially those with chicken or shrimp, are done with the instinctual talent of a Thai native, as are the firm yet tender dumplings filled with bits of scallop. At dessert time, try such offbeat sweets as the delicious Thai sticky rice with mango. Service is brisk and friendly. ⊠ *1438 S. Carrollton Ave., Uptown,* ☎ *504/862–9001. AE, DC, MC, V. No dinner Sun., no lunch Sat.–Mon.*

Traditional Creole

$$$–$$$$ ✕ **Delmonico.** In 1997 celebrity chef Emeril Lagasse bought the very traditional, unpretentious, century-old Delmonico. Millions of dollars later, Delmonico is a large, extravagantly appointed restaurant with the most ambitious revamping of classic Creole dishes in town and formal table-side service from rolling gueridons. The many high-ceiling dining spaces are swathed in upholstered walls and super-thick window fabrics. As the restaurant matures, the menu can be either impressive or disappointing. Oysters baked on the half-shell in various sauces are sinfully good. Barbecue shrimp are reassuringly luscious, as are crawfish in puff pastry and the sautéed fish meunière. But concoctions such as a brochette of oysters and greasy bacon resting on a mound of "dirty rice" or dry "twice-stuffed" potato sitting atop a gristly T-bone steak drenched in marchand de vin sauce are ill-conceived. Desserts range in quality from the superb and bounteous cheesecake with Creole cream cheese to the flabby, forgettable cluster of chocolate crepes. The day when the food and service merit the high prices has yet to arrive. ⊠ *1300 St. Charles Ave.,* ☎ *504/525–4937. AE, D, DC, MC, V.*

Mid-City

Contemporary Creole

$$–$$$ ✕ **Gabrielle.** Bright and energetic and about five minutes by taxi from
★ the French Quarter, Gabrielle is a hit, thanks to chef Greg Sonnier's marvelous interpretations of earthy, spicy South Louisiana dishes. Seating has been expanded with a small add-on dining room that has its own homey atmosphere, complete with lace curtains and framed still-life prints. Regulars come for the spicy rabbit and veal sausages, buttery oysters gratinéed with artichoke and Parmesan, a slew of excellent gumbos and étouffées, and Mary Sonnier's fresh-fruit cobblers and shortcakes. Servings are generous and sauces are rich, so you may want to skip lunch before dining here. ⊠ *3201 Esplanade Ave.,* ☎ *504/ 948–6233. Reservations essential. AE, D, DC, MC, V. Closed Sun. and Mon. No lunch.*

Dessert

$ ✕ **Angelo Brocato's.** Traditional Sicilian fruit sherbets, ice creams, pastries, and candies are the attractions of this quaint little sweetshop that harks back to the time when the French Quarter was peopled mostly by Italian immigrants. The shop has since moved to the Mid-City area, but the cannoli and the lemon and strawberry ices haven't lost their status as local favorites. It closes at 10 PM. ⊠ *214 N. Carrollton Ave.,* ☎ *504/488–1465. No credit cards.*

Seafood

$–$$ ✕ **West End Café.** Seafood restaurants abound on New Orleans's lake-
★   front, but finding an edible meal among them is no piece of cake. The
best of the lot by far is this '40s-style eatery with two no-frills dining rooms
and a sports bar that's usually lined with neighborhood types. At breakfast, lunch, and dinner, the reliably good home-style fare is produced with
solid New Orleans underpinnings: two-fisted omelets; seasonal, expertly
seasoned boiled crabs, shrimp, and crawfish; excellent fried-seafood
platters; gumbos; an old-fashioned crab bisque; and grand versions of
shrimp rémoulade, red beans, hamburger steak, and onion rings. Table
service also is several cuts above the norm for the city's diner-style restaurants. ⊠ *8536 Pontchartrain Blvd.,* ☎ *504/288–0711. AE, DC, MC, V.*

$$ ✕ **Mandina's.** The interior of this white clapboard corner building is
a study in 1940s nostalgia, with its functional bar facing a roomful of
laminated tables set with sugar shakers, hot sauce, and salt and pep-
per. Regulars—a cross section of the population—endure a ¼-hour wait
for a table under a 30-year-old newspaper clipping or the latest art-
work from a St. Louis brewery. Butter, hearty seasonings, and tomato
sauce are the staples. The shrimp rémoulade and old-fashioned gumbo
are the logical appetizers. Broiled trout and shrimp, wading in seasoned
butter, are tasty, as are the fried oysters and shrimp, the seafood or Ital-
ian sausage po'boys, and the sweet bread pudding. Service amounts
to little more than taking and delivering orders. ⊠ *3800 Canal St.,* ☎
504/482–9179. Reservations not accepted. No credit cards.

Steaks

$$$–$$$$ ✕ **Ruth's Chris Steak House.** Ruth's Chris is sacred to New Orleans
★   steak lovers. The all-American menu fairly drips with butter, and the
main draw is aged U.S. prime beef in he-man portions, charbroiled and
served atop a sizzling, seasoned butter sauce. The hefty filet mignon
is often taller than it is wide, and a monstrous porterhouse serves sev-
eral. If the salads lack sparkle, the copious potato dishes are consis-
tently first-rate. Lighter entrées (chicken breast, veal, seafood) mollify
the health-conscious. The large, plush, but unfussy, dining rooms of
the flagship Mid-City restaurant are lined in pale-wood paneling and
understated landscape paintings. Politicians, both actual and aspiring,
are everywhere. ⊠ *711 N. Broad St., Mid-City,* ☎ *504/486–0810;* ⊠
3633 Veterans Blvd., Metairie, ☎ *504/888–3600. Reservations es-
sential. AE, D, DC, MC, V.*

Traditional Creole

$$$ ✕ **Christian's.** A small church in a residential neighborhood has been
★   turned into a front-rank purveyor of Creole cuisine with numerous
French flourishes. On crowded banquettes under stained-glass windows,
regulars devour crunchy, smoked soft-shell crab laced with butter, a
Creole bouillabaisse of local fish and shellfish, and gulf fish sautéed
with fresh oysters and drenched in brown wine sauce. The superb recipe
for skewered fried oysters with bacon comes from Galatoire's (☞
French Quarter, *above*), and the two restaurants, founded by members
of the same family, share other dishes as well. A reservation doesn't
guarantee immediate seating, the bar is tiny, and service can be rushed.
⊠ *3835 Iberville St.,* ☎ *504/482–4924. Reservations essential. AE,
D, MC, V. Closed Sun. No lunch Mon. and Sat.*

Ninth Ward

Traditional Creole

$$–$$$ ✕ **Mandich's.** This many-faceted favorite of locals resists categorizing.
★   It occupies a neat but unremarkable building in a blue-collar neighborhood. The decor—a mix of bright yellow paint, captain's chairs,

and wood veneer—won't win prizes. The food ranges from straight-forward, home-style dishes to ambitious trout and shellfish dishes. Fried oysters are swathed in a finely balanced butter sauce with garlic and parsley. Shrimp and andouille sausages trade flavors on the grill. The trout Mandich (breaded, broiled, and served with a butter, wine, and Worcestershire sauce) has become a classic of the genre, and more garlic boosts slices of buttery roasted potatoes. ⊠ *3200 St. Claude Ave.,* ☎ *504/947–9553. Reservations not accepted. MC, V. Closed Sun., Mon. No lunch Sat., no dinner Tues.–Thurs.*

Tremé

Creole with Soul

$$–$$$ ✕ **Dooky Chase's.** The roots of many of the home-style dishes here go back more than a century. The food, prepared with a technique handed down by generations of local cooks, is served in a warm, elegantly proportioned dining room hung with artwork by local black artists. Crab soup and Creole gumbo are dependable starters. Good meat entrées include the buttery panéed veal and the pork chops sautéed with onions. The sausage jambalaya, stewed okra, and sweet potatoes are delicious and definitive. Late lunch or early dinner at Dooky's on Sunday afternoon has become a tradition for families, and the weekday luncheon buffets are a bountiful bargain. Visitors are advised to use taxis or the secured parking lot adjacent to the restaurant. ⊠ *2301 Orleans Ave.,* ☎ *504/821–2294. AE, MC, V.*

Warehouse District

Cafés and Coffeehouses

$ ✕ **True Brew.** True Brew's three cafés serve a wide selection of teas and unflavored and flavored coffees (rum rhapsody, chocolate-raspberry truffle, and Irish creme supreme are popular). Given equal billing in the Julia Street location are the poetry readings, intimate musical performances, and art exhibitions that take place almost every night. A boutique sells gift baskets, jewelry, and crafts. Closing hours vary at each location from 7 PM to 11 PM. ⊠ *200 Julia St., Warehouse District,* ☎ *504/524–8441;* ⊠ *3133 Ponce de Leon St., Mid-City,* ☎ *504/947–3948;* ⊠ *3242 Magazine St., Uptown,* ☎ *504/899–9453. AE, MC, V accepted at Magazine St.; other locations are cash only.*

Contemporary Creole

$$$$ ✕ **Emeril's.** Although celebrity chef Emeril Lagasse (of the Food Network's *Emeril Live*) makes rare appearances at his original namesake restaurant, you may spot a star or two from the sports and entertainment worlds in these always-jammed dining spaces. Noisy and decidedly contemporary, Emeril's has an ambitious menu that gives equal emphasis to Creole and modern American cooking. On the plate, this translates as a fresh corn crepe topped with Louisiana caviar, grilled andouille sausage in the chef's own Worcestershire sauce, a sauté of crawfish over jambalaya cakes, fresh-fruit cobblers, and a cornucopia of creative dishes. Singles and couples can grab a stool at a food bar and get close-up views of the chef at work. The looks of the place are appropriately avant-garde—brick and glass walls, gleaming wood floors, burnished-aluminum lamps, and a huge abstract-expressionist oil painting. ⊠ *800 Tchoupitoulas St.,* ☎ *504/528–9393. AE, D, DC, MC, V. Closed Sun. No lunch Sat.*

Outside City Limits

Avant-Garde

$$–$$$ ✕ **Vega Tapas Café.** The word *tapas* in the name is deceptive, since the serving sizes at Vega are closer to those of appetizers, with prices

correspondingly lower. The high success rate of chef Alison Vega's dishes, mostly Mediterranean-inspired, enhances the adventure. Lovers of scallops should head straight for the ones seared to a turn and sauced with butter tinged with tomato and saffron. Dark, briny olives join tomato in the white beans that garnish the tasty, pan-roasted tuna. Among the half-dozen full-size entrées are a delectable paella studded with chicken, sausage, and shellfish and a soul-warming braised lamb shank with vegetables in a luscious gravy. Everything is served in a large, minimally decorated room lined with hard surfaces, taking noise levels up a couple of notches. ⊠ *2051 Metairie Rd., Metairie,* ☎ *504/ 836–2007. AE, D, DC, MC, V. Closed Sun. Lunch Fri. only.*

Chinese

$$ ✕ **China Blossom.** The regional Chinese cooking is exemplary in this ★ neat-as-a-pin restaurant, across the Mississippi River from the center of town but quickly accessible via the river bridge. Uncompromising freshness and imagination mark the ingredients, seasonings, and sauces, whether the style is Cantonese, Szechuan, or elegant Hong Kong. These qualities are found not only in a whole, butterflied fried trout and crawfish in spicy lobster sauce but also in such commonplace dishes as egg rolls, lemon chicken, *moo shu* pork, and wonton soup. A few ornamental objects of lacquer, gilt, and mother-of-pearl adorn the white and rust walls of the several dining rooms, and service is by a crisply efficient, affable staff. ⊠ *1801 Stumpf Blvd., at Wright Ave., in the Stumpf Blvd. Shopping Center, Gretna,* ☎ *504/361–4598. AE, D, MC, V. Closed Mon.*

Contemporary Creole

$$–$$$ ✕ **Charley G's Seafood Grill.** One of the few restaurants in the New ★ Orleans suburbs that does justice to contemporary South Louisiana cooking, Charley G's has been a runaway success since its opening in 1992. One reason is the smart, uncluttered look of the split-level dining spaces, simultaneously elegant and festive. Another is the menu, which contains some of the best Creole-Cajun food around. The crab cakes and chicken-and-sausage gumbo would impress the pickiest bayou gastronome. Game dishes, especially duck and quail, are superb, as are the grilled fish and belt-busting desserts. The mostly California wine list is both impressive in range and beautifully organized. ⊠ *Heritage Plaza Bldg., 2nd level, 111 Veterans Blvd., Metairie,* ☎ *504/837– 6408. AE, D, DC, MC, V. No lunch Sat.*

French

$$$ ✕ **La Provence.** It's almost an hour's drive from central New Orleans, ★ but the glorious French provincial food and relaxing atmosphere of this exceptional restaurant are well worth the trip. Owner-chef Chris Kerageorgiu's elegant yet earthy cooking is consistently satisfying. Giant New Zealand mussels, still in their shells under a garlicky butter sauce, arrive on angel-hair pasta; roasted duck with garlic warms the soul; and a thick and hearty quail gumbo with rice and andouille sausage is a revelation. Separating the two dining rooms, hung with pleasant Provençal landscape paintings, is a hearth that welcomes you on damp winter days. In warmer seasons, the tree-shaded deck is almost as congenial. Call for directions. ⊠ *U.S. 190, across Lake Pontchartrain, Lacombe,* ☎ *504/626–7662. Reservations essential. AE, MC, V. Closed Mon., Tues. No lunch Wed.–Sat.*

$$$ ✕ **Le Parvenu.** It's easy to mistake Le Parvenu for a cozy little cottage near the Rivertown historic district on suburban Kenner's Mississippi riverfront. Inside, the homey mood is reinforced by small, pastel-hued dining rooms lined with flouncy drapery and unobtrusive prints. Veteran New Orleans chef Dennis Hutley has created a menu that draws inspiration from elegant Continental sauces and rich Creole flavors. Ramekins of shrimp are immersed in brandy cream. Escallopes of veal enclosing a filling of spinach and ham are lavished with Portobello mushrooms, and rosy grilled salmon is sauced with a basil-tinged hollandaise and lemon vinaigrette. Lemon crepes and crème brûlée are among the very good desserts. ⊠ *509 Williams Blvd., Kenner,* ☎ *504/471–0534. AE, MC, V. Closed Mon. and Tues. No lunch Sat.*

Italian

$$–$$$ ✕ **Brick Oven Café.** A few minutes from the airport is this always-crowded, very laid-back restaurant, which offers what may be the best home-style Italian cooking in the area. Putting meat in minestrone may be flouting tradition, but this minestrone is fabulous. So are the succulent roasted chicken, spaghetti carbonara, veal piccata, and traditional desserts. You may have to wait a half hour or more for a table at peak dinner hours and elbow room is at a premium, but the inconveniences are worth it for food as good as this. The three dining rooms are festooned with all sorts of foodstuffs, tins, jars, and culinary artifacts. The booths are the most desirable seats. ⊠ *2805 Williams Blvd., Kenner,* ☎ *504/466–2097. Reservations not accepted. AE, D, DC, MC, V.*

$$–$$$ ✕ **La Riviera.** This lively and dependable suburban fixture has a lim-
★   ited regional Italian menu, but overall quality is unusually high for a restaurant that can seat a couple hundred. Lots of rich tomato and cream sauces and unusually good pastas keep things interesting. The crabmeat-stuffed ravioli deserves its following, although the shrimp sautéed in wine and herbs with paprika is hard to beat. Top-quality white veal is another favorite, and the buttery piccata and marsala sauces should impress the pickiest veal lover. Space is at a premium in the two dining rooms, which are hung with large oils depicting Italian Riviera seascapes. Table service, by tuxedoed waiters, is often speedier than some diners prefer. ⊠ *4506 Shores Dr., Metairie,* ☎ *504/888–6238. Reservations essential. AE, D, DC, MC, V. Closed Sun. No lunch.*

$$–$$$ ✕ **Mosca's.** Depending on your point of view, the decor here is either
★   charmingly unpretentious or almost primitive. The food—Southern Louisiana ingredients and southern Italian ingenuity—can be good enough to lure city folk to this isolated, simple restaurant in a near-swamp about a half hour from the city. Baked oysters with artichoke, bread crumbs, olive oil, garlic, and herbs approach the summit of Italian-Creole cuisine. The Italian shrimp are cooked in an herbed mix of olive oil and spices, and the roast chicken with rosemary and Italian sausages is flavorful. Getting a table usually means a wait in the bar, even with reservations. The restaurant is difficult to spot along the highway, so call for directions. Reservations are not accepted Friday and Saturday. ⊠ *4137 U.S. 90, Waggaman,* ☎ *504/436–9942. No credit cards. Closed Sun., Mon. No lunch.*

Latin American

$ ✕ **Pupuseria Divino Corazon.** What's a pupuseria? Why, a place that serves pupusas, of course. And Gloria Salmeron is an expert when it comes to making *pupusas,* the soft little pork-and-cheese pies from her native El Salvador. They, and everything else—like the sweet-corn tamales, quesadillas, and fried plantains—are filled with a fresh heartiness not easy to find in Latin American restaurants. The familiar Mexican dishes, especially the nachos chihuahuas, are excellent, too. A large picture of the Sacred Heart of Jesus (the restaurant's namesake) dominates the beautifully tended, wood-panel dining room. This restaurant is across the Mississippi from the heart of town, but quick to get to via the river bridge. ⊠ *2300 Belle Chasse Hwy., Gretna,* ☎ *504/368–5724. Reservations not accepted. D, MC, V. Closed Wed.*

Lebanese

$$ ✕ **Byblos.** Good Middle Eastern cooking is a rarity in New Orleans. So Byblos, just outside the city limits, has the market pretty much to itself, thanks to the freshness of the kitchen's ingredients, used in authentic combinations and admirably spiced and herbed. You'll find such familiar fare as hummus, moussaka, and stuffed grape leaves. Skewered-meat main courses, especially the chicken and beef, are moist and flavorful. Pleasantly seasoned rice accompanies most entrées, and the custardy desserts are very good. The walls of the single lofty dining room are painted to depict soothing country scenes, and the welcome at the door is always warm. To get here, drive northward (toward Lake Pontchartrain) on Canal Street to Metairie Road. Turn left onto Metairie Road and continue about 2 mi to the restaurant. ✉ *1501 Metairie Rd., Metairie,* ☎ *504/834–9773. AE, D, DC, MC, V.*

Traditional Creole

$$$ ✕ **Restaurant des Familles.** No time for a trip to Cajun country? This restaurant about a half-hour's drive from central New Orleans is the next best thing, although you'd best ask for directions when reserving. Just a few yards from the vast windows are the slow-moving waters of Bayou des Familles, offering a primeval tableau. The spectacular view is framed by lush, moss-draped palmettos and other wild greenery. Dramatically illuminated at night, the huge, Acadian-style raised cottage has a kitchen that produces familiar, and very edible, seafoods in the Creole style—shrimp rémoulade, crawfish étouffée, turtle soup, trout meunière, and fried oysters and bacon en brochette. The fried onion rings and pecan pie are worthy of attention, too. ✉ *Rte. 3134, north of the intersection with Rte. 45, Crown Point,* ☎ *504/689–7834. Reservations essential. AE, D, MC, V.*

3 LODGING

A visit to New Orleans can be as much about where you stay as what you see in town. Bed-and-breakfast inns in historic houses are lovingly maintained by proud locals, and fashionable boutique hotels dot the downtown area. Luxury high-rises blend cosmopolitan service with southern charm. You may awaken to the sounds of steam whistles over the Mississippi River and the aroma of European-style bakeries and rich Louisiana coffee.

Updated by
Paul A.
Greenberg

TRAVELERS TO NEW ORLEANS may choose from a variety of accommodations: posh high-rise hotels, antiques-filled antebellum homes, Creole cottages, old slave quarters, or the offerings of the more familiar hotel chains. Lodging options are listed by neighborhood. Downtown areas include the French Quarter—the heart of the city—and the Central Business District (CBD), which is within walking distance of the French Quarter. There are many fine establishments outside downtown that should be considered if you'd like to stay away from the hubbub in a more quiet, residential area—especially if you have a car or don't mind taking a short streetcar or taxi ride. Lodging places in the historic Garden District and Uptown neighborhoods are often on the St. Charles Avenue streetcar route, which extends from downtown to the farthest reaches of Uptown's genteel, oak-lined streets. Mid-City, West-bank, Metairie, and airport locations are farther from downtown.

In part because of the expansion of the city's convention center, new hotels are springing up. Boutique hotels such as International House have become increasingly popular. Another trend is to convert older buildings into creative hotel space. The Ritz-Carlton, for example, occupies the space of a former department store, and a Hampton Inn near the convention center is housed in two former warehouses.

Whatever kind of lodging you prefer, try to reserve well in advance—especially for special events such as Mardi Gras and Jazz Fest. For such events, rates are considerably higher than those listed here; most places require anywhere from a three- to a five-night minimum stay, and some ask for full payment up front. At other times (such as summer), hotels frequently offer special packages at reduced rates.

Guest houses are for those who come to New Orleans with a desire to savor the old-world charm and atmosphere that are so proudly preserved. All have a limited number of rooms, so it is advisable to make reservations as much as a year ahead of time. Bed-and-breakfast means overnight lodging and breakfast in a private residence. Begin by writing or calling a reservation service (☞ Lodging *in* Smart Travel Tips A to Z). The service will send you lists of several B&Bs that meet your needs in terms of price, location, and length of stay.

All of the large hotels offer no-smoking rooms and are in compliance with the Americans with Disabilities Act. Guest houses are mostly in 19th-century structures. If you want to book at a guest house or B&B and will require facilities for persons with disabilities, ask before reserving if the accommodations are suitable.

Good camping facilities close to the city are rare, since open, solid land is at a premium in New Orleans. The two that are listed lie within 20 minutes of the city, depending on traffic. Others can be found farther out or across Lake Pontchartrain.

Fodor's Choice

★ **Soniat House.** Antiques and fine fabrics from every continent enhance the natural splendor of the two historic mansions that make up this supremely comfortable small hotel. *$$$$*

★ **Windsor Court Hotel.** One of the city's top places to stay, this exquisite, eminently civilized lodging has remarkably large rooms with plush carpeting, canopy and four-poster beds, marble vanities, and over-size mirrors. *$$$$*

★ **Fairmont Hotel.** More than a century old, this meticulously maintained grande dame offers a full measure of gracious southern hospitality. The public areas evoke Victorian splendor, and each room is uniquely designed and appointed. *$$$–$$$$*

★ **Hotel Maison de Ville.** You can escape the contemporary bustle of the French Quarter at this small, antiques-furnished gem with a romantic 19th-century ambience. Hideaway seekers can stay in the private Audubon Cottages. *$$$–$$$$*

★ **Monteleone Hotel.** For the authentic French Quarter experience, stay here on historic Royal Street. The service is consistently outstanding, and even though you're in the heart of one of the busiest areas of the city, the rooms are quiet and serene. *$$$–$$$$*

★ **Omni Royal Orleans Hotel.** One of the standard bearers for local hotel excellence occupies a full block in the center of the French Quarter. From the gleaming lobby to the sheer southern elegance of the guest rooms, no other hotel in town has quite the same charm. *$$–$$$$*

★ **Le Richelieu in the French Quarter.** Guests appreciate the friendly atmosphere of this intimate, reasonably priced hotel with luxe accents; it's near the old Ursuline Convent and the French Market. *$$–$$$*

★ **Chimes Bed and Breakfast.** This Uptown residence provides the comforts of home and conveniences of large hotels. High ceilings, hardwood or slate floors, and an airy dining room add to the charm. *$–$$$*

Prices

CATEGORY	COST*
$$$$	over $200
$$$	$150–$200
$$	$100–$149
$	under $100

All prices are for a standard double room, excluding 12% tax.

French Quarter

If New Orleans is the heart of Louisiana, the 96-square-block French Quarter is its soul. Although much of the Quarter is commercially oriented to tourism, elegant but comfortable hotels and B&Bs or guest houses are tucked away in remote residential pockets, and a number of grand, imposing lodgings are placed throughout. If you're staying in a busy part of the Quarter, you may want to request a room away from the side of the building that faces the street.

✉ following the text of a review is your signal that the property has a Web site, where you will find details and, usually, images; for a link, visit www.fodors.com/urls.

Hotels

$$$$ 🏨 **Ritz-Carlton New Orleans.** In keeping with its tradition of elegance, Ritz-Carlton has artfully converted the historic Maison Blanche department store building on Canal Street into a luxurious hotel with touches that recall old New Orleans. Most rooms contain local antiques and have oversize marble bathrooms and exquisite, plush linens. The Club Floor includes 50 rooms and suites with a concierge and a private lounge. The hotel, within walking distances of most attractions and minutes from the convention center, borders the French Quarter and faces the downtown business district. At press time the hotel was set to open in fall 2000. ✉ *921 Canal St., 70112,* ☎ *504/524–1331,* FAX *504/524–7233. 452 room, 37 suites. Restaurant, 3 bars, beauty salon, spa, parking (fee). AE, D, DC, MC, V.* ✉

Downtown New Orleans Lodging

N

440 yds
400 m

Esplanade Ave.
Barracks St.
Gov. Nicholls St.
Ursulines St.
St. Philip St.
Dumaine St.
St. Ann St.
Orleans St.
St. Peter St.
Toulouse St.
St. Louis St.
Conti St.
Bienville St.
Iberville St.
Canal St.
Common St.
Gravier St.
Union St.
Poydras St.
Perdido St.
Girod St.
Lafayette St.

N. Rampart St.
Burgundy St.
Dauphine St.
Bourbon St.
Royal St.
Chartres St.
Decatur St.
N. Peters St.
Clay St.
N. Front St.
Exchange Alley
Dorsiere St.
Clinton St.
Natchez St.
Commercial Al.
Tchoupitoulas St.
Constance St.
Magazine St.
Camp St.
St. Charles Ave.
Carondelet St.
Baronne St.
O'Keefe Ave.
S. Rampart St.
Loyola St.
University Pl.
Penn St.
Carroll St.
North St.

Duncan Plaza
Madison St.
Jackson Square
Wilk Row
Moon Walk
French Market Pl.
Mississippi River

$$$$ ⊞ **W Hotel New Orleans French Quarter.** Close to Jackson Square, Bourbon Street, and Canal Street, this sleekly renovated modern hotel (the former Hotel de la Poste) has one of the best locations in the Quarter. Most rooms are in the main building, and many have balconies that overlook either the courtyard or Chartres Street. Some have French doors that open directly onto a patio. Two of the four carriage-house suites share a cheery sundeck; the others look over a courtyard. The hotel's dining room is Bacco, a stunning, contemporary Italian eatery operated by Ralph Brennan. ⊠ *316 Chartres St., 70130,* ☎ *504/581–1200 or 800/448–4927,* FAX *504/523–2910. 100 rooms, 13 suites. Restaurant, bar, pool, meeting rooms, parking (fee). AE, D, DC, MC, V.* ☙

$$$$ ⊞ **Wyndham New Orleans at Canal Place.** The Wyndham was definitely designed with views in mind. The huge rose Carrara marble lobby, with its European antiques, jardinieres, and grand piano, is on the 11th floor of the Canal Place shopping mall; tea is served in the Riverbend Grill Thursday, Friday, and Saturday afternoons. Its two-story arched windows overlook the great bend in the Mississippi River and the French Quarter. Each room has a marble foyer and marble bath. The perks on the two executive floors include complimentary Continental breakfast and afternoon hors d'oeuvres. The Aquarium, the Canal Street ferry, Riverwalk, and Harrah's casino are a stone's throw away. ⊠ *100 Iberville St., 70130,* ☎ *504/566–7006 or 800/996–3426,* FAX *504/553–5120. 438 rooms, 41 suites. Restaurant, bar, lobby lounge, minibars, room service, pool, parking (fee). AE, D, DC, MC, V.* ☙

$$$–$$$$ ⊞ **Maison Dupuy.** Seven restored 19th-century town houses surround one of the Quarter's prettiest courtyards, anchored by a spectacular fountain. Rooms are on the large side, and some have balconies. Chef-to-watch Dominique Macquet is the guiding force at Dominique, the hotel's restaurant, which specializes in Louisiana cuisine. The adjacent Lautrec Cabaret attracts late-night revelers. The hotel is two blocks from Bourbon Street and the heart of the Quarter. ⊠ *1001 Toulouse St., 70112,* ☎ *504/586–8000 or 800/535–9177,* FAX *504/525–5334. 200 rooms, 7 suites. Restaurant, pool, health club, nightclub, parking (fee). AE, D, DC, MC, V. CP.* ☙

$$$–$$$$ ⊞ **Monteleone Hotel.** The grande dame of French Quarter hotels, with
     ★ its ornate baroque facade, liveried doormen, and shimmering lobby chandeliers, was built in 1886 and has been kept fresh through renovations. It's the Quarter's oldest hotel, operated by the fourth generation of the Monteleone family. Rooms are extra large and luxurious, with rich fabrics and a mix of four-poster beds, brass beds, and beds with traditional headboards. Junior suites are spacious, and sumptuous VIP suites come with extra pampering. The pool and exercise room are on the roof; the slowly revolving Carousel Bar (☞ Nightlife *in* Chapter 4) in the lobby is a local landmark. Local chef Randy Buck prepares superb food in the Hunt Room Grill. ⊠ *214 Royal St., 70140,* ☎ *504/523–3341 or 800/535–9595,* FAX *504/528–1019. 598 rooms, 28 suites. 3 restaurants, bar, pool, exercise room, concierge, business services, meeting rooms. AE, D, DC, MC, V.* ☙

$$$–$$$$ ⊞ **New Orleans Marriott Hotel.** On the cusp of the French Quarter, the Marriott has a fabulous view of the Quarter, the CBD, and the river. It's an easy walk from Riverwalk, the Canal Place mall, and the convention center. The rooms are comfortable, the service is friendly, and there's nightly jazz in the lobby and the Riverview Restaurant, which just happens to have one of the best views of New Orleans anywhere in the city. ⊠ *555 Canal St., 70140,* ☎ *504/581–1000 or 800/228–9290,* FAX *504/523–6755. 1,290 rooms, 54 suites. 3 restaurants, bar, lobby lounge, pool, sauna, health club, meeting rooms, parking (fee). AE, D, DC, MC, V.* ☙

$$–$$$$ 🏨 **Bienville House Hotel.** This small, intimate hotel with the feel of gracious old New Orleans is in an exciting area of the Quarter, amid an influx of shops, restaurants, and entertainment venues. Here you will find one of the most beautiful courtyards in the city and some lovely rooms with balconies overlooking it. Antiques and reproduction pieces furnish the guest rooms. Gamay (☞ French Quarter *in* Chapter 2) is Chef Greg Sonnier's contemporary Creole dining spot. For a special evening, have dinner here one night and then catch a show at House of Blues, just steps away. ⊠ *320 Decatur St., 70130,* ☎ *504/529–2345,* ℻ *504/525–6079. 80 rooms, 3 suites. Restaurant, bar, pool, laundry service, dry cleaning, meeting rooms, parking (fee). AE, D, MC, V. BP.* ✍

$$–$$$$ 🏨 **Chateau Sonesta.** John Kennedy Toole's comic masterpiece, *A Confederacy of Dunces,* begins under the clock of D. H. Holmes department store on Canal Street, now converted to this rather upscale hotel. In Toole's honor, the clock and a statue of the novel's hero, Ignatius J. Reilly, remain. Rooms at the hotel are large, with high ceilings and neutral decor; some have columns and beams, remnants of the original building. Balcony rooms overlook Bourbon Street or Dauphine Street or one of two interior courtyards. The three suites with whirlpool baths are built around an atrium. On the corner is the Storyville District Jazz Club (☞ Nightlife *in* Chapter 4). ⊠ *800 Iberville St., 70112,* ☎ *504/ 586–0800 or 800/766–3782,* ℻ *504/586–1987. 251 rooms, 11 suites. Restaurant, bar, in-room data ports, minibars, room service, pool, exercise room, meeting rooms, parking (fee). AE, D, DC, MC, V.* ✍

$$–$$$$ 🏨 **Holiday Inn–Chateau Le Moyne.** Old-world atmosphere and decor
★ can be found in this quiet hotel one block off Bourbon Street. Eight suites are in Creole cottages off a tropical courtyard; all rooms are furnished with antiques and reproductions, and have coffeemakers, hair dryers, and irons and ironing boards. ⊠ *301 Dauphine St., 70112,* ☎ *504/581–1303 or 800/465–4329,* ℻ *504/523–5709. 160 rooms, 11 suites. Restaurant, lounge, pool, parking (fee). AE, D, DC, MC, V.* ✍

$$–$$$$ 🏨 **Omni Royal Orleans Hotel.** This elegant white-marble hotel, built
★ in 1960 in the heart of the Vieux Carré, is a replica of the grand St. Louis Hotel of the 1800s. Sconce-enhanced columns, gilt mirrors, fan windows, and three magnificent chandeliers blend to re-create the atmosphere of New Orleans more than a century ago. Rooms are well appointed with marble baths and marble-top dressers and tables; some have balconies. The old New Orleans map that covers one wall of the lounge will fascinate anyone interested in history. On the lobby level, the Rib Room has been one of the city's culinary showpieces for 40 years. The rooftop pool has the best overhead view of the French Quarter in the city. ⊠ *621 St. Louis St., 70140,* ☎ *504/529–5333 or 800/843–6664,* ℻ *504/529–7089. 346 rooms, 16 suites. Restaurant, 3 lounges, pool, barbershop, beauty salon, exercise room, business services, meeting rooms, parking (fee). AE, D, DC, MC, V.* ✍

$$–$$$$ 🏨 **Ramada Plaza Inn on Bourbon Street.** This hotel on the site of New Orleans's original French Opera house is not one of the city's most elegant lodgings, but it is well-kept, with colorful rooms. Guest rooms facing the courtyard are quieter, but the 32 rooms with Bourbon Street balconies are coveted during Mardi Gras. The hotel is on one of the busiest blocks of Bourbon Street, so be prepared for clamoring activity virtually 24 hours a day outside and in. ⊠ *541 Bourbon St., 70130,* ☎ *504/524–7611 or 800/535–7891,* ℻ *504/524–8273. 186 rooms, 2 suites. Cafeteria, piano bar, pool, parking (fee). AE, DC, MC, V.* ✍

$$–$$$$ 🏨 **Royal Sonesta Hotel.** Guests step from the revelry of Bourbon Street into the marble elegance of this renowned hotel's lobby, where a cool, serene atmosphere is enhanced with a lush array of plants. Most of the guest rooms are average in size and furnished with light-color antique reproductions; many have French doors that open onto balconies or patios. Rooms with balconies facing Bourbon Street are noisy, but most of the rooms are so soundproof that you wouldn't know you were anywhere near Bourbon Street. One restaurant, Begué's (☞ French Quarter *in* Chapter 2), is a local gem. There's live entertainment in both the Mystick Den cocktail lounge and the Can-Can Café & Jazz Club. ✉ *300 Bourbon St., 70140, ☎ 504/586–0300 or 800/766–3782, ℻ 504/586–0335. 498 rooms, 32 suites. 2 restaurants, bar, minibars, pool, exercise room, nightclubs, concierge floor, business services, parking (fee). AE, D, DC, MC, V.* ☕

$$–$$$ 🏨 **Dauphine Orleans.** This French Quarter property is comfortable but not exceptional. Rooms are average size but have good-quality fabrics; each has an iron and ironing board, a hair dryer, and two bathrobes. Rooms and suites are in the main building, in a smaller building, and in cottages. The lounge is an erstwhile 19th-century bordello and the exercise room is a small, 19th-century Creole cottage just off the pool. ✉ *415 Dauphine St., 70112, ☎ 504/586–1800 or 800/521–7111, ℻ 504/586–1409. 104 rooms, 7 suites. Bar, minibars, pool, outdoor hot tub, exercise room, parking (fee). AE, D, DC, MC, V. CP.* ☕

$$–$$$ 🏨 **Holiday Inn–French Quarter.** Close to Canal Street, this is a good home base for walking into the heart of the French Quarter or the CBD, or for boarding the St. Charles streetcar line. The hotel's restaurant is a TGI Friday's. ✉ *124 Royal St., 70130, ☎ 504/529–7211 or 800/447–2830, ℻ 504/566–1127. 276 rooms, 56 suites. Restaurant, indoor pool, exercise room, parking (fee). AE, D, DC, MC, V.* ☕

$$–$$$ 🏨 **Le Richelieu in the French Quarter.** Tucked in a corner of the French ★ Quarter, close to the Old Ursuline Convent and the French Market, Le Richelieu combines the friendly, personal atmosphere of a small hotel with luxe touches (upscale toiletries, hair dryers)—at a moderate rate. Some rooms have mirrored walls and large walk-in closets, many have refrigerators, and all have brass ceiling fans, irons, and ironing boards. Balcony rooms are the same rates as standard rooms. An intimate bar and café is off the courtyard, with tables on the terrace by the pool. The hotel has many regular customers who would never stay anywhere else than this homey place. ✉ *1234 Chartres St., 70116, ☎ 504/529–2492 or 800/535–9653, ℻ 504/524–8179. 69 rooms, 17 suites. Bar, café, pool, concierge, free parking. AE, D, DC, MC, V.* ☕

$$ 🏨 **Chateau Motor Hotel.** Simple, friendly, and exuding historic charm, this moderately priced hotel only a few blocks from Jackson Square is a find. The original carriageway leads to the guest rooms, which vary in size and decor. Some have king-size four-posters, while others offer painted iron beds. Note that some rooms are a bit small and lack windows, and bathtubs aren't full-size. A number of rooms have antiques, but most are traditional or contemporary; many have balconies, and a few open directly onto the courtyard, which houses the only silo in the Vieux Carré. The silo encloses a spiral stairway to the penthouse suites. A patio suite and a small restaurant are housed in the old slave quarters. ✉ *1001 Chartres St., 70116, ☎ 504/524–9636, ℻ 504/525–2989. 41 rooms, 4 suites. Restaurant, pool, free parking. AE, DC, MC, V. CP.* ☕

Guest Houses and Bed-and-Breakfasts

$$$$ 🏨 **Melrose Mansion.** A stretch limo to fetch guests from the airport; ★ down pillows and fine milled soaps; full breakfast served poolside, in a formal dining room, or in your room; and rooms filled with 19th-century Louisiana antiques (including four-poster beds) are among the attractions of this handsome 1884 Victorian mansion. Rooms and suites are spacious, with high ceilings and polished hardwood floors. Guests gather each evening for cocktails in the formal drawing room. Baths are sumptuous affairs; those in suites have hot tubs. All but one of the rooms has a wet bar, and one has a private patio. ⊠ *937 Esplanade Ave., 70116,* ☎ *504/944–2255,* FAX *504/945–1794. 8 rooms, 4 suites. Pool. AE, D, MC, V. BP.* ✎

$$$$ 🏨 **Soniat House.** This singularly handsome property comprises three
★ meticulously restored town houses built in the 1830s. Polished hardwood floors, Oriental rugs, and American and European antiques are complemented by contemporary artwork. Amenities include Crabtree & Evelyn toiletries, goose-down pillows, and Egyptian cotton sheets. Most rooms and suites have hot tubs and bath phones. There are two secluded courtyards, filled with exotic plants, where afternoon cocktails and a breakfast ($7 extra) of homemade biscuits and strawberry jam, fresh-squeezed orange juice, and café au lait can be taken, weather permitting. An on-site antiques shop carries exquisite European furnishings. ⊠ *1133 Chartres St., 70116,* ☎ *504/522–0570 or 800/544–8808,* FAX *504/522–7208. 20 rooms, 13 suites. Concierge, business services, parking (fee). AE, MC, V.* ✎

$$$–$$$$ 🏨 **Claiborne Mansion.** Enormous rooms with sky-high ceilings,
★ canopy or four-poster beds, polished hardwood floors, and rich fabrics are features of this handsome 1859 mansion in Faubourg Marigny, on the fringe of the French Quarter. The house overlooks Washington Square Park and has a lush, dramatically lighted rear courtyard and pool. The private cottage, separate from the main house, is charming and intimate. Celebrities book it for the privacy, but families appreciate its separate bedrooms and full kitchen. Smoking is not allowed inside the house. ⊠ *2111 Dauphine St., 70116,* ☎ *504/949–7327,* FAX *504/949–0388. 6 rooms, 5 suites, 1 cottage. In-room VCRs, pool. AE, MC, V. BP.*

$$$–$$$$ 🏨 **Hotel Maison de Ville.** This small, romantic hotel lies in seclusion
★ amid the hustle and bustle of the French Quarter. Tapestry-covered chairs, a gas fire burning in the sitting room, and antiques-furnished rooms all contribute to a 19th-century atmosphere. Some rooms are in former slave quarters in the courtyard; others are on the upper floors of the main house. Breakfast is served with a rose on a silver tray, and port and sherry are available in the afternoon. Other meals can be taken at the intimate, adjacent Bistro (☞ French Quarter *in* Chapter 2). Those who seek a special hideaway will love the hotel's Audubon Cottages—off the street, each with a patio—two blocks from the hotel; the pool (for all guests) is here, too. Children under 12 are not accepted. ⊠ *727 Toulouse St., 70130,* ☎ *504/561–5858 or 800/634–1600,* FAX *504/528–9939. 14 rooms, 2 suites, 7 cottages. Restaurant, minibars, pool, parking (fee). AE, D, DC, MC, V. CP.* ✎

$$–$$$$ 🏨 **Hotel Ste. Hélène.** If you can afford one of the lovely, enormous suites (be forewarned that the one with the whirlpool bath does not have a shower) with 14-ft ceilings, fireplaces, chandeliers, and a balcony overlooking Emeril Lagasse's restaurant Nola, by all means book it. This inn has two buildings, one around the corner from the other; each has a courtyard where Continental breakfast is put out daily. In the evening complimentary champagne is served in the brick courtyard of the main building. Standard rooms are functional and clean but are on the small side and lack charm. Both buildings have three floors and no elevators. ⊠ *508 Chartres St., 70130,* ☎ *504/522–5014,* FAX *504/523–7140. 26 rooms, 10 suites. Pool. AE, D, DC, MC, V. CP.* ✎

$$–$$$$ 🏨 **Lanaux Mansion.** This Italianate mansion dates from 1879 and has 14-ft ceilings upstairs and down, as well as some of the original wallpaper, cornices, ceiling medallions, and mantels. The Lanaux Suite, in the main house, and the cottage, in the rear courtyard, are Victorian, with such touches as displays of antique clothing. The house includes the original library, with shelves full of books, and a kitchen with a big open fireplace. Each suite has a refrigerator, microwave, coffeemaker, and fixings for a Continental breakfast. All accommodations have phones with voice mail, irons and ironing boards, hair dryers, and TVs. Smoking is permitted only in the courtyard or on the gallery. ⊠ *547 Esplanade Ave., 70116,* ☎ *504/488–4640 or 800/729–4640,* FAX *504/488–4639. 3 suites, 1 cottage. No credit cards. CP.*

$$–$$$ ☷ **Girod House.** New Orleans's first mayor, Nicholas Girod, built this town house in the 1830s for his son. The suites in the handsomely restored property are spacious, with high ceilings, living rooms, bedrooms, large modern baths, and kitchens. Furnishings are fine European and American antiques; amenities include goose-down pillows and Crabtree & Evelyn toiletries. ⊠ *835 Esplanade Ave., 70116,* ☎ *504/522–5214 or 800/650–3323,* FAX *504/522–7208. 6 suites. Parking (fee). AE, MC, V. CP.* ✎

$$–$$$ ☷ **Lafitte Guest House.** A four-story 1849 French-style manor house, the Lafitte is meticulously restored, with rooms decorated with period furnishings. Room 40 takes up the entire fourth floor and overlooks French Quarter rooftops, and Room 5, the loft apartment, overlooks the beautiful courtyard. Breakfast can be brought to your room, served in the Victorian parlor, or enjoyed in the courtyard, and the owner serves wine and hors d'oeuvres each evening. Smoking is not permitted. ⊠ *1003 Bourbon St., 70116,* ☎ *504/581–2678 or 800/331–7971,* FAX *504/581–2677. 16 rooms, 2 suites. AE, D, DC, MC, V. CP.* ✎

$–$$$ ☷ **Hotel Villa Convento.** Lela and Warren Campo and their son Larry provide round-the-clock service to guests in their four-story 1848 Creole town house. Although it's just blocks from the Quarter's tourist attractions, shopping, and great restaurants, this guest house is on a surprisingly quaint, quiet street, close to the Old Ursuline Convent. Each morning you can have croissants and fresh-brewed coffee on the lush patio. Furnished with reproductions of antiques, rooms vary in price; some have balconies, chandeliers, or ceiling fans. ⊠ *616 Ursulines St., 70116,* ☎ *504/522–1793,* FAX *504/524–1902. 25 rooms. AE, D, DC, MC, V. CP.* ✎

$–$$ ☷ **Bon Maison Guest House.** Quaint accommodations lie within the gates of this 1840 town house on the quiet end of Bourbon Street. Rooms in the former slave quarters, off the lush brick patio with tropical plants, are pleasantly furnished and have ceiling fans. Two large suites with kitchenettes are in the main house. There's no elevator—so be prepared for lots of stair climbing to upper floors. All accommodations have a phone and TV. ⊠ *835 Bourbon St., 70116,* ☎ FAX *504/561–8498. 3 rooms, 2 suites. MC, V.* ✎

$–$$ ☷ **Rue Royal Inn.** A pot of hot coffee and Persian cats greet you in the lobby here. Many rooms in this circa 1830 home are pleasantly oversize; four have balconies overlooking Royal Street and a school playground, two have hot tubs, and each has a coffeemaker and a small refrigerator. The complimentary Continental breakfast comes from the nearby Croissant d'Or (☞ *French Quarter in* Chapter 2). ⊠ *1006 Royal St., 70116,* ☎ *504/524–3900 or 800/776–3901,* FAX *504/558–0566. 17 rooms. Parking (fee). AE, D, DC, MC, V. CP.*

CBD

The CBD will appeal to those who prefer accommodations in luxurious high-rise hotels or in one of the city's ever-increasing collection of smaller boutique hotels. All the hotels listed are within walking distance of the French Quarter, but shuttles, taxis, buses, and the streetcar are readily available. If you're walking in the CBD after dark, it's wise to stay on populated main streets.

Hotels

$$$$ ☒ **Le Meridien New Orleans.** Marble, gleaming brass, beveled mirrors, and stunning displays of fresh flowers create contemporary elegance at this luxury hotel with a European flavor. The staff is friendly, and many rooms have great views. Unfortunately, this hotel could be in any big city, because little has been done to add that special New Orleans touch so commonly found in competing hotels. The hotel is on a busy block of Canal Street across from the French Quarter; the motor entrance is at 609 Common Street. ☒ *614 Canal St., 70130,* ☎ *504/525–6500 or 800/543–4300,* 𝐅𝐀𝐗 *504/525–8068. 494 rooms, 7 suites. Restaurant, no-smoking floors, pool, beauty salon, massage, sauna, aerobics, health club, shops, laundry service, business services, meeting rooms, parking (fee). AE, D, DC, MC, V.* ✎

$$$$ ☒ **Le Pavillon Hotel.** Magnificent chandeliers adorn the European-
★ style lobby of this historic hotel dating to 1907, and a handsome display of artwork lines the corridors. Another dramatic feature is the marble railing in the clubby Gallery Lounge, originally from the Grand Hotel in Paris. The good-size guest rooms have high ceilings and identical traditional decor; suites are particularly luxurious. The elegant Crystal Room has a huge salad and pasta lunch buffet daily. ☒ *833 Poydras St., 70112,* ☎ *504/581–3111 or 800/535–9095,* 𝐅𝐀𝐗 *504/522–5543. 219 rooms, 7 suites. Restaurant, bar, no-smoking floors, pool, hot tub, exercise room, laundry service, parking (fee). AE, D, DC, MC, V.* ✎

$$$$ ☒ **Parc St. Charles.** This upscale Best Western property is on one of the Big Easy's best Carnival corners, at the intersection of Poydras Street and St. Charles Avenue. Rooms in the intimate hotel are decorated with contemporary furniture, and large, plate-glass windows provide lots of light and wide views of the bustling business district. Executive-level rooms come with data ports and a fax/scanner/printer. Gerard Maras is the executive chef at the hotel's restaurant, Gerard's Downtown (☞ Central Business District *in* Chapter 2). ☒ *500 St. Charles Ave., 70130,* ☎ *504/522–9000 or 888/211–3447,* 𝐅𝐀𝐗 *888/211–3448. 120 rooms, 2 suites. Restaurant, bar, in-room safes, minibars, no-smoking rooms, pool, health club, parking (fee). AE, D, DC, MC, V.* ✎

$$$$ ☒ **W Hotel New Orleans.** One of the city's newest entrants in the hotel arena is a sleek, contemporary blend of East Coast sophistication and southern charm. The lobby, called the living room, has a homelike setting but trendy, upscale surroundings. Guest rooms are done in red and black and include first-rate amenities such as Aveda bath products and beds with goose-down pillows and comforters. All rooms have Internet access, and 100 are designated as home office rooms. Just across the street from Harrah's casino, W seems destined to be a favorite alphabet letter in town, and the Randy Gerber–designed cocktail lounge is likely to become a see-and-be-seen spot. (A second W hotel is in the French Quarter; ☞ *above.*) ☒ *333 Poydras St., 70130,* ☎ *504/525–9444 or 800/777–7372,* 𝐅𝐀𝐗 *504/586–9928. 423 rooms, 23 suites. Café, 3 lounges, in-room data ports, pool, health club, parking (fee). AE, D, DC, MC, V.* ✎

$$$$ ☒ **Windsor Court Hotel.** Exquisite, gracious, elegant, eminently civi-
★ lized—these words are frequently used to describe Windsor Court, but all fail to capture the wonderful quality of this hotel. From Le Salon's scrumptious afternoon tea, served daily in the lobby, to the unbelievably large rooms, this is one of *the* places to stay in New Orleans. Plush carpeting, canopy and four-poster beds, stocked wet bars, marble vanities, oversize mirrors, and dressing areas are just some of the pampering touches. The Windsor's Grill Room (☞ Central Business District *in* Chapter 2) is excellent, and the Polo Lounge (☞ Nightlife *in* Chapter 4) has one of the best martini presentations to be found. The hotel is four blocks from the French Quarter. ☒ *300 Gravier St., 70130,* ☎

504/523–6000 or 800/262–2662, FAX *504/596–4513. 58 rooms, 266 suites, 2 penthouses. 2 restaurants, lobby lounge, in-room data ports, pool, hot tub, sauna, steam room, health club, laundry service, parking (fee). AE, D, DC, MC, V.*

$$$–$$$$ ⊡ **Embassy Suites.** If your primary target is the convention center or the contemporary art galleries of the Warehouse District, this is a great choice. The balconied high-rise sits right on Gallery Row. All suites have a bedroom and separate parlor (with a TV in each room and three phones), microwave, and coffeemaker; most have balconies. Room service is available from the Sugar House restaurant. The Lofts at Embassy Suites is in a separate building just around the corner. ⊠ *315 Julia St., 70130,* ☎ *504/525–1993 or 800/362–2779,* FAX *504/525–3437. 347 suites. Restaurant, in-room data ports, refrigerators, wading pool, outdoor hot tub, exercise room, video games, meeting rooms. AE, D, MC, V. BP.*

$$$–$$$$ ⊡ **Fairmont Hotel.** At this grand hotel built in 1893, the marble floor
    ★   and Victorian splendor of the massive, busy lobby evoke a more elegant and gracious era. Rooms have special touches such as down pillows, terry robes, upscale toiletries, and bathroom scales; suites have fax machines. Impressive murals depicting life in the South enliven the walls of the famed Sazerac Bar; the lobby-level Sazerac Grill has an airy, cosmopolitan feel. During the holiday season, the Fairmont's lobby is completely engulfed in strands of white Angel Hair, a tradition that attracts plenty of viewers. Renovations have kept the Fairmont one of the finest hotels in the South. ⊠ *123 Baronne St., 70140,* ☎ *504/529–7111 or 800/527–4727,* FAX *504/529–4764. 700 rooms, 85 suites. 3 restaurants, 2 bars, pool, beauty salon, 2 tennis courts, exercise room, parking (fee). AE, D, DC, MC, V.*

$$$–$$$$ ⊡ **Hotel Inter-Continental.** One of the major convention hotels, the Inter-Continental is a modern rose-granite structure overlooking St. Charles Avenue. Public spaces include a spacious, inviting second-floor lobby and a peaceful sculpture garden. Guest rooms are large and well lighted, with matching quilted spreads and draperies and baths with mini-TVs and hair dryers. The VIP level contains some of the city's finest suites, with antiques from around the world; other special amenities here are TV teleconferencing and complimentary Continental breakfast and afternoon cocktails. The main dining room is the Veranda (☞ Central Business District *in* Chapter 2), showcasing the well-known culinary skills of Willy Cohn. ⊠ *444 St. Charles Ave., 70130,* ☎ *504/ 525–5566 or 800/445–6563,* FAX *504/585–4387. 482 rooms, 20 suites. 3 restaurants, bar, minibars, pool, exercise room, dry cleaning, laundry service, parking (fee). AE, D, DC, MC, V.*

$$$–$$$$ ⊡ **Hyatt Regency New Orleans.** This luxurious Hyatt has a streamlined lobby with fountains, Oriental rugs, and glittering chandeliers. Go for a corner room, where two walls of windows give a sense of space and sometimes a good view. Most rooms in the Lanai Building face the pool, and each one has a private patio or balcony. Special rooms for women travelers are larger, close to the elevators, and come with hair dryers, makeup mirrors, irons, and ironing boards. The revolving Top of the Dome steak house has a great view of the city. A glass atrium connects the hotel with the New Orleans Centre shopping mall and the Superdome, and there's a complimentary French Quarter shuttle. ⊠ *500 Poydras Plaza, 70113,* ☎ *504/561–1234 or 800/233– 1234,* FAX *504/523–0488. 1,184 rooms, 100 suites. 4 restaurants, sports bar, pool, laundry service, parking (fee). AE, D, DC, MC, V.*

$$$–$$$$ ⊡ **New Orleans Hilton Riverside.** This sprawling, multilevel complex is smack on the Mississippi, and rooms in the Riverside and Towers sections have superb river views. Guest rooms have French Provincial furnishings; the 180 rooms that share a concierge have fax machines.

The health club is one of the best in the Gulf South, and there is an excellent business center. Pete Fountain's nightclub (☞ CBD and Warehouse District *in* Chapter 4) is here, and the Riverfront streetcar stops out front. The hotel has a resident golf pro and a 4-hole putting green. ⌧ *Poydras St. at the Mississippi River, 70140,* ☎ *504/561–0500 or 800/445–8667,* ⅧⅩ *504/568–1721. 1,600 rooms, 67 suites. 4 restaurants, 7 lounges, no-smoking floors, 2 pools, beauty salon, outdoor hot tub, massage, saunas, putting green, 8 tennis courts, aerobics, health club, jogging, racquetball, squash, nightclub, business services, parking (fee). AE, D, DC, MC, V.* ☙

\$\$\$–\$\$\$\$ 🏨 **Sheraton New Orleans.** The unique atriumlike lobby of this hotel is large and bright and usually bustling with conventioneers. A tropical atmosphere permeates the Pelican Bar, which presents jazz nightly and offers a fine assortment of cigars. Café Promenade encircles the second level. Executive rooms on the top floors come with many special amenities, but even the regular guest rooms are spacious and well-appointed. Expect top-quality service. The hotel is across Canal Street from one of the city's great downtown eateries, the Palace Café (☞ Central Business District *in* Chapter 2). ⌧ *500 Canal St., 70130,* ☎ *504/525–2500 or 800/253–6156,* ⅧⅩ *504/592–5615. 1,100 rooms, 72 suites. 3 restaurants, bar, lobby lounge, no-smoking rooms, pool, health club, parking (fee). AE, D, DC, MC, V.* ☙

\$\$–\$\$\$\$ 🏨 **Courtyard by Marriott.** Occupying an erstwhile office building, this Marriott has a private feel to it, even though it's in the heart of downtown. Rooms have dark woods and pastel prints; the ones with two double beds are largest and have a desk. Balcony rooms overlooking St. Charles Avenue are much in demand during Mardi Gras—this corner of St. Charles is one of the Carnival hot spots. The restaurant is open for breakfast only, but the hotel is within walking distance of restaurants as well as tourist attractions, good shopping, and the French Quarter. ⌧ *124 St. Charles Ave., 70130,* ☎ *504/581–9005 or 800/321–2211,* ⅧⅩ *504/581–6264. 140 rooms. Restaurant, indoor pool, hot tub, exercise room, parking (fee). AE, D, DC, MC, V.* ☙

\$\$–\$\$\$\$ 🏨 **Doubletree Hotel.** This chain hotel is close to the river, across the street from Canal Place mall, and a block from the French Quarter. The small, comfortable lobby is adorned with flower arrangements and bowls of potpourri, along with the hotel's trademark jar of chocolate chip cookies. Decor is country French, and rooms have an open, airy feeling with pastel draperies and spreads and light-color furniture. Rooms ending in 05 are larger; more than half the rooms are no-smoking. The staff is exceptionally helpful. ⌧ *300 Canal St., 70130,* ☎ *504/ 581–1300 or 800/222–8733,* ⅧⅩ *504/522–4100. 363 rooms, 15 suites. Restaurant, bar, deli, lounge, no-smoking rooms, pool, health club, laundry service, parking (fee). AE, D, DC, MC, V.* ☙

\$\$–\$\$\$\$ 🏨 **Omni Royal Crescent.** Old-fashioned pampering mixes well with state-of-the-art technology in this chic boutique hotel. All guest rooms come with fax machines, plush robes, slippers, Egyptian cotton sheets, iron and ironing board, and umbrella; some king rooms have hot tubs. Some baths and closets, however, are small. The outdoor rooftop pool and well-equipped fitness center are designed along the lines of a Roman bath. ⌧ *535 Gravier St., 70130,* ☎ *504/527–0006 or 800/843–6664,* ⅧⅩ *504/523–0806. 98 rooms, 7 suites. Restaurant, minibars, no-smoking rooms, pool, sauna, health club, dry cleaning, meeting room, parking (fee). AE, D, DC, MC, V.* ☙

\$\$–\$\$\$\$ 🏨 **Pelham Hotel.** A restored four-story office building houses the chic Pelham, which has a sedate yet inviting ambience. This is an ideal place for those who want to be in the center of the CBD—near Riverwalk, Harrah's New Orleans Casino, and the convention center—but who seek a quiet alternative to the bustling convention hotels. The small lobby has a green-marble floor and fresh flowers. Rooms are small; some have four-poster beds and all have marble baths with terry robes and English soaps. Note that the inside rooms, though attractively furnished, have no windows. Guests have use of the fitness center and pool at the nearby Sheraton or at private health clubs. ⊠ *444 Common St., 70130,* ☎ *504/522–4444 or 800/659–5621,* FAX *504/539–9010. 60 rooms, 4 suites. Restaurant, in-room safes, room service, laundry service, dry cleaning, concierge, parking (fee). AE, D, DC, MC, V.* 🐾

$$–$$$$ 🏨 **Wyndham Riverfront Hotel.** A circular drive with a splashing fountain and greenery sweeps to the entrance of the Wyndham, which occupies a full block across the street from the convention center. Four masonry buildings from a former 19th-century rice mill and silo make up the hotel; some of the original cast-iron ornamentation remains on the facade. The lobby is large and light filled. Rooms vary in size and shape; those in the former mill are smaller but have higher ceilings, and rooms in the erstwhile silo, called extended kings, are larger. There's good attention to detail: spreads and drapes match wallpaper in the bath. ⊠ *701 Convention Center Blvd., 70130,* ☎ *504/524–8200 or 800/996–3426,* FAX *504/524–0600. 202 rooms, 2 suites. Restaurant, bar, in-room data ports, no-smoking rooms, room service, exercise room, laundry service, business services, parking (fee). AE, D, DC, MC, V.* 🐾

$$$ 🏨 **Ambassador Hotel.** Guest rooms at this hotel conveniently bordering the CBD and the Warehouse District have real character. Four-poster iron beds, armoires, and local jazz prints are among the furnishings. Exposed brick walls, ceiling fans, and wood floors add to the ambience of the pre–Civil War building. This is a good alternative to huge convention hotels, but it's still just steps from all the major downtown attractions and shopping, as well as the convention center. ⊠ *535 Tchoupitoulas St., 70130,* ☎ *504/527–5271 or 888/527–5271,* FAX *504/599–2110. 114 rooms, 3 suites. Restaurant, lounge, exercise room, meeting rooms, parking (fee). AE, D, DC, MC, V.* 🐾

$$$ 🏨 **Hampton Inn and Suites—Convention Center.** In one of the city's most imaginative renovation projects, two century-old warehouses have been converted into a French colonial–style hotel that is comfortable, architecturally distinctive, and moderately priced. The Grand Lobby has original hardwood floors and exposed brick walls, while the lobby bar overlooks the pool and the lush garden courtyard. Rooms are large and airy, with four-poster beds and wood floors; many overlook a park. The hotel is on the edge of the Warehouse District, directly across the street from the Morial Convention Center. ⊠ *1201 Convention Center Blvd., 70130,* ☎ *504/566–9990 or 800/292–0653,* FAX *504/566–9997. 288 rooms. Bar, deli, pool, exercise room, business services, parking (fee). AE, D, DC, MC, V. CP.* 🐾

$$$ 🏨 **Lafayette Hotel.** This small brick building has housed the Lafayette
★ ever since it was built in 1916. Special features are the handsome millwork, brass fittings, and marble baths throughout. The lobby is tiny but chic, and guest rooms are spacious and sunny. Some rooms have four-poster beds; all have cushy easy chairs and ottomans. Bookshelves filled with books are a homey touch. Some rooms on the second floor have floor-length windows opening onto a balcony; a number overlook Lafayette Square. ⊠ *600 St. Charles Ave., 70130,* ☎ *504/524–4441 or 800/733–4754,* FAX *504/523–7327. 24 rooms, 20 suites. Restaurant, minibars, no-smoking rooms, laundry service, dry cleaning, concierge, parking (fee). AE, D, DC, MC, V.* 🐾

$$–$$$ 🏨 **International House.** The lobby of this unique boutique hotel is an architectural dream with 23-ft-high ceilings, ornate pilasters, marble floors, and seasonally changing decor. Fine linens and fabrics enhance the guest rooms, which, while small, are attractively decorated in a contemporary New Orleans style, with black-and-white photographs of jazz greats and stereo CD players. Bathrooms, some with glass-enclosed double shower stalls, are sleek and contemporary. The hotel holds Loa, one of the most charming and intimate bars in the city; it's across the lobby from Lemon Grass Café, a Vietnamese restaurant (☞ Central Business District *in* Chapter 2). ✉ *221 Camp St., 70130,* ☎ *504/ 553–9550 or 800/633–5770,* FAX *504/553–9560. 119 rooms, 3 suites. Bar, restaurant, exercise room, meeting rooms, parking (fee). AE, D, MC, V.* 🐾

$$–$$$ 🏨 **Queen & Crescent Hotel.** Intimate and tasteful, this hotel two blocks outside the French Quarter is a good alternative to the mega-hotels that surround it. Guest rooms are small but tastefully appointed and come with in-room coffeemakers, hair dryers, and ironing boards. The hotel is within walking distance of Harrah's casino, Riverwalk, and a number of great restaurants. ✉ *344 Camp St., 70130,* ☎ *504/587–9700 or 800/975–6652,* FAX *504/587–9701. 129 rooms. Minibars, in-room safes, no-smoking rooms, exercise room, meeting rooms, travel services, parking (fee). AE, D, DC, MC, V.* 🐾

$–$$$ 🏨 **Quality Inn—Midtown.** A location just west of downtown makes this a popular place to stay during Jazz Fest and City Park golf tournaments. A free shuttle to the French Quarter, the CBD, and the St. Charles streetcar runs throughout the day. Children's Hospital and LSU's and Tulane's medical schools are nearby. ✉ *3900 Tulane Ave., 70119,* ☎ *504/ 486–5541 or 800/228–5151,* FAX *504/488–7440. 96 rooms, 8 suites. Restaurant, bar, no-smoking rooms, pool, hot tub, free parking. AE, D, DC, MC, V.* 🐾

$$ 🏨 **Holiday Inn Downtown—Superdome.** The mural of a 150-ft clarinet on the facade highlights the fact that this hotel is in the neighborhood where jazz was born. Its location, in the heart of the CBD near the Superdome and the French Quarter, makes this a favorite hotel for Saints fans, and it fills up quickly for the Sugar Bowl. Rooms are not exceptional, but the hotel is well-maintained. ✉ *330 Loyola Ave., 70112,* ☎ *504/581–1600 or 800/535–7830,* FAX *504/586–0833. 301 rooms, 3 suites. Restaurant, bar, pool, parking (fee). AE, D, DC, MC, V.* 🐾

$–$$ 🏨 **Comfort Suites Downtown.** A boon for budget travelers, this former office building is four blocks from the French Quarter. It has an uninspiring lobby but large, well-equipped, one-room suites: each has a minirefrigerator, microwave, coffeemaker, hair dryer, and safe; luxury suites have whirlpool baths. The sauna, hot tub, and free morning paper are pleasant surprises, and the first five local calls are free. ✉ *346 Baronne St., 70112,* ☎ *504/524–1140 or 800/524–1140,* FAX *504/523–4444. 102 suites. Bar, in-room safes, hot tub, sauna, exercise room, coin laundry, business services, parking (fee). AE, D, DC, MC, V. CP.* 🐾

$–$$ 🏨 **Hampton Inn.** This moderately priced facility is among several office buildings that have been either totally or partially converted into hotels (the UNO Downtown Center has offices on the second and third floors). The lobby, with lavish furnishings and decor, is an oasis in the midst of a bustling business district. Rooms are large and comfortable, and all baths have hair dryers. Among the safety features are key-access elevators. Two blocks from Bourbon Street, the Hampton Inn is surrounded by great restaurants and tourist attractions. ✉ *226 Carondelet St., 70130,* ☎ *504/529–9990 or 800/426–7866,* FAX *504/529–9996. 186 rooms. Coffee shop, exercise room, concierge, parking (fee). AE, D, DC, MC, V. CP.* 🐾

$–$$ 🏨 **Holiday Inn Select.** This high-end, eight-story Holiday Inn in the Warehouse District is across the street from the convention center. It is built around a three-story atrium and has a handsome lobby with marble floors and wood paneling. All rooms are soundproof and have desks and two phones with voice mail and speed dials. Executive rooms and suites have two phone lines, call waiting, and speakerphones. Other amenities include irons and ironing boards, coffeemakers, and hair dryers. The hotel is within walking distance of Riverwalk and Harrah's casino, as well as a number of great restaurants. ⊠ *881 Convention Center Blvd., 70130,* ☎ *504/524–1881 or 800/465–4329,* FAX *504/528–1005. 167 rooms, 3 suites. Restaurant, bar, in-room data ports, no-smoking rooms, pool, health club, coin laundry, business services. AE, D, DC, MC, V. CP.* ⊗

Garden District/Uptown

These areas are ideal for those who prefer accommodations away from downtown. All the following are on or close to fashionable, mansion-lined St. Charles Avenue, where the St. Charles Avenue streetcar runs (24 hours), making the CBD and the French Quarter a mere 15–20 minutes away during the day, and sometimes longer at night due to less frequent streetcar service. A taxi is a better option if you are out late. Walking in this area after dark is not recommended.

Hotels

$$$–$$$$ 🏨 **Clarion Grand Boutique Hotel.** When Al Copeland (the man behind Popeye's Famous Fried Chicken) renovated this building to house Straya Restaurant and the hotel, local author Anne Rice protested over the neon deco facade, claiming it clashed with Uptown's genteel ambience. Today the flashy structure has become just another part of life on the avenue. The decor of the all-suite hotel is considerably more tame than that in the restaurant downstairs; touches of marble, glass, brass, and wrought iron make it a perfect choice for a romantic weekend getaway. Some suites have in-room hot tubs. Room service is available from Straya Restaurant downstairs. Guests can work off some of that contemporary Creole cuisine at a nearby fitness facility. ⊠ *2001 St. Charles Ave., 70130,* ☎ *504/558–9966 or 800/976–1755,* FAX *504/522–8044. 44 suites. Restaurant, in-room data ports, refrigerators, meeting room, parking (fee). AE, D, DC, MC, V.* ⊗

$$$ 🏨 **Avenue Plaza Hotel.** The spartan lobby belies the amenities found here. Public areas include a romantic lounge with dark wood panels from a French chalet. The spacious rooms have generous dressing areas and kitchenettes with full-size refrigerators. Decor is either traditional or art deco—both are equally appealing. The health club has a Turkish steam bath, Swiss showers, and a Scandinavian sauna, which guests can use for $5 per day. The pool is in a pleasant courtyard setting, and a sundeck and hot tub are on the roof. ⊠ *2111 St. Charles Ave., 70130,* ☎ *504/566–1212 or 800/535–9575,* FAX *504/525–6899. 256 rooms, 80 suites. Restaurant, bar, pool, beauty salon, hot tub, health club, parking (fee). AE, D, DC, MC, V.*

$$–$$$ 🏨 **Pontchartrain Hotel.** Maintaining the grand tradition is the hallmark
★ of this elegant, European-style hotel, which has reigned on St. Charles Avenue since 1927. Accommodations range from lavish, sun-filled suites to small pensione-type rooms with showers only (no bathtubs). The Pontchartrain has been the honeymoon hotel for such couples as Prince Aly Kahn and Rita Hayworth; suite names will tell you who else has passed through. Nowadays, though, more businesspeople than celebrities stay here. ⊠ *2031 St. Charles Ave., 70140,* ☎ *504/524–0581 or 800/777–6193,* FAX *504/524–7828. 84 rooms, 38 suites. 2 restaurants, piano bar, concierge, parking (fee). AE, D, DC, MC, V.* ⊗

$$–$$$ 🏨 **Quality Inn Maison St. Charles.** This is a lovely property in six his-
★ toric buildings that cluster around intimate courtyards. The porte cochere entrance has an attractive mural. A complimentary shuttle to the convention center and 24-hour security are among the amenities.

✉ *1319 St. Charles Ave., 70130,* ☎ *504/522–0187 or 800/831–1783,* ℻ *504/528–9993. 129 rooms, 16 suites. Bar, no-smoking rooms, pool, hot tub, parking (fee). AE, D, DC, MC, V.* ✎

$–$$ 🏨 **Columns Hotel.** This impressive, white-columned 1883 Victorian-style hotel is listed on the National Register of Historic Places. The wide veranda, set with cloth-covered tables for outdoor dining or cocktails, is very inviting, as are the two period-furnished parlors. Dark and intimate, the lounge is a favorite with locals and has excellent live progressive jazz on Tuesday and Thursday. There's also a Sunday jazz brunch. One of the most impressive staircases you will ever climb leads to large, somewhat sparsely furnished rooms that have phones but no TVs. Less expensive rooms share baths. ✉ *3811 St. Charles Ave., 70115,* ☎ *504/899–9308 or 800/445–9308,* ℻ *504/899–8170. 20 rooms, 10 with bath. Bar, dining room. AE, MC, V. CP.*

$ 🏨 **St. Charles Inn.** The canopied entrance to this small Uptown hotel is almost hidden from view, squeezed as it is between a restaurant and a café. It has good-size modern rooms, each with a dressing area and cable TV. Rooms in the front with a St. Charles Avenue view are best unless streetcar noise bothers you. Continental breakfast and a newspaper are brought to your room each morning. The staff is friendly and accommodating. ✉ *3636 St. Charles Ave., 70115,* ☎ *504/899–8888 or 800/489–9908,* ℻ *504/899–8892. 40 rooms. Free parking. AE, D, DC, MC, V. CP.*

Guest Houses and Bed-and-Breakfasts

$$–$$$ 🏨 **Sully Mansion.** New Orleans architect Thomas Sully built this handsome, rambling, Queen Anne–style house more than a century ago. In the foyer, where there is a grand piano, light filters through stunning, pastel-color stained-glass windows that are original to the house. The public rooms have high ceilings, oil paintings, fireplaces, tall windows with swagged, floor-length drapes, and Victorian hand-me-downs. All guest rooms have TVs and phones. Neighbor to other grand mansions, the house is on a pretty, tree-lined street and is a block from the streetcar. ✉ *2631 Prytania St., 70130,* ☎ *504/891–0457,* ℻ *504/899–7237. 5 rooms, 2 suites. AE, D, MC, V. CP.* ✎

$–$$$ 🏨 **The Chimes Bed and Breakfast.** For more than a decade, Jill and
★ Charles Abbyad have welcomed guests in their charming Uptown residence. Rooms in the main house and the converted carriage house have hardwood or slate floors, and there are high ceilings throughout. The Abbyads maintain a homey atmosphere while giving their guests all the conveniences found in large hotels: hair dryers, irons, stereos, coffeemakers, and cable TV, as well as private entrances and phone lines. Continental breakfast is served in the airy dining room; afterward, you can explore Uptown using the Abbyads' homemade guide to the neighborhood or relax in the butterfly garden in the courtyard. English, French, Arabic, and Spanish are spoken in the house, and children are welcome. ✉ *1146 Constantinople St., 70115,* ☎ *504/488–4640 or 800/729–4640,* ℻ *504/488–4639. 5 rooms. No credit cards. CP.*

$$ 🏨 **Park View Guest House.** Adjacent to beautiful Audubon Park, this Victorian guest house has graced St. Charles Avenue as an Uptown landmark since 1884. Rooms on the east side have great views of the park. The general rule here is that you get either antiques or a view: brass beds and ceiling fans are found in the "view" rooms. There is a lounge with TV and fireplace and a bay-window dining room where breakfast is served. ✉ *7004 St. Charles Ave., 70118,* ☎ *504/861–7564,* ℻ *504/861–1225. 23 rooms, 16 with bath. AE, D, MC, V. CP.* ✎

$–$$ 🏨 **Josephine Guest House.** This Italianate mansion, one block from St. Charles Avenue, was built in 1870 and has been perfectly restored. European antiques fill the rooms, and Oriental rugs cover gleaming

Lodging Outside the Downtown Area

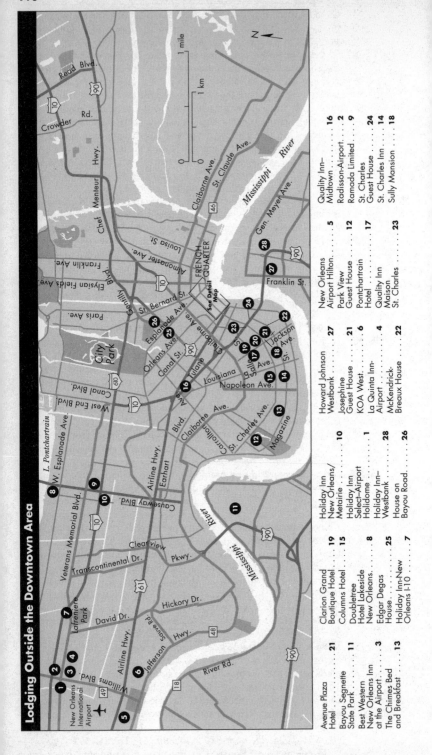

Avenue Plaza Hotel 21
Bayou Segnette State Park 11
Best Western New Orleans Inn at the Airport . . . 3
The Chimes Bed and Breakfast . . . 13
Clarion Grand Boutique Hotel . . . 19
Columns Hotel . . . 15
Doubletree Hotel Lakeside New Orleans . . . 8
Edgar Degas House . . . 25
Holiday Inn–New Orleans I-10 . . . 7
Holiday Inn New Orleans/Metairie . . . 10
Holiday Inn Select–Airport Holidome . . . 1
Holiday Inn–Westbank . . . 28
House on Bayou Road . . . 26
Howard Johnson Westbank . . . 27
Josephine Guest House . . . 21
KOA West . . . 6
La Quinta Inn–Airport . . . 4
McKendrick-Breaux House . . . 22
New Orleans Airport Hilton . . . 5
Park View Guest House . . . 12
Pontchartrain Hotel . . . 17
Quality Inn Maison St. Charles . . . 23
Quality Inn–Midtown . . . 16
Radisson-Airport . . . 2
Ramada Limited . . . 9
St. Charles Guest House . . . 24
St. Charles Inn . . . 14
Sully Mansion . . . 18

hardwood floors. Four rooms and a parlor are in the main house; there are two smaller but still spacious rooms in the *garçonnier* (where the original owners' sons stayed). The bathrooms are impressive in both size and decor. A Creole breakfast of fresh-squeezed orange juice, café au lait, and homemade biscuits can be brought to your room (served on Wedgwood china and a silver tray) or taken on the secluded patio. ✉ *1450 Josephine St., 70130,* ☎ *504/524–6361 or 800/779–6361,* FAX *504/523–6484. 6 rooms. AE, D, DC, MC, V. CP.* ⊛

$–$$ ⊞ **McKendrick-Breaux House.** If you're looking for an alternative to the city's touristy quarters, this Greek Revival guest house in the Magazine Street antiques district is an excellent choice. In fact, the large rooms here, spread throughout the main house and a neighboring building, are one of the best values in the city. They have high ceilings, gorgeous wood floors, fresh flowers, TVs, phones, and voice mail; many have their own entrances on the property's garden courtyard. ✉ *1474 Magazine St., 70130,* ☎ *504/586–1700 or 888/570–1700,* FAX *504/522–7138. 7 rooms. Breakfast room, free parking. AE, MC, V. CP.* ⊛

$–$$ ⊞ **St. Charles Guest House.** Simple and affordable, this European-style pension is in four buildings one block from St. Charles Avenue. Rooms in the A and B buildings are larger. The small "backpacker" rooms share a bath and do not have air-conditioning. A pleasant surprise is the large swimming pool and deck. Proprietors Dennis and Joanne Hilton occasionally delight their guests with an impromptu crawfish boil or an introduction to New Orleans's red beans and rice. ✉ *1748 Prytania St., 70130,* ☎ *504/523–6556,* FAX *504/522–6340. 36 rooms, 28 with private bath. Pool. AE, MC, V. CP.* ⊛

Mid-City

Guest Houses

$$$–$$$$ ⊞ **House on Bayou Road.** This circa 1798 West Indies–style Creole plan-
★ tation home, set on 2 acres of lawns and gardens, has rooms filled with Louisiana antiques, including handsome four-poster feather beds. Accommodations are in the main house as well as in detached cottages. The grand suite in the private cottage has a skylight over the bed, a small kitchenette, bookshelves, and a whirlpool bath. Wind chimes tinkle on the front porch, where there are rocking chairs for lolling. A favorite of celebrities, this inn has hosted Dan Aykroyd, Alfre Woodard, Fran Drescher, and Brad Pitt. A cooking school is conducted here by Gerard Maras, a James Beard–award-winning chef. The house is in a remote setting, and walking in the area is not encouraged. Smoking is allowed only on the porch or patio. ✉ *2275 Bayou Rd., 70119,* ☎ *504/945–0992, 504/949–7711, or 800/882–2968,* FAX *504/945–0993. 4 rooms, 1 suite. Pool. AE, DC. BP.* ⊛

$$–$$$ ⊞ **Edgar Degas House.** Degas, the French Impressionist, stayed in the
★ home of his uncle (both his mother and his grandmother were New Orleans natives) from 1872 to 1873, during which time he produced 17 works. This historic home, built in 1852, has been carefully restored following original floor plans and colors, which include pale peach, celadon, and golden mustard. Second-floor rooms are spacious and have chandeliers that hang from 14-ft ceilings: one room has a whirlpool bath, and another has a balcony. Third-floor garret rooms are small and have no windows, but they are decorated with Degas's works and are less expensive. Parlors on the first floor display reproductions of the artist's works (more than 60 can be seen in the house) and can be visited by nonguests (call for dates and times). Overnighters may enjoy breakfast on a small private rear courtyard. ✉ *2306 Esplanade Ave., 70119,* ☎ *504/821–5009 or 800/755–6730,* FAX *504/821–0870. 6 rooms. Breakfast room. AE, MC, V. CP.* ⊛

Kenner/Airport

Hotels

$$–$$$ 🏨 **New Orleans Airport Hilton.** Directly across from the New Orleans
★ International Airport is this upscale hotel, offering unexpected elegance.
The decor throughout is superb, with muted pastel colors that coordinate well with the soft pink Caribbean-style exterior. Area rugs were
handwoven in England. ⊠ *901 Airline Hwy., Kenner 70062,* ☎ *504/
469–5000 or 800/872–5914,* FAX *504/466–5473. 317 rooms, 2 suites.
Restaurant, bar, pool, putting green, tennis court, exercise room, business services, airport shuttle, parking (fee). AE, D, DC, MC, V.* 🐾

$–$$$ 🏨 **Radisson–Airport.** This chain property offers easy access to I–10 as
well as the airport. The large Esplanade shopping mall, the *Treasure
Chest* riverboat casino, and the Pontchartrain Convention Center are
nearby. There's an oyster bar as well as a restaurant on the premises.
⊠ *2150 Veterans Blvd., Kenner 70062,* ☎ *504/467–3111 or 800/333–
3333,* FAX *504/469–4634. 244 rooms, 3 suites. Restaurant, bar, pool,
meeting rooms, airport shuttle, free parking. AE, D, DC, MC, V.* 🐾

$–$$ 🏨 **Best Western New Orleans Inn at the Airport.** This hotel is convenient to the shops of Williams Boulevard and the Esplanade Mall; the
Treasure Chest riverboat casino is also nearby. It shares its building
with Denny's, which serves as the hotel's restaurant. ⊠ *1021 Airline
Hwy., Kenner 70062,* ☎ *504/464–1644 or 800/333–8278,* FAX *504/469–
1193. 166 rooms, 2 suites. Pool, airport shuttle, free parking. AE, D,
DC, MC, V.* 🐾

$–$$ 🏨 **Holiday Inn Select—Airport Holidome.** Many of the rooms here face
the dome-covered pool area, which is popular with children. It's convenient to I–10 and close to Rivertown, U.S.A., and the *Treasure Chest*
riverboat casino. All rooms have hair dryers, irons, and ironing boards.
⊠ *2929 Williams Blvd., Kenner 70062,* ☎ *504/467–5611 or 800/887–
7371,* FAX *504/469–4915. 303 rooms, 1 suite. Restaurant, bar, indoor
pool, hot tub, sauna, exercise room, meeting rooms, airport shuttle,
free parking. AE, D, DC, MC, V.* 🐾

$ 🏨 **La Quinta Inn–Airport.** This hotel with a southwestern motif offers
free local phone calls and allows children under 18 to stay free in their
parents' room. The Esplanade Mall, *Treasure Chest* casino (accessible
by casino-run shuttle), and Rivertown, U.S.A., are nearby. ⊠ *2610
Williams Blvd., Kenner 70062,* ☎ *504/466–1401 or 800/531–5900,*
FAX *504/466–0319. 150 rooms, 35 suites. No-smoking rooms, in-room
data ports, pool, exercise room, meeting rooms, airport shuttle, free
parking. AE, D, DC, MC, V. CP.* 🐾

Campground

$ 🏕 **KOA West.** There are a few tent sites as well as large back-in sites
for RVs with well-kept grass areas around tree-shaded concrete pads;
reservations are recommended. The campground is close to Rivertown, U.S.A., in Kenner (take the Williams Blvd. exit off I–10). Both
Gray Line and New Orleans Tours pick up here for sightseeing, and
the campground operates a shuttle bus to the French Quarter. ⊠
11129 Jefferson Hwy., River Ridge 70123, ☎ *504/467–1792 or 800/
562–5110,* FAX *504/464–7204. 96 sites, 6 tent sites Picnic area, pool,
playground, coin laundry. AE, D, MC, V.*

Metairie

Hotels

$$$ 🏨 **Doubletree Hotel Lakeside New Orleans.** This upscale hotel with
★ plenty of amenities is part of a glass office complex that towers beside
Lake Pontchartrain. The art deco–style lobby has marble mirrors and
brass touches. Upon arrival guests receive the chain's de rigueur choco-

late chip cookies. There's a free French Quarter shuttle. ⊠ *3838 N. Causeway Blvd., 70002,* ☎ *504/836–5253 or 800/222–8733,* FAX *504/ 836–5262. 198 rooms, 12 suites. Restaurant, bar, no-smoking rooms, beauty salon, 2 tennis courts, health club, meeting rooms, airport shuttle. AE, D, DC, MC, V.* ✎

$–$$ ⊡ **Holiday Inn–New Orleans I–10.** As the name suggests, this hotel is convenient to I–10; it's also across the street from Lafrenière Park, which has barbecue areas, a walking track, sports fields, and duck-filled lagoons. ⊠ *6401 Veterans Blvd., 70003,* ☎ *504/885–5700 or 800/465– 4329,* FAX *504/454–8294. 220 rooms, 3 suites. Restaurant, bar, pool, hot tub, airport shuttle, free parking. AE, D, DC, MC, V.* ✎

$–$$ ⊡ **Holiday Inn New Orleans/Metairie.** There's easy access to I–10 and a free shuttle to the Lakeside Shopping Mall. ⊠ *3400 I–10 Service Rd., 70001,* ☎ *504/833–8201 or 800/522–6963,* FAX *504/838–6829. 193 rooms. Restaurant, bar, pool, free parking. AE, D, DC, MC, V.* ✎

$–$$ ⊡ **Ramada Limited.** Several excellent restaurants are very close, including Ruth's Chris Steak House (☞ Mid-City *in* Chapter 2). Free shuttles will take you to the French Quarter and Lakeside Shopping Mall, except during Mardi Gras and other special events. The hotel is near I– 10; the entrance, a bit hard to find, is at North Causeway and Veterans boulevards. ⊠ *2713 N. Causeway Blvd., 70002,* ☎ *504/835–4141 or 800/874–1280,* FAX *504/833–6942. 138 rooms. Bar, pool, airport shuttle, free parking. AE, D, DC, MC, V. CP.* ✎

Westbank

Hotels

$–$$ ⊡ **Holiday Inn—Westbank.** Don't get confused—the address here is exactly the same as at the Howard Johnson Westbank, but this hotel is a few blocks farther along the expressway, on the opposite side of the expressway when coming off the Crescent City Connection Bridge. Golfers stay here during tournaments at the nearby English Turn Golf and Country Club. ⊠ *100 Westbank Expressway, Gretna 70053,* ☎ *504/366–2361 or 800/465–4329,* FAX *504/362–5814. 311 rooms, 6 suites. Restaurant, bar, pool, free parking. AE, D, DC, MC, V.* ✎

$–$$ ⊡ **Howard Johnson Westbank.** This hotel is just across the Crescent City Connection and near the Oakwood Shopping Mall. ⊠ *100 Westbank Expressway, Gretna 70053,* ☎ *504/366–8531 or 800/635–7787,* FAX *504/362–9502. 168 rooms. Restaurant, bar, pool, free parking. AE, D, DC, MC, V.* ✎

Campground

$ ⚠ **Bayou Segnette State Park.** The campsites in a wooded area of the park have water and electricity, tent pads, picnic tables, and barbecue grills; reservations are not accepted for holiday weekends. Furnished loft cabins that sleep from six to eight have screened porches overlooking the bayou; reservations are required for these. The park, which is home to the state's largest wave pool, is off the Westbank Expressway near the Huey P. Long Bridge. Two comfort stations, a dump station, pay phones, and a boat launch are additional amenities. ⊠ *7777 West Bank Expressway, Westwego 70094,* ☎ *504/736–7140 or 888/677– 2296. 98 sites, 20 cabins. Picnic area, 2 coin laundries. MC, V.*

4 NIGHTLIFE AND THE ARTS

New Orleans is ready for indulgence whenever you are, be it 4 PM or 4 AM. Music is continually in and on the air, pouring out from street ensembles, nightclubs, local radio stations, and riverboat calliopes: jazz, brass bands, marches, Cajun music, zydeco, rhythm and blues, alternative, country, Latin, and gospel. Jazz Fest is the ultimate musical event. Music aside, relaxing and drinking is a prime pastime; teetotalers can get their kicks from abundant java joints. The theatrical scene is active, and you can listen to opera or watch an art film.

NIGHTLIFE

By Jason Berry
and Honey
Naylor

Updated by
Michaela
Morrissey

NO AMERICAN CITY PLACES SUCH A PREMIUM ON pleasure as New Orleans. From the well-appointed lounges of swank hotels to raucous French Quarter bars, to sweaty dance halls and funky dives, to rocking clubs in far-flung neighborhoods, this city is serious about frivolity—and about music.

During Mardi Gras or special events such as the Sugar Bowl, human traffic is tight in the French Quarter. On more relaxed weekends, club-hopping on the old rues can be as charming as tapas-tasting in Madrid. And just as traffic fluctuates, so do "scenes." The presence of Latin groups such as Freddy Omar y Su Banda and Los Hombres Calientes reflects the city's growing Central American community. On the other hand, once-hip Bourbon Street is now trashy and tacky, although many good musicians do play there; other parts of the Quarter still exude a Euro-tropical charm.

Music Around Town

How can you enjoy New Orleans at its best? A lot depends on when you eat. Long, leisurely meals are a tradition here. Many good restaurants are concentrated between Canal Street and Esplanade, and an early dinner reservation allows you to finish in time for the 9 PM set at French Quarter jazz spots or clubs in the adjacent Faubourg Marigny; at a few clubs, such as the Palm Court, the bands actually finish by 11 PM. Farther uptown, music clubs tend to have later opening sets, beginning anytime from 10 to 11 PM. Keep in mind that the lack of a legal closing time means that shows advertised for 11 may not start till after midnight.

"Uptown" encompasses all of New Orleans that follows the upriver curve from the Warehouse District up to Audubon Park. As such it includes the Irish Channel, the Garden District, and the university neighborhoods, extending all the way to the end of the St. Charles streetcar line at the corner of Carrollton and Claiborne avenues. Uptown runs the gamut from elegant residences to rough neighborhoods, and it's often hard to tell which is which. After dark it's best to take a taxi.

Halfway between Lake Pontchartrain and the Mississippi, equidistant from the French Quarter and the suburbs, Mid-City includes the Creole mansions of upper Esplanade Avenue, well-tended middle-class side streets, and the vast green space of City Park. Also here are cozy neighborhood cafés that turn out superb dishes, as well as several notable nightspots. A taxi is recommended to get to this area of town.

The 500 and 600 blocks of Frenchmen Street—just outside the Quarter in the Faubourg Marigny neighborhood—should not be missed. Here you will find an exuberantly funky atmosphere as well as some of the city's hottest music clubs. **Snug Harbor** is a mecca for modern jazz, with patriarch Ellis Marsalis performing regularly. **Café Brasil** showcases reggae, Afro-Caribbean music, jazz, and diverse surprises. It's also a magnet for poets, with readings throughout the year. Frenchmen Street combines the Beat-culture aura of Greenwich Village in the '60s with a lazy semitropical ambience. In this area, hanging out on the street can be as much fun as entering a club: the sidewalks and street are often crowded with revelers with go cups enjoying street performers and taking a breather between sets. The trendy gay and lesbian dance club **Rubyfruit Jungle** is part of the mix.

Music is one of New Orleans's richest resources and biggest drawing cards, with a selection of venues as broad as the types of music you'll find inside them. Famous venues such as **Preservation Hall** and the **Palm Court Jazz Café** carry on the jazz tradition, whereas the modern brass-band renaissance continues to evolve at **Donna's Bar & Grill** and smoky little clubs in Tremé. Swinging singles and happy couples alike dance to toe-tapping Cajun music and zydeco. New Orleans rhythm and blues—which shook the world during the '50s thanks to Fats Domino and Jerry Lee Lewis—still flourishes at such atmospheric corner bars as R&B great Irma Thomas's **Lion's Den** and contemporary institutions like the **House of Blues.** And the epicenter of the local swing music revival can be traced to Uptown's hot yet elegant nightspot, the **Red Room.**

If you have never visited the city before, you should consider the following standouts, which, as with all the clubs mentioned in the introduction, are described in more detail later in the chapter. **Preservation Hall** is an institution; but the same bands can be heard in far more comfortable conditions—including chairs and beverage service—at the **Palm Court Jazz Café.** Next door to Preservation Hall is the internationally known watering hole **Pat O'Brien's,** where the atmosphere is very loud and very lively until very late. The lineup at **Tipitina's** varies nightly, from rhythm and blues to rock, jazz, and funk, with Cajun dancing on Sunday afternoon. For Cajun food and dancing seven nights a week, consider **Mulate's** or **Michaul's**; Cajun music and its black Creole counterpart, zydeco, are frequently presented at the **Maple Leaf, Mid-City Bowling Lanes** (known informally as the Rock 'n' Bowl), **Tipitina's,** and the **House of Blues.** Though the only music at the **Napoleon House** is provided by classical recordings, this ancient bar is enormously popular and is regarded as the epitome of local atmosphere. **Snug Harbor** is a great spot for modern jazz, and young brass band musicians hang out at **Donna's Bar & Grill.**

Bright Lights, Big Easy

One legacy of New Orleans's Caribbean cultural climate that comes as a pleasant shock to many visitors is the city's tolerant attitude toward alcohol. There are bars that stay open all night so long as a crowd is on hand: with 24-hour liquor licenses, closing time is strictly voluntary. Revelers can leave a bar and take their drinks along—as long as it's in a plastic "go cup" rather than a glass or metal container. Whiskey, beer, or wine can be purchased anywhere, anytime, at such unlikely outlets as gas stations or drive-through daiquiri depots.

Many bars advertise the Hurricane—a red rum-and-fruit concoction that is the signature drink at **Pat O'Brien's,** which is the best place to order one. Go cups are ubiquitous in New Orleans, especially in the Quarter, and since Pat's is next door to **Preservation Hall,** which serves neither food nor drink, you can buy a Hurricane-to-go to enjoy in the Hall. Less Hawaiian Punchy than the Hurricane is the light-pink Monsoon, a specialty at **Port of Call** and **Snug Harbor.**

Perhaps the most famous local drink is the Sazerac, brewed of bourbon and bitters, with a coating of ersatz absinthe. The **Sazerac Bar** in the Fairmont Hotel does a stellar job with its namesake.

Practical Matters

In neighborhood clubs featuring music or just drinks, it's best to bring cash. Some take plastic but many more do not. This is a pay-as-you-go kinda town.

Dress codes are as rare as snow in New Orleans, although a few restaurants insist that men wear sport coats. On any given night in the French Quarter, and especially during the Carnival season, you'll see everything from tuxedos and ball gowns to T-shirts and torn jeans. Once you branch out into the city's other neighborhoods, fashions become increasingly casual.

Many bars in the French Quarter, especially on Bourbon Street, entice visitors by presenting live bands and/or strip shows with no cover charge. They make their money by imposing a two-drink minimum, with draft beer or soft drinks—served in small glasses—costing $4 or $5 apiece. Prices range from $5 to $10 a drink in hotel lounges and get cheaper as you move farther away from downtown or the Quarter. Some clubs with a two-drink minimum require that you buy both drinks at once, even if your beer gets warm. Music clubs elsewhere in town generally charge a flat cover of between $5 and $20, with the high-end prices usually reserved for national touring artists.

A **music calendar** is broadcast daily on WWOZ, 90.7 FM, the community radio station devoted to New Orleans music. You can also call the station's "Second Line" for a prerecorded calendar (☎ 504/840–4040). For detailed and up-to-date listings, consult the Friday "Lagniappe" entertainment supplement of the *Times-Picayune* or *Gambit,* the yuppie weekly that appears on Monday and is carried free at major newsstands and many stores. The *TP*'s daily listing covers only the major clubs. The monthly *OffBeat* magazine has in-depth music coverage and listings, and is available at many hotels, stores, and restaurants; remember that bookings printed here may have changed since press time. Many clubs also post entertainment calendars on their Web sites. Never be shy about calling clubs to ask what kind of music a given group plays. It's a good idea to call before going anywhere, since hours may vary from day to day. For further suggestions, *see* Music Venues, *below.*

Fodor's Choice

★ **Café du Monde.** No trip to New Orleans would be complete without a cup of chicory-laced café au lait and a few sugar-dusted beignets at this bustling, open-air institution with views of Jackson Square and Decatur Street.

★ **F&M Patio Bar.** This late-night speakeasy is in Uptown New Orleans (take a taxi). Just try to close it down. . . .

★ **Frenchmen Street.** This bohemian thoroughfare in Faubourg Marigny, the neighborhood just outside the French Quarter, has some of the city's hottest music clubs and venues for poetry readings.

★ **Mid-City Bowling Lanes.** At this combination bowling alley–music club near Uptown, joyful dancers edge into the lanes when a favorite zydeco band takes the stage, earning it the nickname Rock 'n' Bowl. It's open till 3 AM or so.

★ **Preservation Hall.** Although it's grungy and uncomfortable with crude wooden benches and cramped standing room (and only open till midnight), this French Quarter landmark showcases some of the best traditional jazz musicians in the world.

Bars and Lounges

French Quarter

Bombay Club. Those partial to the cocktail, be it shaken or stirred, will appreciate the extensive selection of vodkas, single-malt scotches, ports, and cognacs here—and the martinis approach high art. The plush, paneled interior creates a comfort zone for anyone nostalgic for the glory days of the British Empire. This bar in the Prince Conti Hotel frequently has live piano tunes. ⊠ *830 Conti St.,* ☎ *504/586–0972.*

Carousel Revolving Bar. A veritable institution, this carefree piano bar in the Monteleone Hotel has an authentic revolving carousel that serves as a centerpiece. Some stools revolve, though there's seating beyond the carousel. The mix of loyal, mostly older locals and visitors yields a friendly crowd with an authentic character. Be prepared to join in the sing-alongs. ✉ *214 Royal St.,* ☎ *504/523–3341.*

Crescent City Brewhouse. This laid-back, amiable brewpub is known for its extensive menu of micro and specialty brews; Abita Amber is a local favorite, but ask your server what's good. Live local music is a staple here. The river view from the second-floor balcony is worth a stop. ✉ *527 Decatur St.,* ☎ *504/522–0571.*

Kerry Irish Pub. Here's the spot if you find yourself hankering for the Guinness or a single malt in a casual pub setting. Good live music— which can range from Irish ballads to Delta blues—is staged nightly, and it's free. ✉ *331 Decatur St.,* ☎ *504/527–5954.*

Lafitte's Blacksmith Shop. Very popular with locals, Lafitte's is an atmospheric bar in a rustic 18th-century cottage. There is piano music nightly from 8 PM, and the small patio has a fountain. You do not feel as if you're on Bourbon Street here. ✉ *941 Bourbon St.,* ☎ *504/523–0066.*

Napoleon House Bar and Cafe. This vintage watering hole has long been popular with writers, artists, and various free spirits; locals who wouldn't be caught dead on Bourbon Street come here often. It is a living shrine to the New Orleans school of decor: faded grandeur. Murmuring ceiling fans, diffused light, and a lovely patio create a timeless, escapist mood. The house specialty is a Pimm's Cup cocktail; a menu including sandwiches, soups, salads, and cheese boards is also available. The waiters are unstintingly polite and will never rush you. This is the perfect place for late-afternoon people-watching, an evening nightcap, or the beginning of an up-till-dawn bender. ✉ *500 Chartres St.,* ☎ *504/524–9752.*

Pat O'Brien's. One of the biggest tourist spots in town is also the home of the oversize alcoholic beverage known as the Hurricane. Many people like to take their glass home as a souvenir; be wary of a deposit that is charged at the time of purchase and should be refunded if you don't take the glass home with you. Actually five bars in one, Pat O's claims to sell more liquor than any other establishment in the world. The bar on the left of the entrance is popular with Quarterites, the patio in the rear draws the young (and young at heart) in temperate months, and the piano bar on the right side of the brick corridor packs in raucous celebrants year-round. ✉ *718 St. Peter St.,* ☎ *504/525–4823.*

Port of Call. Dimly lit and warm with barroom comraderies, this casual place is almost an institution for locals. Many claim you'll find the best burger and baked potato in town here. Poised on the edge of the Quarter, the bar draws an even number of visitors and Orleanians. The drink offerings are average, yet many locals crave their tropical Monsoon. ✉ *838 Esplanade Ave.,* ☎ *504/523–0120.*

Tony Moran's Old Absinthe House. This popular watering hole draws mainly out-of-towners from afternoon to late at night, whenever there are too few customers left to stay open. The decor consists of hundreds of business cards pinned to one wall, money papered on another, and absinthe jugs hanging from the ceiling. ✉ *240 Bourbon St.,* ☎ *504/523–3181.*

Central Business District (CBD) and Warehouse District

Fairmont Hotel. The hotel has three distinctive lounges worth a stop. Fairmont Court has varied music on Friday and Saturday nights. Down the hall from the Fairmont Court is the smaller, more elegant Sazerac Bar—with its renowned art deco mural by painter Paul Ninas. Next door, the hotel's famous Sazerac Restaurant features elegant piano music nightly. ✉ *123 Baronne St.,* ☎ *504/529–7111.*

Le Chat Noir. Come to the cabaret for a scintillating mix of revues, chanteuses, theater, piano trills, and pop standards. In the heart of the arts district, this cat is sleek, elegant, and eclectic, with plenty of warm wood and cool tile, all polished to the highest gloss. The patrons, whether in their twenties or fifties, are appropriately urbane. ⊠ *715 St. Charles Ave.,* ☎ *504/581–6333.*

Polo Lounge at the Windsor Court. Paintings of polo ponies and assorted British royalty appoint the posh yet comfy lounge in this upscale hotel. You'll see plenty of people dressed up to take in the top-drawer drinks and service, particularly the signature martini. A jazz trio plays Friday and Saturday; other nights there's a pianist. The Polo ponies up for some of the top jazz talent in town. ⊠ *300 Gravier St.,* ☎ *504/523–6000.*

Top of the Mart. From 33 stories atop the World Trade Center—home of maritime companies, foreign consulates, banks, and other businesses—the city's only revolving lounge makes a complete turn every 1½ hours, giving people a fabulous view of the Mississippi River and the city. The setting is luxe but comfortable. ⊠ *World Trade Center, 2 Canal St. (at the river), 33rd floor,* ☎ *504/522–9795.*

Riverwalk

LeMoyne's Landing. A casual seafood restaurant with an oyster bar, LeMoyne's has a grand view of the Mississippi River as well as live music. The open-air café, adjacent to the Spanish Plaza, has a large fountain and circular seating area. Concerts are held here in warm months; call for details. ⊠ *1 Poydras St.,* ☎ *504/524–4809.*

Uptown

Audubon Hotel. Alternative probably doesn't really describe it. Tucked in among the moonlight and magnolias of the city's stately avenue is this microcosm of arts, street, and bohemian life. The city's wild, seamy side is generally on display and the crowd is always eclectic—24 hours a day. ⊠ *1225 St. Charles Ave.,* ☎ *504/568–1319.*

The Bulldog. The dawg offers 50 different beers on tap as well as an extensive bottled selection. This is a favorite haunt for Gen X, but other age groups are warmly welcomed—particularly if they are trivia buffs. A local group of trivia contestants often battle in informal competition, usually on Sunday night. ⊠ *3236 Magazine St.,* ☎ *504/891–1516.*

Columns Hotel. The Victorian Lounge, with period decor and plenty of decaying elegance, draws a white-collar crowd of all ages. On a given night you might catch a top local jazz combo or flamenco dancers. Take your drink upstairs and relax on the spacious second-story porch. ⊠ *3811 St. Charles Ave.,* ☎ *504/899–9308.*

Dos Jefes Uptown Cigar Bar. Uptown and upscale, this establishment smokes with a menu that includes over 40 premium cigars, single-malt scotches, brandies, whiskeys, ports, and wine by the glass. There's live music nightly. A cab or a car will get you here. ⊠ *5535 Tchoupitoulas St.,* ☎ *504/891–8500.*

F&M Patio Bar. For some people, an all-nighter in New Orleans isn't complete until they've danced on top of the pool table at this perpetually open hangout. There's a loud jukebox, a popular photo booth, and a late-night kitchen (it gets going around 8 and keeps serving until early in the morning), and the tropical patio can actually be peaceful at times. You'll need a car or a taxi to get here. ⊠ *4841 Tchoupitoulas St.,* ☎ *504/895–6784.*

Pontchartrain Hotel. The Bayou Bar, a lovely lounge, is just off the lobby as you enter this elegant European-style hotel that dates to the 1920s. Popular with businesspeople and Uptown residents, the bar is easy to reach by streetcar. ⊠ *2031 St. Charles Ave.,* ☎ *504/524–0581.*

Coffeehouses

Cafe Marigny. At the center of the Faubourg Marigny triangle, this is the perfect place to grab a cappuccino and bagel before dancing on Frenchmen Street; you'll also find sandwiches, pasta salads, and a sinful assortment of pastries. The warm, friendly atmosphere makes it a comfortable place to sit and read all afternoon. Best of all, the café is just outside the French Quarter, making it a welcome respite from all the hustle and bustle of the Vieux Carré. ⊠ *1913 Royal St.,* ☎ *504/945–4472.*

Neutral Ground Coffee House. This one-of-a-kind 1960s-style coffeehouse that attracts artistic and intellectual types operates as a co-op. Sofas, chess boards, laid-back counter service, and a bulletin board encourage an intimacy unmatched in most other cafés. On Sunday night there's an open mike for any aspiring musician. On other nights (except Monday, when it's closed), the city's best singer-songwriters and contemporary or traditional folk artists perform. It's a short cab ride from downtown. ⊠ *5110 Danneel St.,* ☎ *504/891–3381.*

P. J.'s Coffee & Tea Cafés. This chain of coffeehouses has locations throughout New Orleans; a popular one is on Frenchmen Street in Faubourg Marigny. You can enjoy muffins, cakes, and java and indulge in people-watching. ⊠ *634 Frenchmen St.,* ☎ *504/949–2292;* ⊠ *7624 Maple St.,* ☎ *504/866–7031;* ⊠ *5432 Magazine St.,* ☎ *504/895–0273;* ⊠ *637 N. Carrollton Ave.,* ☎ *504/482–4847.*

Royal Blend. In the French Quarter, with a beautiful outdoor patio, this spot serves exotic coffees, desserts, and muffins from early in the morning until 10 PM. ⊠ *623 Royal St.,* ☎ *504/523–2716.*

Rue de la Course. Pressed tin and polished wood create the comfortable, slightly worn look of 19th-century Europe. This is what a coffeehouse should be: hip and un-yuppified, with plenty of hot java choices and cool tunes. ⊠ *1500 Magazine St.,* ☎ *504/529–1455;* ⊠ *3128 Magazine St.,* ☎ *504/899–0242;* ⊠ *219 N. Peters St.,* ☎ *504/523–0206;* ⊠ *401 Carondelet St.,* ☎ *504/525–5200.*

True Brew Café/True Brew Theater. You can enjoy live music and eclectic theater (at night) with lots of local character in an intimate setting while you choose from exotic coffees, teas, and pastries. This Warehouse District spot is open from 6:30 AM on weekdays, 7:30 AM on weekends. ⊠ *200 Julia St.,* ☎ *504/524–8441.*

Gambling

Though gambling would appear natural for an indulgent town such as New Orleans, it has been a volatile issue since 1993, when the state legislature approved riverboat gambling on state waterways and in one land-based casino in New Orleans. By law, the boats must cruise while gamblers are on board, but they rarely do because of various loopholes; now they're even more likely to stay put on account of the dangers of heavy river traffic. After an earlier venture in the city went bankrupt, Harrah's reemerged, phoenixlike, in fall 1999 with a resplendent land-based palace; time will tell if it will succeed. Three riverboat casinos also continue to operate in the metro area, but it's best to check ahead. Note that admission to all the casinos is free, but you must be 21 or older to play. The casinos are all open 24 hrs daily.

Bally's Casino Lakeshore Resort. Docked on the south shore of Lake Pontchartrain, a few minutes from downtown, *Bally's Casino* has 30,000 square ft of gaming on two levels and a 250-seat buffet; 46 gaming tables and 1,213 slot machines provide plenty of action. Live concerts are staged nightly, often with nationally known acts. ⊠ *1 Stars and Stripes Blvd.,* ☎ *504/248–3200 or 800/572–2559.*

Boomtown Belle Casino. On the west bank of the Mississippi River, the *Boomtown Belle* is docked at the Harvey Canal, 10 mi from New Orleans. The vessel has 30,000 square ft of gaming space and accommodates 1,600 passengers. Besides the 1,100 slots and 46 gaming tables, the casino has a café, arcade, and lounge. Cajun music and country tunes are a hallmark, dancing lessons are available. This is a popular spot for locals. ⊠ *4132 Peters Rd., Harvey,* ☎ *504/366–7711.*

Harrah's New Orleans Casino. Commanding the foot of Canal Street, this Beaux Arts–style palace is clearly the largest such facility in the South. Its 100,000 square feet hold 2,900 slots and 120 gaming tables. The themed decor evokes the spirit of the Crescent City in five distinct courts. Fifty-five-ft ceilings, a five-story "live" oak tree slung with Spanish moss, and realistic stars and fireflies set the mood for the Jazz Court. Live, high-quality entertainment is a sure bet; some of the town's hottest talents gig at Harrah's from time to time. Three elaborate parades pass through the Mardi Gras Court every night. The Smuggler's Court and the Court of the Mansion create two additional scenes for gaming fantasy. If you need a break, head for the café, food court, or lounge. There's even valet parking. ⊠ *512 S. Peters St.,* ☎ *504/533–6000 or 800/427–7247.*

Treasure Chest Casino. Only seven minutes from the airport on Lake Pontchartrain, the Treasure Chest features Las Vegas–style gaming entertainment with 900 slot machines, 50 gaming tables, and the area's largest poker room. There's a no-smoking gaming area. The kitchen here serves Louisiana specialties; a free shuttle operates to and from nearby hotels. ⊠ *5050 Williams Blvd.,* ☎ *504/443–8000 or 800/298–0711.*

Gay Bars and Nightclubs

New Orleans, in particular the French Quarter and Faubourg Marigny, has a sizable gay and lesbian community. The inside scoop on local goings-on appears in *Impact* and *Ambush,* local biweekly newspapers that provide lists of current events in addition to news and reviews. *Impact* also publishes a slick glossy called *Eclipse* that contains all its nightlife coverage. All three publications are available in many of the establishments listed below and at the gay and lesbian **Faubourg Marigny Bookstore** (⊠ 600 Frenchmen St., ☎ 504/943–9875).

Many of the gay bars are on or near Rampart, St. Ann, and Dumaine streets in the vicinity of Armstrong Park. The neighborhoods around the park are not the safest, so be very careful, and don't go into the park at night unless there's a major event.

Bars
Bourbon Pub. This 24-hour video bar, with its mostly young male clientele, has been popular for two decades. ⊠ *801 Bourbon St.,* ☎ *504/529–2107.*

Café Lafitte in Exile. Gay men have been gathering for ages at this large and lively 24-hour bar, best known for its balcony overlooking Bourbon Street. ⊠ *901 Bourbon St.,* ☎ *504/522–8397.*

Footloose. This appropriately named 24-hour neighborhood spot attracts lesbians, gays (including the leather and Levi's crowd), transvestites, and transsexuals, as well as straight clientele. Happy hour is 4–8 daily. ⊠ *700 N. Rampart St.,* ☎ *504/524–7654.*

The Mint. This place showcases local comedians and musical entertainment; it's a great place to catch drag shows. The clientele is predominantly but not exclusively gay. Call for show times. ⊠ *940 Elysian Fields Ave.,* ☎ *504/944–4888.*

Rawhide. As the name indicates, this is a rowdy—and somewhat sexually charged—leather-and-Levi's bar. It's two blocks from Bourbon Street and is open around the clock. ⊠ *740 Burgundy St.,* ☎ *504/525–8106.*

Dance Bars

Oz. This dance-and-cruise bar is one of the Quarter's most popular spots for young gay men and, to a lesser degree, lesbians—24 hours a day. ⊠ *800 Bourbon St.,* ☎ *504/593–9491.*

Parade Disco. This glitzy, high-energy disco draws a young crowd of men and women; there are also well-attended tea dances on Sunday at 3 PM. ⊠ *801 Bourbon St., above Bourbon Pub,* ☎ *504/529–2107.*

Rubyfruit Jungle. Named for one of the works by lesbian novelist Rita Mae Brown, Rubyfruit—in Faubourg Marigny—has weekend dancing to DJ-spun tunes that attracts mostly women but plenty of gay guys and straights, too. It's popular for pool and socializing on weekdays. ⊠ *640 Frenchmen St.,* ☎ *504/947–4000.*

Music Venues

For a city of only 473,000 (the metro area is 1,263,000), New Orleans has a vast selection of live music. To list every club and bar would be a massive undertaking: the clubs selected here host good bands on a regular basis, usually most nights of the week. Venues come and go in the precarious music business, so check the city's various publications to keep up-to-date.

Many hotels have piano bars. Some hotels present live music, especially New Orleans jazz, either on a seasonal basis, at the evening cocktail hour, or for Sunday jazz brunches. New Orleans also has a good selection of neighborhood restaurants or taverns that periodically have live music on weekends.

The heaviest concentration of live music is in the French Quarter, and high standards of musicianship prevail despite the at-times tawdry atmosphere. Most people discover the Quarter's hot spots as they explore the district on foot. Some of the descriptions in this section of neighborhood clubs outside the Quarter and downtown are a bit longer, as these places are generally less familiar to out-of-towners.

Show times can vary greatly. French Quarter clubs with Dixieland or traditional jazz get rolling early in the evening, usually by 8 PM; several present music in the afternoons as well, especially on weekends. The first set at most neighborhood clubs usually begins about 10 PM; unless a club has wee-hours music on a regular basis, the last set usually ends around 2 AM. But it's advisable to call ahead to double-check times and ask for directions if you need them. Remember that in a city with no closing time there is also no compulsion to start punctually, no matter what you are told over the phone.

French Quarter and Faubourg Marigny

Café Brasil. If a popular band such as the Iguanas is playing, then it's strictly standing and dancing inside—under cramped conditions. Tables line the sidewalk, though, and the music pours through the open doors. On a hot night it may be far more pleasant to hang and dance outside. Modern jazz tends to draw a much smaller crowd of serious listeners who sit at comfortably spaced tables. All kinds of music and people come to this bohemian hot spot, and it's also a popular place to show off costumes on Mardi Gras. ⊠ *2100 Chartres St., Faubourg Marigny,* ☎ *504/947–9286.*

Cajun Cabin. Here is reasonably authentic Cajun music and Cajun food in the midst of the garish fantasy that is Bourbon Street. There is a one-drink minimum. It's open daily from 11:30 AM until people are ready for the last waltz. ⊠ *503 Bourbon St.,* ☎ *504/529–4256.*

Cat's Meow. Locals and visitors alike flock to this lively karaoke spot, which also has videos, "hand jive," "hokey pokey," and other diversions. ⊠ *701 Bourbon St.,* ☎ *504/523–1157.*

Checkpoint Charlie's. This bustling French Quarter corner bar draws young locals who shoot pool and listen to late-night blues and rock—24 hrs a day, 7 days a week. There's also a paperback library and a fully functioning Laundromat. The 1993 film *The Pelican Brief* included several scenes shot here. ⊠ *501 Esplanade Ave.,* ☎ *504/947–0979.*

Chris Owens Club. A famous French Quarter figure, Chris Owens is an energetic female dancer and entertainer with a slightly risqué act. The late Al Hirt often played here. ⊠ *500 Bourbon St.,* ☎ *504/523–6400.*

Court of Two Sisters. If you want to catch jazz in the daytime, head to this restaurant, which has the largest courtyard in the French Quarter and serves a jazz buffet brunch 9 AM–3 PM daily—not just on weekends. ⊠ *613 Royal St.,* ☎ *504/522–7261.*

Donna's Bar & Grill. A barbecue joint, Donna's is the hottest place in town to hear the city's young brass bands in an informal neighborhood setting. ⊠ *800 N. Rampart St.,* ☎ *504/596–6914.*

Dragon's Den. This most bohemian of music cafés, located above a Thai restaurant, provides pillows on the floor and features live music every night—as well as such offerings as New Orleans poet John Sinclair and the Blues Scholars. ⊠ *435 Esplanade Ave.,* ☎ *504/949–1750.*

Ernie K-Doe's Mother-in-Law Lounge. Ernie K-Doe is a rhythm and blues legend as well as one of the city's most eccentric personalities—no small achievement in New Orleans. This small neighborhood bar is named for K-Doe's biggest hit and is a shrine to his career. It's a great spot to enjoy classic R&B in a '50s time-warp atmosphere. K-Doe performs frequently and many of his colleagues drop by to sit in. This bar is in Tremé, a neighborhood adjacent to the French Quarter. The area is not safe for walking, but taxis from the Quarter are quick and inexpensive. ⊠ *1500 N. Claiborne Ave.,* ☎ *504/947–1078.*

Esplanade. One of the most elegant piano bars in the city, the Esplanade, in the Royal Orleans hotel, serves cocktails, desserts, and postprandial liqueurs. ⊠ *621 St. Louis St.,* ☎ *504/529–5333.*

Famous Door. Music has been pouring out of this place for more than 30 years; the patio is a fairly recent addition. There's Dixieland 5 PM–9 PM and R&B from 9 until the pedestrian traffic finally thins out, which can be late indeed. ⊠ *339 Bourbon St.,* ☎ *504/522–7626.*

Funky Butt at Congo Square. Named after jazz pioneer Buddy Bolden's home club and housed in Art Deco splendor, this club took a scant two years to distinguish itself as one of the top spots for top contemporary jazz. Local talent and local connoisseurs are both found in plentiful supply here. ⊠ *714 N. Rampart St.,* ☎ *504/558–0872.*

Gazebo Café and Bar. Near the French Market, this popular tourist spot has a relaxed local ambience, outdoor dining, good drinks, and spirited performances of jazz and R&B. ⊠ *1018 Decatur St.,* ☎ *504/522–0862.*

House of Blues. Part-owner Dan Aykroyd opened this club, a link in a growing chain, in 1994. Despite its name, blues is a relatively small component in the booking policy, which also embraces rock, jazz, country, soul, funk, world music, and more, performed by everyone from local artists to international touring acts. A gospel brunch is a rousing Sunday staple. In the bar you can absorb blues history on CD-ROM and take in a rich assortment of Southern folk art. The adjoining restaurant has an eclectic menu, including vegetarian dishes and classic southern cuisine, served in ample portions at reasonable prices. ⊠ *225 Decatur St.,* ☎ *504/529–2583 concert line.*

Maison Bourbon. Come here for a variety of live jazz nightly, including the Bourbon Brass Band. ⊠ *641 Bourbon St.,* ☎ *504/522–8818.*

Margaritaville Café. Yes, it's named after *that* song. Jimmy Buffett's devoted fans, called "parrotheads," flock to this shrine to the singer-songwriter-author that has live music by local and regional blues, rock, and zydeco performers. Menu items such as Cheeseburger in Paradise derive from Buffett songs, and there are several varieties of the salt-rimmed signature drink. Decor consists mainly of Buffett photos, and the man himself does appear occasionally. ✉ *1104 Decatur St.,* ☎ *504/592–2565.*

O'Flaherty's Irish Channel. Irish brothers Patrick and Danny O'Flaherty hold court in Gaelic in this Celtic-style pub and cultural center. There is live music nightly—be prepared to sing along. ✉ *514 Toulouse St.,* ☎ *504/529–1317.*

Palm Court Jazz Café. Banjo player Danny Barker immortalized this restaurant in his song "Palm Court Strut." The best of traditional New Orleans jazz is presented in a classy setting with tile floors, exposed brick walls, and a handsome mahogany bar. There are decent creature comforts here, compared with Preservation Hall (☞ *below*); regional cuisine is served, and you can sit at the bar and rub elbows with local musicians. A wide selection of records, tapes, and CDs are on sale. ✉ *1204 Decatur St.,* ☎ *504/525–0200.*

Preservation Hall. The jazz tradition that flowered in the 1920s is enshrined in this cultural landmark by a cadre of distinguished New Orleans musicians, most of whom were schooled by an ever-dwindling group of elder statesmen who actually played with Louis Armstrong et al. There is limited seating—many patrons end up squatting on the floor—and no beverages are served. Nonetheless, the legions of satisfied customers regard an evening here as a transcendent New Orleans experience. ✉ *726 St. Peter St.,* ☎ *504/522–2841 or 504/523–8939.*

Rhythms. Home to Willie Lockett and the Blues Krewe, Rhythms has a spacious courtyard and live blues. ✉ *227 Bourbon St.,* ☎ *504/523–3800.*

Shim Sham. Sixties-era Vegas meets the Vieux Carré in a riot of leopard and zebra print—and hot hipster sound. Retro-themed acts, such as Sam Butera (Louis Prima's original sax man), are a specialty. The era is captured down to the most perfect, plastic detail, topped off by a tiki lounge upstairs. Thursdays make a separate statement with a glam goth night that evokes Orwell's *1984.* ✉ *615 Toulouse St.,* ☎ *504/565–5400.*

Snug Harbor. This intimate club just outside the Quarter is one of the city's best rooms for soaking up modern jazz, blues, and R&B. It is the home base of such esteemed talent as vocalist Charmaine Neville and pianist/patriarch Ellis Marsalis (father of Wynton and Branford). The dining room serves good local food but is best known in town for its burgers. Budget-conscious types can listen to the band from the bar without paying the rather high cover charge. ✉ *626 Frenchmen St., Faubourg Marigny,* ☎ *504/949–0696.*

Storyville District Jazz Club. Named after the notorious red-light district that witnessed the birth of New Orleans jazz, this new venue at the foot of Bourbon Street came out singin' and swingin' in 1999. Its 12,000-square-ft multistage jazz club and restaurant celebrate jazz and other local music with authentic—as well as contemporary—aplomb. The District serves up continuous live entertainment, including a jazz brunch and tribute to the life and music of Louis Armstrong on Sunday and sizzling jam sessions that cook every night. The project was developed by Jazz Fest producer Quint Davis and local restaurateur Ralph Brennan, among others. ✉ *125 Bourbon St.,* ☎ *504/410–1000.*

Tipitina's. The Quarter branch of this legendary spot (☞ Uptown, *below*) books good local talent.

CBD and Warehouse District

Howlin' Wolf. A former grain and cotton warehouse holds a club that's popular with locals. Live music offerings include an acoustic open mike on Monday and a grab bag of alternative rock and progressive country the rest of the week. Visiting musicians often hang out and may sit in. ✉ *828 S. Peters St.,* ☎ *504/523–2551.*

Mermaid Lounge. This funky-but-chic hangout—a combination bar, art gallery, and part-time health-food restaurant—presents a wide variety of acts including local rock, funk, brass bands, and classic country. Call for current schedule. ✉ *1102 Constance St.,* ☎ *504/524–4747.*

Michaul's Live Cajun Music Restaurant. Spacious and homey, Michaul's has a huge dance floor on which patient teachers give free Cajun dance lessons nightly except Sunday, mostly to visitors, though locals check it out from time to time. The Cajun food is authentic if not inventive. ✉ *840 St. Charles Ave.,* ☎ *504/522–5517.*

Mulate's. Just across the street from the convention center, this large restaurant seats 400, and the dance floor quickly fills with couples twirling and two-stepping to authentic Cajun bands from the countryside. The home-style Cajun cuisine (☞ Breaux Bridge *in* Chapter 7) is quite good. You'll see mostly visitors here. ✉ *201 Julia St.,* ☎ *504/522–1492.*

Pete Fountain's. The renowned Dixieland clarinetist plays one show from 10 PM to 11:15 PM on Tuesday, Wednesday, Friday, and Saturday in his plush club on the third floor of the Hilton, when he's not booked out of town. The schedule varies, so call ahead. Wear your good duds. ✉ *2 Poydras St. at river,* ☎ *504/523–4374 or 504/561–0500.*

Vic's Kangaroo Café. The Australian-born owner combines down-under food with local blues and rock; bands start around 10 PM. It's a relaxed place with a dart board and a good selection of beers. This is home court to gentleman harmonica player Rockin' Jake. ✉ *636 Tchoupitoulas St.,* ☎ *504/524–4329.*

Uptown

Carrollton Station. Small and cozy, this club showcases such acts as blues guitarist John Mooney and the beloved chanteuse L'il Queenie with her latest group, Mixed Knots. Sunday's acoustic songwriters' night presents a lesser-known side of the rich New Orleans music scene. You can take the streetcar here. ✉ *8140 Willow St.*

Jimmy's Club. Next to Carrollton Station and across the street from the streetcar barn, this club presents rock, rap, reggae, and more, both local and national acts. The hours and schedule vary widely, so call ahead. ✉ *8200 Willow St.,* ☎ *504/861–8200.*

Maple Leaf. Down-home and funky, with pressed-tin walls and over-worked ceiling fans, this is an atmospheric if cramped place to listen and dance to blues, zydeco, R&B, and more. There's a romantic, tropical patio out back, and the sidewalk out front is often filled with dancers. Poetry readings are held on Sunday at 3 PM. Although the club is only a few blocks from the Oak and Carrollton streetcar stop, it's best to take a cab. ✉ *8316 Oak St.,* ☎ *504/866–9359.*

Red Room. Many New Orleanians remember the Restaurant de la Tour Eiffel, which was in a St. Charles Avenue building constructed from metalwork that originally housed the restaurant on the *deuxième étage* of the Eiffel Tower. Years later, this unique structure has been converted to the oh-so-swank Red Room. Six days a week (closed Sunday), live music is played in the octagonal main dining room; piano music begins at 6:30 PM, followed by main-stage acts at 8 PM. Swing music has taken the nation by storm again, and the Red Room is the driving force behind the local swing scene. Arrive early for contemporary cuisine from chef Carlos H. Guia: steaks, fish, and chops come with ambitious sauces. Dress nicely: T-shirts, jeans, shorts, and tennis shoes are not allowed. Valet parking is available, although the club is on the streetcar line. ✉ *2040 St. Charles Ave.,* ☎ *504/528–9759.*

The River Shack. Across River Road from the levee, this vintage road-house presents blues, rock, country, and rockabilly, usually with no cover charge, even for national acts. It has the feel of a rural honky-tonk that's a few decades back in time. The River Shack is also a popular lunch spot for burgers and po'boys, and the kitchen stays open till the place closes every day. Take a taxi; it's about 25 minutes from downtown and a bit hard to find. ⊠ *3449 River Rd., Jefferson,* ☎ *504/834–4938.*

Tipitina's. The original Tip's was founded in the mid-'70s as the home base for Professor Longhair, the pioneering rhythm-and-blues pianist and singer who died in 1980; the club takes its name from one of his most popular songs. A bust of "Fess" stands prominently between the bar and short-order grill, and a tapestry portrait hangs behind the stage. As the multitude of concert posters on the walls indicates, Tip's hosts a wide variety of local and global acts. For about a decade Bruce Daigrepont has played a weekly Cajun dance on Sunday 5 PM–9 PM; free red beans and rice are served. And Tip's has opened a location in the French Quarter, which offers the same classic New Orleans music that's made it a legendary institution. ⊠ *501 Napoleon Ave., Uptown,* ☎ *504/897–3943;* ⊠ *233 N. Peters St., French Quarter,* ☎ *504/566–7095.*

Mid-City

Lion's Den. This is a place to drift away from the mainstream and immerse yourself in an authentic New Orleans atmosphere, particularly if Miss Irma Thomas, an inspiration to the early Rolling Stones, is here. When she's not on tour, the city's undisputed R&B queen often performs at her own club. Call first to see what's on and take a cab here. Music usually starts at 10 PM. ⊠ *2655 Gravier St.,* ☎ *504/821–3745.*

Mid-City Bowling Lanes & Sports Palace. The saying "Only in New Orleans . . ." applies to this combination bowling alley/music club near Uptown, in Mid-City. Dancers may spill over into the lanes when a favorite band such as zydeco legend Boozoo Chavis takes the stage. Blues, R&B, rock, and Cajun music are all presented. Wednesday and Thursday are zydeco nights, bringing the best Creole musicians in from rural Louisiana. Be sure to ask club owner John Blancher for a dance lesson. The Rock 'n' Bowl, as it's known, is fun, fun, fun. ⊠ *4133 S. Carrollton Ave.,* ☎ *504/482–3133.*

Rollin' on the River

The audience for these themed cruises is 90% visitors, including busloads of tour groups. The food is acceptable, but the city is so rich with high-quality musicians that you can count on taking in some good music along with the scenery.

Creole Queen Paddle Wheeler. Among the various cruises on the Big Muddy is a "Dinner on the River & All That Jazz" outing. Boarding and a Creole buffet begin at 7 PM; cruises are 8–10. The band features the renowned clarinetist Otis Bazoon, who has played with the late Al Hirt, among others. ⊠ *Poydras St. Wharf at Riverwalk,* ☎ *504/529–4567 or 800/445–4109.* ☉ *Departures daily.*

Steamboat Natchez. The city's only authentic steamboat stern-wheeler does an evening excursion featuring traditional jazz by the Dukes of Dixieland and a Cajun-Creole buffet. Boarding is at 6 PM; the cruise is from 7 to 9. Day cruises also showcase live jazz. ⊠ *Toulouse St. Wharf behind Jax Brewery,* ☎ *504/586–8777 or 800/233–2628.* ☉ *Departures daily; Fri. and Sat. only Thanksgiving–Mardi Gras.*

THE ARTS

The performing arts are alive and well in New Orleans. A number of small theater and dance companies present an impressive variety of fare. Keep in mind, however, that the stage in New Orleans—although entertaining, reasonably priced, and generally good—can't and shouldn't be compared with that in New York. And don't forget: although most are not listed here, local colleges and universities such as Tulane, Loyola, Dillard, Xavier, and the University of New Orleans have sizable fine arts departments. Many performances are of outstanding caliber. For current listings, consult the daily calendar in the *Times-Picayune* and its "Lagniappe" Friday entertainment section. *OffBeat, Where,* and *Gambit* are free publications (distributed in hotels and other public places) that also have up-to-date entertainment news.

Ticket prices for theater and for concerts vary widely, from $20 for performances at smaller venues to $100 for top acts at major halls. You can purchase tickets from box offices. **Ticketmaster** (☎ 504/522–5555) also handles many venues.

Dance

New Orleans Ballet Association. The only major professional dance troupe in the city presents a diverse slate of performances—including ballet, modern, and tap—in the Mahalia Jackson Theater of the Performing Arts from September through May. ⊠ *Theater, Armstrong Park at Basin St.,* ☎ *504/565–7470; 504/522–0996 for ballet association.*

Film

Canal Place Cinemas. Art films and less well-known works, along with first-run films, are screened at this comfortable cinema in the fashionable mall. ⊠ *Canal Place, 333 Canal St.,* ☎ *504/581–5400.*

Film Buffs Institute. This Loyola University program screens an excellent selection of art and foreign films during the school year. ☎ *504/ 865–2152.*

Movie Pitchers. Art, foreign, and second-run films are shown in a laid-back setting that includes sandwiches and drinks. Get here early for the comfortable easy chairs. At press time the word was that the building might be razed; call before setting out. ⊠ *3941 Bienville St.,* ☎ *504/488–8881.*

N. O. Film and Video Festival. The N. O. Film and Video Society presents this one- to two-week festival in early October, bringing in top international films and visits from directors and scriptwriters. ☎ *504/ 523–3818.*

Zeitgeist. This place offers New Orleanians some of the most outstanding independent, experimental, and foreign films in release. Zeitgeist also displays visual art in its large space on lower Magazine Street's unofficial gallery row. ⊠ *2010 Magazine St.,* ☎ *504/524–0064.*

Music Venues

Free year-round musical events are held in the city's parks and universities. Louisiana also has a glorious tradition of festivals of all types, including music. Any weekend is bound to hold a fest somewhere around the bayou. New Orleans is no exception, the most famous examples being Mardi Gras and Jazz Fest (☞ Close-Up: All That Jazz). The French Quarter Festival, in early April, is attracting some kickin' musical talent. So when you're scanning the events calendar, check out the festivals.

The city has several major concert facilities, including the **Louisiana Superdome** (⊠ 1 Sugar Bowl Dr., ☎ 504/587–3663), the **Mahalia Jackson Theater of the Performing Arts** (⊠ Armstrong Park at Basin St., ☎ 504/565–7470), the **Municipal Auditorium** (⊠ Armstrong Park at Basin St., ☎ 504/565–7470), the **Saenger Performing Arts Center** (⊠ 143 N. Rampart St., ☎ 504/524–2490), and the **Kiefer UNO Lakefront Arena** (⊠ 6801 Franklin Ave., ☎ 504/280–7171) of the University of New Orleans.

ALL THAT JAZZ

JAZZ FEST IS, IN ITSELF, REASON enough for a trip to New Orleans. Each year during the last weekend in April and the first weekend in May (2001 dates are April 27–May 6), just as the summer heat is threatening to set in, the New Orleans Jazz & Heritage Festival roars through town, bursting with more music, food, and fun than any single person could possibly take in. The festival exuberantly exceeds the boundaries of its name, focusing on all aspects of Louisiana music and culture and featuring national performers as well as local ones. In addition to jazz, you'll hear blues, rhythm and blues, Cajun, zydeco, gospel, pop, rock, Latin, and world music.

Founded in 1970, the festival has grown into a giant, drawing some half-million visitors a year and showcasing some 6,000 performers, cooks, and craftspeople. Regulars make the annual pilgrimage from spots all over the country, and sometimes the world, to sit in the middle of a field with thousands of others, listening to good music and chowing on Creole and Cajun food. Even rain can't sour this crowd: they tramp gleefully through the track, digging their toes into the mud and listening to the same good music.

The festival is divided into two parts: its heart and soul is the Heritage Fair, held at the New Orleans Fair Grounds Race Track, right in the middle of town, from 11 AM to 7 PM on Friday through Sunday of the first weekend and Thursday through Sunday of the second weekend. The Fair Grounds' grandstand and grassy infield together hold 12 stages, each of which sees six or seven different performers a day. Each stage has a special bent: Congo Square for African and African-influenced music, the Fais-do-do Stage for Cajun and zydeco music, the Gospel Tent, the Jazz Tent, and others. Big-name local acts like the Neville Brothers and Dr. John, as well as national stars like Santana and Ziggy Marley, grace the Ray Ban and Sprint PCS/Fox 8 stages. The trick here is not to get too hung up on seeing any one performance. Favorite Fest memories inevitably recall the little-known Cajun group you happened upon while on your way to the mango ice stand.

Jazz Fest's offerings don't stop with the music. Restaurants from all over Louisiana vie for space in the food stalls, where you will find boudin, boiled crawfish, jambalaya, gumbo, and every variety of po'boy (including alligator), for starters. Come hungry. Nearby, artisans exhibit and sell crafts, clothing, jewelry, and furniture. Under the crafts tents and in the grandstand you might find Mardi Gras Indians sewing elaborately beaded costumes, craftspeople carving pirogues, or chefs giving cooking demonstrations—and samples.

When the Fair Grounds close at 7 PM, the other part of Jazz Fest takes over: the evening concerts. These are held in locations throughout town, and ticket prices vary widely ($20–$45 for most), depending on the venue and performer. If you still have energy left after the full day, you can catch a full set by groups you may have shortchanged during the day, or occasionally see musicians who are performing at night only.

Jazz Fest's line-up is announced in February; a brochure goes out in March. But don't wait that long to make room reservations: many people make their plans a full year in advance and eagerly pay the higher prices rooms command during the festival. To get on the mailing list, contact **New Orleans Jazz & Heritage Festival** (✉ 1205 Rampart St., New Orleans 70116, ☎ 504/522–4786) or visit the festival's official website: **www.nojazzfest.com.** Tickets (a bargain at $20 a day for all stages; evening concerts are separate) are available through mail order to the festival (certified check or money order) or through ☎ Ticketmaster (☎ 800/488–5252 or 504/522–5555). Parking at the Fair Grounds is extremely limited. Park on the street near the festival, take a taxi, or take advantage of the **festival shuttles** (☎ 504/592–0500 or 800/366–8882) that serve major hotels, spots downtown, and City Park. The **Regional Transit Authority** (☎ 504/569–2700) runs city buses that can also get you there.

— Baty Landis

Opera

New Orleanians have had a long love affair with opera (the first grand opera staged in North America was performed here), but since the French Opera House burned down in 1919, the city has not had an aria arena per se.

New Orleans Opera Association. The October–March season generally showcases five operas; performances are given annually at the Mahalia Jackson Theater of the Performing Arts. ⊠ *Theater, Armstrong Park at Basin St.,* ☎ *504/565–7470; 504/529–2278 for association.*

Jefferson Performing Arts Society. The society frequently stages operatic offerings, including classic European operas, works by contemporary American composers, and lively operettas. ⊠ *400 Phlox St., Metairie,* ☎ *504/885–2000.*

Xavier University. The university has an opera school in its music department and stages occasional student productions. ☎ *504/486–7411.*

Orchestra

New Orleans has a rich history in classical music and spawned a distinguished 19th-century composer and pianist, Louis Moreau Gottschalk.

Louisiana Philharmonic Orchestra. Always good and sometimes excellent, the orchestra performs a wide range of classical works in the Orpheum Theater (⊠ 129 University Pl.) and has a Casual Classics Series at the Pontchartrain Center (⊠ 4545 Williams Blvd., Kenner). Guest conductors and artists are often top-notch. The flexible programming includes children's concerts and free concerts in park. ⊠ *305 Baronne St., Suite 600,* ☎ *504/523–6530.*

Theater

Contemporary Arts Center. The center has two theaters that stage experimental works, productions by local playwrights, musical performances, and multimedia events. ⊠ *900 Camp St.,* ☎ *504/523–1216.*

Jefferson Performing Arts Society. This active, ambitious community theater (☞ Opera, *above*) stages musicals, dramas, and orchestral productions year-round. ⊠ *400 Phlox St., Metairie,* ☎ *504/885–2000.*

Junebug Productions. One of the region's most accomplished African-American theater companies presents outstanding productions at venues around the Crescent City. Call to find out what's currently on the boards. ☎ *504/524–8257.*

Le Petit Théâtre. The oldest continuously running community theater in the United States occupies a historic building in the French Quarter. It has a children's corner in addition to its usual fare of classics, musicals, and dramas. Events for the Tennessee Williams Festival take place here in March. ⊠ *616 St. Peter St.,* ☎ *504/522–2081.*

Movie Pitchers. Live comedy improv and plays share the bill with a cinematic schedule (☞ Film, *above*). Call ahead; this place may be moving—or closing. ⊠ *3941 Bienville St.,* ☎ *504/488–8881.*

New Rivertown Repertory Theatre. This community theater stages contemporary musicals, comedy, and drama year-round. ⊠ *1903 Short St., Kenner,* ☎ *504/468–7221.*

NORD Theater. A division of the New Orleans Recreation Department presents local playwrights and the Dashiki Players at Gallier Hall (⊠ 545 St. Charles Ave.) in the CBD. ☎ *504/565–7860.*

Saenger Performing Arts Center. A splendidly restored theater built in 1927, the Saenger showcases national and international talent. Broadway revivals and road shows come here, and pop and rock performers also often take the stage. ⊠ *143 N. Rampart St.,* ☎ *504/524–2490.*

Southern Repertory Theater. This company presents an annual season of regional plays and classics such as works by Tennessee Williams. The actors are always competent, though the quality of the plays themselves can vary. ✉ *Canal Place, 3rd level, 333 Canal St.,* ☎ *504/861–8163.)*

Theatre Marigny. Now in its second successful decade, Theatre Marigny stages avant-garde plays in an intimate setting just outside the French Quarter. ✉ *616 Frenchmen St.,* ☎ *504/944–2653.*

5 OUTDOOR ACTIVITIES AND SPORTS

There's plenty to do fitness-wise in the city, even though you're probably more apt to work up a sweat at a jazz bar at 2 AM. Enjoyable ways to work off the inevitable overindulgence of food and drink are trading a wooden seat on the St. Charles Avenue streetcar for a bicycle or jogging under canopies of live oaks in Audubon Park. And for those who like to overindulge and burn energy at the same time, bowl with a Dixie in hand at the Mid-City Bowling Lanes, or see a rockin' band and dance, dance, dance.

W HILE THE SPIRIT of a true Orleanian may soar higher on a dance floor, those who seek outdoor pursuits are rewarded with some pretty spectacular scenery as they jog, bike, canoe, lob, and putt. In the early spring and fall, the humidity is much lower than it is during the hot, sticky summer months, which makes breathing a bit easier. In June, July, and August, you won't have trouble remembering to confine rigorous outdoor activities to early morning and late afternoon. If you enjoy watching sports, college and professional teams provide plenty of options year-round.

Updated by
Honey Naylor

PARTICIPANT SPORTS AND FITNESS

Biking

Instead of riding the streetcar, you can bike at your own pace past the mansions of St. Charles Avenue to lush Audubon Park. City Park and the lakefront are other good alternatives. The **Crescent City Cyclists** bike hot line (☎ 504/276–2601) gives information on biking events.

The **Linear Parkway** along Lake Pontchartrain is a 7½-mi path for biking and hiking along the south shore of the lake (☞ Bayou St. John–Lakefront *in* Chapter 1).

Rentals (a major credit card is required for deposit) are available at **Bicycle Michael's.** ⊠ 622 Frenchmen St., ☎ 504/945–9505. ⊠ $3.50 per hr, $12.50 per day.

Boating

Pedal boats, rowboats, and canoes have been available to use in the semitropical lagoons that wind through the 1,500 acres of **City Park** (☎ 504/482–4888). In 2000 the park moved the boating concession from the Timken Center (formerly the casino), but a new dock must be built. Call the park for an update and current prices and hours.

Lake Pontchartrain awaits the boating enthusiast. **Tim Murray Sailboats** has a Pierson 26 that you can rent for the day. ⊠ 402 Roadway St., ☎ 504/283–2507.

Bowling

Two popular lanes are **Don Carter's All Star Lanes** (⊠ 3640 Williams Blvd., Kenner, ☎ 504/443–5353) and **Fazzio's Rainbow Lanes** (⊠ 5555 Bullard Ave., ☎ 504/241–2695).

Mid-City Bowling Lanes & Sports Palace is the rockin'est bowling alley in the South. Every weekend is Rock 'n' Bowl, when the whole neighborhood turns out for bowling and dancing to live music. The alley was built in 1946 and has been carefully maintained. A bar and eating area offer good drinks and local food specials at old-time prices. ⊠ 4133 S. Carrollton Ave., ☎ 504/482–3133. ⊠ $8 per hr, $10 after 6 PM; shoe rental $1. ☉ Daily noon–1 AM.

Canoeing

Bayou Sauvage National Wildlife Refuge, within the eastern limits of New Orleans, is a 22,000-acre marshland preserve administered by the U.S. Fish and Wildlife Service. Free guided canoe trips are available at the refuge; these include canoes and gear. ⊠ Off I–10, ☎ 504/646–7555 for directions. ⊠ Free. ☉ Weekdays 7:30–4.

For information about canoeing in **City Park,** *see* Boating, *above.*

The 20,000 acres of forest, swamp, and marsh in the Barataria Unit of **Jean Lafitte National Historical Park** include 20 mi of waterways that are good for canoeing. A local rental shop delivers canoes to the park. The park service hosts a free guided canoe tour Sunday 8:30–11:30 AM (reservations required). ⊠ *7400 Rte. 45, Marrero, 45-min drive south of New Orleans,* ☎ *504/589–2330.* ☜ *Free.* ☉ *Daily 9–5.*

Fishing

Nonresidents intending to fish around New Orleans must purchase a license. Seven-day licenses ($5.50) are issued separately for saltwater (which includes Lake Pontchartrain) and freshwater fishing; these are required whether fishing from shore or from a boat. Certain types of crabbing and shrimping also require a license, but crawfishing does not. For licenses or information about fishing regulations, contact the **Louisiana Department of Wildlife and Fisheries** (⊠ Box 98000, Baton Rouge 70898, ☎ 225/765–2800).

Bayou Sauvage National Wildlife Refuge (☞ Canoeing, *above*) offers some of the best fishing of local brackish and freshwater species. The refuge is open year-round, with superior fishing from winter to early spring.

For $2 per day **City Park** (☞ Boating, *above*) issues one-day permits (sunup to sundown) that allow fishing for perch, catfish, and bass from the shore of the stocked streams in the park. A state license ($5.50) is also required and can be purchased at the same time.

Golf

The public can golf at the following courses in the New Orleans area.

Across the street from Tulane and Loyola universities, **Audubon Park** has an 18-hole golf course (par-68 for men, par-69 for women), a pro shop, and a snack bar. ⊠ *473 Walnut St.,* ☎ *504/865–8260.* ☜ *Greens fee: weekdays $9, weekends $12.*

Ten miles south of downtown New Orleans, between Terrytown and Tall Timbers on the west bank of the Mississippi River, the **Brechtel Golf Course** is a basic 18-hole, par-70 course; amenities include a pro shop, driving range, and snack bar. ⊠ *3700 Behrman Pl.,* ☎ *504/362–4761.* ☜ *Greens fee: weekdays $7.75, weekends $10.*

City Park, trimmed in moss-draped live oak trees, has four 18-hole courses, all under the banner **Bayou Oaks Golf Courses.** Facilities include a lighted, 100-tee double-decker driving range, a pro shop, and a restaurant. The par-72 Championship Course is the best. ⊠ *1040 Filmore Ave.,* ☎ *504/483–9396.* ☜ *Greens fee: $11–$17 depending on the course and the day of the week.*

In eastern New Orleans, about 12 mi from downtown, the **Joe Bartholomew Golf Course** has an 18-hole, par-72 course and a pro shop. ⊠ *6514 Congress Dr.,* ☎ *504/288–0928.* ☜ *Greens fee: weekdays $7.75, weekends $11.*

The **Oak Harbor Country Club,** about 25 mi northeast of downtown, has a very good 18-hole, par-72 course and a pro shop, snack bar, and driving range. Prices include cart rentals. ⊠ *201 Oak Harbor Blvd., Slidell,* ☎ *504/646–0110.* ☜ *Greens fee: Mon.–Thurs. $39–$49; Fri. $49–$59; weekends $59–$69.*

Health and Fitness Clubs

Many hotels and even some guest houses have exercise rooms, but if yours does not, a number of clubs welcome guests.

In the CBD, the **Rivercenter Racquet & Health Club** (⊠ New Orleans Hilton Riverside, 2 Poydras St., ☎ 504/561–0500) charges nonguests $10 per day for the use of its Nautilus equipment, free weights, jogging track, sauna, pools, 4-hole putting green and driving range, and tennis, squash, and racquetball courts.

Le Meridien New Orleans (⊠ 614 Canal St., ☎ 504/525–6500) charges nonguests $12 per day for using its health club, with its Nautilus equipment, sauna, dumbbells, pool, and beauty salon.

For a daily charge of $8, nonmembers may use the facilities of the **YMCA Lee Circle** (⊠ 920 St. Charles Ave., ☎ 504/568–9622), which has an Olympic-size pool, free weights, walking and running tracks, basketball and volleyball courts, and saunas.

The **Mackie Shilstone Pro Spa** (⊠ 2111 St. Charles Ave., ☎ 504/679–7691), in the Avenue Plaza Hotel in the Garden District, charges $9 per day for use of its facilities and services, which include treadmills, stair climbers, bikes, rowing machines, weights, a sauna, massages, and herbal wraps.

Hiking

The Barataria Unit of **Jean Lafitte National Historical Park** (☞ Canoeing, *above*) has 8 mi of boardwalk and hard-surface trails that explore Louisiana's delta wetlands and important archaeological sites. A park ranger gives a guided tour daily at 1:15.

The **Linear Parkway** that runs along the south shore of Lake Pontchartrain is a popular 7½-mi route for hiking and biking (☞ Bayou St. John–Lakefront *in* Chapter 1).

Louisiana Nature and Science Center (⊠ 11000 Lake Forest Blvd., New Orleans East, ☎ 504/246–9381) plans hiking and backpacking excursions into areas around New Orleans; call for details.

Horseback Riding

Cascade Stables in Audubon Park rents horses for riding within the boundaries of the park. Located east of the zoo, off a one-way side road that runs into Magazine Street, the stables are hard to find the first time, but most people in the area will be happy to give directions. ⊠ 6500 Magazine St., ☎ 504/891–2246. 🎫 1-hr ride with guide $20. ☉ Daily 9–5; last trail ride at 4.

Ice-skating

Holiday Ice Rink, the city's only outdoor rink, is adjacent to the Wisner Tennis Center in City Park. Besides skating sessions for the public, there are lessons, figure-skating exhibitions, and hockey demonstrations. Admission includes skate rental for a 90-minute session. ⊠ Victory Ave. at Dreyfous Dr., ☎ 504/522–7465. 🎫 $9. ☉ Mid-Nov.–early Mar., Sun.–Thurs. 10–10, Fri.–Sat. 10–midnight.

Jogging

Audubon Park, between St. Charles Avenue and Magazine Street, has a 2-mi jogging path that passes several scenic lagoons as it encircles the golf course. Exercise stations parallel the trail. **City Park** (⊠ Dreyfous Dr.) is popular for jogging. The Mississippi River levee, especially at **Woldenberg Riverfront Park** from Canal Street to Esplanade Avenue, is an appealing place to run.

Locals sometimes jog in the streetcar tracks, facing the direction from which the streetcar approaches. This is because sidewalks are often uneven due to cracks in the pavement caused by oak roots; and streets are not generally well lighted. Several organized running events held in New Orleans are open to the public (☞ Spectator Sports, *below*).

Tennis

Audubon Park has 10 courts at the back of the park, off Tchoupitoulas Street. ☎ 504/895–1042. ☒ *$6.* ☾ *Daily 8–dark.*

City Park has 36 lighted courts and a pro shop. ☒ *Dreyfous Dr.,* ☎ *504/483–9383.* ☒ *$5.50–$6.50.* ☾ *Weekdays 7 AM–10 PM, weekends 7 AM–6 PM.*

Volleyball

Coconut Beach Volleyball Complex (☒ 7360 W. Roadway, West End, ☎ 504/286–0333), near Lake Pontchartrain, is an open-air sandlot where locals meet for coed games. Unless leagues or tournaments are scheduled, playing is open to anyone for a small fee. Visitors are welcome.

SPECTATOR SPORTS

Baseball

The **New Orleans Zephyrs** (☒ 6000 Airline Hwy., Metairie, ☎ 504/734–5155), the triple-A farm club of Major League Baseball's Houston Astros, play home games from early April until late August at a 10,000-seat stadium across from the NFL Saints' training camp. Tickets cost $5–$9.

Tulane University (☎ 504/865–5005), the **University of New Orleans** (☎ 504/280–6357) and **Delgado Community College** (☎ 504/483–4381) also field top-flight collegiate teams in the spring.

Basketball

The collegiate **Sugar Bowl Basketball Tournament** is held at the Louisiana Superdome (☒ 1 Sugar Bowl Dr., ☎ 504/525–8573 for tournament information) in late December, preceding the annual football classic. The University of New Orleans plays NCAA Division I competition; other schools, including Delgado Community College, Dillard, Xavier, and Southern University, also have teams that play home games at gyms and field houses on their respective campuses. Tulane's home games are split between the on-campus Fogelman Arena and the New Orleans Arena (☒ 1501 Girod St.), behind the Superdome.

Football

The Louisiana Superdome (☒ 1 Sugar Bowl Dr.) is the place for football. On Sunday the **New Orleans Saints** (☎ 504/731–1700) of the National Football League play their home games. Preseason games start in August; the regular season runs from early September through late December. Tickets are $65–$95. ☾

On Saturday afternoon you can usually catch **Tulane University's** (☎ 504/865–5355) home games. The famed LSU–Tulane game is played at the Superdome in odd-number years. Grambling and Southern universities renew their annual rivalry in the **Bayou Classic** each Novem-

ber. On New Year's Day the Superdome hosts the **Sugar Bowl** (☎ 504/
525–8573). In 2002, the **Super Bowl** (☎ 504/566–5011 for information) will be played in New Orleans.

Golf

In April the nation's top professional golfers compete in the PGA's **Entergy Classic** at English Turn Country Club (✉ Rte. 406, East Canal,
English Turn, ☎ 504/831–4653), which has a Jack Nicklaus–designed
golf course.

Horse Racing

At the **Fair Grounds,** the third-oldest racetrack in the nation, the sea-
son opens Thanksgiving Day and runs through mid-April. Big races
include the New Orleans Handicap for older horses and the Louisiana
Derby for three-year-olds, a major warm-up for the Kentucky Derby.
Both are run in March. ✉ *1751 Gentilly Blvd.,* ☎ *504/944–5515.* ☉
Post time Thanksgiving–mid-Apr., daily 12:30 PM.

Ice Hockey

The **New Orleans Brass** is a minor league club in the East Coast
Hockey League. At press time the International Hockey League and
the National Hockey League were in negotiations for fielding a pro
hockey team in New Orleans. The Brass plays home games in the New
Orleans Arena (✉ 1501 Girod St., ☎ 504/522–7825), behind the
Louisiana Superdome. The season runs from mid-October until late
March or early April; tickets are $8–$20.

Running

Tad Gormley Stadium/Alerion Field (✉ Off Marconi Blvd., ☎ 504/483–
9496), in City Park, is a state-of-the-art track facility for local and national events.

Many organized runs take place in New Orleans every year. These include the **Mardi Gras Marathon** in January, the **Crescent City Classic** in
March or April, **Witches Moonlight Run** the night before Halloween,
and the **Corporate Run** in December.

For information on running events and marathons in the city, contact
the **Southern Runners** (☎ 504/891–9999).

6   SHOPPING

New Orleans makes a strong impression:
it's no surprise that travelers want to take a
bit of the city home with them. You can try
your luck at duplicating jambalaya, gumbo,
or beignets with packaged mixes, spices,
and cookbooks; re-create Mardi Gras with
masks, beads, and doubloons; and replay
the sounds of the city with recordings of
jazz, blues, and zydeco. Voodoo dolls also
make fun gifts (just make sure you're on
good terms with the recipient).

Updated by
Honey Naylor

THE FUN OF SHOPPING IN NEW ORLEANS is in the many regional items available throughout the city, in the smallest shops or the biggest department stores. You can take home some of the flavor of the city: its pralines (pecan candies), seafood (packaged to go), Louisiana red beans and rice, coffee (pure or with chicory), and Creole and Cajun spices (cayenne pepper, chili, and garlic). There are even packaged mixes of such local favorites as jambalaya, gumbo, beignets, and the sweet red local cocktail called the Hurricane. A variety of cookbooks also share the secrets of preparing distinctive New Orleans dishes.

Beautiful posters celebrating Mardi Gras, the New Orleans Jazz & Heritage Festival, and the Crescent City Classic all are issued each year and quickly become collector's items. Ceramic or feather masks can serve as attire during Mardi Gras and as attractive wall hangings during the rest of the year. Mardi Gras costumes, beads, and doubloons make wonderful gifts, too. Posters, photographs, and paintings on canvas and slate capture scenes in New Orleans. Jewelry, antiques, ceramics, carved wooden toys, kites, jazz umbrellas, and wreaths of dried flowers are often handmade and make lovely gifts and souvenirs.

The sounds of New Orleans are available in music stores and in certain live-music venues (such as Preservation Hall) throughout the city. There is a wide spectrum, including old Dixieland jazz, contemporary jazz, swinging Cajun and zydeco, and the hot, sweet wail of rhythm and blues.

All major bookstores carry books about the city; local history and photography books are especially popular. Good bets are cookbooks, guides to special-interest sightseeing, and books that specialize in local ethnic history. The city has a number of small, independently operated bookshops where perseverance can yield some real finds in local literature and lore. Stock in these shops often includes old photographs, posters, and postcards.

There are many clothing shops that offer items popular in the semitropical heat: Panama hats, lacy lingerie, and the ubiquitous T-shirt and sports clothes. Designer fashions are available in such national department stores as Macy's and Saks Fifth Avenue, and delightful vintage clothing is sold in several shops.

Shopping guides can be found in most of the tourist magazines available in hotel rooms and lobbies. The Welcome Center of the New Orleans Metropolitan Convention and Visitors Bureau on the St. Ann Street side of Jackson Square also has pamphlets on shopping.

For information on store hours, *see* Business Hours *in* Smart Travel Tips A to Z. If you're visiting from outside the United States, *see* Taxes *in* Smart Travel Tips A to Z for information about a sales-tax rebate.

Shopping Areas

The main shopping areas in the city are the French Quarter, with its narrow streets lined with specialty, gift, and antiques shops and art galleries; the Central Business District (CBD), including Canal Street, which has department stores and clothing and jewelry shops; Magazine Street, known for its antiques shops and galleries; the Warehouse District, popular for Julia Street's contemporary arts galleries; and Uptown, with its neighborhood and specialty shops in several fashionable shopping areas.

Blitz Tours

Study your map and then plunge into one of the following shopping itineraries arranged by special interest.

Mardi Gras Shopping Blitz

New Orleans during Mardi Gras is not for the faint of heart. Even if you think you're bashful, get a couple of parades under your belt and you'll be out bagging beads with the rest of 'em, hollering and scrambling. Carnival is a time for letting down your hair and just generally getting down. Way down. No, you don't have to make a complete fool of yourself, but hey! Everybody else does. Maybe you'll enter the Mardi Gras Mask-A-Thon on Canal Street, a Fat Tuesday tradition. Having now made the decision to get into the swing of things, you'll want to choose your costume and mask. In the French Quarter, a good starting place is the **Community Flea Market** (⊠ French Market Pl.), where face-painters go hog-wild and fanciful duds might be found. From there, walk over to Chartres Street to check out the wigs and way-out make-up at **Fifi Mahoney's** (⊠ 828 Chartres St.). A few doors over from Fifi's you can root through the bear suits and belly-dance gear at the **Mardi Gras Center** (⊠ 831 Chartres St.). Around the corner, you can find stunning handmade masks at the **Little Shop of Fantasy** (⊠ 523 Dumaine St.). There are masks and more masks over on Royal Street, at **Rumors** (⊠ 513 Royal St.) and its sister shop, **Rumors Too** (⊠ 319 Royal St.). You won't be far from Canal Place, where you can look over the locally made masks at **Rhino.** Nearby are still more beautifully crafted masks at **Masks and Make Believe** (⊠ Riverwalk Marketplace). If you've decided to costume in vintage clothing, take the Magazine Street bus and browse through the threads at **Ragin' Daisy** (⊠ 3125 Magazine St.). Just remember, the Lord of Misrule rules during Mardi Gras, so suit up, step out, and have a ball.

N'Awlins to Go—Food Shopping Blitz

Face it: there's no way you're going to make it to all of those famous New Orleans restaurants. But you can take a taste of the city home with you, boxed though it may be. It's almost unheard of for anyone to leave town without at least one box of sweet-sweet pralines. Locals and tourists alike turn up at all hours for café au lait and sugary beignets at **Café du Monde** (⊠ 800 Decatur St.), which sells Creole coffee and boxed beignet mix. It will ship anywhere in the country, so you can try your hand at making these hole-less doughnuts. (There are branches in Riverwalk Marketplace and Kenner's Esplanade Mall; ⊠ 1401 W. Esplanade Ave.) Across Decatur Street is **Louisiana Products** (⊠ 507 St. Ann St., on Jackson Sq.), which sells coffee and beignet mix, as well as Cajun and Creole spices. Quarterites think the best pralines in town are those made at the **Old Town Pralines** (⊠ 627 Royal St.). Before continuing on Royal, walk over to **Gumbo Ya-Ya** (⊠ 219 Bourbon St.), which sells spices, coffee, and beignet mix. Head back to Royal to **Laura's Original Fudge and Praline Shoppe** (⊠ 115 Royal St.) to study the options there. You'll then be at Royal and Canal streets, close to **Riverwalk Marketplace,** which is loaded with candy shops. And if you can't quite duplicate the taste of N'Awlins beignets and pralines—well, you'll just have to return to N'Awlins. Like everybody else.

CBD

Canal Place (⊠ 333 Canal St., ☎ 504/587–0739) draws fashionable shoppers to 60 shops that include Saks Fifth Avenue, Gucci, Williams-Sonoma, the Pottery Barn, Laura Ashley, and Brooks Brothers. The **New Orleans Centre** (⊠ 1400 Poydras St., ☎ 504/568–0000), a shopping complex between the Superdome and the Hyatt Regency hotel, houses Macy's and Lord & Taylor.

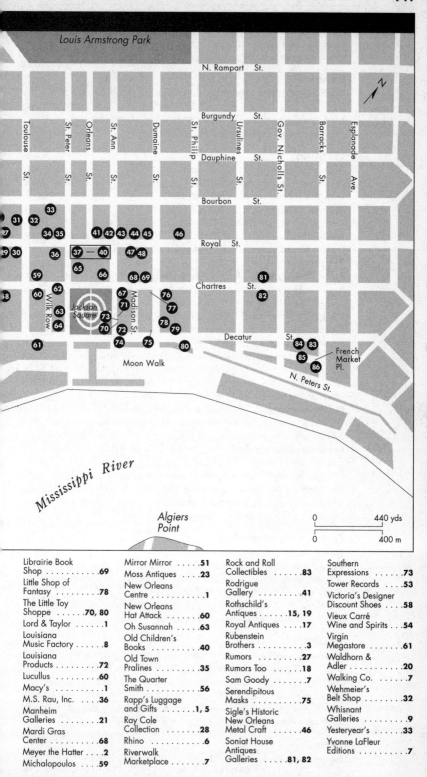

Riverwalk Marketplace (✉ 1 Poydras St., ☎ 504/522–1555), along the riverfront (☞ Foot of Canal Street and Algiers Point *in* Chapter 1), has a ½-mi-long marketplace with 180 local and nationally known shops and restaurants, including Café du Monde.

Books

Deville Books and Prints (✉ Riverwalk Marketplace, ☎ 504/595–8916; ✉ 344 Carondelet St., ☎ 504/525–1846), a locally owned bookstore specializing in New Orleans books and collectibles, is the place for local literary memorabilia.

Clothing

Abercrombie & Fitch (✉ Riverwalk Marketplace, ☎ 504/522–7156) carries fine sportswear and casual clothes that have become popular with the alternative and Gen X crowds.

Banana Republic (✉ Riverwalk Marketplace, ☎ 504/523–684; ✉ Canal Place, ☎ 504/581–2478) displays stylish, tailored casual wear.

Brooks Brothers (✉ Canal Place, ☎ 504/522–4200) is internationally known for classic, tailored clothing for men; you'll find women's wear here, too.

Cajun Clothing Co. (✉ Riverwalk Marketplace, ☎ 504/581–6746), an outlet of Perlis (☞ Magazine Street, *below*), carries clothing for men, women, and children, as well as novelty items.

Clarks (✉ Riverwalk Marketplace, ☎ 504/568–0070), with footwear for men and women, is a good place to look for Havana Joe, Birkenstock, Rockport, and BeautiFeel shoes.

Gap (✉ Riverwalk Marketplace, ☎ 504/529–4962) and its siblings GapKids and Baby Gap (✉ Riverwalk Marketplace, ☎ 504/522–5828) are great places to shop for comfortable, straightforward fashions for infants, children, and young adults.

Meyer the Hatter (✉ 120 St. Charles Ave., ☎ 504/525–1048 or 800/882–4287), which has been in operation for more than a century, has a large selection of Stetsons, Dobbs, Biltmore hats, and baseball caps.

Rubenstein Brothers (✉ 102 St. Charles Ave., ☎ 504/581–6666), a local, family-owned men's clothier, carries casual and formal attire by Gucci, Giorgio Armani, Donna Karan, and other designers.

The Walking Co. (✉ Riverwalk Marketplace, ☎ 504/522–9255) carries sturdy men's and women's shoes and canvas hats, as well as hiking staffs and orthopedic walking sticks.

Department Stores

Lord & Taylor (✉ New Orleans Centre, 1400 Poydras St., ☎ 504/581–5673) sells designer and casual clothes with a classic look for men, women, and children and carries other department store fare.

Macy's (✉ New Orleans Centre, 1400 Poydras St., ☎ 504/592–5985) is a New York–headquartered department store that sells fashions for all ages, linens, housewares, and more.

Food

Riverwalk Marketplace (☞ *above*) has many local restaurants and food retailers. Evans Creole Candies (☎ 504/581–4641) sells pralines and other goodies. Creole Delicacies (☎ 504/586–8832) is among the best places to shop for local food products. Godiva Chocolatiers (☎ 504/522–1269) is renowned the world over for its elegantly shaped and packaged chocolates, even if they aren't a local specialty.

Gifts

Rapp's Luggage and Gifts (✉ 604 Canal St., ☎ 504/568–1953; ✉ New Orleans Centre, ☎ 504/566–0700; ✉ 1628 St. Charles Ave., ☎ 504/524–5400) is a locally owned variety store, specializing in fine leather goods and unusual gift items such as a briefcase that serves as a portable bar.

Rhino (✉ Canal Place, ☎ 504/523–7945) has locally made handicrafts, including Mardi Gras masks, paintings, jewelry, and ceramics.

Riverwalk Marketplace (☞ *above*) has dozens of specialty shops with dazzling displays of toys, crafts, cards, and curios. Look for Masks and Make Believe (☎ 504/522–6473), Kites, Tails and Toys (☎ 504/529–3247), The Great Train Store (☎ 504/581–3531), and The New Orleans Cat House (☎ 504/581–1479).

Jewelry

Adler & Sons (✉ 722 Canal St., ☎ 504/523–5292) is a family-owned local store with top-of-the-line jewelry, watches, and silver.

Bernard K. Passman Gallery (✉ Riverwalk Marketplace, ☎ 504/525–4581) displays black-coral jewelry and collectibles crafted by the eponymous artist, who's in his eighties.

Music

Sam Goody (✉ Riverwalk Marketplace, ☎ 504/588–1385), part of the nationwide chain, has a large inventory of records, CDs, and tapes, including Dixieland, historical jazz, and rhythm and blues.

French Quarter

The charm of this area and its fascinating merchandise should be enjoyed at a leisurely pace. Remember, there's always a bistro or café nearby for a rest stop. Rents in the Quarter have risen sharply, forcing some small shops to relocate. Bourbon Street, alas, is lined with souvenir shops that sell postcards, T-shirts, and plenty of ticky-tacky stuff.

Jackson Brewery Corporation (✉ 600 Decatur St., ☎ 504/586–8015) operates three indoor malls that house a mix of local shops and national chains. The Brewhouse, on Decatur Street across from Jackson Square, occupies a historic building in which Jax beer was once brewed. A Planet Hollywood restaurant and a Virgin Megastore loaded with books and music each occupy considerable square footage in the Brewhouse. Adjacent to the Brewhouse, and connected by indoor and outdoor walkways, is the Millhouse. Two blocks toward Canal Street, the Marketplace is in the 400 block of North Peters Street.

Antiques

The French Quarter is well known for its fine antiques shops, located mainly on Royal and Chartres streets. **The Royal Street Guild** (☎ 504/949–2222), a merchants' association, places informative brochures in shops and hotels.

Local antiques shopping consultant **Macon Riddle** (☎ 504/899–3027) conducts half- and full-day shopping expeditions by appointment.

Diane Genre Oriental Art and Antiques (☎ 504/595–8945) showcases Chinese furniture and Japanese textiles and woodblock prints, and a major collection of Japanese cloisonné. Obtain the store's address by phoning for an appointment.

French Antique Shop (✉ 225 Royal St., ☎ 504/524–9861) displays a large selection of European chandeliers and furniture, sconces, mirrors, porcelain objects, and marble mantels.

Lucullus (✉ 610 Chartres St., ☎ 504/528–9620; ✉ 3932 Magazine St., ☎ 504/894–0500) carries 17th- to 19th-century Continental and English furniture, art, and cookware, all relating to the culinary arts.

M. S. Rau, Inc. (✉ 630 Royal St., ☎ 504/523–5660 or 800/544–9440), a tremendous source for Victorian furniture, stocks American, French,

English, and Asian furniture, as well as china (including Wedgwood), American cut glass, silver, ornamental ironwork, and estate jewelry.

Manheim Galleries (⊠ 403–409 Royal St., ☎ 504/568–1901) has porcelains, paintings, silver, stunning jade, and a large collection of antique English, Continental, Asian, and custom-made furnishings. This is the agent for the porcelain Boehm Birds.

Mirror Mirror (⊠ 301 Chartres St., ☎ 504/566–1990), aptly named, gleams with mirrors from the Victorian and Art Deco eras as well as more contemporary pieces.

Moss Antiques (⊠ 411 Royal St., ☎ 504/522–3981) has a large selection of walking sticks and antique and estate jewels, as well as fine French and English furnishings, paintings, boxes, and bric-a-brac.

Rothschild's Antiques (⊠ 241 and 321 Royal St., ☎ 504/523–5816) carries English and French furniture, and an extensive selection of silver, jewelry, mantels, and clocks from the 18th through the 20th centuries.

Royal Antiques (⊠ 307–309 Royal St., ☎ 504/524–7033) specializes in French and English 18th- and 19th-century furnishings.

Soniat House Antiques Galleries (⊠ 1130, 1138, and 1139 Chartres St., ☎ 504/522–0570), run by the owner of the Soniat House hotel (☞ French Quarter *in* Chapter 3), sells mostly European antiques such as furniture, chandeliers, and mirrors.

Waldhorn & Adler (⊠ 343 Royal St., ☎ 504/581–6379) is New Orleans's oldest antiques store, established in 1881. It sells English furniture, Victorian and other jewelry, and English porcelain and silver.

Whisnant Galleries (⊠ 222 Chartres St., ☎ 504/524–9766) carries delightfully eclectic antique jewelry, African sculptures, art, furniture, and unusual pieces.

Art and Crafts Galleries

Animal Art (⊠ 617 Chartres St., ☎ 504/529–4407), a good source for Majolica and Palissy ware, specializes in fine furniture, paintings, and ceramics, all depicting animals.

Bergen Galleries (⊠ 730 Royal St., ☎ 504/523–7882) showcases collectibles and the city's largest display of posters, including ones for Mardi Gras and Jazz Fest, by local artists.

The Black Art Collection (⊠ 309 Chartres St., ☎ 504/529–3080) focuses on the works of major local and national black artists; inventory includes posters, jazz images, and antique African artifacts.

Circle Gallery (⊠ 316 Royal St., ☎ 504/523–1350) sells paintings, sculptures, and graphics by internationally known artists, including Vaskely, Lebadang, and Peter Max, as well as jewelry by Erté and drawings by Walt Disney.

The Crabnet (⊠ 925 Decatur St., ☎ 504/522–3478) has a large collection of wood ducks and decoys, mostly by Louisiana carvers and wildlife artists.

Dyansen Gallery (⊠ 433 Royal St., ☎ 504/523–2902) displays a comprehensive collection of Erté's sculpture, lithographs, and serigraphs, as well as art by Paul Wegner, Martinique, and Sasonne.

Elliott Galleries (⊠ 540 Royal St., ☎ 504/524–8696), a long-established, locally owned gallery, exhibits and sells works of contemporary European artists such as Theo Tobiasse, Max Pappart, and James Coignard. Formerly Nahan Galleries, it is still operated by the same family.

Eye on the Square (⊠ 514 St. Peter St., ☎ 504/522–9988) has an extensive collection of African-American art, including ceramics, paintings, masks, and figurines.

A Gallery for Fine Photography (⊠ 322 Royal St., ☎ 504/568–1313), bastion of local fine-art photographer Joseph Pailet, sells works by lead-

When it Comes to Getting
Cash at an ATM,
Same Thing.

Whether you're in Yosemite or Yemen, using your Visa® card or ATM card with the PLUS symbol is the easiest and most convenient way to get cash. Even if your bank is in Minneapolis and you're in Miami, Visa/PLUS ATMs make getting cash so easy, you'll feel right at home. After all, Visa/PLUS ATMs are open 24 hours a day, 7 days a week, rain or shine. And if you need help finding one of Visa's 627,000 ATMs in 127 countries worldwide, visit **visa.com/pd/atm**. We'll make finding an ATM as easy as finding the Eiffel Tower, the Pyramids or even the Grand Canyon.

It's Everywhere You Want To Be.®

ONE LAST TRAVEL TIP:

Pack an easy way to reach the world.

Wherever you travel, the MCI WorldCom Card℠ is the easiest way to stay in touch. You can use it to call to and from more than 125 countries worldwide. And you can earn bonus miles every time you use your card. So go ahead, travel the world. MCI WorldCom℠ makes it even more rewarding. For additional access codes, visit www.wcom.com/worldphone.

EASY TO CALL WORLDWIDE

1. Just dial the WorldPhone® access number of the country you're calling from.

2. Dial or give the operator your MCI WorldCom Card number.

3. Dial or give the number you're calling.

Aruba (A) ÷	800-888-8
Australia ◆	1-800-881-100
Bahamas ÷	1-800-888-8000
Barbados (A) ÷	1-800-888-8000
Bermuda ÷	1-800-888-8000
British Virgin Islands (A) ÷	1-800-888-8000
Canada	1-800-888-8000
Costa Rica (A) ◆	0800-012-2222
New Zealand	000-912
Puerto Rico	1-800-888-8000
United States	1-800-888-8000
U.S. Virgin Islands	1-800-888-8000

(A) Calls back to U.S. only. ÷ Limited availability. ◆ Public phones may require deposit of coin or phone card for dial tone.

EARN FREQUENT FLIER MILES

ing American and European photographers, past and present, as well as rare 19th-century photographs and books.

Hanson Galleries (⊠ 229 Royal St., ☎ 504/566–0816) concentrates on contemporary master graphics and originals by internationally known artists (Miró, Calder, Tamayo), and also carries some local works.

Kurt E. Schon, Ltd. (⊠ 510 St. Louis St., ☎ 504/524–5462) stocks art from the 17th through the 20th centuries and has a stunning collection of landscapes and portraits. The staff is very knowledgeable.

LMS Fine Art & Antiques (⊠ 729 Royal St., ☎ 504/529–3774) displays Russian furnishings and objets d'art, including the popular marioshka (stacked) dolls.

Michalopoulos (⊠ 617 Chartres St., ☎ 504/558–0505) presents New Orleans architecture and street scenes captured in the oil paintings and lithographs of James Michalopoulos.

Rodrigue Gallery (⊠ 721 Royal St., ☎ 504/581–4244 or 800/899–4244) showcases the work of internationally known Cajun artist George Rodrigue. His "blue dog" paintings are especially popular.

Southern Expressions (⊠ 521 St. Ann St., Jackson Sq., ☎ 504/525–4530) carries paintings, prints, and watercolors by local artists.

Books

Cookbooks and local history books are available in gift shops throughout the Quarter. Fun for any collector are the various musty used-book shops that proliferate in this area.

BookStar (⊠ 414 N. Peters St., ☎ 504/523–6411), owned by Barnes & Noble, is a huge store with an extensive inventory, including works by local and regional writers.

Faulkner House Books (⊠ 624 Pirate's Alley, ☎ 504/524–2940), in the house where William Faulkner lived and wrote in the 1920s, is stocked with rare and out-of-print books by Southern authors. It's a real find for bibliophiles.

Librairie Book Shop (⊠ 823 Chartres St., ☎ 504/525–4837) has the Quarter's largest selection of local lore in books, old posters, and postcards.

Old Children's Books (⊠ 734 Royal St., ☎ 504/525–3655) stocks antiquarian and out-of-print children's literature.

Clothing and Accessories

Fifi Mahoney's (⊠ 828 Chartres St., ☎ 504/525–4343) carries Urban Decay and other cosmetics, as well as wigs and other fun accessories.

Fleur de Paris (⊠ 712 Royal St., ☎ 504/525–1899), an innovative and elegant women's apparel shop, sells designer dresses, custom hats, and silk lingerie.

New Orleans Hat Attack (⊠ Jackson Brewery Millhouse, 600 Decatur St., ☎ 504/523–5770), a fun place to visit, is New Orleans's last word in headgear for men and women.

Ray Cole Collection (⊠ 503 Royal St., ☎ 504/588–1194) showcases the award-winning designer's paintings of local scenes on silk dresses and scarves. Look for his voodoo doll motifs.

Victoria's Designer Discount Shoes (⊠ 532 Chartres St., ☎ 504/568–9990; ⊠ 7725 Maple St., ☎ 504/861–8861) carries famous-name shoes, such as Charles David, Madsen Mason, and Enzo, at substantial discounts.

Wehmeier's Belt Shop (⊠ 719 Toulouse St., ☎ 504/525–2758) displays finely crafted alligator and exotic leather goods, including belts, wallets, handbags, boots, and shoes.

Food and Gift Packages

Café du Monde (⊠ 800 Decatur St., ☎ 504/525–4544), a French Quarter landmark, sells its delicious Creole coffee in 15-ounce cans

(13-ounce cans for the decaf). Also available is the mix for beignets, the French doughnuts that accompany the coffee. The shop will ship anywhere in the country.

Coffee, Tea, or . . . (✉ 630 St. Ann St., ☎ 504/522–0830) stocks teas, spices of the world, and gift items.

Farmers' Market (✉ N. Peters St. in the French Market, ☎ 504/522–2621) is an open-air emporium where Louisiana's farmers sell their produce. The variety of local fruits and vegetables available in season includes pecans, sugarcane, mirlitons, Creole tomatoes, and okra. Garlic wreaths hang from the rafters of the building where the great chefs of New Orleans shop for their kitchens.

Gumbo Ya-Ya (✉ 219 Bourbon St., ☎ 504/522–7484) carries pralines, spices, cookbooks, and gift packages.

Laura's Original Fudge and Praline Shoppe (✉ 115 Royal St., ☎ 504/525–3886) has pralines (made fresh daily), hand-dipped chocolates, Creole spices, and other local favorites.

Louisiana Products (✉ 507 St. Ann St., on Jackson Sq., ☎ 504/524–7331) showcases Cajun and Creole foods, Mardi Gras beads, local crafts, and novelties. Gift boxes of food items can be shipped anywhere.

Old Town Pralines (✉ 627 Royal St., ☎ 504/525–1413) has pralines that many locals believe are the best in town. You can buy them individually or by the box, and they'll ship them for you.

Vieux Carré Wine and Spirits (✉ 422 Chartres St., ☎ 504/568–9463) serves wine by the glass and has frequent wine-tasting events. The store offers a large selection of imported and domestic beers, wines, spirits, and cheeses. Gift baskets are available.

Jewelry

Currents . . . (✉ 305 Royal St., ☎ 504/522–6099) is a chic store in which Terry and Sylvia Weidert create their own designs in 14- and 18-karat gold and platinum.

Gerald D. Katz Antiques (✉ 505 Royal St., ☎ 504/524–5050) showcases antique and estate jewelry, as well as decorative arts.

Joan Good Antiques (✉ 809 Royal St., ☎ 504/525–1705) has beautiful garnets, cameos, blue topaz, and marcasite creations, as well as some antique Japanese pieces.

The Quarter Smith (✉ 535 St. Louis St., ☎ 504/524–9731) carries estate jewelry; Ken Bowers will also create a piece of your own design.

Masks

The masks worn at Mardi Gras are popular as gifts, souvenirs, and decorative pieces. Be careful of cheap imitations; the better handcrafted, locally made masks bear the artist's insignia and are more expensive than the mass-produced ones. A good ceramic or feather mask starts at around $10 and can run as high as $1,000, depending on the materials, artistry, and size of the mask.

Little Shop of Fantasy (✉ 523 Dumaine St., ☎ 504/529–4243) showcases the handmade leather-and-feather masks of Mike Stark.

Mardi Gras Center (✉ 831 Chartres St., ☎ 504/524–4384) is where locals serious about Carnival go for custom-made masks, costumes, and accessories. Hundreds of masks, including animal ones, make this a great place to browse.

Rumors (✉ 513 Royal St., ☎ 504/525–0292) and **Rumors Too** (✉ 319 Royal St., ☎ 504/523–0011) both have large selections of top-of-the-line ceramic and feather masks.

Serendipitous Masks (✉ 831 Decatur St., ☎ 504/522–9158) has an excellent selection of feather masks made by artists on the premises. The shop carries an extensive array of ornate Mardi Gras headdresses, and masks can be made to order.

Yesteryear's (⊠ 626 Bourbon St., ☎ 504/523–6603) is a welcome alternative to the T-shirt and poster shops on Bourbon Street. Owner Teresa Latshaw makes her own elaborate feather masks. Voodoo dolls and folklore items are also sold.

Music

GHB Jazz Foundation (⊠ 1204 Decatur St., ☎ 504/525–0200) operates eight record labels and publishes the quarterly *Jazzbeat*. The music store is in the Palm Court Jazz Café (☞ Nightlife *in* Chapter 4).

Louisiana Music Factory (⊠ 210 Decatur St., ☎ 504/586–1094) showcases regional music and carries videos, posters, books, and T-shirts. And if that isn't enough, they also have the occasional jam session.

Rock and Roll Collectibles (⊠ 1214 Decatur St., ☎ 504/561–5683) buys, sells, and trades an array of records, tapes, CDs, and videos. The shop specializes in rock and roll, especially by local artists.

Tower Records (⊠ 408 N. Peters St. ☎ 504/529–4411), a huge branch of the national chain, sells records, CDs, and DVDs. Nearby is Tower Video.

Virgin Megastore (⊠ Jackson Brewhouse, 620 Decatur St., ☎ 504/671–8100) has four floors of records, CDs, DVDs, videos, and books, including a good selection of Louisiana music and books.

Novelties and Gifts

Angel Wings (⊠ 710 St. Louis St., ☎ 504/524–6880), a whimsical Victorian shop, displays handcrafted and unique items, including wearable ceramics, art gifts, crystals, and hair sticks.

Café Havana (⊠ 842 Royal St., ☎ 504/569–9006 or 800/860–2988) sells cigars and cigar accoutrements, and operates a bar as well.

Coghlan Gallery (⊠ 710 Toulouse St., ☎ 504/525–8550), housed in the historic Lion's Court, has a peaceful courtyard with displays of locally crafted fountains, statuary, and other garden accessories.

Community Flea Market (⊠ The French Market at Gov. Nicholls St., ☎ 504/596–3420) is an open-air market with dozens of tables displaying everything imaginable: jewelry, antiques, clothing, leather goods, and local crafts. It's open daily 7 AM–8 PM, though hours vary with weather and season.

Crafty Louisianians (⊠ 813 Royal St., ☎ 504/528–3094), which resembles a local crafts fair, showcases New Orleans and Louisiana wares, such as carved ducks and birds, cypress knees, Mississippi mud dolls, and designs on slate.

Esoterica (⊠ 541 Dumaine St., ☎ 504/581–7711) specializes in "Tools of the Occult Arts and Sciences," such as gris-gris, potions, and books on the occult. The shop also offers tarot readings.

The Idea Factory (⊠ 838 Chartres St., ☎ 504/524–5195) stocks one-of-a-kind gifts, such as miniature steamboats, streetcars, and antique cars, as well as puzzles and puzzle boxes. Most items are handmade by owner Kenny Ford.

Importico's (⊠ 736 Royal St., ☎ 504/523–0306; ⊠ 517 St. Louis St., ☎ 504/523–3100, ⊠ Riverwalk Marketplace, ☎ 504/581–5333; ⊠ 5523 Magazine St., ☎ 504/891–6141) imports handcrafted items, such as jewelry, chess sets, lamps, and clothing, from Indonesia, Mexico, Bali, and other exotic spots.

Sigle's Historic New Orleans Metal Craft (⊠ 935 Royal St., ☎ 504/522–7647) sells original cast-iron wall planters, handcrafted since 1938; these are often seen on Quarter balconies and patios.

Perfumes

Bourbon French Parfums (⊠ 525 St. Ann St., ☎ 504/522–4480) has been custom-blending fragrances since 1843. It carries a line of more than 30 women's and men's fragrances.

Hové Parfumeur, Ltd. (✉ 824 Royal St., ☎ 504/525–7827) creates and manufactures fine fragrances for men and women. Oils, soaps, sachets, and potpourri are made to order on the premises. This local family-run business has been around since 1932.

La Belle Epoque (✉ Jackson Brewery Millhouse, 600 Decatur St., ☎ 504/271–3577) is the creator of Can-Can, Creole Rose, and other New Orleans fragrances.

Toys

Boyer Antiques (✉ 241 Chartres St., ☎ 504/522–4513) carries delightful antique dolls and dollhouses.

Ginja Jar (✉ 611 Royal St., ☎ 504/523–7643) has a large collection of Palmary and Madame Alexander dolls, McCrory bears, and hand-carved walking sticks.

Hello Dolly (✉ 815 Royal St., ☎ 504/522–9948) stocks one of the largest collections of regional dolls. The Gambina doll is a specialty.

The Little Toy Shoppe (✉ 900 Decatur St., ☎ 504/522–6588; ✉ 513 St. Ann St., ☎ 504/523–1770) carries a large selection of children's toys, books, and posters. The store has beautiful, locally produced Gambina dolls and Madame Alexander dolls. Many regional items for children of all ages are also for sale.

Oh Susannah (✉ 518 St. Peter St., ☎ 504/586–8701) showcases pricey collector's dolls from the likes of Annette Hinestedt and Hildegard Gunzel. Dolls of all types are ubiquitous in the French Quarter, but this shop has the edge.

Le Petit Soldier Shop (✉ 528 Royal St., ☎ 504/523–7741) stocks whole armies of beautifully crafted, hand-painted toy soldiers that may well become heirlooms.

Magazine Street

Magazine Street is one of the oldest and most diverse shopping districts in New Orleans. Named for the French word for shop—*maga-sin*—this street runs parallel to St. Charles Avenue (although several blocks closer to the river) and passes through old, established neighborhoods. Along Magazine Street's 5 mi, you can find dozens of intriguing antiques shops, bric-a-brac vendors, used clothing and furniture stores, art galleries, and specialists in furniture restoration, interior decorating, and pottery.

The main stretch of shops begins at the intersection of Melpomene and Magazine streets. The Magazine Street bus runs there from Canal Street, and the St. Charles streetcar stops within blocks of this shopping district. The best and safest way to shop on Magazine Street is by car; shops are in clusters and the sections between them can be somewhat unsafe for those not familiar with them.

Macon Riddle (☎ 504/899–3027, FAX 504/891–2703), a local antiques expert, offers personalized, guided shopping expeditions of Magazine and Royal streets.

Antiques

Ann Koerner Antiques and Interiors (✉ 4021 Magazine St., ☎ 504/899–2664) displays a great collection of 19th century southern and French antiques, including sideboards, chests, chairs, and linens.

Antebellum Antiques (✉ 2011 Magazine St., ☎ 504/558–0208) showcases 19th-century furnishings, including American beds and parlor sets.

Antiques Magazine (✉ 2028 Magazine St., ☎ 504/522–2043) is the place to go for piano babies, lighting from the 1850s to the 1940s, and all things Victorian.

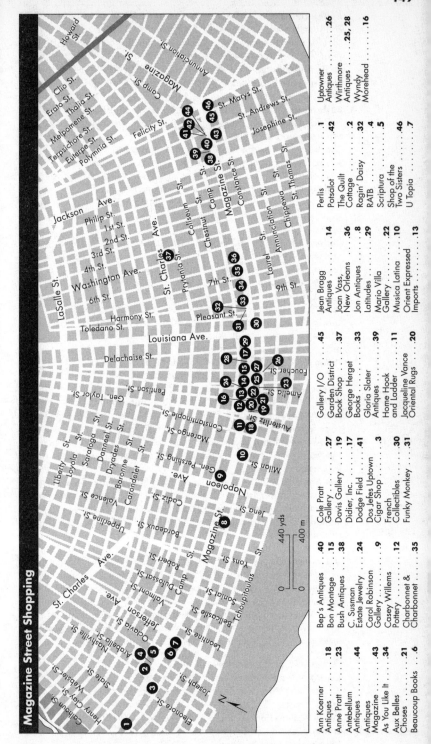

Magazine Street Shopping

As You Like It (✉ 3025 Magazine St., ☎ 504/897–6915 or 800/828–2311) sells a wide selection of discontinued and hard-to-find sterling silver tea services, trays, and flatware—including Victorian, Art Nouveau, and Art Deco pieces.

Bep's Antiques (✉ 2051 Magazine St., ☎ 504/525–7726) is a great browsing place for English tables and chairs and antique glass bottles, porcelain, and crockery.

Bush Antiques (✉ 2109–2111 Magazine St., ☎ 504/581–3518) carries French, English, and American furniture, antique beds, religious art, ironwork, and chandeliers.

Charbonnet & Charbonnet (✉ 2728 Magazine St., ☎ 504/891–9948), where there is an on-site cabinet workshop, specializes in large mid-19th-century cupboards and chests made from Irish and English pine. It also carries brackets, cornices, and stained glass.

Didier, Inc. (✉ 3439 Magazine St., ☎ 504/899–7749) sells fine American furniture from the 1800s to the 1850s as well as paintings and prints.

Dodge Fjeld (✉ 2033 Magazine St., ☎ 504/581–6930) is a well-established shop that focuses on American Empire and Art Deco furnishings, decorative pieces, and clocks, clocks, clocks.

French Collectibles (✉ 3424 Magazine St., ☎ 504/897–9020) specializes in 18th- and 19th- century Italian and English, as well as French, furnishings: armoires, chairs, mirrors, and smaller objects.

Gloria Slater Antiques (✉ 2115 Magazine St., ☎ 504/561–5738) stocks a charming collection of 19th-century French antiques, armoires, chandeliers, and mirrors.

Home Hook and Ladder (✉ 4100 Magazine St., ☎ 504/895–4480) is a source for delightful children's chairs, as well as pillows and lamps.

Jacqueline Vance Oriental Rugs (✉ 3944 Magazine St., ☎ 504/891–3304) sells a large variety of fine antique and contemporary rugs.

Jean Bragg Antiques (✉ 3901 Magazine St., ☎ 504/895–7375) has vintage linens, sewing tools, christening dresses, jewelry, porcelain, silver, picture frames, and banquet napkins at good prices. Also here are Newcomb and George Ohr pottery and Louisiana art, including works by Clementine Hunter.

Jon Antiques (✉ 4605 Magazine St., ☎ 504/899–4482), known for boxes and Staffordshire porcelain, also sells English furniture, porcelain, mirrors, lamps, tea caddies, and other bric-a-brac.

Latitudes (✉ 3701 Magazine St., ☎ 504/895–9880) carries top-quality imported Indonesian, Chinese, and Tibetan furnishings, accessories, and decorative arts.

Uptowner Antiques (✉ 3828 Magazine St., ☎ 504/891–7700) displays an outstanding selection of 18th- and 19th-century French antiques, mirrors, and Aubusson and needlepoint pillows.

Wirthmore Antiques (✉ 3900 Magazine St., ☎ 504/899–3811; ✉ 3727 Magazine St., ☎ 504/269–0660) has carefully selected 18th- and 19th-century country furniture from France and England; there's always a good selection of armoires and gold-leaf mirrors.

Art and Crafts Galleries

Carol Robinson Gallery (✉ 840 Napoleon Ave., at Magazine St., ☎ 504/895–6130) has a wide selection of paintings and sculptures by regional artists.

Casey Willems Pottery (✉ 3919 Magazine St., ☎ 504/899–1174) welcomes you to view the potter as he creates his imaginative ceramics, from berry bowls to lamps.

Cole Pratt Gallery (✉ 3800 Magazine St., ☎ 504/891–6789) exhibits paintings, sculptures, and ceramics crafted by contemporary regional and nationally recognized artists.

Davis Gallery (✉ 3964 Magazine St., ☎ 504/897–0780) carries rare African, pre-Columbian, and ethnographic art for collectors and museums.

Gallery I/O (✉ 1804 Magazine St., ☎ 504/899–9900) is a showcase for well known local artist Thomas Mann's ultramodern furnishings and one-of-a-kind pieces of jewelry—"Sculptures for the Body."

Mario Villa Gallery (✉ 3908 Magazine St., ☎ 504/895–8731) exhibits the internationally known artist's innovative furniture, as well as other Louisiana artists' sculpture, photography, pottery, and paintings.

Potsalot (✉ 2029 Magazine St., ☎ 504/524–6238) is the pottery studio and shop of Alex and Cindy Williams, whose works include attractive bread bowls and Mad Hatter tea cups. You can watch them at work and take classes here, too.

Wyndy Morehead (✉ 3926 Magazine St., ☎ 504/269–8333) offers a comfortable, welcoming setting for the eponymous owner's eclectic collection of art. An admitted color "addict," she leans toward the representational in art, particularly works in bold, bright colors.

Books

Beaucoup Books (✉ 5414 Magazine St., ☎ 504/895–2663) specializes in travel, fiction, and foreign language books; has a children's room; and hosts author signings and readings.

Garden District Book Shop (✉ 2727 Prytania St., ☎ 504/895–2266) stocks a good selection of regional, rare, and old books. Sometimes the novelist Anne Rice autographs her books here.

George Herget Books (✉ 3109 Magazine St., ☎ 504/891–5595) is a treasure shop with thousands of rare books, including many regional titles, along with rare postcards, records, sheet music, and Civil War memorabilia.

Clothing

Anne Pratt (✉ 3937 Magazine St., ☎ 504/891–6532) creates interesting Mexican-style jewelry in silver and 18- and 22-karat gold, as well as popular iron furniture.

Funky Monkey (✉ 3127 Magazine St., ☎ 504/899–5587) sells wigs, beaded bags, vintage hats and clothing, feather boas, lamé opera gloves, and harlequin glasses. Around Halloween, you can find pointed witches' hats here.

Joan Vass, New Orleans (✉ 2917 Magazine St., ☎ 504/891–4502 or 800/338–4864) is one of only six outlets in the country devoted exclusively to the designer, with a full line of women's ready-to-wear clothing, mostly in soft knits with simple, classic lines.

Perlis (✉ 6070 Magazine St., ☎ 504/895–8661), a New Orleans institution, is the home of the trademark Louisiana crawfish–embroidered shirts and ties. The shop sells top-quality men's and women's clothing.

Ragin' Daisy (✉ 3125 Magazine St., ☎ 504/269–1960) stocks vintage threads from the heyday of the rock and roll era, including dress-up duds, accessories, and jewelry.

RATB (✉ 5509 Magazine St., ☎ 504/897–0811 or 800/826–7282) displays pins, necklaces, bracelets, and other jewelry by local artisan Ruby Ann Tobar-Blanco (her initials give the store its name), whose designs also can be seen in stores nationwide. This is a great place to create your own designs and have her execute them.

U Topia (✉ 5408 Magazine St., ☎ 504/899–8488) stocks one-of-a-kind block-print cotton knits; the owners also make tie-dyed wearables. This is a retail shop for the company's nationally marketed lines.

Jewelry

C. Susman Estate Jewelry (✉ 3933 Magazine St., ☎ 504/897–9144) carries Magazine Street's best collection of Art Nouveau and Art Deco estate jewelry; the store also stocks art pottery, art glass, and collectibles.

Music
Musica Latina (⊠ 4226 Magazine St., ☎ 504/895–4227) is one of the oldest Latin American businesses in the city and a must for anyone serious about Latin music and local color.

Novelties and Gifts
Aux Belles Choses (⊠ 3912 Magazine St., ☎ 504/891–1009) has an eclectic assortment of dried-flower arrangements, notepaper, pottery, linens, soaps imported from France and England, and other beautiful things.

Bon Montage (⊠ 3719 Magazine St., ☎ 504/897–6295) specializes in custom-made dollhouses, dolls, glassware, children's clothes, and lamps.

Dos Jefes Uptown Cigar Shop (⊠ 5700 Magazine St., ☎ 504/899–3030) purveys cigars, humidors, and other cigar paraphernalia.

Orient Expressed Imports (⊠ 3905 Magazine St., ☎ 504/899–3060) has a wide selection of Asian pottery and ceramics, plus children's clothing and jewelry.

The Quilt Cottage (⊠ 801 Nashville St., off Magazine St., ☎ 504/895–3791) is the place to look for new and antique quilts and handmade gift items. Quilting services are available.

Scriptura (⊠ 5423 Magazine St., ☎ 504/897–1555) carries a large inventory of pretty stationery, ornate writing implements and letter openers, picture frames, photo albums, and books on calligraphy.

Shop of the Two Sisters (⊠ 1800 Magazine St., ☎ 504/524–6213 or 504/525–2747) displays a wonderful collection of miniatures, boxes, antique books, and decorative arts.

Maple Street/Riverbend

There's an old-fashioned small-town feeling in this area, where most of the shops are housed in turn-of-the-century cottages. On Maple Street, the shops run for six blocks, from Carrollton Avenue to Cherokee Street; in Riverbend, they dot the streets surrounding the shopping center on Carrollton Avenue. To reach both areas from Downtown, ride the streetcar until St. Charles Avenue becomes Carrollton Avenue; then get off at the first stop, the corner of Maple Street and Carrollton Avenue.

Art and Crafts Galleries
Nuance (⊠ 728 Dublin St., ☎ 504/865–8463) is the glass-blowing studio and showroom for Arden Stewart, a New Orleanian who creates traditional iridescent art glass and contemporary sculpture pieces.

The Sun Shop (⊠ 7722 Maple St., ☎ 504/861–8338) sells pottery, jewelry, Native American masks, and handwoven rugs, blankets, and wall hangings. For more than 20 years the proprietor has been traveling all over the United States and Central America to select handcrafted works by Native Americans. The shop is closed July and August.

Books
Maple Street Book Shop (⊠ 7523 Maple St., ☎ 504/866–4916) has outlets around the city; this store is the original. The staff is knowledgeable about the local literary scene past and present.

Maple Street Children's Book Shop (⊠ 7529 Maple St., ☎ 504/861–2105), next door to the Maple Street Book Shop, is the best place in town for children's literature. Bring the kids—there's a reading and activity area for them.

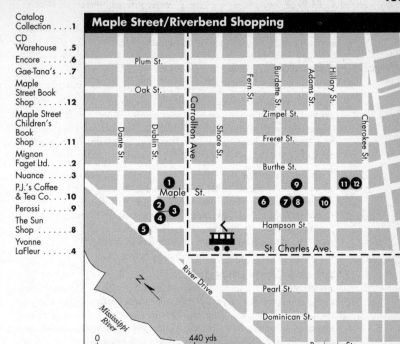

Clothing

Catalog Collection (✉ 8141 Maple St., ☎ 504/861–5002) stocks men's, women's, and children's clothing from J. Crew, Guess, and other labels at discounts of 25% to 75%.

Encore Shop (✉ 7814 Maple St., ☎ 504/861–9028), the resale shop of the Louisiana Philharmonic Orchestra, carries a very large selection of formal and casual women's wear, including bridal gowns and veils, costume jewelry, shoes, and accessories.

Gae-Tana's (✉ 7732 Maple St., ☎ 504/865–9625) sells casual, contemporary, and designer-label clothing at 30%–50% discounts.

Perossi (✉ 7725 Maple St., ☎ 504/866–1092) stocks women's formal and casual clothing, with labels such as BCBG, Relais, Jane Doe, and To The Max!

Yvonne LaFleur (✉ 8131 Hampson St., ☎ 504/866–9666) sells innovative custom-design fashions, French lingerie, and an array of shoes and accessories (including a spectacular selection of hats). LaFleur is a New Orleans designer whose boutique in Esplanade Mall (☞ Shopping Centers, *below*) is distinctive in its quality and range.

Food

P. J.'s Coffee & Tea Co. (✉ 7624 Maple St., ☎ 504/866–7031), a local chain, imports coffee beans and exotic teas. Pastries can be purchased in the café and enjoyed at umbrella-covered tables on the patio with cups of freshly brewed coffee or tea.

Jewelry

Mignon Faget Ltd. (✉ 710 Dublin St., ☎ 504/865–7361; ✉ 4300 Magazine St., ☎ 504/891–7545) is a custom-design jeweler whose signature pieces include Greek columns, king cakes, and alligators. There's a nice selection of accessories and toiletries, too.

Music
CD Warehouse (✉ 8200 Hampson St., ☎ 504/864–0444) has a wide selection of regional music on CDs and tapes.

Warehouse District

Since the first smattering of artists began moving into the Warehouse District in the mid-1970s, Julia Street has grown from a few isolated art and crafts galleries to the premier avenue of the arts for New Orleans; the excellent Louisiana Children's Museum (☞ Foot of Canal and Algiers Point *in* Chapter 1) is here, too. If you intend to visit them all, fortify yourself with food or drink at one of the many eateries here.

Each month in the Warehouse District new galleries open . . . and some close. There are other galleries in adjacent areas, too. An excellent publication, "Walking Tours of the Warehouse District and Lafayette Square," available free of charge at most galleries, can be your guide to further explorations. Most galleries are open Tuesday–Saturday 10–5, but some are open on Monday as well. It's best to call to confirm a gallery's opening and closing times.

Art and Crafts Galleries
Ariodante (✉ 535 Julia St., ☎ 504/534–3233) has elegant, custom-made display cases in which the gallery sets forth its high-end contemporary crafts. But even the best items—the beautiful glass, for example—are reasonably priced. Almost everything here—bowls, jewelry, vases, and more—is both beautiful and practical.

Arthur Roger Gallery (✉ 432 Julia St., ☎ 504/522–1999) is one of the best-known New Orleans galleries nationally. The gallery represents many fine contemporary Louisiana artists, including Lin Emery, Jacquelyn Bishop, and Willy Birch, and shows are often provocative and imaginative. The gallery also shows artists of national stature.

The **Contemporary Arts Center** (✉ 900 Camp St., ☎ 504/523–1216), although not on Julia Street itself, is the mother of all Warehouse District galleries, with a spectacular lobby. The CAC is focusing more and more on local and regional artists, while not neglecting national trends. The Cyber Café here can cure temporary gallery-hopping exhaustion.

Estudio Gallery (✉ 630 Baronne St., ☎ 504/524–7982) is a gallery as well as a studio for local artists Zella Funck and Martin Laborde. Funck, a painter and teacher, joined forces with Laborde, a gentle man who has hit the big time with his paintings of a little magician who remains inscrutable and mysterious.

Galerie Simonne Sterm (✉ 518 Julia St., ☎ 504/529–1118) was the creation of a remarkable Frenchwoman who died far too young. Her legacy lives on in the gallery director's commitment to showcasing the finest Louisiana contemporary artists, interspersed with well-known national artists. You can't see inside from the street, but don't let that deter you: the gallery and its staff are most welcoming.

George Schmidt Gallery (✉ 608 Julia St., ☎ 504/592–0201) is a one-of-a-kind showplace for the works of George Schmidt. Fabled for fascinating and outrageous conversation, Schmidt creates shows of "history painting, narrative art, and other reactionary works on canvas and paper." From small-scale monotypes to mural-size depictions of historic moments, his work fascinates with the scope of its subjects and its attention to detail.

Heriard-Cimino Gallery (✉ 440 Julia St., ☎ 504/525–7300) conveys a minimalist sensibility, featuring, in general, sparse, abstract works—whether paintings or sculpture—which nevertheless can engage the senses with color and, sometimes, a sense of humor. The national and inter-

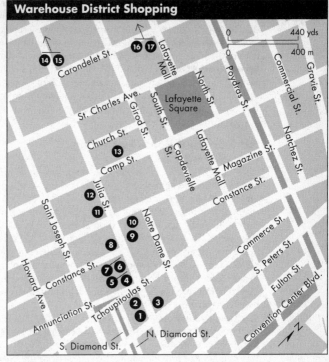

Warehouse District Shopping

national roster of artists guarantees a broad spectrum of styles and techniques within the minimalist credo.

Jonathan Ferrara Gallery (⊠ 816 Baronne St., ☎ 504/522–5471), a fresh, open space, assembles a variety of abstract paintings, sculpture, and glass. The Greek-column pedestals add an elegant note to the surroundings. This could be a spot to watch, as the selection of works is imaginative and the taste of the designer/installer impeccable.

LeMieux Gallery (⊠ 332 Julia St., ☎ 504/522–5988) is distinguished by what its director refers to as "Third-Coast Art," the work of artists along the Gulf Coast from Louisiana to Florida. It displays both fine arts and crafts from these artists, and also represents the works of the late Paul Ninas, one of New Orleans's finest abstract artists.

Marguerite Oestreicher Fine Art (⊠ 626 Julia St., ☎ 504/581–9253) packs a punch in a small space. The gallery seeks out some of the most interesting painters, printmakers, and sculptors from around the country. The enthusiastic staff assists the owner in assembling contemporary art with a difference: you can always count on being amused or challenged—or both—by what you see on these walls.

New Orleans School of GlassWorks and Printmaking Studio (⊠ 727 Magazine St., ☎ 504/529–7277) is the South's largest glassblowing and printmaking studio. Here you'll find imaginative glass—both practical and art pieces—as well as metal sculptures. You may have the opportunity to view glassblowers at work.

628 Gallery (⊠ 628 Baronne St., ☎ 504/529–3306) is where a new style began. Artist Jana K. Napoli started working with children from nearby Rabouin vocational school. Covering furniture with brilliant color and design, these young artists found themselves featured as the new wave in national magazines. Young artists, young aspirations = YA/YA. Orleanians say "YES/YES" to what they've achieved in their bold furniture and splashy murals.

Still-Zinsel Gallery (✉ 328 Julia St., ☎ 504/588–9999), a spacious, high-ceiling gallery, assembles an eclectic mix of local and nationally produced art, particularly by young emerging and mid-career artists whose work shows promise. Several artists represented have other careers in the art world as teachers, which adds perspective to their work.

Sylvia Schmidt Gallery (✉ 400 Julia St., ☎ 504/522–2000) represents some of the finest contemporary realist painters of the region, displaying their imaginative paintings, sculptures, and works on paper. Abstract works are not ruled out, and the whimsical fantasies of artist-cartoonist Walter Wade Welch should not be missed.

Furniture and Home Furnishings

Christopher Maier Studio (✉ 329 Julia St., ☎ 504/586–7097) showcases the work of the eponymous distinguished local furniture maker, and the furniture he makes is substantial—no thin-legged, trendy tables here. Maier specializes in furniture with historic, mythological, or regional interest; some armoires resemble the aboveground tombs in the city's cemeteries. His workshop is on the premises.

Necessities (✉ 832 Baronne St., ☎ 504/581–2333), a showcase for home furnishings by New Orleans craftsmen, lives up to its name, providing such necessities as custom woodwork and upholstery on-site. You probably didn't bring Grandma's tattered armchair with you to have reupholstered in New Orleans, but you can order something new here to replace it.

Ray Langley Interiors (✉ 434 Julia St., ☎ 504/522–2284) is "Truth or Dare" land. Are you ready for the Madonna lifestyle? Do you want to pretend that you live in one of the trendy South Beach hotels in Miami? Ray Langley can provide you with oversize furniture in outrageous colors, and accessories to boot. You'll probably find it hard to resist.

Shopping Centers

These are a few of greater New Orleans's better shopping centers not previously discussed in this chapter. These centers are open Monday through Saturday 10–9, Sunday 12:30–5:30.

Esplanade Mall (✉ 1401 W. Esplanade Ave., Kenner, ☎ 504/468–6116), with about 135 shops and department stores such as Macy's and Dillard's, has locally owned stores such as Yvonne LaFleur (elegant women's fashions; ☞ Maple Street/Riverbend, *above*) and a branch of the Café du Monde.

Lakeside Shopping Center (✉ 3301 Veterans Memorial Blvd., Metairie, ☎ 504/835–8000) has 145 stores and a food court. Here you will find JCPenney, Dillard's, Bailey Banks & Biddle Jewelers, five cinemas, Ruby Tuesday's restaurant, Café du Monde, and Popeye's Famous Fried Chicken (a New Orleans original).

Oakwood Shopping Center (✉ 197 Westbank Expy., Gretna, ☎ 504/362–1900), anchored by Dillard's, Mervyn's, and Sears, has more than 100 shops, including a large Books-a-Million store, and a food court.

The Plaza at Lake Forest (✉ 5700 Read Blvd., ☎ 504/246–1500) is where you'll find Dillard's and Gordon's Jewelers, among 95 stores.

7 SIDE TRIPS

If the Tara replica on St. Charles Avenue
has whetted your appetite for the real thing,
head west on the Great River Road to tour
antebellum plantation homes; some are
bed-and-breakfasts. Also outside the city's
parameters are swamps, where you
can come face-to-face with gators and
experience the eerie stillness of the bayous.
A tour of Cajun Country will reward you
with fantastic music and food and a chance
to race your pet pig. Bird-watchers and
people who fish are in heaven here.

By Macon Fry
and Honey
Naylor

Updated by
Michaela
Morrissey

ALTHOUGH **NEW ORLEANS** has never been a typical Dixie city, the word "Dixieland" was coined here in the early 19th century. And you have but to look away, look away to the west of town to see that old times here are not forgotten. Rare is the visitor to New Orleans who does not wheel out to see at least a couple of the restored antebellum homes that line the Great River Road between New Orleans and Baton Rouge.

Other popular day trips are tours of the swamps and bayous that surround New Orleans. *Bayou* comes from a Native American word that means "creek." The brackish, slow-moving waters of South Louisiana were once the highways and byways of the Choctaw, Chickasaw, and Chitimacha. Two centuries ago Jean Lafitte and his freebooters easily hid in murky reaches of swamp, which were covered with thick canopies of subtropical vegetation; pirate gold is said to be still buried here. Ancient, gnarled cypresses with gray shawls of Spanish moss rise out of quiet waters. The state has an alligator population of about 500,000, and most of them laze around in the meandering tributaries and secluded sloughs of South Louisiana. Wild boars, snow-white egrets, bald eagles, and all manner of other exotic creatures inhabit the swamps and marshlands. (For swamp tour operators, *see* Sightseeing *in* Smart Travel Tips A to Z.)

Southern Louisiana, cradle of the Cajun population, is decidedly French in flavor. In smaller communities along the coast and in the upland prairie, fluent Cajun French remains the primary tongue, although just about everyone also speaks English. After a hard day's work fishing or working crawfish ponds, rural residents of Cajun Country often live up to the motto *laissez les bon temps rouler,* which means, *cher,* let the good times roll.

You can, of course, combine aspects of both the River Road and Cajun Country during a visit, perhaps allotting an afternoon for a swamp tour, too. Just head out from New Orleans on I–10 and take I–310 to U.S. 61 (Airline Highway) or to River Road and stop at the plantations that interest you; then you can continue on to Cajun Country. If you have the time, take Route 18 (also known as LA 18), on the west bank and overnight along the way.

Pleasures and Pastimes

Dining

It's easy to find steaks and fries, but part of the considerable charm of the region is the Cajun food, popularized by Cajun chef Paul Prudhomme, a native of Opelousas. This is jambalaya, crawfish pie, and filé gumbo country, and nowhere on earth is Cajun food done better than in the region in which it originated. Cajun food is often described as the robust, hot-peppery country kin of Creole cuisine. Ubiquitous sea critters turn up in a wide variety of exotic concoctions, such as étouffées, bisques, and boulettes, and on almost every Acadian menu are jambalaya, gumbo, and some blackened fish. Alligator meat is a great favorite, as are boudin and andouille, which are hot, hot sausages. Cajun food is very rich, and portions tend to be ample. Biscuits and grits are breakfast staples, and many an evening meal ends with bread pudding. (For explanations of many Cajun foods, *see* Chapter 2.)

Approximate costs are as follows:

CATEGORY	COST*
$$$$	over $35
$$$	$25–$35
$$	$15–$24
$	under $15

per person, excluding drinks, service, and 9% tax

Lodging

Some of the handsome antebellum mansions along River Road are also B&Bs in which you may roam the high-ceiling rooms before bedding down in a big four-poster or canopied bed. The greatest concentration of accommodations in Cajun Country is in Lafayette, which has an abundance of chain properties. In nearby towns there are charming B&Bs, where friendly hosts can give you insider tips about touring the region.

Approximate costs are as follows:

CATEGORY	COST*
$$$$	over $120
$$$	$90–$120
$$	$50–$89
$	under $50

All prices are for a standard double room, excluding 8% tax.

Music

Music beats at the heart of Cajun life. Only the cuisine rivals it as an expression of this unique culture. The ensembles of fiddles, washboards, accordions, and sometimes guitars and drums produce eminently danceable music. Songs are usually sung in Cajun French. Zydeco music, closely related to Cajun, has more intricate rhythms. The songs of both are plaintive and exuberant, describing the nature of life on the plains, swamps, and bayous.

Plantation Houses

A drive along the winding River Road is a study in contrasts. The sweeping artistry of the grand plantation houses stands in the eerie shadow of massive chemical plants that operate on the Mississippi today. The houses themselves vary greatly, reflecting the area's long history. Some are low-slung, Creole-style structures that are relatively humble, while others are grandly columned mansions. A number are more beautiful outside than inside. If you're planning to take house tours, be aware that the level of knowledge among tour guides varies widely; it's the luck of the draw here.

THE GREAT RIVER ROAD

The Old South is in a state of grace along the Great River Road, between New Orleans and Baton Rouge, where elegant and beautifully restored antebellum plantations are filled with period antiques, ghosts of former residents, and tales of Yankee gunboats.

Alas, the Great River Road itself is not as scenic as it once was. Along some stretches industrial plants mar the landscape on one side of the road, and on the other side the levee obstructs a view of the Mississippi. However, you can always park your car and climb up on the levee for a look at Ol' Man River. The Great River Road is also called, variously, Route or LA 44 and 75 on the east bank of the river, and Route or LA 18 on the west bank. LA and Route are interchangeable; Fodor's uses Route throughout this chapter. Alternatives to the Great River Road are I–10 and U.S. 61; both have signs marking exits for various plantations. All of the plantations described are listed in the National Register of Historic Places, and some of them are B&Bs. Plantation touring can take anywhere from an hour to two days, depending upon how many houses you want to see.

Numbers in the margin correspond to points of interest on the River Road Plantations map. ✎ following the text of a review is your signal that the property has a Web site, where you will find details and, usually, images; for a link, visit www.fodors.com/urls.

Destrehan Plantation

❶ *23 mi west (upriver) of New Orleans.*

Destrehan is an appropriate place to begin a River Road ramble: the oldest plantation left intact in the lower Mississippi Valley, this simple West Indies–style house, built in 1787 by a free man of color, is typical of the homes built by the earliest planters in the region. The plantation is notable for the handhewn cypress timbers that were used in its construction and for the insulation in its walls, made of *bousillage,* a mixture of horsehair and Spanish moss. An annual Fall Festival is held during the second weekend in November. Some scenes from *Interview with a Vampire* were filmed here. ✉ 13034 River Rd., Destrehan, ☎ 504/764–9315. 🎫 $8. ✹ Daily 9–4.

San Francisco

❷ *15 mi west of Destrehan Plantation, 35 mi west of New Orleans.*

An elaborate Steamboat Gothic house completed in 1856, San Francisco presents an intriguing variation on the standard plantation styles. The house was once called St. Frusquin, a name derived from a French slang term, *sans fruscins,* which means "without a penny in my pocket"—the condition its first owner, Edmond Bozonier Marmillion, found himself in after paying exorbitant construction costs. The galleries outside resemble the decks of a ship, and the house has cypress wood beautifully painted to resemble wood and marble. Louisiana novelist Frances Parkinson Keyes used the site as the model for her book, *Steamboat Gothic.* Purchased by Marathon Oil in the 1980s, the house is authentically furnished with antiques. ✉ Rte. 44, Reserve, ☎ 504/535–2341 or 888/322–1756. 🎫 $8. ✹ Daily 10–4.

Dining

$–$$ ✗ **Airline Motors.** From the huge neon sign to the glass-brick facade and long curving counter, this 1940s relic is a step back in time. Be sure to try the smoky chicken andouille gumbo, and follow it with a simple po'boy or fried seafood platter. The restaurant is open 24 hours daily, except late on Sunday and Monday nights. ✉ 221 E. Airline Hwy. (U.S. 61), LaPlace, ☎ 504/652–9181. D, MC, V.

St. James Historical Society Museum

❸ *10 mi west of San Francisco Plantation, 45 mi west of New Orleans.*

From Native American mounds to lumber mills to sugar plantations, the St. James Historical Society presents a colorful overview of the changing face of life on River Road through artifacts and photographs. This quintessential small-town museum housed in a cottage is also the best place to get information on the St. James Bonfire tradition. Around Christmas, on the weekend before the winter solstice, communities along the river torch large log tepees that they build along the levee while bands play and food is served (☞ When to Go *in* Smart Travel Tips A to Z for more information). In St. John, St. Charles, St. James, and Ascension parishes, these bonfires have been a tradition for more than

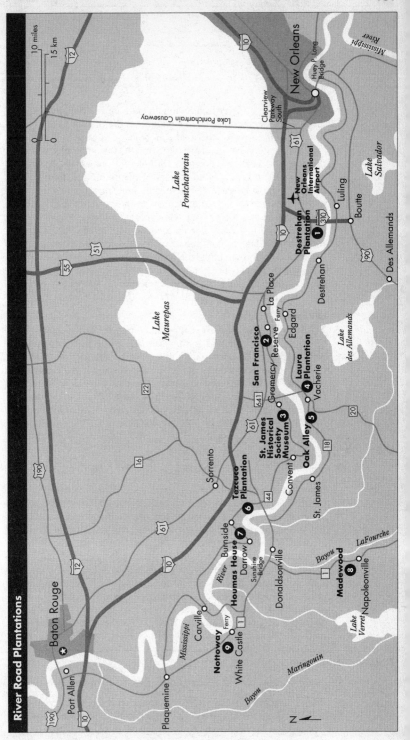

River Road Plantations

200 years. ⊠ *River Rd., Gramercy,* ☎ *504/869–9752.* ⊡ *Free.* ☉ *Weekdays 9–4.*

Laura Plantation

★ **❹** *8 mi southwest of St. James Historical Society Museum, 57 mi from New Orleans.*

Nowhere else on River Road will you get a more intimate, well-documented presentation of Creole plantation life than at Laura Plantation. The narrative of the guides is built on first-person accounts, estate records, and original artifacts from the Locoul family, who built the simple, Creole-style house in 1805. Laura Locoul, granddaughter of the builders, kept a detailed diary of plantation life, family fights, and the horrors of slavery. The information from Laura's diary and the rugged slave cabins out back provide an unvarnished glimpse into the institution of slavery. Senegalese slaves at Laura are believed to have first told folklorist Alcee Fortier the tales of B'rer Rabbit; his friend, Joel Chandler Harris, used the stories in this Uncle Remus tales. Since its purchase by preservationist Norman Marmillion in the early 1990s, the house has slowly been undergoing restoration to its original state. B&B accommodations are planned for a large outbuilding by 2005. ⊠ *2247 Rte. 18, Vacherie,* ☎ *225/265–7690.* ⊡ *$8.* ☉ *Daily 9–5.* ✎

Dining

$ ✕ **B&C Cajun Deli.** A small restaurant adjoining the deli counter at B&C serves the tastiest seafood gumbo ever ladled into a Styrofoam bowl. Try it with a dash of hot sauce and a sprinkle of filé, or sample the alligator and garfish po'boys. Finish with a scoop of soft and chewy bread pudding. The deli has fresh and frozen catfish, crawfish, alligator, and turtle meat harvested from the nearby swamps. You can buy seafood packed to travel. ⊠ *2155 Rte. 18, beside Laura Plantation, Vacherie,* ☎ *225/265–8356. AE, D, MC, V. Closed Sun.*

Oak Alley

★ **❺** *3 mi west of Laura Plantation, 60 mi west of New Orleans.*

Built between 1837 and 1839 by Jacques T. Roman, a French Creole sugar planter from New Orleans, Oak Alley is the most famous of all the antebellum homes in Louisiana and an outstanding example of Greek Revival architecture. The 28 gnarled oak trees that line the drive and give the columned plantation its name were planted in the early 1700s. Be sure to take in the view from the upper gallery of the house and to spend time exploring the grounds, which may seem more impressive than the interior. The house and the grounds have been used in several Hollywood movies, including *Interview with the Vampire* and *Primary Colors.* A number of late-19th-century cottages provide simple overnight accommodations. ⊠ *Rte. 18, Vacherie,* ☎ *225/265–2151 or 800/442–5539.* ⊡ *$10.* ☉ *Daily 9–5.* ✎

Tezcuco Plantation

❻ *20 mi northwest of Oak Alley, 55 mi west of New Orleans.*

Tezcuco is a graceful raised cottage, Greek Revival in style and adorned with elaborate wrought-iron–trimmed galleries and ornate friezes. Built by Benjamin Tureaud over a five-year period, this is one of the last plantations constructed prior to the Civil War. Original outbuildings on the large, sprawling property include a chapel and blacksmith's shop, which now serve as an antiques store and Civil War museum. Cottages and rooms can be booked (ahead of time) for overnight accommodations (☞ Lodging, *below*). Tezcuco is also home to the **River Road African American Museum & Gallery,** which examines the antebellum slave culture. ✉ *Rte. 44, just north of Sunshine Bridge, Darrow,* ☎ *225/562–3929.* ⬛ *$8; $4 to tour grounds only.* ☉ *Daily 9–5; museum Wed.–Sun. 1–5.* ✎

Lodging

$$–$$$$ ⊡ **Tezcuco Plantation.** The renovated wood-frame cottages behind the main house at Tezcuco resemble a small village. Interiors range from homey to lavishly formal; some have fireplaces. You can walk the grounds after the last visitors have departed and sip a glass of wine in the gardens or rock on your own porch. Two elaborately furnished rooms are also available in the main house. There's a restaurant on premises but it is not recommended. ✉ *Rte. 44, just north of the Sunshine Bridge, Darrow 70725,* ☎ *504/562–3929,* ⅁ᴬˣ *504/562–3923. 2 rooms, 19 cottages. Restaurant. AE, D, MC, V. BP.* ✎

Houmas House

❼ *2½ mi west of Tezcuco, 58 mi west of New Orleans.*

Houmas Plantation was a tract of land along the Mississippi River purchased from the Houmas people in colonial times by Maurice Conway and Alexander Latil. The house here is actually two buildings of quite different styles, joined together. In 1790 Latil built the smaller rear house, which has characteristics of both Spanish and rural French architecture. A grand Greek Revival mansion was built in 1840 by John Smith Preston and his wife, Caroline. Her father, Revolutionary War hero General Wade Hampton of South Carolina, had bought the property in 1812. The Prestons preserved the original four-room dwelling at the rear, and it was later attached to the big house by an arched carriageway. Today, docents in antebellum garb guide you through this beautiful structure, which includes a three-story spiral staircase. ✉ *Rte. 942, Burnside, ½ mi off Rte. 44,* ☎ *225/473–7841.* ⬛ *$8.* ☉ *Feb.–Oct., daily 10–5; Nov.–Jan., daily 10–4.*

Dining

$–$$ ✕ **The Cabin.** Yellowed newspapers cover the walls and ancient farm implements dangle here and there in a 150-year-old slave cabin–cum-restaurant. Crawfish étouffée and other seafood items are a specialty, but you can choose among po'boys, burgers, and steaks, too. ✉ *Rte. 44 and Rte. 22, Burnside,* ☎ *504/473–3007. AE, D, MC, V. No dinner Sun.–Wed.*

Madewood

❽ *20 mi south of Houmas House, 74 mi west of New Orleans.*

This galleried, 21-room Greek Revival mansion with its massive white columns was designed by noted architect Henry Howard and completed in 1854. The house has an enormous freestanding staircase and 25-ft ceilings, and is best experienced overnight (☞ Lodging, *below*): the tour can be disappointing but the B&B experience is magnificent. ✉ *4250 Rte. 308, Napoleonville, 2 mi south of town,* ☎ *504/369–7151 or 800/ 375–7151.* ⬛ *$6.* ☉ *Daily 10–5.*

Lodging

$$$$ ⊡ **Madewood.** Expect gracious hospitality, lovely antiques, canopied beds, and a homey atmosphere in both the 21-room main house and Charlet House, a smaller structure on the plantation grounds. The cost includes breakfast and a southern meal in a candlelit formal dining room. ✉ *4250 Rte. 308, Napoleonville 70390,* ☎ *800/375–7151. 5 rooms, 3 suites. AE, D, MC, V. MAP.* ✎

Nottoway

★ ⑨ *33 mi northwest of Madewood, 70 mi west of New Orleans.*

The South's largest plantation house, Nottoway, should not be missed. Built in 1859, the mansion is in a class by itself, a gem of Italianate and Greek Revival style, the epitome of luxury and magnificence. With 64 rooms, 53,000 square ft of space, 22 columns, and 200 windows, this white castle (the nearby town of White Castle was named for it) was the pièce de résistance of architect Henry Howard. It was saved from total destruction during the Civil War by a northern gunboat officer (a former guest of the owners, Mr. and Mrs. John Randolph). Nottoway has a white ballroom that is famed in these parts for its original crystal chandeliers and hand-carved Corinthian columns. You can also stay here overnight (☞ Lodging, *below*), and a rather formal restaurant serves three meals daily. ☒ *30907 Rte. 405, White Castle, 2 mi north of White Castle,* ☏ *225/545–2730.* ⛋ *$10.* ☉ *Daily 9–5.* ☜

Lodging

$$$$ ☷ **Nottoway.** The largest antebellum plantation in the South, this stunner is fun to wander around at night. You can sit on the upstairs balcony and watch the ships go by on the river. In this antiques-filled B&B, three suites come with a bottle of champagne; guests in the other rooms—in the main house, its wings, and surrounding cottages—receive a complimentary glass of sherry. Mornings begin with a Continental breakfast in bed, followed by a full breakfast in the dining room. ☒ *30907 Rte. 405, White Castle 70788,* ☏ *225/545–2730. 13 rooms, 3 suites. Restaurant, pool. AE, D, MC, V. BP.* ☜

The Great River Road A to Z

Getting Around

BY CAR

From New Orleans, take I–10 west to I–310 to Exit 6, River Road. Driving time to the nearest plantation (Destrehan) is about 20 minutes from the airport. Alternatives to the Great River Road are to continue on either I–10 or U.S. 61 west; both have signs marking exits for various plantations. Route 18 runs along the west bank of the river.

BY FERRY

Several car and passenger ferries cross the Mississippi River. The **Edgard–Reserve** ferry, near San Francisco Plantation, operates daily 5 AM–9 PM, leaving the west bank on the hour and half hour, and the east bank on the quarter and three-quarter hour. There's a $1 toll.

The **White Castle–Carville** ferry, near Nottoway Plantation, runs weekdays, 5 AM–7:45 AM and 3:30 PM–7:30 PM, leaving the west bank on the hour and half hour and the east bank on the quarter and three-quarter hour. The toll is $1.

Guided Tours

For information about guided plantation tours that depart from New Orleans, *see* Sightseeing Tours *in* Smart Travel Tips A to Z.

LAFAYETTE

Lafayette, 128 mi west of New Orleans and the largest city in Cajun Country, is a major center of Cajun lore and life, even if it does lack the charm and rusticity of smaller, outlying villages. Excellent restaurants and B&Bs make it a good jumping-off point for exploring the region. Cajun Mardi Gras in Lafayette is second only to its sister celebration in New Orleans.

The surrounding countryside is dotted with tiny towns and villages where antiques seekers and explorers can poke around blissfully. Live oaks with ragged gray buntings of Spanish moss form canopies over the bottle-green bayous. Country roads follow the contortions of the Teche (pronounced *tesh*), the state's longest bayou, and meander through villages where cypress cabins rise up out of the water on stilts and moored fishing boats and pirogues scarcely bob on the sluggish waters.

Numbers in the text correspond to numbers in the margin and on the Lafayette map.

Downtown Lafayette

The city's downtown (called Lafayette Centre) is an amalgam of Victorian, Art Deco, and modern structures centered around the intersection of Main and Jefferson streets. The district has survived the explosive growth of suburbs on all sides and supports a lively turn-of-the-century commercial section, a growing museum complex, and a couple of very soulful lunchrooms.

A Good Walk

Park on St. John Street (a quarter buys a full hour of metered street parking) and begin your walk on the northern edge of downtown at **St. John the Evangelist Cathedral** ①. From the steps of the cathedral, head two blocks east on Main Street to the **Lafayette Courthouse** ②, where the clerk displays a huge collection of historic photographs. Exit the courthouse onto Lafayette Street and walk south two blocks to **Lafayette Museum** ③, with its Acadian and Civil War artifacts. Stroll east two blocks on Convent Street to reach Jefferson Street, the main commercial thoroughfare of downtown Lafayette. Presiding over this intersection are the deco-style Le Centre Internationale de Lafayette and a glowering statue of native son and Confederate Civil War hero Alfred Mouton. Four blocks north on Jefferson Street are three classic Louisiana **murals** ④.

TIMING

To see all the sites downtown including the museum allow a half day (museum tours take about a half hour). If you visit on weekends, some of the municipal buildings will be closed. You might also wish to allow time for breakfast or lunch at one of the eateries on Jefferson Street.

Sights to See

Artists' Alliance. The oldest commercial building in downtown Lafayette, constructed before 1890, was formerly a hardware store. Now works by local artists and traveling exhibits hang on the walls, and there are occasional dance and performance art shows. ⊠ *121 W. Vermilion St.,* ☎ *337/233–7518.* 🎫 *Free.* ☉ *Wed.–Fri. 11–5, Sat. 1–5.*

❷ **Lafayette Courthouse.** The courthouse contains an impressive collection of more than 2,000 historical photographs of life in the Lafayette area. There are images of famous politicians such as Dudley LeBlanc and Huey Long working the stump and scenes from the great flood of 1927. Many of the pictures are on display on the second floor. ⊠ *800 Buchanan St.,* ☎ *337/233–0150.* ☉ *Weekdays 8:30–4:30.*

❸ **Lafayette Museum.** Built in 1800 as the *maison dimanche,* or "Sunday house," of town founder Jean Mouton, this galleried town house with a mid-19th-century addition now preserves local history. The older section is an excellent example of early Acadian architecture and contains artifacts used by settlers. The main museum contains Civil War–era furnishings and memorabilia and a Mardi Gras exhibit. ⊠ *1122 Lafayette St.,* ☎ *337/234–2208.* 🎫 *$3.* ☉ *Tues.–Sat. 9–5, Sun. 3–5.*

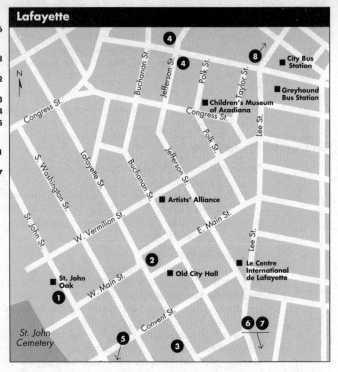

Lafayette

❹ **Murals.** There are three outdoor murals by Robert Dafford in Lafayette Centre. A Cajun accordion is on the side of the **Lee Furniture** store (✉ 314 Jefferson St.), a Louisiana swamp scene is across from Dwyer's Café (☞ Dining, *below*) at 407 Jefferson, and splashy cars are on the **Jefferson Tower Building** (✉ 556 Jefferson St.). The microcosm of Lafayette inside the garage at Parc Auto du Centre Ville, at the corner of Polk and Vermilion streets, is the work of local artist Tanya Falgout.

❶ **St. John the Evangelist Cathedral.** This cathedral, constructed in 1913, is a Romanesque structure with Byzantine touches. Union troops encamped on the grounds during the Civil War. In the cemetery beside the church are aboveground tombs of town founder Jean Mouton, Civil War hero General Alfred Mouton, and Cidalese Arceneaux. Arceneaux is believed to be the daughter of Gabriel, the lost love of Longfellow's Evangeline. Next to the cathedral is the 400-year-old St. John Oak, one of the charter members of the silent but leafy Louisiana Live Oak Society. ✉ *914 St. John St., ☎ 337/276–4576.*

Greater Lafayette

Outside the small downtown area, the only way to see Lafayette is by car. To the east on the banks of Bayou Vermilion (called the Vermilion River in the countryside), the Vermilionville Theme Park and the Acadian Cultural Center offer entertaining presentations on Cajun history and culture. Acadian Village is about 8 mi away and focuses on the early 1800s when the French-Canadians fled from Nova Scotia to Louisiana.

A Good Drive

From I–10, head south on Johnston Street (U.S. 167), the main route connecting Lafayette with the village of Abbeville to the south. From the intersection of Jefferson Street in downtown Lafayette, drive south

½ mi and turn left onto St. Mary Boulevard. Here you will enter the campus of the University of Southwestern Louisiana, with its many deco-style buildings. Travel four blocks and turn right on Girard Park Drive, which skirts the edge of Girard Park.

Turn left on Auditorium Street before making an immediate left onto College Road. Take the first left again onto Coolidge Street to enter the **Oil Center** ⑤, a bizarre cluster of single-story '50s-style offices and shops that was the original home of Louisiana's offshore oil industry.

From Harding Street turn right on Oil Center Boulevard, go three blocks and turn left on West Pinhook Road. Travel a mile and turn right on the Evangeline Thruway (U.S. 90). Take a left at University Avenue, which will be the first light after crossing the Vermilion River. On the left, across from Lafayette Regional Airport, look for the signs for the **Acadian Cultural Center** ⑥, a museum with information on all aspects of Cajun culture. Beside the Cultural Center is **Vermilionville Theme Park** ⑦, a simulated Acadian village on the banks of the Vermilion River.

At the entrance to the Acadian Cultural Center, University Avenue becomes Surrey Street, a winding road that passes through the working-class neighborhoods of north Lafayette. Turn left on Surrey Street, go 1½ mi, and turn right on Louisiana Avenue. Travel 2 mi on Louisiana Avenue and turn right onto Alexander Street. Less than a mile east of Louisiana Avenue, on the left side, is the heavily forested **Acadiana Park Nature Station** ⑧.

TIMING

The drive may be completed in an hour and a half, but allot at least an extra half hour for each museum and two hours to see Vermilionville Theme Park.

Sights To See

❻ **Acadian Cultural Center.** A unit of the Jean Lafitte National Historical Park and Preserve, the center traces the history of the area through numerous audiovisual exhibits of food, music, and folklore. Be sure to watch the introductory film, which is a dramatization of the Acadian exile. Black-and-white clips from the 1929 movie *The Romance of Evangeline* are incorporated in the film; aficionados of old motion pictures will love it. ⊠ *501 Fisher Rd.,* ☎ *337/232–0789 or 337/232–0961.* ☞ *Free.* ☉ *Daily 8–5.*

OFF THE
BEATEN PATH

ACADIAN VILLAGE — A re-creation of an early 19th-century bayou settlement, the village is on 10 wooded acres with a meandering bayou criss-crossed by wooden footbridges. Each of the houses—authentic but built elsewhere in the early 1800s and moved to this site—represents a different style of Acadian architecture and is decorated with antique furnishings. The rustic general store, blacksmith shop, and chapel are all replicas of 19th-century buildings. ⊠ *Greenleaf Rd., south of downtown,* ☎ *337/981–2489 or 800/962–9133.* ☞ *$5.50.* ☉ *Daily 10–5.*

❽ **Acadiana Park Nature Station.** Naturalists are on hand in the interpretive center at this three-story cypress structure that overlooks a 40-acre park. Discovery boxes help children get to know the wildflowers, birds, and other outdoorsy things they'll see on the 3½-mi nature trail. ⊠ *E. Alexander St.,* ☎ *337/291–8448.* ☞ *Free.* ☉ *Weekdays 9–5, weekends 11–3.*

❺ **Oil Center.** This 16-square-block conglomeration of odd one-story offices and stores was the center of Louisiana's offshore oil industry for three decades. Many companies have moved to Houston or New Orleans and have been replaced with eateries, cigar and wine stores, and upscale shops. A great bookstore to search out is Lilly's for Books (☞ Shopping, *below*). ✉ *Bordered by Girard Park Dr., Oil Center Dr., Heymann Blvd., and Audubon Blvd.*

❼ Vermilionville Theme Park. Directly behind the **Acadian Cultural Center** (☞ *above*) a living-history village re-creates the early life of the region's Creoles and Cajuns, focusing on the late 1800s to early 1900s. There are exhibits in 22 Acadian structures, including a music hall in which live Cajun music is played weekdays 1:30–3:30 and weekends 12:30–2. A large, rustic restaurant serves "whatever Mama's cooking today," and cooking demonstrations are presented weekdays at 11 and 1:30, weekends 11:30 and 1:30. ✉ *1600 Surrey St.,* ☎ *337/233–4077 or 800/992–2968.* ⬚ *$8.* ⊙ *Daily 10–5; tours 10:15, 12:30, and 3.*

Dining

$$$–$$$$ ✕ **Café Vermilionville.** This 19th-century inn with crisp white napery and old-brick fireplaces serves French and Cajun fare. Among the specialties are pecan-crusted tilapia, Louisiana Crab Madness (crabmeat prepared au gratin or as an étouffée), and snapper Anna (fillets sautéed in white wine and butter and laced with crawfish tails, mushrooms, and artichoke hearts). ✉ *1304 W. Pinhook Rd.,* ☎ *337/237–0100. AE, D, DC, MC, V. No lunch Sat., no dinner Sun.*

$$–$$$ ✕ **Prejean's.** Oyster shuckers work in a cozy bar at this local favorite
★   in a cypress house with a wide front porch and a 50-ft shrimp boat parked outside. People gather at tables with red-and-white-check cloths to partake of Prejean's seafood platter (gumbo, fried shrimp, oysters, catfish, and seafood-stuffed bell peppers) as well as Cajun rack of elk, American buffalo au poivre, and steak and chicken prepared in various ways. There's live Cajun music nightly. ✉ *3480 U.S. 167N, south of Evangeline Downs,* ☎ *337/896–3247. AE, D, DC, MC, V.*

$ ✕ **Creole Lunch House.** Retired high school principal Merline Hebert serves spicy plate lunches. The baked chicken and dirty rice is good but be sure to try Hebert's patented specialty, Creole Stuffed Bread. Service is cafeteria-style and seating is in a six-table dining room or on an outdoor patio. Despite the name, the Creole Lunch House opens at 5 AM for breakfast. ✉ *713 12th St., in the Northgate Mall,* ☎ *337/232–9929. AE, MC, V. No dinner.*

$ ✕ **Dwyer's Café.** People jam this diner as early as 5 AM, having hot biscuits and grits. It serves red beans and rice, jambalaya, pot roast, burgers, and omelets, and has been going strong since 1927. ✉ *323 Jefferson St.,* ☎ *337/235–9364. AE, MC, V. Closed Sun. No dinner.*

$ ✕ **T-Coon's Cafe.** This lively diner serves hearty (half-orders are recommended) Cajun lunches such as smothered rabbit or stuffed pork chops with two vegetables, rice, and gravy. Locals gather in the back room for conversation, jokes, and raucous songs in French. ✉ *740 Jefferson St.,* ☎ *318/232–3803. AE, MC, V. No dinner.*

Lodging

$$$–$$$$ ▥ **Bois Des Chênes Inn.** This B&B is in a 19th-century carriage house at the rear of the Mouton Plantation, which dates from about 1820. The upstairs suite, which can accommodate five adults, has early Acadian antiques; downstairs, the Louisiana Empire Suite has a queen-size bed, and the Victorian Suite has a tester double bed. Two suites are in the main house. Included in the rate are a welcoming glass of wine and a tour of the plantation house. Proprietor Coerte Voorhies conducts great boat tours through the surrounding swamps and bayous. ✉ *338 N. Sterling St., 70501,* ☎ FAX *337/233–7816. 5 suites. AE, MC, V. BP.*

$$–$$$$ ⬚ **Lafayette Hilton & Towers.** Mirrored pillars and medieval tapestries
★ fill the ballroom-size lobby, and guest rooms seem only slightly smaller.
Traditional furnishings outfit the standard rooms; rooms on concierge
floors come with hot tubs and wet bars. Riverside rooms have a view
of the Bayou Vermilion, upon whose banks this high-rise rises. ✉
1521 Pinhook Rd., 70505, ☎ *337/235–6111 or 800/332–2586,* 𝖥𝖠𝖷 *318/
261–0311. 327 rooms. Restaurant, bar, pool, exercise room, concierge
floors, airport shuttle, helipad. AE, D, DC, MC, V.* 🐾

$$–$$$ ⬚ **T'Frere's House.** Built in 1880 of native cypress and handmade
★ bricks, "little brother's house" has been a B&B since 1985. About 2
mi south from the Oil Center (☞ *above*), the Acadian-style house
with Victorian trim is furnished with French and Louisiana antiques.
Additional accommodations are in an Acadian-style cottage behind the
main house. Guests are greeted with a complimentary "T" julep" and
"Cajun canapés," hors d'oeuvres made with boudin. ✉ *1905 Verot
School Rd., 70508,* ☎ *337/984–9347 or 800/984–9347. 4 rooms, 1
cottage. Hot tub, coin laundry. AE, D, MC, V. BP.* 🐾

Nightlife and the Arts

Nightlife

Pick up a copy of the *Times of Acadiana* and check the "On the Town"
listings for fais-do-dos, zydeco dances, and other events. This free
newspaper is available in hotels, restaurants, and shops.

Major concerts are held at the **Cajundome** (✉ 444 Cajundome Blvd.,
☎ 337/265–2100) and at the **Heymann Performing Arts Center** (✉ 1373
S. College Rd., ☎ 337/291–5540).

At **Back to Back** (✉ Northgate Mall, Evangeline Thruway, ☎ 337/232–
9500 or 337/232–0272), which is two clubs in one, folks slow dance
to swamp pop (a mix of country, New Orleans–style R&B, and blue-
eyed soul) and Louisiana standards Thursday–Sunday. On Friday af-
ternoon from April through June and September through November,
Downtown Alive! (✉ Jefferson St. at Main St.) draws dancing crowds
to downtown Lafayette, where bands play on an open-air stage. **El Sido's**
(✉ 1523 Martin Luther King Jr. Dr., ☎ 337/235–0647) is a family-
run zydeco club. Sid Williams manages the club while his brother's band,
Nathan Williams and the Zydeco Cha-Chas, performs frequently. **Four
Seasons Lodge** (✉ 4855 W. Congress St., ☎ 337/989–2421) has been
Lafayette's premier swamp pop dance hall for 40 years; the smoke is
thick and the dancing close.

Grant Street Dance Hall (✉ 1113 W. Grant St., ☎ 337/237–2255), like
Tipitina's in New Orleans, features roots and rock and roll music by
local and touring bands. Call and check out their prerecorded concert
line. **Hamilton's** (✉ 1808 Verot School Rd., ☎ 337/984–5583) is a
weather-beaten, country-style zydeco dance hall that has been around
since the 1920s. Play dates are erratic; call before heading out. **Ran-
dol's** (✉ 2320 Kaliste Saloom Rd., ☎ 337/981–7080 or 800/962–2586),
a Cajun "fern restaurant" (with lots of ferns and hanging plants), has
music and dancing nightly.

Festivals

The biggest bash in this neck of the woods is **Cajun Mardi Gras** (Febru-
ary or March), which showcases colorful parades and King Gabriel and
Queen Evangeline. Lafayette's **Festival International de Louisiane** (✉
Box 4008, 70502, ☎ 337/232–8086), which takes place on the third
weekend of April, is a free event that fills the streets with entertainers,
artisans, and chefs from French-speaking nations and communities. The
annual September **Festival Acadiens** is a huge music-and-food fest in

CAJUN AND ZYDECO MUSIC

I T'S 9 AM ON A TYPICAL SATURDAY morning in the Cajun prairie town of Mamou, and Fred's Lounge (☞ Nightlife and the Arts *in* Eunice) is already so full that people are spilling out the door. Inside, Cajun singer Donald Thibodeaux gets a nod from the radio announcer, squeezes his accordion, and launches into a bluesy rendition of "Pine Grove Blues." Oblivious to the posted warning, THIS IS NOT A DANCEHALL, the packed bar begins to roil. Fred's Lounge may not be a "formal" dance hall, but plenty of dancing is done here; it gets pretty lively during Mamou's Mardi Gras and Fourth of July celebrations. And every Saturday morning for more than 40 years, live Cajun radio shows have been broadcast from the late Fred Tate's lounge. Cajuns who have chank-a-chanked late Friday night pack into Fred's on Saturday morning, waltzing around the ropes and keeping the bartender busy. Things get revved up at 8 am and keep going till 1 pm, and the show is aired on Ville Platte's KVPI radio (1250 AM).

You needn't be a detective to find indigenous music in South Louisiana. Just spin the radio dial, or roll down your window while driving past an old bar on some country road, and you are likely to hear the wheeze of a Cajun accordion or the scrape of spoons on a zydeco rubboard.

Music has been an integral expression of Cajun culture since early Acadian immigrants unpacked string instruments and gathered in homes for song and socializing. With the growth of towns these house parties—called "fais-do-dos"—were supplanted by dance halls. Accordions, steel guitars, and drums were added and amplified to be heard over the noise of crowded barrooms. The term fais-do-do (pronounced *fay*-doh-doh, from "go to sleep" in French) comes from words mothers murmured to put their babies to sleep while the fiddlers tuned up before a dance.

Cajun music went through some lean years in the 1940s and '50s when the state attempted to eradicate the use of the Cajun French language, but today folks of all ages can enjoy Cajun music at street festivals and restaurants such as Randol's, Prejean's, and Mulate's, which serve equal portions of seafood and song. These places not only provide an opportunity for the music and dance tradition to be passed on to a new generation but also serve as magnets for Cajun dance enthusiasts from around the world.

Z YDECO, THE HIGHLY RHYTHMIC dance music of South Louisiana's black Creole people, can be a bit harder to find than Cajun music, usually requiring a trip to one of the rural dance halls where the music is played on weekends. Modern zydeco and Cajun music are both accordion-based, but zydeco tends to be faster and more syncopated. Many bands have incorporated electric guitars, drums, and even saxophones as well as accordions. Bands often play soul- and rhythm and blues–inflected tunes sung in Creole French. The beat is thrashed out on a corrugated rubboard (called a *frottoir*), which is struck with honed spoons.

Whatever music you find in Cajun Country, you can expect a warm welcome and a full dance floor. South Louisiana music is dance music, and many folks are surprised when there is no applause. Appreciation is best shown in lively two stepping and waltzes. Dance is the universal language of Cajun Country, but don't worry if you're not fluent; there is always someone happy to lead you around the floor and leave you feeling like a local.

If you'd like to hear some Cajun and zydeco tunes before (or after) your trip, *see* What to Read, Watch, & and Listen To Before You Go *in* Chapter 8.

Lafayette. Contact the **Lafayette Convention and Visitors Commission** (⊠ 1400 N.W. Evangeline Thruway, ☎ 337/232–3808 or 800/346–1958) for information on all events.

Shopping

Antiques

Antiques hunting is a favorite pastime in these parts. You can root around **Ruins & Relics** (⊠ 802 Jefferson St., ☎ 337/233–9163). **The Crowded Attic** (⊠ 400 Plantation Rd., ☎ 337/237–5559) has a good selection. Locals enjoy sorting through **Solomon's Splendor Antique Mall** (⊠ 731 Rue de Belier, ☎ 337/984–5776). A good browsing place is the **Lafayette Antique Market** (⊠ 2015 Johnston St., ☎ 337/269–9430).

Art and Crafts

Seventeen vendors sell works by local artists and craftspeople in **Jefferson Street Market** (⊠ 538 Jefferson St., ☎ 337/233–2589), including folk art and items such as turned cypress bowls, hand-spun and handwoven textiles, bent-willow furniture, and model boats.

Lafayette Art Gallery (⊠ Oil Center, 412 Travis St., ☎ 337/269–0363) showcases and sells paintings, pottery, jewelry, and glass made by local artists. It's open Tuesday–Friday noon–5 and Saturday by appointment.

Books

Lilly's for Books (⊠ 913 Harding St., Oil Center, ☎ 337/232–2764) specializes in books on regional topics and has many signed editions by local authors and photographers.

Food

Restaurants all over the country serve their own versions of Cajun food, but you can take some of the real thing home with you. The **Cajun Country Store** (⊠ 401 E. Cypress, ☎ 337/233–7977 or 800/252–9689) sells Cajun gift packages.

Lafayette A to Z

For travel information and contacts and resources that will be useful in Lafayette and throughout Cajun Country, *see* Elsewhere in Cajun Country A to Z, *below*.

ELSEWHERE IN CAJUN COUNTRY

French Louisiana, lying amid the bayous, rice paddies, and canebrakes to the west of New Orleans, has become famous in the rest of the country through its food (po'boys and blackened fish) and music (both Cajun and zydeco). The Cajun culture dates from about 1604 when French settlers colonized a region they called l'Acadie in the present-day Canadian provinces of Nova Scotia and New Brunswick. The British seized control of the region in the early 18th century and the French were expelled. Their exile was described by Henry Wadsworth Longfellow in his epic poem "Evangeline." Many Acadians eventually settled in 22 parishes of southwestern Louisiana. Their descendants are called "Cajun," a corruption of "Acadian"; some continue the traditions of the early French settlers, living by fishing and fur trapping.

Cajun French is an oral tradition, a 17th-century French that differs significantly from what is spoken in France. Still, students of French should be able to participate without much difficulty. English is also spoken throughout Cajun Country, but you will hear Gallic accents and see many signs that read ICI ON PARLE FRANÇAIS (French spoken here).

In Mamou and Eunice in Acadia Parish, the *Courir de Mardi Gras* (Mardi Gras run) is a wild affair with masked and costumed horseback riders following *le capitain* for a mad dash through the countryside in search of gumbo ingredients.

Numbers in the margin correspond to points of interest on the Cajun Country map.

Grand Coteau

❾ *11 mi north of Lafayette.*

Grand Coteau nestles against a sweeping ridge that was a natural levee of the Mississippi River centuries ago. The tiny village (about 10 square blocks) of 1,100 residents may be the most serene place in South Louisiana. More than 70 structures are listed on the National Register of Historic Places, including Creole cottages, early Acadian-style homes, and the grand Academy of the Sacred Heart. Martin Luther King Drive (Route 93) is the main thoroughfare.

A magnificent avenue of pines and moss-hung oaks leads to the entrance of the **Academy and Convent of the Sacred Heart,** founded in 1821 and the site of the only Vatican-certified miracle to occur in the United States. The miracle occurred when a very ill novitiate at the convent said novenas to John Berchmans, who appeared to her twice. The novitiate, Mary Wilson, was cured, and Berchmans was canonized in 1888. Visitors may enter a **shrine** on the exact site of the miracle and (by appointment only) tour a **museum** with artifacts dating to the school's occupation by Union troops during the Civil War. ✉ *End of Church St.,* ☎ *337/662–5275.* 🎟 *$5.* ☉ *Weekdays 9–5.*

In one of Grand Coteau's historic cottages, the **Kitchen Shop** specializes in regional cookbooks and cooking supplies. It also has prints and greeting cards by famed local photographer John Slaughter. In a tea room, pastry chef Nancy Brewer prepares scones, cookies, and a rich tart she calls pecan-na-na. ✉ *Martin Luther King Dr. at Cherry St.,* ☎ *318/662–3500.* ☉ *Mon.–Sat. 10–5, Sun. noon–4.*

Dining

$$–$$$ ✕ **Catahoula's.** This stylish yet simple restaurant in an old dry-goods store serves ambitious contemporary cuisine prepared with Mediterranean flair. In a signature starter course, firm gulf shrimp are dressed with grilled onions, poblano peppers, and feta cheese, then wrapped in a flour tortilla. For a pure Louisiana experience, try the smoked seafood–stuffed soft-shell crab with strawberry-fig butter. ✉ *234 Martin Luther King Dr.,* ☎ *337/662–2275. AE, MC, V. Closed Mon. No dinner Sun.*

Opelousas

❿ *15 mi north of Grant Coteau.*

Opelousas is the third-oldest town in the state—Poste de Opelousas was founded in 1720 by the French as a trading post. At the intersection of I–49 and U.S. 190, look for the **Opelousas Tourist Information Center** (☎ *337/948–6263*), where you can get plenty of information; arrange for tours of historic homes; and see memorabilia pertaining to Jim Bowie, the Alamo hero who spent his early years in Opelousas.

Nightlife and the Arts

Plaisance, near Opelousas, holds a **Zydeco Festival** in September.

"That's the place that the people love," sings popular zydeco musician Beau Jocque, about **Richard's Club** (✉ U.S. 190, Lawtell, ☎ 337/543–6596), a rural, wood-frame zydeco club west of Opelousas. **Slim's Y-**

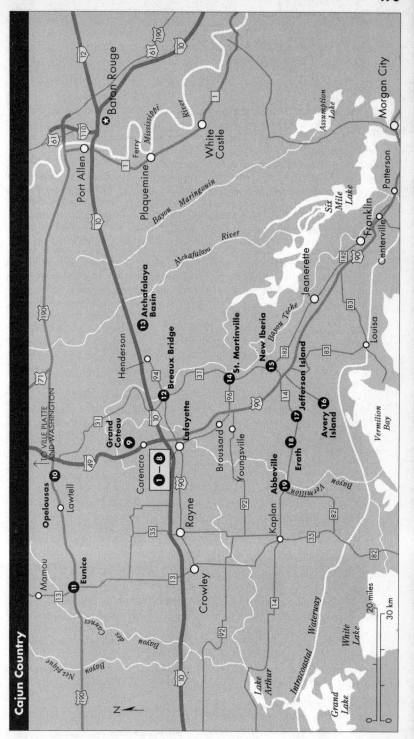

Cajun Country

OUT ON THE WATER

LEGEND HAS IT THAT SOMEWHERE in the Atchafalaya swamp lives a catfish more than 6 ft long. Although that "whopper" may or may not be true, what can't be disputed is Louisiana's claim as the Sportsmen's Paradise. Ever since Chef Paul Prudhomme blackened his first redfish caught in local waters, the secret has been out—there's plenty of fish to be had almost everywhere in Louisiana.

The **Gulf of Mexico** and its brackish-water coastal marsh region have made Louisiana famous for shrimp, blue crab, oysters, and fish. And folks are looking for much more than just oil out at the rigs in the Gulf. Whether you choose to troll around the rigs or to anchor for some casting, you'll find brag-size lemonfish, cobia, snapper, yellowfin tuna, speckled trout, Spanish and king mackerel, sailfish, wahoo, and even pompano. Many of the marinas in Grand Isle, Cocodrie, and Venice offer charter fishing trips that include all fishing tackle, fuel, soft drinks, ice, and someone to bait your hook during the trip and clean your fish when it's over. Prices range from $200 to $500 a day depending on where you fish and for how long. Trips range from 4 to 8 hours or overnight. If you're not inclined to pay for a charter, there are plenty of piers, wharves, bridges, and jetties like those at Grand Isle State Park to give you easy access to the open water.

If you're lucky enough to be in Louisiana during the second to last weekend in July, you may want to try your hand at one of the great fishing events in the world, the **Grand Isle Tarpon Rodeo** (☎ 504/763–6400). Every year, records are broken in several categories including redfish, grouper, shark, flounder, and—of course—tarpon.

If saltwater fishing isn't your thing, don't worry: there's plenty of freshwater to go around. Top spots include the **Atchafalaya Basin,** Louisiana's magnificent 800,000-plus-acre natural swampland with facilities at Lake Fausse Point State park; and **Toledo Bend Reservoir,** a 186,000-acre bass fishing paradise lined with campgrounds, marinas, and North Toledo Bend State Park. There are numerous oxbow lakes such as **False River,** north of Baton Rouge, and **Lake Bruin** where you can find scads of bream, goggle-eye, and perch.

Also very popular are the **swamp and gator tours.** Most tour operators offer convenient departure time (usually mid-morning and mid-afternoon) and hotel pick-ups in New Orleans. Most tour operators use pontoon boats, but—depending on the size of the group—a bass boat might be used. Anticipate from 1 to 2 hours on the water and 45 minutes commute time to and from New Orleans. Prices generally range from $15 to $20 per person. Expect to see coypu or nutria, a member of the rodent family that resembles a beaver in appearance and size, egrets (a white, long-necked heron with flowing feathers), turtles, and the occasional snake. During the warmer months, alligator sightings are commonplace; many of the guides use either chicken or marshmallows to attract them. Plant life includes Spanish moss, cypress, water oaks, and water hyacinths (a member of the lily family). Swamp tours are readily available in New Orleans, Lafayette, and Houma (☞ Sightseeing Tours *in* Smart Travel Tips A to Z).

FOR INFORMATION ON FISHING licenses, contact the **Louisiana Department of Wildlife and Fisheries** (✉ Box 98000, Baton Rouge 70898-9000, ☎ 225/765–2800). For lake maps, call **Louisiana Conservationists** (☎ 225/765–2934). The New Orleans Metropolitan Convention & Visitor Center (☞ Visitor Information *in* Smart Travel Tips A to Z) can provide a list of charter fishing companies.

Ki-Ki (⊠ U.S. 182, ☎ 337/942–9980), a rural zydeco club since 1947, has huge industrial fans to cool down the regular dance crowd.

Shopping

For Cajun and zydeco music recordings and related products, **Floyd's Record Shop** (⊠ 434 E. Main St., Ville Platte, ☎ 337/363–2138) is well worth the drive.

The largest antiques and collectibles flea market in Acadiana is held each weekend at the **Washington School Mall Flea Market** (⊠ Vine and Church Sts., Washington, ☎ 337/984–5776). Every classroom in the old schoolhouse as well as the gymnasium out back is stuffed with the exotic, rare, and campy.

Eunice

⓫ *20 mi west of Opelousas.*

Tiny Eunice is home to the Cajun radio show *Rendez-Vous des Cajuns* (☞ Nightlife and the Arts, *below*) and a number of other attractions. The **Eunice Museum** is in a former railroad depot and contains displays on Cajun culture, including Cajun music and Cajun Mardi Gras. ⊠ *220 S. C. C. Duson Dr.,* ☎ *337/457–6540.* ⊡ *Free.* ⊘ *Tues.–Sat. 8–noon and 1–5.*

The large **Prairie Acadian Cultural Center,** part of the Jean Lafitte National Historical Park, has good exhibits that trace the history and culture of the Prairie Acadians, whose lore and customs differ from those of the Bayou Acadians around Lafayette. Food, crafts, and music demonstrations are held from time to time. ⊠ *250 W. Park Ave.,* ☎ *337/457–8490 or 337/457–8499.* ⊡ *Free.* ⊘ *Daily 8–5.*

The **Savoy Music Center and Accordion Factory** includes a music store and, in back, a Cajun accordion workshop. Proprietor Marc Savoy's factory turns out about five accordions a month for people around the world. On Saturday morning, accordions and other instruments tune up during jam sessions in the shop. Musicians from all over the area drop in, and there's beer and two-stepping. ⊠ *U.S. 190, 3 mi east of town,* ☎ *337/457–9563.* ⊡ *Free.* ⊘ *Tues.–Fri. 9–5, Sat. 9–noon.*

The area surrounding Eunice is the major stomping ground for an annual event, **Courir de Mardi Gras,** which takes place the Sunday before Fat Tuesday (Mardi Gras Day). Costumed horseback riders on dash through the countryside, stopping at farmhouses along the way to shout, *"Voulez-vous recevoir cette bande de Mardi Gras* (Do you wish to receive the Mardi Gras band)?" The answer is always yes, and the group enlarges and continues, gathering food for the street festivals that wind things up. For information, contact the **Lafayette Convention and Visitors Bureau** (☎ 800/346–1958).

Nightlife and the Arts

In addition to showcasing the best Cajun and zydeco bands, **Rendez-Vous des Cajuns,** a two-hour variety program, presents local comedians and even a "Living Recipe Corner." The show, mostly in French, has been dubbed the Cajun Grand Ole Opry; it's broadcast weekly on local radio and TV from a 1924 movie house. ⊠ *Liberty Center for the Performing Arts, 2nd St. and Park Ave.,* ☎ *337/457–6577.* ⊡ *$2.* ⊘ *Show Sat. at 6.*

Fred's Lounge (☞ Close-Up: Cajun and Zydeco Music) hops on Saturday morning when live radio shows are broadcast from here. Drive north from Eunice on Route 13 to Mamou, a town so small you can drive around for 5 minutes and find Fred's. ⊠ *420 6th St., Mamou,* ☎ *337/468–5411.* ⊡ *Free.*

Breaux Bridge

★ ⑫ *10 mi east of Lafayette, 20 mi southeast of Grand Coteau.*

A dyed-in-the-wool Cajun town, Breaux Bridge is known as the Crawfish Capital of the World. During the first full weekend in May, the Crawfish Festival draws more than 100,000 visitors to this little village on Bayou Teche. Once a wild place, old Breaux Bridge has attracted a small arts community that includes renowned Louisiana photographer Debbie Fleming Caffery, and has traded its honky-tonks for B&Bs, antiques shops, and restaurants.

This town of 6,500 has a Main Street (Route 31) that has changed little over the years; still in evidence are a range of watering holes and card rooms left over from its heyday during Prohibition. Main Street, in addition to Bridge Street on both sides of the bayou, constitutes downtown. You can pick up a city map and information at the **Chamber of Commerce** (⊠ Huval Insurance Company Bldg., 111 Rees St., ☎ 318/ 332–5406). Rees Street (Route 328) is about ½ mi south of I–10.

Dining and Lodging

$$–$$$ ★ ✕ **Café des Amis.** The culinary heart and soul of downtown Breaux Bridge rests in this renovated old store just a block from Bayou Teche. In warm weather the doors are flung open and locals and visitors gather to enjoy hospitality that is second only to the food. Sample the ambience over cocktails or coffee at the bar, or take a table and try the shrimp and okra gumbo and the eggplant wheels topped with crawfish. Three ice-box pies are served daily. Breakfast here should be savored, from the fresh-squeezed orange juice to the pastry-wrapped boudin, couscous, and black java. ⊠ *140 Bridge St.,* ☎ *318/332–5273. AE, D, MC, V. Closed Mon. No dinner Tues., Wed., or Sun.*

$$–$$$ ★ ✕ **Mulate's.** A roadhouse with flashing yellow lights outside and red-and-white plastic tablecloths inside, Mulate's is a Cajun eatery, a dance hall (live Cajun music every weekday during lunch and daily during dinner), and a family gathering place that has been featured on many national TV programs. A dressed-down crowd digs into the likes of stuffed crabs and the Super Seafood Platter. ⊠ *325 Mills Ave. (Rte. 94),* ☎ *337/ 332–4648, 800/634–9880 in LA, 800/422–2586 elsewhere. AE, MC, V.*

$$ 🏠 **Maison des Amis.** The owners of Café des Amis (☞ *above*), Cynthia and Dickie Breaux, renovated this 19th-century house on the banks of Bayou Teche with comfort and perhaps romance in mind. Each room has a private entrance and a queen bed covered with luxurious linens and huge pillows. A pier and gazebo are perfect for watching moonlight over the bayou. The complimentary Cajun breakfast at Café des Amis is not to be missed. ⊠ *140 Bridge St., 70517,* ☎ *337/ 322–5273. 3 rooms, 1 suite. AE, D, MC, V. BP.* ✒

Nightlife

Harry's (⊠ 519 Parkway Dr., ☎ 337/332–6852) resembles a high school gym more than a dance hall, but every Sunday at 5—when the house lights go down and the beer signs flicker on—the dance floor fills with old-timers. Harry's is ½ mi south of I–10. **La Poussière** (⊠ 1212 Grand Point Rd., ☎ 337/332–1721), an ancient Cajun honky-tonk, is where local favorite Walter Mouton plays every Saturday.

Atchafalaya Basin

⑬ *5 mi east of Breaux Bridge, 12 mi east of Lafayette.*

The Atchafalaya Basin is an eerily beautiful 800,000-acre wilderness swamp, characteristic of South Louisiana's exotic wetlands. Boating enthusiasts, bird-watchers, photographers, and nature lovers are drawn by vast expanses of still water, cypresses standing knee-deep in water and dripping with Spanish moss, and blue herons taking flight. The basin is best viewed from one of the tour boats that ply its waters, but it is possible to explore around its edges on the 7 mi of Henderson's Levee Road (also known as Route 5; I–10, Exit 115), which provides several opportunities to cross the levee and access swamp tours, bars, and restaurants on the other side.

Pontoon boats at **McGee's Landing** take passengers daily for 1½- to 2-hour tours of the Atchafalaya Basin. You can also rent a boat and fishing gear and hire a guide here. McGee's is a 25-minute drive east of Lafayette. ⊠ *Levee Rd., Henderson (from I-10, Exit 115 at Henderson; 1 block south of the highway turn left on Rte. 352 and follow it 7 mi east over Bayou Amy; turn right atop the levee onto Levee Rd.),* ☎ *337/228–2384.* ⌨ *Tour $8.50.*

Angelle's Whiskey River Landing (⊠ 1¾ mi south of Rte. 352, on the Levee Rd. on the left) is the departure point for **Angelle's Swamp Tours** (☎ 337/228–8567, $8.50) and the site of the lively **Angelle's Atchafalaya Basin Bar** (☎ 337/228–8567). On Sunday afternoon when the last tour boat comes in, Cajun bands play in a dance hall right over the water. The music usually starts around 4 PM and attracts a crowd of fishermen, locals, and visitors. Beer and burgers are served.

You can explore the swamp on your own in a rented canoe ($12 per day) or motorboat ($30 per day) from **Wiltz Landing** (⊠ Levee Rd., Henderson, ☎ 337/228–7880), which is less than 1 mi south of the Bayou Amy Bridge.

St. Martinville

⑭   *15 mi south of Breaux Bridge.*

St. Martinville, along winding Bayou Teche, is in the heart of Evangeline country. It was founded in 1761 and became a refuge for royalists who escaped the guillotine during the French Revolution. Known as Petit Paris, this little town was once the scene of lavish balls and operas. It's a worthwhile stop, but neighboring towns are better for dining and nightlife.

Longfellow's poem about the star-crossed lovers Evangeline and Gabriel is based on a true story. According to the oft-told tale, the real-life lovers, Emmeline Labiche and Louis Arceneaux, met for the last time under the **Evangeline Oak** (⊠ Evangeline Blvd. at Bayou Teche). As in Longfellow's poem, the lovers were separated during the arduous Acadian exodus. Louis arrived in St. Martinville, a major debarkation port for the refugees, but it was many years before Emmeline came. The legend has it that the two saw each other by chance just as she stepped ashore. He turned deadly pale with shock and told her that, having despaired of ever seeing her again, he was betrothed to another. *The Romance of Evangeline* was filmed in St. Martinville in 1929. The privately owned movie was never distributed, but clips from it are incorporated in the film presentation at the Jean Lafitte National Historical Park Acadian Cultural Center (☞ Acadian Cultural Center *in* Lafayette, *above*). Its star, Dolores Del Rio, posed for the bronze statue of Evangeline that the cast and crew donated to St. Martinville; it is in the cemetery behind the church of St. Martin de Tours (☞ *below*), near the final resting place of Emmeline Labiche.

Shaded by giant live oaks draped with Spanish moss, the 157-acre **Longfellow-Evangeline State Commemorative Area** has picnic tables and pavilions, a boat launch, and early Acadian structures. The Evangeline legend claims that Louis Arceneaux, on whom Gabriel was based, lived in the **Acadian House** on the park's grounds, but there is no evidence that he did. The house was built in the mid-18th century of handmade bricks and it contains Louisiana antiques. ⊠ *Rte. 31 and Bayou Teche (½ mi north of St. Martinsville),* ☎ *337/394–3754.* ≈ *$2.* ⊙ *Park daily 9–5, house Wed.–Sun. 9–4:30.*

St. Martin de Tours (⊠ 123 S. Main St., ☎ 337/394–2233) is the Mother Church of the Acadians and one of the country's oldest Catholic churches; the 1836 building was erected on the site on an earlier church. Inside is a replica of the Lourdes grotto and a baptismal font said to have been a gift from Louis XVI. Emmeline Labiche is buried in the cemetery.

The **Petit Paris Museum** on the church (St. Martin de Tours) square contains historical records, Carnival costumes, a video history of Mardi Gras, and a chariot exhibit. The chariots are from an annual one-of-a-kind event, the **Chariot Parade**—a colorful procession of wagons, made by children, that depict anything from a streetcar to a castle. The children and their fanciful chariots circle the church square, beginning at dusk on the third Sunday of August. ⊠ *103 S. Main St.,* ☎ *337/394–7334.* ≈ *$1.* ⊙ *Daily 9:30–4:30.*

Lodging

$$ 🏨 **Old Castillo Hotel/La Place d'Evangeline.** In the late-19th century the Castillo Hotel, a two-story redbrick building next to the Evangeline Oak and Bayou Teche, was an inn for steamboat passengers and a gathering place for French royalists. Guest rooms are large and have hardwood floors, early Louisiana antiques, and decorative touches such as marble table-tops, cheval mirrors, and pitchers and washbowls. The restaurant here is not recommended. ⊠ *220 Evangeline Blvd., 70582,* ☎ *337/394–4010 or 800/621–3017,* 𝖥𝖠𝖷 *337/394–7983. Restaurant. AE, MC, V. BP.* 🍴

New Iberia

★ ⑮   *14 mi south of St. Martinville.*

New Iberia is known as the Queen City of the Teche because of its proximity to the adjacent bayou and its high profile in the sugar industry. Spanish settlers founded the town in 1779, naming it after the Iberian Peninsula. The grand homes of sugarcane planters dominate the residential section of Main Street. Park downtown or stay in one of the classy B&Bs here and you can easily walk to the bayou, restaurants, and attractions in the historic business district. Downtown stretches eight blocks east and west on Main Street (Route 182) from the intersection of Center Street (Route 14). Shadows on the Teche (☞ *below*) is at this intersection and is a good place to park.

Shadows-on-the-Teche, one of the South's best-known plantation homes, was built on the bank of the bayou for wealthy sugar planter David Weeks in 1834. Surrounded by 2 acres of lush gardens and moss-draped oaks, the two-story rose-hued house has white columns, exterior staircases sheltered in cabinets (cabinetlike enclosures), and a pitched roof pierced by dormer windows. Shadows, a museum property of the National Trust for Historic Preservation, is authentically restored and furnished. ⊠ *317 E. Main St.,* ☎ *337/369–6446.* ≈ *$8.* ⊙ *Daily 9–4:30.*

The **Gerbert Oak** (⊠ 541 E. Main St.) is a member in good standing of the Live Oak Society. Planted in 1831 and dripping with ferns and moss, this massive tree stretches over almost an entire lawn. It is named for a family that once lived on the property, although the tree was originally planted to mark the grave of a child whose surname was Morse.

The **Conrad Rice Mill** is the country's oldest rice mill still in operation, dating from 1912, and it produces a distinctive wild pecan rice. ⊠ *307 Ann St., ☎ 337/367–6163 or 800/551–3245. ⊉ $2.75. ☉ Weekdays 9–5; tours at 10, 11, 1, 2, and 3.*

The tour boats at **Airboats Inc.** (⊠ Loreauville, 11 mi northeast of New Iberia, ☎ 337/229–4457) will take you across miles of lotus-covered water to a majestic stand of 200-year-old cypresses before they skid into shallow alligator ponds. Powered by an airplane propeller attached to a car engine, airboats are faster and louder than any other tour craft and can run on very shallow water. Tours are by appointment.

Dining and Lodging

$$–$$$ ✕ **Lagniappe Too.** Lighter fare than you'd expect in Cajun Country is served at this casual café just a block from Shadows-on-the-Teche. The owners' paintings and oversize stuffed dolls add personal touches. Fresh and spicy green salads or marinated chicken salad dotted with pecans and olives are great starters. Sandwiches are carefully prepared; for something richer, try the steaks and the bread pudding. ⊠ *204 E. Main St., ☎ 337/365–9419. AE, MC, V. Closed Sun. No dinner Mon.–Thurs.*

$$$ ✕🖬 **leRosier.** Chef Hallman Woods III has won kudos for the new Acadian cuisine he has introduced at the elegant leRosier, a 19th-century house across from Shadows-on-the-Teche plantation. Dinner ($$$–$$$$; Fri.–Sat. only) in the small rear dining room is the best entertainment in town. Crawfish spring rolls with ginger and beurre blanc, and grilled duck with sweet-potato hay are typical of the creative fare. Guest rooms have their private entrances and are in an original outbuilding. Although rooms are small and have few windows, each has a king bed; two have hot tubs. ⊠ *314 Main St., ☎ 337/367–5306 or 888/804–7673. 6 rooms. Restaurant. AE, MC, V. BP.* ✑

$$–$$$ 🖬 **Bayou Teche Guest Cottage.** There could scarcely be a better way to appreciate the Queen City of the Teche than to spend a night in this refurbished 18th-century cottage right on the banks of the bayou, only four blocks from downtown attractions. You can explore the 3 acres of quiet grounds or sit in the front porch rocking chairs and watch towboats ply the waters. The two-room cottage, which sleeps two, is simply furnished; you may prepare meals in the kitchen. ⊠ *100 Teche St., ☎ 337/364–1933. 1 cottage. MC, V.*

Shopping

Konriko Company Store, adjacent to the Conrad Rice Mill (☞ *above*), sells Cajun crafts and foods and has a sight-and-sound show. It's open the same hours as the mill.

Books Along the Teche (⊠ 110 E. Main St., ☎ 337/367–7621), a prime destination for Louisiana bookworms, specializes in titles of regional interest. The store is occasionally visited by local literary legend James Lee Burke, whose Cajun detective Dave Robichaux prowls the streets of New Iberia and New Orleans. You will find not only signed copies of Burke's novels but also a free map of local sites mentioned in his books, paired with relevant quotations.

Avery Island

🔟 *9 mi south of New Iberia.*

The Louisiana coastline is dotted with "hills" or "domes" that sit atop salt mines, and Avery Island is one of these. They are covered with lush vegetation, and because they rise above the surface of the flatlands, they are referred to as islands.

Avery Island is the birthplace of Tabasco sauce, which pleases the Cajun palate and flavors many a Bloody Mary. Tabasco was invented by Edmund McIlhenny in the mid-1800s, and the **Tabasco Factory** is presided over by the fourth generation of the McIlhenny family. You can take a factory tour here. The Jungle Gardens and Bird City (☞ *below*) are adjacent. ⊠ *Rte. 329,* ☎ *337/365–8173.* ⌸ *Free.* ☉ *Weekdays 9–4, Sat. 9–noon.*

☾ The 200-acre **Jungle Gardens** has trails through wisteria, palms, lilies, irises, and ferns. Birdlife includes ducks and geese, and there's also a 1,000-year-old statue of Buddha. These gardens belonged to Edward Avery McIlhenny, who brought back flora from his travels: lotus and papyrus from Egypt, bamboo from China. **Bird City,** a bird sanctuary on the southeast edge of Jungle Gardens, is sometimes so thick with egrets that it appears to be blanketed with snow. The largest egret colony in the world (20,000) begins nesting here in February or March, and their offspring remain until winter. Herons and other birds find refuge here as well. ⊠ *Rte. 329,* ☎ *337/369–6243.* ⌸ *Jungle Gardens and Bird City $5.75.* ☉ *Daily 8–5:30.*

Jefferson Island

⑰ *9 mi south of New Iberia.*

Jefferson Island, named for the actor Joseph Jefferson, who toured the country in the 19th century portraying Rip van Winkle, is, like Avery Island (☞ *above*), one of the many salt domes in the area.

In 1870 Jefferson purchased 5,000 acres here on which he built a winter home: a three-story Steamboat Gothic house with Moorish flourishes, opulent furnishings, and rocking chairs on the wide veranda. Twenty acres, including Jefferson's house, now constitute **Rip van Winkle Gardens,** beautiful formal gardens and groves of oaks, crape myrtle, camellias, and azaleas. A café in the reception area overlooks Lake Peigneur; there are also antique duck decoys and an art gallery with traveling exhibits. An introductory video has incredible footage of the geologic disaster that occurred at Jefferson Island in the early 1980s, when an oil drill punctured the salt dome and drained the entire contents of neighboring Lake Peigneur. ⊠ *5505 Rip van Winkle Rd., off Rte. 14,* ☎ *337/365–3332 or 800/375–3332.* ⌸ *Self-guided garden tour $6.50; house and garden $9.* ☉ *Daily 9–5.*

Erath

⑱ *9 mi west of Jefferson Island.*

The little town of Erath is a quintessential tiny Cajun village. The several rooms of the **Acadian Museum** are filled to the rafters with memorabilia donated by local folks—everything from antique radios and butter churns to patchwork quilts and yellowed newspaper clippings. ⊠ *203 S. Broadway,* ☎ *337/233–5832 or 318/937–5468.* ⌸ *Free; donations suggested.* ☉ *Weekdays 1–4.*

"Factory" conjures up images of assembly lines and high-tech equipment, but **D. L. Menard's Chair Factory** (☎ *337/937–5471*) fits no such description, and the chairs made by Mr. Menard are very much in demand in this part of the country. Mr. Menard is also a songwriter, a musician (he plays the guitar, and has been touring the world with his Cajun band since 1973), a raconteur, and a *traiteur,* or healer. Ladderbacks, old-fashioned rockers, stools, and Early American kitchen chairs are made by hand. The factory is a family business, with Mr. Menard's son making porch swings and his wife and daughter doing the weaving for the rush-seat chairs. Call for directions.

Nightlife

Wilbert "Smiley" Menard operates the most popular Cajun dance hall—**Smiley's Bon Ami** (⊠ Rte. 14 between Erath and Delcambre, ☎ 337/937–4591)—in coastal Louisiana. On a warm Saturday night, cars park on the moist meadow outside this 1950s-style hall. An older crowd fills the dance floor, gliding in the way that only the elder generation of Cajun dancers seems to have mastered. There are jam sessions on Friday and an early show especially popular with seniors on Sunday after mass. Smiley's is open Friday 8 PM–midnight, Saturday 9 PM–1 AM, and Sunday 2 PM–6 PM.

Abbeville

⑲ *5 mi west of Erath, 15 mi south of Lafayette.*

Abbeville has a number of historic buildings and two pretty village squares anchoring the center of downtown. The town sponsors the annual Giant Omelette Festival each November, when some 5,000 eggs go into the concoction. At other times, oysters are the culinary draw.

You can pick up a self-guided walking-tour brochure at the **Abbeville Main Street Program Office** (⊠ 101 N. State St., ☎ 318/898–4110). Many buildings in the 20-block Main Street district are on the National Register of Historic Places. **St. Mary Magdalen Catholic Church** (⊠ N. Main and Père Megret Sts.) is a fine Romanesque Revival building with stunning stained-glass windows.

For more than 100 years critters from mules to pigs have pounded the turf at **Cajun Downs** (⊠ Rte. 338, off the Rte. 14 bypass, ☎ 318/893–8160 or 318/893–0421). The "bush track"—so called because it's in the bush—is next to a cane field. There's nothing fancy here; the official betting window is a cash box under a ramshackle shed. Every Sunday morning, weather permitting, Cajuns back their pickups right up to the dirt track, turn their radios up, and watch the goings-on from lawn chairs in the back of their trucks. The Cajun Runyonesque crowd is nothing if not colorful and friendly. You can get beer, burgers, and such in an extremely rustic "clubhouse." There are usually a half dozen races or more on Sunday, but call to see if the races are on.

Dining

$–$$ ✕ **Black's.** Fresh, salty oysters are the specialty at this restaurant in a
★ vast, high-ceiling building opposite the St. Mary Magdalen Church. Fresh seafood reigns supreme here; the only offerings for red-meat eaters are a lone burger and a rib eye. Shrimp and oysters dominate the appetizer list; po'boys include catfish loaf and soft-shell–crab loaf. Seafood platters, fried blue-channel catfish, and stuffed crabs are entrées tucked amid the array of shrimp and oyster dishes. ⊠ *319 Père Megret St.,* ☎ *318/893–4266. AE, MC, V. Closed Sun., Mon.*

$–$$ ✕ **Richard's Seafood Patio.** Richard's (pronounced Ree-charz) is a family-style place, not far from Cajun Downs. It's well-known in these parts for superb boiled crawfish, shrimp, and crabs. ⊠ *1516 S. Henry St.,* ☎ *318/893–1693. MC, V. No lunch.*

$–$$ ✕ **Shucks!** To folks throughout Cajun Country, Abbeville means oysters, and the owners at Shucks! have been serving cold bivalves longer than any of the other purveyors in town. The buttery oyster stew, spiked with oyster juice and stuffed oysters, is recommended. Oysters are ridiculously inexpensive in this part of Louisiana, and two dozen of them with a cold beer is a perfect Cajun three-course meal. ⊠ *701 W. Port St.,* ☎ *318/898–3311. AE, MC, V. Closed Sun.*

Elsewhere in Cajun Country A to Z

Arriving and Departing

BY BUS

Greyhound (☎ 800/231–2222) has numerous daily departures from New Orleans to Lafayette. The trip takes 3–3½ hours because of frequent stops along the way.

BY CAR

I–10 runs east–west across the state and through New Orleans. Take I–10 west to the Lafayette exit, 128 mi from New Orleans. The interstate route will take about two hours. If you wish, return to New Orleans via U.S. 90, down through Houma, to take advantage of many scenic stopovers.

BY TRAIN

Amtrak (☎ 800/872–7245) connects New Orleans and Lafayette. Trains make the three- to four-hour scenic trip each way three times a week.

Getting Around

The best way to travel around Cajun Country is by car, as other options are very limited.

Contacts and Resources

EMERGENCIES

Dial **911** for assistance. The **Medical Center of Southwest Louisiana** (✉ 2810 Ambassador Caffery Pkwy., Lafayette, ☎ 318/981–2949) has an emergency room.

GUIDED TOURS

Allons à Lafayette (☎ 318/269–9607) provides guides for escorted, customized tours. **Tours by Isabelle** (☎ 504/367–3963) offers customized tours from New Orleans to Cajun Country.

24-HOUR PHARMACY

Eckerd (✉ 4406 Johnston St., Lafayette, ☎ 318/984–5220).

VISITOR INFORMATION

Lafayette Convention and Visitors Commission (✉ 1400 N.W. Evangeline Thruway (Box 52066), Lafayette 70505, ☎ 318/232–3808 or 800/346–1958) is open weekdays 8:30–5 and weekends 9–5.

La Remise (✉ 127 New Market St., ☎ 337/394–2233), the St. Martinville visitor center, is across the street from the Evangeline Oak Park, just behind the Church Square. It's open daily 9–5.

8 BACKGROUND AND ESSENTIALS

Portraits of New Orleans

Books, Films, and Music

Smart Travel Tips A to Z

NEW ORLEANS: A HISTORY

Known to generations as the Crescent City and more recently as the Big Easy, New Orleans is a city whose magical names conjure up images of a Gallic-Hispanic and Caribbean heritage in a predominantly Anglo-Saxon culture, an amalgamation that forms a unique city and people. It was founded by the French on the banks of the Mississippi River in 1718, taken over by the Spanish in 1762, regained by Napoléon in 1800, and sold to the United States in 1803.

During its nearly 300 years of history, New Orleans has survived yellow fever and cholera epidemics, Indian wars, slave uprisings, economic depressions, revolts, conspiracies, hurricanes, floods, the American and French revolutions, the Civil War and Reconstruction, racial riots, and political corruption. Today its jazz, Vieux Carré (the French Quarter), cuisine, Mardi Gras, and port are known worldwide.

New Orleans is a city whose mystique has captured the imaginations of generations of writers and motion picture and television producers; a city of tourists, beignets, Creoles, aboveground cemetery tombs, William Faulkner's French Quarter, Tennessee Williams's *A Streetcar Named Desire,* Walker Percy's *The Moviegoer,* and John Kennedy Toole's *A Confederacy of Dunces.* It stands like a curious island of Roman Catholicism (of the Mediterranean variety) in a southern sea of hardshell Protestantism that looks upon New Orleans as "Sin City." Novelist Walker Percy once wrote that to reach New Orleans the traveler must penetrate "the depths of the Bible Belt, running the gauntlet of Klan territory, the pine barrens of south Mississippi, Bogalusa, and the Florida parishes of Louisiana. Out over a watery waste and there it is, a proper enough American city, and yet within the next few hours, the tourist is apt to see more nuns and naked women than he ever saw before."

As San Francisco is often called the most Asian of cities in the Western world, New Orleans could be considered the most Caribbean of American cities. Perhaps journalist A. J. Liebling characterized it best when he described New Orleans as a cross between Port-au-Prince, Haiti, and Paterson, New Jersey, with a culture not unlike that of Genoa, Marseilles, Beirut, or Egyptian Alexandria. Colonial New Orleans was very much a part of the economic, political, and social milieu of the French and Spanish Caribbean; its earliest population consisted of lesser French and Spanish gentry, tradesmen, merchants, prostitutes, criminals, clergy, farmers from the fields of France and Germany, Acadians from Canada, Canary Islanders, Indians, Africans, English, Irish, and English-Americans. Later came the Italians, Greeks, Cubans, Vietnamese, Central Americans, and others from the Earth's four corners, who have made New Orleans one of the nation's most cosmopolitan cities.

Because of the large Irish, German, and Yankee immigration into this river-port city during the middle of the last century, visitors are likely to hear a Brooklyn-style accent spoken in one section of the city while hearing an interesting blend of New England and southern accents in another. Tune your ear for the familiar "choich" for church and "zink" for sink, and particularly for the "downtown" greeting, "Where y'at!" New Orleans's southern accent has a lot less magnolia and mint julep than a Mississippi or Georgia accent.

It all began on Mardi Gras day in 1699 when a small French-Canadian expedition dropped anchor near the mouth of the Mississippi to explore and colonize "La Louisiane." For the next few years the expedition built a series of posts and fortifications along the river and the Gulf Coast, including what are today Mobile, Alabama, and Biloxi, Mississippi. By 1718, a permanent settlement was deemed necessary to hold France's claim to the Mississippi; the British and Spanish had their eyes on the vast Mississippi Valley. When French-Canadian Jean Baptiste le Moyne, Sieur de Bienville, established that settlement, it must have seemed only natural (and politically wise) to name it after Philippe, Duc d'Orléans, who was ruling France as regent for young Louis XV. Local legend has it that Bienville gave the settlement the feminine form of the adjective "new" and called it Nouvelle Orléans because the duke, who was a little effeminate, preferred to wear women's clothes.

New Orleans has had its glories and problems over the years, with two major standouts—hurricanes and politics. Contrary to orders from France, Bienville insisted upon building his settlement where New Orleans still stands today. He claimed the site was high and dry and protected from hurricanes, but during its first four years, the little village was wiped out four times by hurricanes. Politics have been an equally stormy art form here since the city's beginning; even the naming of the first city streets was a stroke of diplomatic genius. As historian John Chase notes in his delightful book on the origins of New Orleans street names, *Frenchmen Desire Good Children* (each name in the title is a street name), Bourbon, Orleans, Burgundy, and Royal streets were so named in honor of the royal families of France. Also honored were the Conti, Chartres, and Condé families, cousins to the Bourbons and Orleanses. (Conde Street was once a section of Chartres Street from Jackson Square to Esplanade Avenue before the name was dropped in 1865; Chartres now extends from Canal Street to Esplanade.) St. Peter Street was named for an ancestor of the Bourbon family; Louis IX, the Saint-King, was honored with St. Louis Street; Louis XIII's widowed Queen Ann got St. Ann Street; and Toulouse and Dumaine streets were named for Louis XIV's politically powerful royal bastard children.

The best place to get a real feel for the city's unique history is Jackson Square, the heart of the French Quarter, where you are surrounded by the river, St. Louis Cathedral, the colonial Cabildo and Presbytere, and the Pontalba Apartments. Called the Place d'Armes by the French and Plaza de Armas by the Spanish, this was the town square where the militia drilled and townsfolk met. It also was where public hangings, beheadings, "breakings at the wheel," and brandings were carried out.

The Place d'Armes, site in 1803 of the Louisiana Purchase ceremony, was renamed Jackson Square in the 1850s in honor of Andrew Jackson, the hero of the Battle of New Orleans in the War of 1812 and seventh president of the United States. In the center of the square is an equestrian statue of Jackson erected in 1856, one of three cast: a second stands in Lafayette Park in front of the White House in Washington, DC, and a third, in Nashville, Tennessee, Jackson's hometown. Today Jackson Square springs to life each day with artists, street musicians, jugglers, and a host of wandering minstrels who follow the sun and tourist trade.

The old city, fanning out from the square, is filled with the legends and romances of an ever-changing people. Although the French Quarter is a living city and not a re-created fantasy world, history and time hang over the Vieux Carré like the thick, damp fogs that roll in from the river. You see the past everywhere—through the wrought-iron gates and down the ancient alleys, in the steamy courtyards tucked out of sight, in the graceful colonial dwellings that hang over narrow streets. You find it in museums and the old stories about Madame Lalaurie's tortured slaves, the romantic drama surrounding the Baroness Pontalba; Père Antoine; pirate Jean Lafitte; voodoo and its queen, Marie Laveau; revolutions; the Civil War; and yellow fever.

The history of New Orleans is inseparable from the port of New Orleans. The port is why the city was founded and why it survived. France wanted to colonize Louisiana and built New Orleans to reap imagined riches from the vast interior of North America. Despite the expectations of the first explorers and the French crown, gold and silver did not come pouring out of the North American wilderness; different treasures waited. Quantities of tobacco, lumber, indigo, animal hides, and other indigenous products were floated downriver on flatboats to the new city, where ships from France, Spanish Florida, the West Indies, and the British colonies waited to trade for them with spices, cloth, cutlery, wine, utensils, foods, and other such goods. New Orleans became a commercial center, connecting Europe and the West Indies with the backcountry and upper regions of the Mississippi.

Trade was not without its difficulties. Storms, poorly built ships, privateers, colonial wars, and financially shaky entrepreneurs all added risks to commerce. There were other troubles as well; by the mid-18th century, serious international problems were brewing.

In 1754 the long-running dispute between France and England over who owned what in America erupted into war. Dubbed the Seven Years' War in Europe and the French and Indian War in the British colonies along the Atlantic seaboard, it ultimately eliminated France as a colonial power in America. Despite an alliance with Spain (organized in the war's last years), France was defeated, and in 1763 it ceded to England all French territory east of the Mississippi River, keeping for itself just two small islands in the St. Lawrence Seaway.

Not included in the package, however, was New Orleans. Along with all the Louisiana territory west of the Mississippi River, the port had been signed over to Louis XV's cousin, King Carlos III of Spain, in the secret Treaty of Fontainebleau in 1762. (Perhaps that's where the long tradition of back-room deals got its start in Louisiana.) Louis gladly turned Louisiana over to his Spanish cousin. The colony was costing him his royal shirt, and the merchant class in France wanted nothing more to do with it. Carlos III, for his part, accepted the unprofitable holding as a buffer to keep the British away from nearby Mexico.

The Louisiana French, however, generally opposed the change to Spanish rule. When the first Spanish governor, Don Antonio de Ulloa, arrived, he did little to court their favor. After a few breaches in local etiquette and several commercial edicts that hurt the colony's already sagging economy, the settlers drove Ulloa out in a bloodless coup in October 1768. (Local historians, trying to upstage the British colonies along the Atlantic, claim this was the first revolution on American soil against a foreign monarch.)

Retaliation from the mother country was quick and complete. In July 1769 the Spanish fleet dropped anchor at the mouth of the Mississippi, with 2,600 Spanish soldiers under the command of General Alexander O'Reilly, an Irishman in Spanish service. O'Reilly quashed the short-lived rebellion, set up a new government in the colony, and executed the ringleaders of the rebellion.

The American Revolution afforded two of O'Reilly's successors, Unzaga and Galvez, the opportunity to attack their British colonial rival. Through the Louisiana colony, the Spanish sent supplies and munitions to the American rebels and allowed American raiding parties to launch forays into British West Florida. Galvez attacked and captured the British forts at Pensacola, Mobile, and Baton Rouge, and while the British were kept busy with the rebellious colonies, the Spanish took the opportunity to regain West Florida, which they had lost to the British during the French and Indian War.

The Spanish governors of Louisiana opened New Orleans's gates to a great variety of peoples by establishing an open-minded immigration policy that welcomed British-Americans escaping the Revolution as well as French Acadians (whose descendants are Louisiana's famous Cajuns) fleeing the British in Canada. (The Cajuns later moved on to south-central and southwest Louisiana.) Canary Islanders came and settled just below New Orleans, where their descendants still live and speak their ancient language today.

Spanish New Orleans weathered several storms during the last decades of the 18th century, including the French Revolution. Mobs roamed the streets calling New Orleans governor Carondelet a *cochon de lait* (suckling pig) and shouting, "Liberty, Equality, and Fraternity." Carondelet brought in troops and outlawed publications concerning the Revolution in France. Diplomatically, he also gave refuge to French aristocrats fleeing the carnage, which won him back some favor with the Louisiana French.

Carondelet also had problems upriver with the westward-expanding Americans (usually Kentuckians, called Kaintocks). During the American Revolution, the rebels had assured the Spanish that they had no designs on Louisiana. But by the 1790s their assurances had begun to carry less weight; Americans' use of the river had grown, and so, too, had American desire for free navigation along its length.

As time passed, the situation worsened. Spanish officials in New Orleans occasionally seized American flatboats; the Americans responded by rattling sabers, urged on by the Kaintocks, who called for an invasion of the Louisiana colony. War between the United States and Spain over Louisiana was narrowly averted in 1795 upon the signing of the Pinckney Treaty.

By the end of the 18th century, New Orleans had become a major North American port handling cargo from all over the world, with a population close to 10,000 and a well-earned reputation as a vibrant, colorful city. Mardi Gras was celebrated (though it wasn't yet the extravagant carnival of parades seen today), and Creole food—that unique combination of French, Spanish, West Indian, and African cuisines for which New Orleans is so famous—had found its place on local palates. Unfortunately, much of the old colonial city was destroyed by fire in 1788 and 1794, but each time it was quickly rebuilt; most of the French Quarter of today was constructed during the Spanish colonial days and after the Louisiana Purchase in 1803. The oldest building in the French Quarter, and the only one remaining from French colonial years, is the former Ursuline Convent on Chartres Street, constructed in the 1730s.

For all the changes of the 18th century, the opening of the 19th was to bring even more. In France, Napoléon had reestablished the country as a formidable military force on the Continent. In 1800 he forced Spain to retrocede Louisiana to the French; New Orleans was back in the hands of its first colonial parent, though Spanish officials continued to run the colony for the next three years.

This news sat poorly with U.S. president Thomas Jefferson, who feared that war with France had become inevitable. The issue that concerned him was free navigation along the Mississippi River. To solve the problem, he resolved to buy New Orleans and a portion of West Florida bordering the Mississippi, including Baton Rouge. Napoléon, anxious for money to finance his imminent war against England (and reasonably sure that he would lose the land to England or the United States when war came), went Jefferson one better; he offered to sell the entire Louisiana colony.

On April 29, 1803, American emissaries agreed to pay $11,250,000 for Louisiana and, at the same time, to write off $3,750,000 in French debts, setting the territory's cost at $15 million. Short on cash, the United States borrowed the money to buy the territory from banking houses in London and Amsterdam. After the sale, Napoléon commented: "This accession of territory affirms forever the power of the United States, and I have just given England a maritime rival that sooner or later will lay low her pride."

The Americanization of New Orleans moved quickly during the first decade of the 19th century. The city's first suburb, Faubourg St. Mary (today's Central Business District), sprang up and bustled with construction and commerce; this was the American Section. Mississippi flatboatmen made their way downriver from the Missouri and Ohio rivers to sell their cargoes in New Orleans, then made their way home overland along the Natchez Trace.

The year 1812 brought statehood to Louisiana and, almost equally important, the arrival of the first steamboat, the *New Orleans,* captained by Nicholas Roosevelt, ancestral kinsman of the two presidents; 1812 also brought war against Britain. Though its first effects on New Orleans were slight, the War of 1812 eventually came hard to the city. In 1815 Andrew Jackson, with a ragged army of Louisianans and the assistance of Jean Lafitte, Lafitte's Baratarian pirates, and Tennessee and Kentucky volunteers, fought the British and stopped them in a bloody battle at Chalmette Plantation, a few miles downriver from the city. Although casualty estimates for the Battle of New Orleans conflict somewhat, reports placed American losses at 13 killed and 39 wounded, and British losses at 858 killed and 2,468 wounded. Ironically, the battle took place two weeks after the United States and Britain signed a treaty ending the war. Every January 8 local historical groups reenact the victory at Chalmette Battlefield, which is now a national park.

The years between the Battle of New Orleans and the Civil War were the city's golden era. By 1820 the population had reached 25,000; during the next 10 years it doubled. By 1840 it had doubled again, with a census count of 102,000 people within New Orleans; about half were black, both free and slave. The city was a major center for slave auctions. The burgeoning port was choked with seagoing ships and riverboats laden with sugar, molasses, cotton, raw materials from upriver, and refined goods from Europe and the Northeast.

The golden age also gave birth to one of New Orleans's most famous pastimes: the Mardi Gras parade. Mardi Gras had been celebrated on the European continent, one way or another, for centuries. The parades, however, originated in Mobile, Alabama, but later moved to New Orleans, where the custom flourished. Begun in the 1820s when bands of maskers marched through the streets throwing confetti and flour (and sometimes lye) in the faces of onlookers, the parades were first staged by Americans in the American Section and not by the French or Spanish populace, who preferred their gala balls. Vehicles were first used in 1839, and the first carnival organization, the Mistick Krewe of Comus, was formed in 1857.

Through the years of prosperity and celebration, disease continued to stalk the city. The almost yearly visits of yellow fever, cholera, and typhus— encouraged by widespread poverty— took thousands of lives; 8,000 fell to yellow fever in 1853 and another 2,700 in 1856. In that same year cholera claimed the lives of more than 1,000 people, and tuberculosis killed 650. New Orleans was known as one of the unhealthiest cities in the Northern Hemisphere.

If the 18th century can be seen as New Orleans's childhood, then the antebellum period was its adolescence and young adulthood; by its end, the city had reached full maturity. Prosperous and growing, it possessed an international personality that distinguished it from every other city on the North American continent.

But the Civil War was to change that. On January 26, 1861, Louisiana seceded from the Union. It was a difficult choice for New Orleanians, many of whom had strong commercial and family ties with the Northeast and Midwest. Less than three months after secession, the war began when Southern troops, under the command of New Orleans's own General Pierre Gustave Toutant Beauregard, opened fire on Fort Sumter in Charleston harbor. A month later a Union fleet blockaded the mouth of the Mississippi

River, causing severe economic hardship in the city.

The Confederate flag waved barely a year over New Orleans before it fell to Union forces under "Damn the Torpedoes" Admiral David Glasgow Farragut in April 1862. When the Union fleet arrived and trained its guns on a panicked city, the mayor refused to surrender; Farragut threatened to bombard the city but backed down. After a brief standoff, a naval squad went ashore and lowered the Confederate flag. New Orleans, the Confederacy's largest city, had fallen, and Reconstruction had begun.

New Orleans had the dubious distinction of being under Reconstruction longer than any other place in the Confederacy—from May 1862 to April 1877. The city's port and nearby fertile plantations were sources of immense profits for corrupt politicians under Reconstruction; the social and political upheaval it brought on was often violent, with bloody street battles between New Orleans natives and factions of the military-backed Reconstruction government. Withdrawal of federal troops in 1877 brought an end to 15 years of Reconstruction; it also ended a flicker of hope that blacks in New Orleans would enjoy the same constitutional rights and protections as whites. With the end of Reconstruction came home rule and New Orleans's Gilded Age.

The last two decades of the century saw an era of conscious boosterism, economic booms and busts, corruption and reform, labor unrest, and racial retrenchment. With a population of more than 216,000, New Orleans was still the largest city in the South. Large and elaborate Victorian homes, decorated with mass-produced gingerbread frills, sprang up along major avenues and thoroughfares.

New Orleans entered the 20th century with an air of optimism. North and South put aside their differences to defeat the Spanish in the Spanish-American War in 1898. Uptown continued to grow with new mansions along St. Charles Avenue, and skyscrapers in the Central Business District hovered over the early 19th-century buildings of the old American Section. The New Orleans World Cotton Exposition of 1884 clearly forecast a century of new promises.

The prosperity continued until the Great Depression of the 1930s as skyscrapers towered even higher above the old city. World War II, however, was a turning point. Although the city prospered during the war years, its population began to fall behind that of other American and southern cities. By 1950 it was no longer the South's largest city, falling to second place behind Houston. By 1970 the Crescent City had dropped to fifth place in the South, and the 1980 and 1990 censuses showed it slipping even further behind.

Census returns those years also showed a decline in the urban population, while surrounding suburbs grew dramatically. Since the early 1960s, tens of thousands of middle-class white and black families have moved to the sprawling suburban communities surrounding the city; thousands of acres of soupy marshlands have given way to tract housing and shopping centers. Unfortunately, the flight to suburbia has destroyed most of New Orleans's old neighborhoods.

Many New Orleanians, however, especially young and affluent couples, have refused to abandon the city, preferring to stay behind to buy and renovate old homes in the declining Victorian neighborhoods. Their work, courage, and good taste have revitalized entire sections of the city. The restoration craze has even spread to the Central Business District, which is experiencing its biggest construction boom since the 1850s. During the 1960s and 1970s, developers thought everything old had to be razed to make way for the new; scores of buildings dating from the 1850s and earlier gave way to the wrecker's ball. In more recent years, however, developers have found it profitable to adapt pre–Civil War buildings and warehouses to modern use, with magnificent results, especially in what has become known as the Warehouse District.

The construction of the Louisiana Superdome in the early 1970s and the 1984 New Orleans World's Fair also had considerable impact on the Central Business District. One glance at the city's skyline quickly reveals that the Central Business District is taking on all the trappings of a Sun Belt city. During the last decade the district has experienced phenomenal growth, despite the downturn in the region's oil and gas industries, with more than a dozen new skyscrapers rising above New Orleans's early 19th-century suburb. Major oil companies have built regional corporate offices here, and big-name hotel chains, including Hyatt, Hilton, Marriott, Ritz-Carlton, Meridien, Wyndham, and Sheraton, have constructed luxurious high-rise hotels in the district.

More than 280 years have passed since Bienville's engineers and work crews built the first palmetto huts at the crescent in the Mississippi River. Today New Orleans—the Crescent City, the Big Easy—is scarred and somewhat decayed, but it can be the most beautiful and charming of hostesses. Its people, history, cuisine, and alluring 19th-century mystique and Caribbean-like culture make it resemble no other city in the nation.

— John R. Kemp

John R. Kemp has written several books about the city, including New Orleans: An Illustrated History.

CARNIVAL

What could persuade a prominent New Orleans businessman to wear a pageboy wig, gold crown, jeweled tunic, and white tights in public—and consider it the honor of a lifetime? Or cause people to ask with interest, "Who found the baby in the king cake?" Or prompt little old ladies to jostle strangers and shout that phrase New Orleanians learn at mama's knee—"Throw me something, Mister!"

Come to New Orleans during Carnival and find out.

Carnival is a mad game in which New Orleanians beg masked men on passing floats to toss them handfuls of plastic beads, go cups, or aluminum doubloons (known generically as "throws") that eventually are recycled, pitched into the trash, or mailed to family members who have married Yankees and moved away.

Don't be smug: if you visit, you'll catch the fervor. After a few moments of astonished gaping, you'll yell for throws, too, draping layers of beads around your neck, sipping from a plastic cup as you prance along the street, bebopping with the marching bands, and having a grand old time—assuming you like crowds.

Get one thing straight right away: there is a difference between Mardi Gras and Carnival—always with a capital C to differentiate it from carnivals that set up portable Ferris wheels and dart booths in vacant lots.

Carnival refers to an entire season that begins January 6 with an elegant debutante ball called Twelfth Night (as in "twelfth night after Christmas") and a separate, less aristocratic ball held on a streetcar by a group of Carnival devotees calling themselves Phunny Phorty Phellows.

Lasting for one to two months, Carnival explodes in its final days into a party that envelops the entire city and suburbs, with balls in every hall and hotel room on the final two weekends, and parades day and night, all of them organized and paid for by members of private clubs called krewes. Since the parades are free (although most of the balls are strictly by invitation), New Orleanians refer to Carnival as "the greatest free show on earth."

During Carnival just about everybody overdoses on king cake, a sweet-dough coffee cake shaped like a wreath and topped with icing or sugar sprinkles in the Carnival colors of green, gold, and purple. Baked inside is the mysterious "baby," a fingernail-long pink plastic baby doll. Whoever bites into the baby is supposed to give the next king cake party or bring the next king cake to the office.

Mardi Gras (French for Fat Tuesday) is the final day of Carnival, the only day that it is legal to wear costumes, face paint, and masks in the streets. It's the final bash-of-a-celebration before Ash Wednesday, the beginning of Lent—that period of fasting for 40 days (and six Sundays that don't count) that leads up to Easter. Mardi Gras is an official city holiday, with just about everyone but the police taking the day off.

It's also the day that a middle-age man in a pageboy wig reigns over the parade of Rex—the most important of the 50 or more parades—and 100 or so Carnival balls (all with their own maids and queens accompanying their own draped and bewigged kings).

But there is only one Rex (the king of this krewe is also known as Rex, Latin for king), and he is always an outstanding citizen who has done some high-profile volunteer work and who is a member of the men's group sponsoring the parade. Unlike kings of some of the less socially prominent balls, who sometimes pay hundreds or even thousands of dollars to their organizations for the honor (and for their costumes), Rex pays nothing to be king, and his club owns his outfit.

The queen of Rex is a young debutante chosen by the group's leaders on the basis of her father's prominence. Rex and his queen are considered the monarchs of the entire Carnival celebration. Their identities are kept secret until the day before Mardi Gras, when they are announced publicly.

The queen of Rex watches the parade from a grandstand in front of a hotel; though she wears a traditional white suit, she waves her arms for throws like everyone else. That night the king and queen of Carnival wear jeweled clothes as they promenade around the white-cloth-covered floor at a ball in the Fairmont Hotel. At the end of the evening, they leave the Rex ball and cross to the other side of the auditorium to join the ball of the Mistick Krewe of Comus, the oldest and most exclusive of all Carnival balls in New Orleans. (The identity of Comus is never publicly revealed—a tradition that all the aristocratic krewes except Rex follow.)

The kings swap queens and all sit together on a throne, then leave the floor grandly, one at a time, in a regal ceremony that used to be televised but is now open only to invited guests. And that is the end of Mardi Gras. Midnight is the witching hour when downtown streets are cleared: police cars cruise through the French Quarter, loudspeakers blaring, "Mardi Gras is over."

The next morning, Ash Wednesday, more than half of the New Orleanians who are Roman Catholic go to church to receive the sign of the cross on their foreheads in ashes. And Lent begins.

The city's residents are of two minds about Carnival. Most think it's the grandest thing since the invention of beer; the rest leave town. So many locals seek exile skiing in Colorado that they call themselves the Krewe of Aspen.

There are complications to Mardi Gras. First there's the matter of the date, which changes yearly because it is based on the movable feast of Easter. Mardi Gras can occur from early February to early March, and, whenever it is, New Orleanians invariably say, "Mardi Gras is early this year" or "Mardi Gras is late this year." Mardi Gras falls on February 27, 2001, and February 12, 2002.

How it all started no one is absolutely sure. Some say the Carnival celebration is an offshoot of pagan holidays. Others point to the Middle Ages. The faithful abstained from meat, eggs, and milk during Lent and partied at vast feasts before the fasting began. There were rowdy celebrations in Rome during the Renaissance; in fact, festivities were held in most Christian countries, including France. So when French-Canadian explorer Pierre le

Moyne, Sieur d'Iberville, landed on a plot of ground near the mouth of the Mississippi River on Mardi Gras, March 3, 1699, he named it Pointe du Mardi Gras.

There's not much in history books about early Louisiana Carnival celebrations until the 1800s, when private balls were held by the Creole descendants of French and Spanish settlers, the city's aristocracy in those days. And there were "quadroon" balls where wealthy white men mingled with beautiful "free women of color" who were one-quarter black.

There also were street processions of the raucous sort. Young men from the so-called good families (as well as the not so good) wore masks and costumes and sometimes dumped flour on passersby, more intent on getting drunk than anything else. Occasionally the parades were splendid, but more often they were coarse. Then, on February 24, 1857, Mardi Gras changed.

At 9 PM, 60 or so men dressed like demons paraded in the streets with two floats in a torchlighted cavalcade. The group called itself the Mistick Krewe of Comus, after the god of revelry. Arthur Burton LaCour wrote in his classic 1952 book *New Orleans Masquerade* that the men were Creoles from the French Quarter and Saxons (as LaCour referred to the nouveau riche Americans) from the other side of Canal Street across the so-called neutral ground (a name still used in New Orleans to refer to the median of a wide street).

Comus, LaCour wrote, was started by 13 New Orleanians and six men from Mobile, Alabama, where Mardi Gras parades had begun a few years earlier. Wanting to observe the holiday more fully, they formed a secret men's society, went to Mobile for costumes, and sent 3,000 invitations to a ball held at New Orleans's Gaiety Theater. They had begun a tradition.

As time passed (with lapses for the Civil War), invitations to the Comus ball became so coveted that one year the krewe captain advertised a $2,000 reward for two missing invitations. Comus crowned Robert E. Lee's daughter, Mildred Lee, as its first queen in 1884.

Through the years, other groups of men organized Carnival krewes. Then, in 1872, 40 businessmen founded Rex and sponsored a daytime parade for the Mardi Gras visit of His Imperial Highness, the Grand Duke Alexis of Russia. They chose as Carnival colors green for faith, gold for power, and purple for justice. Today's standard Carnival song, "If Ever I Cease to Love," was in a play called *Bluebeard,* which featured an actress who infatuated the grand duke, and bands of the day played it ceaselessly. The first Rex parade was thrown together quickly with borrowed costumes, but there was no ball. The first reception was not until the next year, when a queen was chosen on the spot at a public ball. Eventually invitations and formal dress became required.

As more and more Carnival organizations were founded, young white girls who made debuts at afternoon teas held by their grandmothers were invited to be queens and maids. Traditionally, debutantes wear subdued white dresses, giving the 18 or so socially elite balls the nickname whitegown balls. The queens and maids of less socially prominent balls may be teenagers, young single women of debutante age (typically college juniors), or married women; they tend to wear lavish costumes depicting some aspect of the ball's theme. As with the kings, debutantes of the social balls pay only for their dresses, whereas the mock royalty in less prestigious balls may also pay several hundred dollars for their right to reign.

Balls were strictly segregated by race; even Jews and Italians were banned from guest lists of the exclusive older balls (known as the old-line krewes). Some balls still keep up the practice—even now, among the ultrasocial krewes, only Rex invites black guests. So other segments of society started clubs of their own.

A black butler and dance instructor from Chicago started the Illinois

Club in 1895, copying the format of the old-line balls. Though this club split into two krewes—the Original Illinois Club and the Young Men Illinois Club—the African-American debutantes, usually high school seniors or college freshmen, still perform the founder's dance, the Chicago Glide, in parallel black galas. The Illinois clubs don't sponsor parades, but the Zulu Social and Pleasure Club, organized in 1909 by working-class black men, does. The Zulu king (Louis Armstrong reigned in 1949) and his entourage toss glitter-covered coconuts to the crowds. In days gone by, the Zulu parade would wander wherever the drivers chose, stopping at various bars along the way; these days it's more organized. Doctors and bishops mingle with blue-collar members at a splashy, racially integrated party, and the parade follows a route published in city newspapers.

After the Depression and World War II, Carnival clubs started popping up everywhere. Some were for doctors, others for businessmen, some for residents of certain neighborhoods, for military men, or for gays. Organizations for women include the krewe of Iris, made up partially of former old-line debutantes. The gay balls are splendid extravaganzas, but invitations for straights are scarce. Even mothers of debutantes have been known to beg for invitations from their gay hairdressers for these lavish productions, featuring court members in drag and with headdresses so heavy that some krewe members have trouble standing up straight.

Membership fees in krewes can range from $150 to $600, but joining parading krewes costs much more, because members must buy the trinkets they throw.

Though new krewes proliferated after the Depression, their members, revering the traditions of the older groups, never dreamed of competing for status with them. Then, in 1969, an upstart group of businessmen looking to entertain tourists the Sunday before Mardi Gras founded Bacchus,

named after the god of wine. The sassy group stunned the city by setting new rules and strutting out with a show as stupendous as the Rex gala. The Bacchus floats (designed by Blaine Kern, who also creates the Rex parade) were bigger than any seen before, and the king was Danny Kaye, not a homegrown humanitarian but a famous entertainer. The party was in the old Rivergate Convention Center (since razed to make way for the newly constructed Harrah's New Orleans Casino), not at Municipal Auditorium or a hotel ballroom. There was no queen, no court, and the party was called a rendezvous, not a ball. All guests could dance, not just members and their wives, as was the custom in old-line balls, where nonmembers merely watched the proceedings. The floats rode right into the Rivergate, and you didn't have to be socially prominent to join—or even white.

The crowds have loved Bacchus from day one, and guessing which celebrities will follow the likes of Ron Howard, Tom Arnold, and Drew Carey has become almost as popular as wondering about the identity of Rex.

In 1974 another krewe of businessmen, Endymion, borrowed some of Bacchus's ideas and took over an abandoned slot in the Saturday-night parade lineup. Nationally known celebrities are invited to be grand marshal and to entertain at a party for 10,000 called the Extravaganza, now held in the Louisiana Superdome. Endymion has super floats, a local king (drawn in a members' raffle at $25 a chance), and a court consisting of daughters of members. It can cost a queen's father $15,000 in expenses that include an elaborate dress and party. By the time members of Bacchus and Endymion buy throws and pay dues, they've dished out $2,000 to $3,000 each.

The last weekend before Mardi Gras is a whirlwind of parades and parties. Some krewes stage Carnival balls for convention groups willing to pay to see a simulated version of the real thing. Occasionally, lucky out-of-towners can buy extra tickets to the Bacchus or Endymion party. Or they may be able to obtain invitations (always invitations, never tickets) to Rex, the most accessible of the old-line balls, if they happen to know a prominent New Orleanian with connections.

The best parades tend to be near the end of Carnival. A favored (and crowded!) spot to watch the floats and marching bands is downtown on Canal Street, where the parades end around 8 to 9 PM. Families tend to prefer watching Uptown, particularly on St. Charles Avenue between Napoleon and Jackson avenues. A proliferation of new parades in the suburbs of Metairie, Kenner, Gretna, St. Bernard Parish, and Covington now keeps many families in their own neighborhoods even on Mardi Gras itself. Argus, for example, which parades in Metairie on Mardi Gras, always has a local or national celebrity rider.

The parades begin in earnest two weekends before Mardi Gras, and the public part of the celebration really goes into gear the Thursday before Mardi Gras with the procession of the Knights of Babylon, the so-called doctors' krewe, whose path is lighted by flambeaux (torches) carried by young black men who dance as they collect change thrown by onlookers. Though some think it demeaning, the tradition remains.

Other traditions, though, are in transition. In 1992 there was much hubbub concerning a city ordinance forbidding racial and sexual discrimination in krewes that parade through New Orleans and use city police, fire, and sanitation services (though they do pay a fee for parading). Nobody denies that discrimination exists. With few exceptions, krewes are all male, all female, all white, or all black. City leaders later rescinded the sexual mix part of the ordinance and weakened the rest to the simple requirement that krewe leaders sign a statement that their krewes do not discriminate.

The ordinance was directed at the socially elite old-line organizations, particularly Comus, Momus, Proteus, and Rex—all limited to white men. Rex complied, reportedly inviting three black civic leaders to join the organization, which puts on the main parade of the season on Mardi Gras. Two black men joined—or so members say, since membership in all of the organizations is supposedly secret. But Comus and Momus both decided not to parade in 1992 (they said they feared for their safety), and Proteus joined them in 1993. These old-line krewes rebelled at the notion of being forced to accept members, when they could tell stories of sons and brothers of members (even of officers) who had been denied membership.

In 1992 the city was split over the issue. About 55% of the city's black residents told one pollster that they objected to the ordinance. People here accept Mardi Gras with all its limitations, many said, because everybody enjoys the parades.

In 1993 the principal mutterings of discontent came from the white social elite and from a few historians who hated to see the oldest traditional krewes cease parading. In a letter to *New Orleans Magazine,* Comus, Momus, and Proteus (which still held their private Carnival balls) stated, "Be certain, our Societies will endure. . . . Adieu, Fair City, until the coming of some happy day when the Furies are done and the Fates call us to ride again to greet you." Whether they will ever actually parade again is anyone's guess. Other krewes have taken over Momus's and Proteus's traditional parade dates, and on Fat Tuesday 1998, at the hallowed hour of Comus, a new outfit called the Krewe of America paraded up and down Canal Street. Geared for tourists, to entertain other tourists, the highly touted America sought members from each of the United States; the cost of joining the krewe was $4,800, including round-trip airfare, hotel room, throws, and a spot on one of the 25 floats. The whole thing horrified many Orleanians, who no doubt were relieved when the new krewe failed dramatically to meet its goals. Only 300 members joined, instead of the projected 1,000; only 14 floats were mustered; and, as a last resort, the krewe was offering "starter packages" for $250. Krewe of America organizers maintain optimism for the coming years.

A new celebration, Lundi Gras, has turned the formerly dull Monday before Mardi Gras into a day of music, food, and activities centered on welcoming the kings of Rex (actually, you're never supposed to say "king of Rex," since literally it's saying "king of King") and of Zulu, which parades before Rex on Mardi Gras. A celebrity-studded krewe called Orpheus was organized by locals including District Attorney Harry Connick Sr., whose superstar crooning son and other celebrities ride in the Mardi Gras eve parade. The krewe's big bash is at the convention center, and it's open to the public.

Tuesday is Mardi Gras. Zulu and Rex are followed by parades of trucks decorated by anyone who wants to organize a group of friends. Walking clubs (they march instead of ride on floats), including the Jefferson City Buzzards and Pete Fountain's Half Fast Marching Club, zigzag all over town, stopping in bars and swapping kisses for paper flowers and beads. The Krewe of America parades in the late afternoon.

The Mardi Gras Indians also roam the city, particularly near Orleans and Claiborne avenues. The Indians are neighborhood groups of black men who stitch and glue their own stupendous feathered costumes. Creole Wild West, the oldest gang, chants "Wild, Wild West" to a beat that's part blues, part Afro, part Caribbean. In the French Quarter, people in improbably flashy costumes saunter about. Though the Quarter is crowded, wild, and drunken, it's worth seeing the mind-boggling costumes that frequently are the result of

a year's work. If a woman is in a particularly stunning costume, look twice—she may be a he.

A word of warning to women is unfortunately necessary here. During Mardi Gras, many men from all over the country and all over the world descend on New Orleans in groups. Packs of guys together with a lot of alcohol can sometimes spell trouble. A common demand women will hear is "Show your tits!" More women than you would imagine flash as barter for good beads. But if you are groped or feel threatened in any way, be assured that a police officer will probably be in your sight range. The force is ubiquitous and arrest-happy during Mardi Gras.

Mardi Gras Publications
For anyone serious about planning for Carnival, Arthur Hardy's annual *Mardi Gras Guide* is a must. *$6.50 (including shipping).* ✉ *Box 19500, New Orleans 70179,* ☎ *504/838–6111.*

The New Orleans daily newspaper, the *Times-Picayune,* publishes an annual Carnival guide a few weeks before Mardi Gras each year. In some cases it is more accurate than the *Mardi Gras Guide* (☞ *above*) because it is published closer to the actual date. If you're planning your trip to Mardi Gras far in advance, buy a copy of the guide and later secure a copy of the *Times-Picayune*'s section and compare parade dates and times. The newspaper's section is likely to be more up-to-date. Contact the Special Sections Department, *The Times-Picayune* (✉ 3800 Howard Ave., New Orleans 70140, ☎ 504/826–3464).

Gambit (✉ 4141 Bienville St., New Orleans 70119, ☎ 504/486–5900) an alternative newsweekly, also publishes parade guides in the weeks before Mardi Gras.

— Millie Ball

Millie Ball is the travel editor of the New Orleans *Times-Picayune.*

THE CRADLE OF JAZZ

Music is the soul of New Orleans. Since the 1890s her melodies, rhythms, and musicians have enriched America's artistic heritage, and today the city's musical texture is an inter-weaving of jazz, rhythm and blues, gospel, rock and roll, Latin beat, and then some.

The sound of New Orleans extends from the classic jazz of the early 1920s through the sterling sound of Louis Armstrong and his mates; from the mid-century dance-hall beat of Fats Domino, Professor Longhair, and a le-gion of rhythm-and-bluesmen to the polished modern improvisations of Wynton Marsalis and the young jazz lions of the 1980s.

As a distinctive sound, New Orleans's music is marked by a parade-time backbeat on drums; rocking, vocally suggestive horns; and a percussive piano style with liberal shadings of the blues.

The root of this sound is called the "second line"—the waves of march-ing dancers who engulf the brass bands with a dazzling body language of gyrating steps, following the mu-sicians as they parade through the streets. Above all, it's music to make you clap your hands and move your feet.

The power of New Orleans's music has always come from the neighbor-hoods. Like Brazilian samba and the Beatles' Liverpool rock, jazz polyrhythms rose like a vox populi from working-class environs of this port city. Louis Armstrong in his mem-oir, *Satchmo*, recalled with a mea-sure of tenderness the Back-o'-Town streets where he was raised. "The toughest characters in town used to live there," he wrote, ". . . as did churchpeople, gamblers, hustlers, cheap pimps, thieves, prostitutes, and lots of children."

But the seedbed of jazz music and its later offshoots lay in distant reaches of the past, at Congo Square, the early 19th-century grassy plain (on what is now Louis Armstrong Park) where each Sunday slaves gathered for drum-and-dance celebrations that drew crowds of varied onlookers, in-cluding landed gentry.

Congo Square was the cultural trans-shipment point where African per-cussions and tribal dance steps, akin to those developing across the Caribbean map, began the long, slow march into European instrumenta-tion and melody that would culminate a century later in the birth of jazz.

By the 1930s Armstrong had given the music a grand voice, with lovely lyri-cal flourishes and gritty blueslike voic-ings. Since then, New Orleans has produced a continuing line of distin-guished musicians. On October 22, 1990, the cover of *Time* featured trumpeter Wynton Marsalis, a virtu-oso superstar and eloquent advocate of jazz, as a metaphor of democracy. As Armstrong had done two genera-tions earlier, the 29-year-old Marsalis became the spokesman of America's indigenous art form.

The seeds of New Orleans jazz first took root in the 1890s. New Orleans was then legally segregated but was a town where rare degrees of social intercourse prevailed. It was a soci-ety of many layers—Creole descen-dants of European settlers, Italians, Irish, Germans, blacks, Native Amer-icans, and Creoles of color (or *gens de couleur*).

Music held a common currency among these peoples. Outdoor festi-vals and indoor dances followed the calendar of Catholic feasts, the biggest of which was Mardi Gras, "Fat Tues-day," ushering in 40 days of Lent. The society orchestras and smaller ensembles that performed for parties and other events were playing syn-copated rags; French quadrilles and polkas were popular, too.

A more potent influence, at least for the impetus of jazz, was the brass bands—groups that marched in uni-forms, playing parade music with new rhythmic flavorings that reflected an African percussive tradition.

The musicianship of black Creoles was a primary factor in the emergence of jazz. They were a distinct caste, descendants of African mothers and fathers of French or Spanish ancestry; many first arrived from Haiti in the early 1800s, settling in the Treme neighborhood (behind what is now Louis Armstrong Park) and, in later years, the Seventh Ward, which lies downtown, well beyond the French Quarter. The lines of racial intermixture were perpetuated by New Orleans aristocrats who kept mulatto mistresses and often supported second, "shadow" families.

Some Creoles amassed great wealth before the Civil War and even owned slaves. They were generally better educated than the blacks who lived in uptown wards, upriver from the French Quarter. By the end of Reconstruction and with the tightening of racial laws, the sturdy familial lines and artisan skills of the downtown Creoles had produced a burgeoning tradition of families who taught music and performed professionally.

One such professor, James Brown Humphrey, played a variety of instruments and was a catalyst for jazz. In 1887 he began regular trips to outlying plantation communities to teach poor blacks, a number of whom moved to town to join brass bands. In 1987 two of his grandsons, Willie and Percy Humphrey, were regular performers in Preservation Hall.

A more legendary figure—universally deemed the first great jazzman—was Buddy Bolden, who played cornet (a smaller version of the trumpet) with strong, bluesy currents. Though his music was popular, Bolden suffered a mental breakdown in 1907 and never recorded.

In time, the musical division between blacks, who learned to play by ear—listening to songs, replicating what they heard—and Creoles, who read sheet music, began to blur. Meanwhile, a red-light district called Storyville gave piano professors like Jelly Roll Morton quite a venue until its closure in 1917.

The year 1917 was a milestone for another reason: in New York, a group of white New Orleans musicians led by Nick LaRocca, the Original Dixieland Jazz Band, recorded the first jazz disk. Jazz was an idiom rooted in the African improvisational genius; many white practitioners, whose style became known as Dixieland, began to flourish in New Orleans as well.

The first generation of New Orleans jazzmen produced three brilliant artists—Louis Armstrong, Jelly Roll Morton, and Sidney Bechet—each of whom left the city to establish his reputation. Morton, a Creole with great talent as a composer-pianist, was a peripatetic figure who died in 1941, down on his luck. Bechet, also a Creole, was a virtuoso clarinetist who left behind a string of memorable recordings. He settled near Paris, where he became a celebrity, and died in 1959.

Armstrong's life was a rags-to-riches odyssey. Records show that Armstrong was born August 4, 1901—however, he preferred the more romantic, fabricated birthday of July 4, 1900. He grew up in the Back-o'-Town ghetto and, after a stint in the Colored Waifs Home, found an early mentor in Papa Joe Oliver, the popular cornetist and bandleader also known as King Oliver. In 1918 Armstrong began traveling the Mississippi, playing on riverboats, refining his technique. In 1922 he left New Orleans to join Oliver's band in Chicago, and for the next half-century he traveled the globe, elevating jazz to an international art form.

The music stylizations and recordings of Armstrong, Morton, and Bechet had an enormous influence, yet to all but aficionados of jazz, the historical sensibility they shared is frequently overlooked. Each man worked hard on a biography; their books are solid works of literature as well as classics of jazz history—Armstrong's *Satchmo: My Life in New Orleans,* Bechet's *Treat It Gentle,* and Morton's *Mister Jelly Roll* (written by

Alan Lomax, but based on long interviews with Morton).

The sounds of jazz continued to flow in New Orleans through the '30s and '40s. The tidal shift toward a new idiom came after World War II: rhythm and blues.

A blues sensibility ran deep in New Orleans, and the many lyrics about love lost, love found were fashioned into a style, enhanced by gospel techniques, the soaring choirs and drums of the churches, and saxophones and trumpets that blasted like preachers and moaned like bluesmen.

Fats Domino put R&B on the map. In 1949 "The Fat Man," with his rocking piano style and rolling, mellifluous voice, triggered a line of golden records that made teenagers put on their dancing shoes.

Domino had the advantage of a highly skilled producer, trumpeter-bandleader Dave Bartholomew, who molded Fats's sound for the Imperial label. His biggest hit, "Blueberry Hill," was a country boy's song that wedded Fats's appeal to an audience of blue-collar workers and rural folk.

The other influential early rhythm-and-bluesman was Henry Roeland Byrd, who took the stage name Professor Longhair in 1949 and who played in Domino's shadow most of his life. Fess, as he was fondly known among locals, was quite a ticket. A tap dancer in his youth, he made the rounds of Rampart Street honkytonks in the depression, studying the blues piano of Champion Jack Dupree and Sonny Boy Williamson.

Professor Longhair called his own style "a mixture of mambo, rumba, and calypso." He infused the dance steps of his youth into an intricate, percussive keyboard style, and he sang with the deep heart of a bluesman. He simulated the street pace of Carnival in "Mardi Gras in New Orleans" and "Go to the Mardi Gras," which became local anthems. "Big Chief" was his homage to the Mardi Gras Indians, groups of blacks who create grand Native American costumes and still parade in neighborhood tribes through New Orleans's back streets.

In a sense, Professor Longhair's death in 1980 marked the end of the post-war R&B era. His unique style never caught on as a national chart buster, but he had enormous influence on younger musicians. Even before his death, younger jazzmen in the brass bands had begun performing his Carnival tunes.

Domino and Longhair divided New Orleans R&B into two stylistic camps—one a building block of rock and roll, the other a more improvisational, Afro-Caribbean beat. Between these styles was a generation of exceptional musicians.

Allen Toussaint harnessed the talents of a stable of singers in the 1960s. A skilled pianist with a seasoned lyrical touch, Toussaint composed songs for Irma Thomas ("Queen of the Blues"); Aaron Neville, a brawny balladeer with a falsetto reach that chills the spine; Ernie K-Doe, an extravagant stage performer and blues shouter who scored a hit with "Mother-in-Law"; and Benny Spellman, a hefty ex-football player for whom Toussaint penned the memorable "Fortune Teller."

The music of the 1950s fit a new urban groove. White teenagers were the big market; of the many New Orleans artists who reached the kids, Huey "Piano" Smith did it with a colorful entourage known as the Clowns. Drawing on nursery rhymes, Huey wrote uncomplicated, if offbeat, lyrics—"I got the rockin' pneumonia and the boogie-woogie flu"—and the dancers loved it.

When the Beatles and Rolling Stones swept America in the 1960s, the New Orleans R&B scene fell into decline. In the early 1970s, the annual Jazz & Heritage Festival ignited a revival.

One of the most talented 1950s session artists, Mac Rebenneck, played piano and guitar and penned dozens of compositions before hitting pop stardom in 1968 as Dr. John. James Booker, who dubbed himself the Piano Prince, also had commanding talent; he could jump from classical chords into R&B bounces with sizzling heat and witty lyrics. Booker, Dr. John, and Art Neville were prime exponents of a piano idiom that roamed the bridge between the Longhair-Domino styles. Booker's death in 1983 was greatly felt in New Orleans's jazz community.

In 1977 Art joined his brothers to form the Neville Brothers band, today the city's preeminent pop group. Charles plays saxophone; Cyril sings and plays congas; Aaron, whose 1966 hit "Tell It Like It Is" is still a showstopper, sings and plays hand percussions. The Nevilles' four-part harmonies, set against Afro-Caribbean lines, gave R&B a warm new shading. At the same time, the Nevilles wrote a new chapter in popular music through their association with the Wild Tchoupitoulas, a Mardi Gras Indian tribe led by their uncle, George Landry.

The Nevilles hit their stride in 1990, winning a Grammy for "Yellow Moon." The following year, Aaron Neville took another Grammy for his vocal duet with Linda Ronstadt and in 1992 won his first gold record, "Warm Your Heart," which sold 500,000 copies. His odyssey from stevedore work on the river docks of the Mississippi to musical celebrity is one of the most poignant artistic careers in New Orleans.

There are approximately 25 black neighborhood groups that masquerade as Indians each Mardi Gras; the folk tradition dates to Reconstruction. As Big Chief Jolley, Landry founded the Wild Tchoupitoulas in the uptown neighborhood where he and his nephews lived. A 1976 LP, *The Wild Tchoupitoulas,* combined the instrumental prowess of the Nevilles and the Meters bands with Jolley's hearty vocals, based on the old a capella tribal chants, to become a classic. By the time Landry passed away in 1980, Mardi Gras Indian music was emblematic of the Neville sound.

In the 1980s New Orleans experienced a jazz renaissance led by the brilliant trumpet work of a young Wynton Marsalis, the product of yet another musical family. As high school students, Wynton and his brothers studied at the New Orleans Center for the Creative Arts, where Ellis Marsalis, their father, directed the jazz program. With brother Branford on saxophone, Wynton emerged as a national star by the time he was 20 and in 1984 won two Grammy awards. Branford has also worked with rock star Sting for several years and contributed to the score of *Do the Right Thing,* the Spike Lee film.

A gifted composer-pianist in his own right, Ellis Marsalis molded three other young talents who have since achieved national recognition: trumpeter Terence Blanchard and saxophonist Donald Harrison, who perform together, and pianist Harry Connick Jr., who in 1987 released his debut album at age 19. Connick began dazzling audiences with a polished blend of jazz piano and a golden mellifluous singing voice that drew comparisons with Frank Sinatra. He also became a heartthrob in the youth market, a rare feat for a jazz artist. Connick has now emerged as a superstar vocalist, touring with a big band known for its lush arrangements. He has also acted in such films as *Memphis Belle, Little Man Tate,* and *Independence Day.*

The young lions of the 1980s are products of a teaching tradition and a society rooted in musical families. Their myriad innovations draw from a large canvas of sounds. The Dirty Dozen and Rebirth bands have led the brass-band resurgence, a fourth generation of young musicians improvising with blues, bebop, R&B, and jazz.

Yet a new line of young jazz talents emerged in 1991—trumpeter Nicholas Payton, son of esteemed bassist Walter Payton; drummer Brian Blade, who learned music in a Shreveport gospel church; and bassist Chris Thomas, a University of New Orleans (UNO) jazz student, among others. The impact of the UNO program under Ellis Marsalis is the most important musical development in the city in years. Molding professional artists, Marsalis and Harold Battiste, a pioneer of the post–World War II heritage jazz, are laying the groundwork for a much more sophisticated approach to the business of music.

Although a full-blown recording industry has yet to emerge, New Orleans is making dramatic strides as a music city. New Orleans in no way rivals Nashville as a production and song-publishing center. Yet tourists flock here by the millions each year, especially for the annual Jazz & Heritage Festival that runs from late April to early May. There's a heightened activity in local studios and a sturdy club circuit signals growth in the entertainment economy. The main obstacle to building a bona fide music industry is capturing a record distribution base.

Artists who make it big often head for New York, such as Armstrong, Dr. John, Wynton Marsalis, and Harry Connick Jr. Yet for all those who moved, many more choose to live here—including some of the city's best talent, such as Fats Domino, the Nevilles, and younger groups such as the Dirty Dozen and Rebirth brass bands—while playing long stretches on concert tours each year.

Despite its drawbacks, a distinctive cultural sensibility—more Latin and African than Anglo-American—has endowed New Orleans with a unique musical society. As saxophonist Harold Battiste, a pioneer of 1950s heritage jazz that came out of small clubs around the Magnolia housing project, once put it: "Musicians come and go, and their creations always seem directed at the city. Because after all is said and done, *New Orleans* is the star."

–Jason Berry

Jason Berry is the author of *Amazing Grace: With Charles Evers in Mississippi* and the coauthor of *Up from the Cradle of Jazz: New Orleans Music Since World War II.*

VOODOO AND THE LIFE OF SPIRITS IN NEW ORLEANS

Imagine New Orleans in the colonial era. Rain-sodden, prone to yellow fever epidemics, it is a remote port whose plantation economy turns on the toil of African slaves. Indian communities dot swampy woodlands that are well removed from the great estates where Creole aristocrats, their society wedded to interests of the Church, eat sumptuously and party well.

Voodoo charges the territory with powerful impulses, bewildering planter and priest. Away from the plantation house, in the secluded woods near river and bayou, booming drums summon slaves to torch-lighted ceremonies in the night. Men and women gyrate to the percussive rhythms as a cult priest chants. Slap goes his knife, slicing through a chicken's neck—up gushes the blood, covering his hands. Around and around the worshipers dance, shouting in response to the priest's African chants.

Voices pulsate to the beat of hands and sticks on drums, pulsating on and on until the spirit hits and a woman is possessed by a current of psychic energy. Her shoulders shake, her body twists, her tongue speaks words no white man understands. The cultists gather round, calming her till the possession passes and she is released from her spell. Now the drumbeats become more insistent and the ceremony resumes.

In the nearby mansion, a Creole planter does not like what he hears; he tells himself he treats his slaves well. But what do those cries mean? A foreboding seeps into his night.

In the 18th century, voodoo was the most dramatic symbol of division between master and slave, and it loomed as a sinister threat to the ruling class. In 1782 the governor of Louisiana, fearing rebellious uprisings of the cults, put a clamp on voodoo-worshiping slaves imported from the Caribbean island of Martinique. But by then it was too late—voodoo had taken root.

Voodoo was a religion that had journeyed to the New World in the hearts and minds of African slaves uprooted from the animist culture of their homeland. Its origins lay in West Africa, particularly in the ancient kingdom of Dahomey (today the People's Republic of Benin) and in neighboring Yorubaland (what is now Nigeria).

In the 1720s, millions of Africans were captured by West African kings and sold as slaves to foreign merchants. Chained and hungry, the hostages were shipped in the holds of large ships that crossed the ocean. The Africans, as beheld by Caribbean and southern planters, were people without religion, redeemed from the savage world they had left behind.

In reality, they came from large, extended families. Their African culture revolved around communal ceremonies that honored the spirits of departed ancestors. Music and dance rituals recognized the dead as existential presences; devotees wore masks to embody ancestral figures, deities, animals, and forces of nature.

The Yoruba believed that existence consists of three interconnected zones: the living, the dead, and the unborn. In rituals (still performed today) masked figures danced to percussive rhythms that evoked the ancients, or *orisas*.

The tone of the "talking drums" communicated the tribal vocabulary. The drum voice and dancer's mask formed a continuum—one gave language through music, and the other an image of the spirit. Voodoo was the faith, the center of gravity for the tribe, and it, along with its followers, crossed the Atlantic Ocean in the overloaded slave holds. However, the masks would now lie buried in the savannas of the mind: communications with the orisas in the white man's land would be dangerous and difficult.

The deepest implanting of voodoo occurred on the island of Saint Domingue, as Haiti was known before 1804. The Fon, natives of Dahomey, cast a large influence over the island's slave communities. Just as the Yoruba evoked their orisas, the Fon summoned their spirits, called *loa*. To the Fon, "vodun" meant "god" or "protective spirit."

Indoctrinated as Catholics, slaves on Haiti used the Mass in melding African spirits with visages of Christian saints. The Mass provided a New World ritual for voodoo's elastic reach; cultists could forsake the knife from chicken or goat and transform their worship in a less bloody rite while maintaining its inner core complete with sacrificial gods and drumbeats.

On the night of August 22, 1791, while a storm raged through Saint Domingue, a cult priest named Boukman led a voodoo incantation, drank blood from a pig, and, as reported by historian C. L. R. James, told his followers: "The gods of the white man inspire him with crime. . . . Our god who is good to us orders us to revenge our wrongs." Boukman was killed, but his revolt was one in a succession of slave rebellions culminating with the overthrow of French forces in 1804 and the founding of the Republic of Haiti.

During the next decade, waves of planters, free Creoles of color, and slaves reached New Orleans, many via Cuba, scattering seeds that sprouted new voodoo cults. By then nearly a century had passed since the first slaves had arrived in Louisiana; the vocabulary of African drum voices had been effectively erased, but the religious sensibility had found a new cultural passageway.

In the early 1800s, land along the ramparts of New Orleans (what is now Louis Armstrong Park) became known as Place Congo, or Congo Square. On Sunday, slaves gravitated there for massive drum-and-dance convocations. They were not actual voodoo ceremonies, though the underlying impulse was similar, and white planters and their wives gawked at these spectacles performed in the open sunlight. These congregations in Congo Square were outlawed about 1835; however, the sustained impact of tribal drums and dancing created for the slaves a link to their African past.

New Orleans was fast becoming a culture *métissage*—a mixture of bloodlines. Segregation was the law, but social intercourse was fluid among the peoples, especially between Creole planters and the mistresses they found among the mulatto women. As the antebellum era wore on, the voodoo sensibility—adaptive to the culture in which it found itself— worked its way into the thoughts and culture of aristocratic white society.

In the 1820s voodoo queen Marie Laveau (believed to have been of black, Indian, and white blood) worked as a hairdresser in white homes, where she gathered secrets of the Creole elite by utilizing domestic servants to spy on whites, many of whom sought her advice as a spiritual counselor. A practicing Catholic, she nevertheless frequently prescribed the sticking of a pin into a voodoo doll to provoke trouble for someone's nemesis or magical gris-gris dust (spell-casting powder) as a curative or protective hex. Her influence with blacks was greater by virtue of her sway over whites.

Marie made quite a living as a spiritual guide, selling her hexes and charms; she also made regular visits to the local prison. She groomed her daughter Marie to carry on the voodoo tradition; it was the second Marie whose exotic ceremonies of the night became legendary. Sex orgies reportedly occurred during voodoo rites of the late 19th century.

Dr. John, another important voodoo legend, was a towering black man (reputed to be a Senegalese prince in his former life) who owned slaves and was apparently a polygamist. He cultivated his own network of informants among slaves and servants who worked for whites. Aristocrats are said to have sought his advice, making him a legendary figure to blacks, but an outright cult priest he apparently was not.

In New Orleans today, voodoo is a bare whisper of its former self, a shadow along the margins of a different spirit world, grounded in the folkways of black Christian churches. As voodoo waned with early 20th-century urbanization, spiritualistic religions took root in New Orleans's churches. In these mostly small chapels, blacks honored the presence of St. Michael the Archangel, Black Hawk the Indian, Leith Anderson, Mother Catherine, and other benevolent figures. Although the base religion was Christianity, Haitian voodoo had turned African deities into images of Catholic saints; the spiritualistic churches transformed the faces once again, finding North American spirits to fit the visages of the new pantheon. Spirits may change as culture goes through upheavals, but the coil of memory springs the imagination, triggering messages in music and dance, myth and symbol.

American Indian tribes shared this imaginative process. Black Hawk was a powerful Sauk chief in Illinois who died in 1838. As Yoruba and Fon spirits resurfaced in Haiti, so the spirit of Black Hawk coursed through the mental chambers of a people with Native American heritage. In 1919 the consciousness of Black Hawk reached New Orleans's spiritualistic churches through Leith Anderson, a woman of black and Indian ancestry who had come from Chicago.

In a WPA interview conducted during the Depression, Mother Dora, another spiritualistic leader, recalled Leith Anderson: "She wanted us to pray to Black Hawk because he was a great saint for spiritualism only. . . . Ah think he came to her one time and said dat he was de first one to start spiritualism in dis country way before de white men come heah."

A Black Hawk cult flourishes in spiritualist churches today. Mother Leith Anderson—also called Leafy—is memorialized as well. The trancelike possessions are powerful testimony to the belief system—a benevolent Christian vision of spirits-as-seed-carriers of culture across space and time.

In 1967 a crusty rock-and-roller named Mac Rebenneck adopted the stage name and persona of Dr. John. He sported bone and teeth necklaces, face paint, and a turban with billowing colored feathers. Confronting this bizarre persona, Mac's mother, a good Catholic lady, fretted, "I didn't want him for his soul's sake to be doing this. But actually, I could see the creativeness of what he was doing."

In "Gris-Gris Gumbo Ya-Ya," Mac sang as Dr. John: "Got a satchel of gris-gris in my hand / Got many clients that come from miles around."

Perhaps the most visible emblem of voodoo's hold on the popular imagination today is the number of visitors who flock to the tomb of Marie Laveau in St. Louis Cemetery #1 and to the Voodoo Museum in the French Quarter. There is no dearth of voodoo walking tours during which a guide will go into further detail about the history of the religion while pointing out Marie Laveau's house and grave, Congo Square, and other places of interest.

— Jason Berry

WHAT TO READ, WATCH, & LISTEN TO BEFORE YOU GO

Books

For a good mixture of romance and adventure with an eccentric cast of characters, pick up *Bandits* by Elmore Leonard. Frances Parkinson Keyes's *Dinner at Antoine's* is a charming murder mystery. In Sarah Shankman's *Now Let's Talk of Graves*, a journalist-detective travels to New Orleans for a Mardi Gras holiday and investigates a possible murder.

Julie Smith won an Edgar Award for her first murder mystery set in New Orleans. *New Orleans Mourning* introduced policewoman Skip Langdon to readers in 1990. Tony Dunbar has been turning out highly regarded murder mysteries with a southern twist, most featuring flawed crime solver, Tubby Dubonnet. Dunbar's *City of Beads* is considered his best. Of course, James Lee Burke started all this with his Dave Robicheaux series. Burke's *Neon Rain* is a good example of the genre.

The Muse is Always Half-Dressed in New Orleans is a witty collection of droll philosophical essays from Andrei Codrescu, the transplanted Romanian and National Public Radio commentator who happens to call New Orleans home.

A Feast of All Saints, by Anne Rice, describes the lives of the "free people of color" (a localism for blacks who were not enslaved prior to Emancipation) in pre–Civil War New Orleans. Rice's best-selling *Vampire Chronicles* also often use New Orleans as a background.

Other novels set in the city include *Lives of the Saints*, by Nancy Lemann, a fun novel about a wacky New Orleans family; Kate Chopin's *The Awakening*, a serious story about the life of a New Orleans woman in

the mid-1800s; *The Moviegoer*, by Walker Percy, full of details about the city as it follows a charming, neurotic native of New Orleans; and *A Confederacy of Dunces*, by John Kennedy Toole, a Pulitzer Prize–winning novel about another neurotic New Orleanian—this time, though, he is not so charming. Robert Penn Warren's *All the King's Men*, a thinly veiled story of Huey Long, is an American classic, a beautifully written, insightful look at southern-fried politics.

Bethany Ewald Bultman's *New Orleans*, a Compass American Guide, has color photos and plenty of cultural essays and historical material. For an interesting history of the city—through an explanation of New Orleans street names—read *Frenchmen Desire Good Children*, by John Chase. Al Rose's *Storyville* gives a good account of the origins of jazz and New Orleans's once infamous red-light district. The pocket-size history *The Free People of Color of New Orleans*, by Mary Gehman, explains the contributions of that unique group, today often referred to as Creoles.

Films

Eve's Bayou (1997) was hailed by critic Roger Ebert as the best movie of 1997. Lynn Whitfield and Samuel L. Jackson shine in this film steeped in mystery, betrayal, and voodoo and shot almost exclusively on the Northshore of New Orleans. *Interview with the Vampire* (1994), based on the novel by Anne Rice, has vampires Tom Cruise and Brad Pitt appearing around the French Quarter, in Lafayette Cemetery, and at Oak Alley plantation. In *The Pelican Brief* (1993), based on the John Grisham best-seller, Julia Roberts plays a Tulane law school student who discovers why two supreme court justices have been murdered. In *JFK* (1991),

New Orleans district attorney Jim Garrison (Kevin Costner) tries to prosecute a city businessman (Tommy Lee Jones) for conspiracy in the assassination of President John F. Kennedy. *The Big Easy* (1987) features Lake Pontchartrain, the Piazza d'Italia, and a catchy zydeco music soundtrack as it unfolds its tale of a wise-guy police lieutenant (Dennis Quaid) who uncovers corruption in the New Orleans police force.

Other films shot in New Orleans include: *Double Jeopardy* (1999); *Hard Target* (1994); *Undercover Blues* (1993); *Storyville* (1992); *Miller's Crossing* (1990); *Tune in Tomorrow* (1990); *Blaze* (1989); *Angel Heart* (1987); *Tightrope* (1984); *Cat People* (1982); *Pretty Baby* (1978); *Easy Rider* (1969); and *Panic in the Streets* (1950). For a glimpse of Cajun country, take a look at *The Apostle* (1997), *Passion Fish* (1992), *Belizaire the Cajun* (1986), and *No Mercy* (1986).

Music

It would be impossible to prepare fully for the incredible variety of music you will hear pouring from shops, restaurants, bars, and clubs in New Orleans. Far and away the best source for local and regional music is the **Louisiana Music Factory** (✉ 210 Decatur St., New Orleans 70130, ☎ 504/586–1094), a mecca for musicians passing through New Orleans and an important force in the local music community. The staff will help you identify that great band you heard the night before, and some local CDs are available only here. Saturday afternoons bring live in-store concerts. The store also ships anywhere.

Louis Armstrong laid the foundation of a classic style that New Orleans musicians—and jazz artists worldwide—still draw upon today. Any CD from the series *The Hot 5s and 7s* (CBS Records) is a good bet; the whole set is now available as a four-CD box set (JSP 100). The clarinet playing that seduced Paris is captured on *The Best of Sidney Bechet* (Blue Note 28891). The Preservation Hall Jazz Band still plays each night at Preservation Hall; hear their tradi-

tional jazz on *Songs of New Orleans, Parts I and II* (Preservation Hall Records 5). Danny Barker's all-acoustic and entertaining *Save the Bones* (Orleans Records 1018) captures the folk element in traditional New Orleans music.

Piano virtuosity has a long and rich history in New Orleans. Good examples of Jelly Roll Morton's ragtime art are found on *The Piano Rolls* (Nonesuch 79363) and *The Pearls* (Bluebird 6588). Professor Longhair, who developed his own unique "rumba-boogie" style and influenced every local pianist to come after him, has a slew of recordings; a couple of the best are *Rock and Roll Gumbo* (Dancing Cat 3006) and *Mardi Gras in Baton Rouge* (Rhino 70736). The dazzling, intensely intellectual playing of James Booker can be sampled on *Junco Partner* (Hannibal 1359) and *The Lost Paramount Tapes* (DJM 10010). In the rhythm and blues camp, you'll find many of Fats Domino's jaunty favorites on *The Fat Man* (EMI 52326). More good New Orleans R&B is available on Lee Dorsey's *Working in the Coalmine* (Collectables 5082).

Some of the best artists to come out of New Orleans are still playing local clubs today. Dr. John's raspy mysticism comes through especially well on *Gumbo* (Atco 7006). The funky Meters (currently playing as "The Funky Meters") have a number of good albums, including *The Very Best of the Meters* (Rhino 72642), and the two-CD *Funkify Your Life* (Rhino 71869). The Neville Brothers have a new greatest hits album, *Uptown Rulin'* (A&M Records 490403), which traces the trajectory of their funk-R&B development. That unique New Orleans genre, Mardi Gras Indian music, gets a good hearing on the Wild Magnolias' *I'm Back at Carnival Time* (Rounder 2094). The Rebirth Brass Band is the local favorite among contemporary brass bands; their *Feel Like Funkin' it Up* (Rounder 2092) and *Take it to the Street* (Rounder 2115) provide a good sense of this dynamic, modern sound that falls somewhere between traditional jazz and hip-hop.

Though Cajun country lies upriver from New Orleans, its unique French-language folk music is very popular in town, too. For a good introduction, try *The Balfa Brothers Play Traditional Cajun Music* (Swallow Records 6011) and David Doucet's *Quand j'ai parti* (Rounder 1640) or *"1957"* (Rounder 6088). Zydeco, Cajun's bluesier near-relation, is best exemplified by the classic recordings of Clifton Chenier, including *Louisiana Blues and Zydeco* (Arhoolie 329) and *Bogalusa Boogie* (Arhoolie 347); hot albums by zydeco's newest generation include Geno Delafose's *French Rockin' Boogie* (Rounder 612131) and Nathan and the Zydeco Cha-Chas' *Creole Crossroads* (Rounder 612137).

— Baty Landis

ESSENTIAL INFORMATION

ADDRESSES

New Orleans expands from an 8-mi stretch between the Mississippi River and Lake Pontchartrain. The downtown includes the the Vieux Carré (Old Square), or the French Quarter; the Central Business District (CBD); and the riverfront. Addresses in a city that bases its compass on the bends of the river can be confusing. Canal Street, a long avenue that runs from the river to the lake, divides the city roughly into uptown and downtown sections. Locals will most likely give you directions in terms of so many blocks downriver or upriver on the lake side or river side. Streets to the north of Canal are named North and run downtown; those to the south of Canal are named South and run uptown. Addresses begin at 100 on either side of Canal St. Only the French Quarter is laid out in a grid pattern. Street numbers begin at 400 in the Quarter on the river side. It's helpful to keep a map handy.

AIR TRAVEL TO AND FROM NEW ORLEANS

BOOKING

When you book **look for nonstop flights** and **remember that "direct" flights stop at least once.** Try to avoid connecting flights, which require a change of plane.

CARRIERS

➤ MAJOR AIRLINES: **American** (☎ 800/433–7300). **Continental** (☎ 800/525–0280). **Delta** (☎ 800/221–1212). **Northwest** (☎ 800/225–2525). **TWA** (☎ 800/221–2000). **United** (☎ 800/241–6522). **US Airways** (☎ 800/428–4322).

➤ SMALLER AIRLINES: **America West** (☎ 800/235–9292). **Southwest** (☎ 800/435–9792). **AirTran** (☎ 770/994–8258 or 800/825–8538).

➤ FOR DIRECT FLIGHTS FROM THE U.K.: **American** (☎ 0845/778–9789) via Chicago or Dallas. **British Airways** (☎ 0845/722–2111) via Philadelphia. **Delta** (☎ 0800/414–767) via Atlanta or Cincinnati. **United** (☎ 0800/888–555) via Washington. **Virgin Atlantic** (☎ 01293/747–747) via Miami or Washington.

CHECK-IN & BOARDING

Assuming that not everyone with a ticket will show up, airlines routinely overbook planes. When everyone does, airlines ask for volunteers to give up their seats. In return, these volunteers usually get a certificate for a free flight and are rebooked on the next flight out. If there are not enough volunteers, the airline must choose who will be denied boarding. The first to get bumped are passengers who checked in late and those flying on discounted tickets, so **get to the gate and check in as early as possible,** especially during peak periods.

Always **bring a government-issued photo I.D. to the airport.** You may be asked to show it before you are allowed to check in.

CUTTING COSTS

The least expensive airfares to New Orleans must usually be purchased in advance and are non-refundable. It's smart to **call a number of airlines, and when you are quoted a good price, book it on the spot**—the same fare may not be available the next day. Always **check different routings** and look into using different airports. Travel agents, especially low-fare specialists (☞ Discounts & Deals, *below*), are helpful.

Consolidators are another good source. They buy tickets for scheduled international flights at reduced rates from the airlines, then sell them at prices that beat the best fare available directly from the airlines, usually without restrictions. Sometimes you can even get your money back if you need to return the ticket. Carefully read the fine print detailing penalties for changes and cancellations, and **confirm your consolidator reservation with the airline.**

When you **fly as a courier,** you trade your checked-luggage space for a ticket deeply subsidized by a courier service. There are restrictions on when you can book and how long you can stay.

➤ CONSOLIDATORS: **Cheap Tickets** (☎ 800/377–1000). **Discount Airline Ticket Service** (☎ 800/576–1600). **Unitravel** (☎ 800/325–2222). **Up & Away Travel** (☎ 212/889–2345). **World Travel Network** (☎ 800/409–6753).

ENJOYING THE FLIGHT

For more legroom, **request an emergency-aisle seat.** Don't sit in the row in front of the emergency aisle or in front of a bulkhead, where seats may not recline. If you have dietary concerns, **ask for special meals when booking.** These can be vegetarian, low-cholesterol, or kosher, for example. On long flights, try to maintain a normal routine, to help fight jet lag. At night, **get some sleep.** By day, **eat light meals, drink water** (not alcohol), and **move around the cabin** to stretch your legs.

FLYING TIMES

Flying time is 2½ hours from New York, 2¼ hours from Chicago, 3½ hours from San Francisco, and 10 hours from London.

HOW TO COMPLAIN

If your baggage goes astray or your flight goes awry, complain right away. Most carriers require that you **file a claim immediately.**

➤ AIRLINE COMPLAINTS: U.S. Department of Transportation **Aviation Consumer Protection Division** (✉ C-75, Room 4107, Washington, DC 20590, ☎ 202/366–2220, airconsumer@ost.dot.gov, www.dot.gov/airconsumer). **Federal Aviation Administration Consumer Hotline** (☎ 800/322–7873).

AIRPORTS & TRANSFERS

The major gateway to New Orleans is New Orleans International Airport (MSY), 15 mi west of the city in Kenner. There's an airport exit off I-10.

➤ AIRPORT INFORMATION: **New Orleans International Airport** (✉ 900 Airline Dr., Kenner, ☎ 504/464–0831).

AIRPORT TRANSFERS

Shuttle bus service to and from the airport and downtown hotels is available through New Orleans Tours Airport Shuttle. Buses leave regularly from the ground-floor level near the baggage claim. To return to the airport, call at least two hours in advance of flight time. One-way cost is $10 per person and the trip takes about 40 minutes.

Louisiana Transit also runs a bus between the airport and the Central Business District (CBD). The trip costs $1.50 in exact change and takes about 45 minutes. From the CBD, departures for the airport are every 10 to 20 minutes from Elks Place and Tulane Avenue across from the city library. The last bus leaves at 6:30 PM.

Taxis cut about 15 minutes from the trip but cost $25 for the first two people and $8 for each additional person.

By car, take the I–10 Expressway (from the CBD, go west to the Airport exit). Allow an hour for the drive during afternoon rush hour.

➤ TAXIS & SHUTTLES: **New Orleans Tours Airport Shuttle** (☎ 504/522–3500). **Louisiana Transit** (☎ 504/818–1077).

BOAT & FERRY TRAVEL

The ferry ride across the river to a part of New Orleans called Algiers is an experience in itself, offering great views of the river and the New Orleans skyline as well as the heady feeling of being on one of the largest and most powerful rivers in the world (☞ Foot of Canal Street and Algiers Point *in* Chapter 1). Pedestrians climb the stairs (there is no elevator) near the Spanish Plaza and the Riverwalk shopping area and board the Canal Street Ferry from above, while bicycles and cars board from below on the left of the terminal. The trip takes about 10 minutes; ferries leave on the hour and half hour and run from 6:30 AM to midnight. Hours at night may vary, so be sure to check with the attendants if you are crossing in the evening—it is no fun to be stranded on the other side. The fare is $1 round-trip per car, free for pedestrians. Keep in mind, too, that there are no rest room facilities in the terminals or on the ferry itself, and no food or drink concessions. Special arrangements for people with disabilities must be made with an attendant.

FARES & SCHEDULES

➤ BOAT & FERRY INFORMATION: **Canal Street Ferry** (Foot of Canal, ☎ 504/364–8100).

BUS TRAVEL AROUND NEW ORLEANS

Within New Orleans, the Regional Transit Authority (RTA) operates a public bus transportation system with interconnecting lines throughout the city. The buses are generally clean and on time.

FARES & SCHEDULES

Bus and streetcar fare is $1.25 plus 25¢ for transfers. Visiting senior citizens 65 or over who have a valid Medicare ID card may ride public transit for only 50¢. Visitor passes available at hotels apply to buses as well as streetcars and cost $5 for one day, $12 for three days of unlimited rides.

➤ BUS INFORMATION: **RTA** (☎ 504/248–3900, 504/242–2600 for automated information).

PAYING

Exact change is required.

BUS TRAVEL TO AND FROM NEW ORLEANS

Greyhound has one terminal in the city, in the Union Passenger Terminal in the CBD. Ask about special travel passes. Check with your local Greyhound ticket office for prices and schedules.

➤ BUS INFORMATION: **Greyhound** (Union Passenger Terminal, 1001 Loyola Ave., ☎ 504/525–6075 or 800/231–2222).

BUSINESS HOURS

BANKS AND OFFICES

Banks are open weekdays 9–3; some may be open in the morning on Saturday. ATMs are abundant, however. Business offices are typically open weekdays 9–5.

MUSEUMS

Many museums are closed on Monday, and some are not open Sunday as well. Very few have evening hours. Hours of sights and attractions are denoted in the book by the clock icon, ☉.

PHARMACIES

Pharmacies generally open at 9 or 10 AM and close between 5 and 9 PM.

SHOPS

Store hours are generally from 10 to 5:30 or 6 Monday–Saturday, with shorter hours—from noon to 5—on Sunday. In areas with active nightlife, such as the French Quarter and at shopping malls, many stores stay open until 9 PM. Sunday is a good shopping day in heavily trafficked areas, though some of the smaller shops and boutiques may not be open.

CAMERAS & PHOTOGRAPHY

New Orleans welcomes cameras in most places, but **remember that no flashes allowed in churches and art museums.** Many people will want a photo of Jackson Square and the distinctive wrought iron that decorates many buildings in the French Quarter; the St. Charles Avenue streetcar and the riverfront are other distinctive sights.

➤ PHOTO HELP: **Kodak Information Center** (☎ 800/242–2424). *Kodak Guide to Shooting Great Travel Pictures,* available in bookstores or from Fodor's Travel Publications (☎ 800/533–6478; $16.50 plus $5.50 shipping).

EQUIPMENT PRECAUTIONS

Always **keep your film and tape out of the sun.** Carry an extra supply of batteries, and **be prepared to turn on your camera or camcorder** to prove to security personnel that the device is real. Always **ask for hand inspection**

of film, which becomes clouded after repeated exposure to airport X-ray machines, and **keep videotapes away from metal detectors.**

CAR RENTAL

Rates in New Orleans begin at $44 per day and $143 per week for an economy car with air conditioning, an automatic transmission, and unlimited mileage. This does not include tax on car rentals, which is 12%.

➤ MAJOR AGENCIES: **Alamo** (☎ 800/327–9633; 020/8759–6200 in the U.K.). **Avis** (☎ 800/331–1212; 800/879–2847 in Canada; 0870/606–0100 in the U.K., 02/9353–9000 in Australia; 09/525–1982 in New Zealand). **Budget** (☎ 800/527–0700; 0144/227–6266 in the U.K.). **Dollar** (☎ 800/800–4000; 020/8897–0811 in the U.K., where it is known as Eurodollar; 02/9223–1444 in Australia). **Hertz** (☎ 800/654–3131; 800/263–0600 in Canada; 020/8897–2072 in the U.K.; 02/9669–2444 in Australia; 03/358–6777 in New Zealand). **National InterRent** (☎ 800/227–7368; 0845/722–2525 in the U.K., where it is known as Europcar InterRent).

CUTTING COSTS

To get the best deal, **book through a travel agent who will shop around.** Also **price local car-rental companies,** although the service and maintenance may not be as good as those of a major player. Remember to ask about required deposits, cancellation penalties, and drop-off charges if you're planning to pick up the car in one city and leave it in another. If you're traveling during a holiday period, also make sure that a confirmed reservation guarantees you a car.

Do **look into wholesalers,** companies that do not own fleets but rent in bulk from those that do and often offer better rates than traditional car-rental operations.

➤ WHOLESALERS: **Auto Europe** (☎ 207/842–2000 or 800/223–5555, FAX 800/235–6321). **Kemwel Holiday Autos** (☎ 914/835–5555 or 800/678–0678, FAX 914/835–5126).

INSURANCE

When driving a rented car you are generally responsible for any damage to or loss of the vehicle as well as for any property damage or personal injury that you may cause. Before you rent see what coverage your personal auto-insurance policy and credit cards already provide.

For about $15 to $20 per day, rental companies sell protection, known as a collision- or loss-damage waiver (CDW or LDW), that eliminates your liability for damage to the car. In most states you don't need a CDW if you have personal auto insurance or other liability insurance. However, **make sure you have enough coverage to pay for the car.** If you do not have auto insurance or an umbrella policy that covers damage to third parties, purchasing liability insurance and a CDW or LDW is highly recommended.

REQUIREMENTS & RESTRICTIONS

In New Orleans you must be 21 to rent a car, and rates may be higher if you're under 25. You'll pay extra for child seats (about $3 per day), which are compulsory for children under five, and for additional drivers (about $2 per day). Non-U.S. residents will need a reservation voucher, a passport, a driver's license, and a travel policy that covers each driver, when picking up a car.

SURCHARGES

Before you pick up a car in one city and leave it in another, **ask about drop-off charges or one-way service fees,** which can be substantial. Note, too, that some rental agencies charge extra if you return the car before the time specified in your contract. To avoid a hefty refueling fee, **fill the tank just before you turn in the car,** but be aware that gas stations near the rental outlet may overcharge.

CAR TRAVEL

Having a car in New Orleans is no problem—except at Mardi Gras. Then the whole French Quarter is closed to traffic, and cars parked on parade routes get whisked away. A car is not needed for sightseeing around the most visited areas of the city, however. You can get around many popular areas on foot or by streetcar or taxi. For excursions to surrounding areas, cars are advisable.

I–10 runs from Florida to California and passes directly through the city. To get to the CBD, exit at Poydras Street near the Louisiana Superdome. For the French Quarter, look for the Vieux Carré exit.

Gas stations are not plentiful within the city of New Orleans. The downtown area is particularly short on stations. Most stations in the city and suburbs open early and stay open late. Some all-night stations are available.

CHILDREN IN NEW ORLEANS

Be sure to plan ahead and **involve your youngsters** as you outline your trip. When packing, include things to keep them busy en route. On sightseeing days try to schedule activities of special interest to your children.

New Orleans for Kids ($5 from the New Orleans Metropolitan Convention and Tourist Bureau) is an activity book and tour guide; it includes puzzles and pictures for coloring as well as a whole host of suggestions about where to take children in New Orleans.

If you are renting a car, don't forget to **arrange for a car seat** when you reserve.

➤ LOCAL INFORMATION: **New Orleans Convention and Visitors Bureau** (✉ 1520 Sugar Bowl Dr., 70112, ☎ 504/566–5031).

BABY-SITTING

➤ AGENCIES: **Accent on Arrangements** (☎ 504/524–1227). **Dependable Kid Care** (☎ 504/486–4001).

FLYING

If your children are two or older **ask about children's airfares.** As a general rule, infants under two not occupying a seat fly at greatly reduced fares or even for free.

Experts agree that it's a good idea to use safety seats aloft for children weighing less than 40 pounds. Airlines set their own policies: U.S. carriers usually require that the child be ticketed, even if he or she is young enough to ride free, since the seats must be strapped into regular seats. Do **check your airline's policy about using safety seats during takeoff and landing.** And since safety seats are not allowed just everywhere in the plane, get your seat assignments early.

When reserving, **request children's meals or a freestanding bassinet** if you need them. But note that bulk-head seats, where you must sit to use the bassinet, may lack an overhead bin or storage space on the floor.

LODGING

Most hotels in New Orleans allow children under a certain age to stay in their parents' room at no extra charge, but others charge for them as extra adults; be sure to **find out the cutoff age for children's discounts.**

SIGHTS & ATTRACTIONS

Places that are especially appealing to children are indicated by a rubber duckie icon in the margin.

CONCIERGES

Concierges, found in many hotels, can help you with theater tickets and dinner reservations: a good one with connections may be able to get you seats for a hot show or prime-time dinner reservations at the restaurant of the moment. You can also turn to your hotel's concierge for help with travel arrangements, sightseeing plans, services ranging from aromatherapy to zipper repair, and emergencies. Always, **always tip** a concierge who has been of assistance (☞ Tipping, *below*).

CONSUMER PROTECTION

Whenever shopping or buying travel services in New Orleans, **pay with a major credit card** so you can cancel payment or get reimbursed if there's a problem. If you're doing business with a particular company for the first time, **contact your local Better Business Bureau and the attorney general's offices** in your own state and the company's home state, as well. Have any complaints been filed? Finally, if you're buying a package or tour, always **consider travel insurance** that includes default coverage (☞ Insurance, *below*).

➤ BBBs: **Council of Better Business Bureaus** (✉ 4200 Wilson Blvd., Suite 800, Arlington, VA 22203, ☎ 703/276–0100, FAX 703/525–8277 www.bbb.org).

CRUISE TRAVEL

The Delta Queen Steamboat Company offers 3- to 12-day excursions up the Big Muddy and environs aboard the *Delta Queen,* a National Historic Landmark built in the 1920s; the *Mississippi Queen,* built in 1976; or the *American Queen,* the largest paddle wheeler ever built. Cruises up the Mississippi focus on the river's effect on history and historic onshore sites such as antebellum plantation houses, Vicksburg, and Natchez. Founded in 1890, the company operates out of an enormous and efficient waterfront terminal complex adjacent to the Ernest M. Morial Convention Center. Several of the larger cruise lines, such as Carnival and Commodore also stop in New Orleans.

➤ CRUISE LINES: *Delta Queen* Steamboat Company (✉ Robin Street Wharf, ☎ 504/586–0631 or 800/543–1949).

CUSTOMS & DUTIES

When shopping, **keep receipts** for all purchases. Upon reentering the country, **be ready to show customs officials what you've bought.** If you feel a duty is incorrect or object to the way your clearance was handled, note the inspector's badge number and ask to see a supervisor. If the problem isn't resolved, write to the appropriate authorities, beginning with the port director at your point of entry.

IN AUSTRALIA

Australian residents who are 18 or older may bring home $A400 worth of souvenirs and gifts (including jewelry), 250 cigarettes or 250 grams of tobacco, and 1,125 ml of alcohol (including wine, beer, and spirits). Residents under 18 may bring back $A200 worth of goods. Prohibited items include meat products. Seeds, plants, and fruits need to be declared upon arrival.

➤ INFORMATION: **Australian Customs Service** (Regional Director, ✉ Box 8, Sydney, NSW 2001, ☎ 02/9213–2000, ⅎ 02/9213–4000).

IN CANADA

Canadian residents who have been out of Canada for at least 7 days may bring home C$500 worth of goods duty-free. If you've been away less than 7 days but more than 48 hours, the duty-free allowance drops to C$200; if your trip lasts 24–48 hours, the allowance is C$50. You may not pool allowances with family members. Goods claimed under the C$500 exemption may follow you by mail; those claimed under the lesser exemptions must accompany you. Alcohol and tobacco products may be included in the 7-day and 48-hour exemptions but not in the 24-hour exemption. If you meet the age requirements of the province or territory through which you reenter Canada, you may bring in, duty-free, 1.14 liters (40 imperial ounces) of wine or liquor *or* 24 12-ounce cans or bottles of beer or ale. If you are 16 or older you may bring in, duty-free, 200 cigarettes and 50 cigars. Check ahead of time with Revenue Canada or the Department of Agriculture for policies regarding meat products, seeds, plants, and fruits.

You may send an unlimited number of gifts worth up to C$60 each duty-free to Canada. Label the package UNSOLICITED GIFT—VALUE UNDER $60. Alcohol and tobacco are excluded.

IN NEW ZEALAND

Homeward-bound residents 17 or older may bring back $700 worth of souvenirs and gifts. Your duty-free allowance also includes 4.5 liters of wine or beer; one 1,125-ml bottle of spirits; and either 200 cigarettes, 250 grams of tobacco, 50 cigars, or a combination of the three up to 250 grams. Prohibited items include meat products, seeds, plants, and fruits.

➤ INFORMATION: **New Zealand Customs** (Custom House, ✉ 50 Anzac Ave., Box 29, Auckland, New Zealand, ☎ 09/359–6655, ⅎ 09/359–6732).

IN THE U.K.

From countries outside the EU, including New Orleans, you may bring home, duty-free, 200 cigarettes or 50 cigars; 1 liter of spirits or 2 liters of fortified or sparkling wine or liqueurs; 2 liters of still table wine; 60 ml of perfume; 250 ml of toilet water; plus £136 worth of other goods, including gifts and souvenirs. If returning from outside the EU, prohibited items include meat products, seeds, plants, and fruits.

➤ INFORMATION: **HM Customs and Excise** (✉ Dorset House, Stamford St., Bromley, Kent BR1 1XX, ☎ 020/7202–4227).

IN THE U.S.

➤ INFORMATION: **U.S. Customs Service** (✉ 1300 Pennsylvania Ave. NW, Washington, DC 20229, www.customs.gov; inquiries ☎ 202/354–1000; complaints c/o ✉ Office of Regulations and Rulings; registration of equipment c/o ✉ Resource Management, ☎ 202/927–0540).

DINING

New Orleans is known worldwide for its food. The introduction to Chapter 2 provides a good overview of the dining scene and some local specialties; there is even a glossary of food terms.

Most places accept all major credit cards.

MEALTIMES

Unless otherwise noted, the restaurants listed in this guide are open daily for lunch and dinner. Lunch is normally taken between 11 and 2, dinner between 7 and 10.

RESERVATIONS & DRESS

Reservations are always a good idea: we mention them only when they're essential or not accepted. We mention dress only when men are required to wear a jacket or a jacket and tie.

Most restaurants in New Orleans accept reservations, and many of the very popular places become quickly booked, especially on Friday and Saturday nights. The best strategy is to reserve as soon as you decide where and when you'd like to go; several weeks ahead of time is not too far in advance to reserve for trips during Mardi Gras, Jazz Fest, or other special events. Reconfirm as soon as you arrive. If you must cancel, let the reservations desk know immediately.

If you're eating in a luxury restaurant, or one of the old-line, conservative Creole places, dress appropriately. If you don't know whether jackets are required or jeans are frowned upon, telephoning to find out is a simple matter. You'll probably be more comfortable, and so will the restaurant's other customers. Also, you may avoid being turned away at the door. Unless otherwise noted, restaurants listed in this book allow casual dress. Reviews mention dress only when men are required to wear a jacket or a jacket and tie.

WINE, BEER & SPIRITS

Liquor laws in New Orleans are liberal, although the drinking age is 21 in Louisiana. Liquor is available around the clock, and you can carry open alcoholic beverages on the street (in a cup but not in a bottle or can) and from one establishment to another. It is not, however, permissible to drive under the influence of alcohol, although the suburbs feature drive-through daquiri shops.

DISABILITIES & ACCESSIBILITY

Curbs are cut on most corners in the French Quarter and CBD: Decatur Street from Canal Street to Esplanade Avenue (on river side only, not on lake side); Chartres, Royal, and Bourbon streets from Canal to St. Ann streets; and St. Peter and St. Ann streets, from Decatur (river side) to Bourbon streets.

In the Garden District, the terrain is flat but not all curbs are cut and the sidewalks are badly cracked due to the roots of the many live oaks. Audubon Zoo, the Aquarium of the Americas, riverboats, and swamp boats are all accessible. Gray Line (☞ Sightseeing, *below*) has tour buses that accommodate visitors with mobility, hearing, and sight impairments.

➤ LOCAL RESOURCES: **Advocacy Center for the Elderly and Disabled** (✉ 225 Baronne St., Suite 2112, 70112, ☎ 504/522–2337 [also TTY]; 800/960–7705 [also TTY]). **The Easter Seal Society of Louisiana for Children and Adults with Disabilities** (✉ 305 Baronne St., 4th floor, Box 8245, New Orleans, 70112, ☎ 504/455–5533 (and TTY); 800/695–7325 (and TTY).

RESERVATIONS

When discussing accessibility with
an operator or reservations agent,
ask hard questions. Are there any
stairs, inside *or* out? Are there grab
bars next to the toilet *and* in the
shower/tub? How wide is the doorway to the room? To the bathroom?
For the most extensive facilities
meeting the latest legal specifications,
opt for newer accommodations.

➤ COMPLAINTS: **Disability Rights
Section** (✉ U.S. Department of Justice, Civil Rights Division, Box
66738, Washington, DC 20035-6738,
☎ 202/514–0301 or 800/514–0301;
TTY 202/514–0301 or 800/514–
0301, FAX 202/307–1198) for general
complaints. **Aviation Consumer
Protection Division** (☞ Air Travel,
above) for airline-related problems.
Civil Rights Office (✉ U.S. Department of Transportation, Departmen-
tal Office of Civil Rights, S-30, 400
7th St. SW, Room 10215, Washington, DC 20590, ☎ 202/366–4648,
FAX 202/366–9371) for problems with
surface transportation.

TRAVEL AGENCIES

In the United States, the Americans
with Disabilities Act requires that
travel firms serve the needs of all
travelers. Some agencies specialize in
working with people with disabilities.

➤ TRAVELERS WITH MOBILITY PROB-
LEMS: **Access Adventures** (✉ 206
Chestnut Ridge Rd., Rochester,
NY 14624, ☎ 716/889–9096, dl-
travel@prodigy.net), run by a former
physical-rehabilitation counselor.
CareVacations (✉ 5-5110 50th Ave.,
Leduc, Alberta T9E 6V4, ☎ 780/
986–6404 or 877/478–7827, FAX 780/
986–8332, www.carevacations.com),
for group tours and cruise vacations.
Flying Wheels Travel (✉ 143 W.
Bridge St., Box 382, Owatonna, MN
55060, ☎ 507/451–5005 or 800/
535–6790, FAX 507/451–1685,
thq@ll.net, www.flyingwheels.com).
Hinsdale Travel Service (✉ 201 E.
Ogden Ave., Suite 100, Hinsdale, IL
60521, ☎ 630/325–1335, FAX 630/
325–1342, hinstrvl@interaccess.com).

➤ TRAVELERS WITH DEVELOPMENTAL
DISABILITIES: **New Directions** (✉ 5276
Hollister Ave., Suite 207, Santa Bar-

bara, CA 93111, ☎ 805/967–2841 or
888/967–2841, FAX 805/964–7344).

DISCOUNTS & DEALS

Be a smart shopper and **compare all
your options** before making decisions.
A plane ticket bought with a promotional coupon from travel clubs,
coupon books, and direct-mail offers
may not be cheaper than the least
expensive fare from a discount ticket
agency. And always keep in mind that
what you get is just as important as
what you save.

DISCOUNT RESERVATIONS

To save money, **look into discount
reservations services** with toll-free
numbers, which use their buying
power to get a better price on hotels,
airline tickets, even car rentals. When
booking a room, always **call the
hotel's local toll-free number** (if one is
available) rather than the central
reservations number—you'll often get
a better price. Always ask about
special packages or corporate rates.

➤ AIRLINE TICKETS: ☎ **800/FLY-4–
LESS.** ☎ **800/FLY-ASAP.**

➤ HOTEL ROOMS: **Accommodations
Express** (☎ 800/444–7666, www.
accommodationsexpress.com). **Central Reservation Service (CRS)**
(☎ 800/548–3311). **Hotel Reservations Network** (☎ 800/964–6835,
www.hoteldiscounts.com). **RMC
Travel** (☎ 800/245–5738, www.rm-
cwebtravel.com). **Steigenberger Reservation Service** (☎ 800/223–5652,
www.srs-worldhotels.com). **Tur-
botrip.com** (☎ 800/473–7829,
www.turbotrip.com).

PACKAGE DEALS

Don't confuse packages and guided
tours. When you buy a package, you
travel on your own, just as though
you had planned the trip yourself.
Fly/drive packages, which combine
airfare and car rental, are often a
good deal. In cities, ask the local
visitors' bureau about hotel packages
that include tickets to major museum
exhibits or other special events.

EMERGENCIES

➤ DOCTORS & DENTISTS: For referrals, contact the **New Orleans Dental
Association** (✉ 3101 W. Napoleon

St., Suite 119, Metairie, ☎ 504/834–6449). **Elk Place Dental Center** (✉ 144 Elk Pl., ☎ 504/561–5771) takes walk-ins. **Charity Hospital & Medical Center of Louisiana** (☞ Hospitals, *below*) provides 24-hour dental emergency treatment. **Touro Infirmary** (☞ Hospitals, *below*) has a physician-referral service (☎ 504/897–7777), available weekdays 8–5.

➤ EMERGENCY SERVICES: Dial ☎ 911 for police, fire, and ambulance.

➤ HOSPITALS: **Charity Hospital & Medical Center of Louisiana** (✉ 1532 Tulane Ave., ☎ 504/568–2311 or 504/568–3572). **Touro Infirmary** (✉ 1401 Foucher St., ☎ 504/897–7011 or 504/897–8250). **Tulane University Medical Center** (✉ 1415 Tulane Ave., ☎ 504/588–5268 or 504/588–5711).

➤ PHARMACIES: **Royal Pharmacy** (✉ 1101 Royal St., ☎ 504/523–5401), in the French Quarter, open Monday–Saturday 9–6. **Walgreens** (✉ 900 Canal St., ☎ 504/568–9544), open Monday–Saturday 7 AM–9 PM, Sunday 9–7. **Walgreens** (✉ 3311 Canal St., ☎ 504/822–8070), open 24 hours. **Eckerd Drugs** (✉ 3400 Canal St., ☎ 504/488–6661), open until 10 PM Monday–Saturday, until 6 PM on Sunday.

GAY & LESBIAN TRAVEL

New Orleans has a large gay and lesbian population spread throughout the metropolitan area. The most gay-friendly neighborhood is the French Quarter, followed by the Faubourg Marigny, just outside the Quarter. Most gay bars are within these neighborhoods. A Gay Heritage Tour, a walking tour scheduled Wednesdays and Saturdays at 2, begins at a shop called Alternatives. Throughout the year a number of festivals (☞ When to Go, *below*) celebrate gay culture. The city also has gay-friendly guest houses and bed-and-breakfasts. *Impact* and *Ambush,* local biweekly newspapers, provide lists of current events in addition to news and reviews. *Impact* also publishes a slick glossy called *Eclipse* with all its nightlife coverage. These publications

are found in many gay bars and in the Faubourg Marigny Bookstore. For full information about services, accommodations, and events, contact the Gay and Lesbian Community Center.

➤ GAY- & LESBIAN-FRIENDLY TRAVEL AGENCIES: **Different Roads Travel** (✉ 8383 Wilshire Blvd., Suite 902, Beverly Hills, CA 90211, ☎ 323/651–5557 or 800/429–8747, FAX 323/651–3678, leigh@west.tzell.com). **Kennedy Travel** (✉ 314 Jericho Turnpike, Floral Park, NY 11001, ☎ 516/352–4888 or 800/237–7433, FAX 516/354–8849, main@kennedy-travel.com, www.kennedytravel.com). **Now Voyager** (✉ 4406 18th St., San Francisco, CA 94114, ☎ 415/626–1169 or 800/255–6951, FAX 415/626–8626, www.nowvoyager.com). **Skylink Travel and Tour** (✉ 1006 Mendocino Ave., Santa Rosa, CA 95401, ☎ 707/546–9888 or 800/225–5759, FAX 707/546–9891, skylinktvl@aol.com, www.skylink-travel.com), serving lesbian travelers.

➤ LOCAL SOURCES: **Alternatives** (✉ 909 Bourbon St., 70116, ☎ 504/945–6789). **Faubourg Marigny Bookstore** (✉ 600 Frenchmen St., ☎ 504/943–9875). **Gay and Lesbian Community Center** (✉ 2114 Decatur St., 70116, ☎ 504/945–1103).

HEALTH

The intense heat and humidity of New Orleans in the height of summer can be a concern for anyone unused to a semitropical climate. It's best to pace yourself to avoid problems such as dehydration. Walk at a reasonable pace, stop frequently, and drink plenty of water. Know your own limits and select indoor activities in the middle of the day; you'll find the locals doing the same thing.

HOLIDAYS

Major national holidays include New Year's Day (Jan. 1); Martin Luther King, Jr., Day (3rd Mon. in Jan.); President's Day (3rd Mon. in Feb.); Memorial Day (last Mon. in May); Independence Day (July 4); Labor Day (1st Mon. in Sept.); Thanksgiving Day (4th Thurs. in Nov.); Christmas Eve and Christmas Day (Dec. 24 and 25); and New Year's Eve (Dec. 31).

INSURANCE

The most useful travel insurance plan is a comprehensive policy that includes coverage for trip cancellation and interruption, default, trip delay, and medical expenses (with a waiver for preexisting conditions).

Without insurance you will lose all or most of your money if you cancel your trip, regardless of the reason. Default insurance covers you if your tour operator, airline, or cruise line goes out of business. Trip-delay covers expenses that arise because of bad weather or mechanical delays. Study the fine print when comparing policies.

British and Australian citizens need extra medical coverage when traveling overseas. Always **buy travel policies directly from the insurance company**; if you buy them from a cruise line, airline, or tour operator that goes out of business you probably will not be covered for the agency or operator's default, a major risk. Before making any purchase, **review your existing health and homeowner's policies** to find what they cover away from home.

➤ TRAVEL INSURERS: In the U.S.: **Access America** (✉ 6600 W. Broad St., Richmond, VA 23230, ☎ 804/285–3300 or 800/284–8300, FAX 804/673–1583, www.previewtravel.com), **Travel Guard International** (✉ 1145 Clark St., Stevens Point, WI 54481, ☎ 715/345–0505 or 800/826–1300, FAX 800/955–8785, www.noelgroup.com). In Canada: **Voyager Insurance** (✉ 44 Peel Center Dr., Brampton, Ontario L6T 4M8, ☎ 905/791–8700; 800/668–4342 in Canada).

➤ INSURANCE INFORMATION: In the U.K.: **Association of British Insurers** (✉ 51–55 Gresham St., London EC2V 7HQ, ☎ 020/7600–3333, FAX 020/7696–8999, info@abi.org.uk, www.abi.org.uk). In Australia: **Insurance Council of Australia** (☎ 03/9614–1077, FAX 03/9614–7924).

LODGING

The lodgings we list are the cream of the crop in each price category. We always list the facilities that are available—but we don't specify whether they cost extra: when pricing accommodations, always ask what's included and what costs extra. All rooms have private baths unless otherwise noted. Properties marked ✗☐ are lodging establishments whose restaurants warrant a special trip.

When you book a room, be sure to mention if you have a disability or are traveling with children, if you prefer a certain type of bed, or if you have specific dietary needs or other concerns.

Assume that hotels operate on the **European Plan** (EP, with no meals) unless we specify that they use the **Continental Plan** (CP, with a Continental breakfast), **Breakfast Plan** (BP, with a full breakfast), **Modified American Plan** (MAP, with breakfast and dinner), or the **Full American Plan** (FAP, with all meals).

➤ LODGING ASSISTANCE: **Housing Bureau** (☎ 504/566–5021) or the **New Orleans Metropolitan Convention & Visitors Bureau** (☎ 504/566–5011).

APARTMENT RENTALS

If you want a home base that's roomy enough for a family and comes with cooking facilities, **consider a furnished rental.** These can save you money, especially if you're traveling with a group. Home-exchange directories sometimes list rentals as well as exchanges.

B&BS

Bed-and breakfasts provide an intimate alternative to hotels and motels, and New Orleans has many charming accommodations of this kind. For information on B&Bs, *see* Chapter 3. Hazel Boyce at Bed & Breakfast, Inc.—Reservations Service represents a variety of accommodations in all areas of New Orleans. Sarah-Margaret Brown at New Orleans Bed & Breakfast and Accommodations represents properties citywide including private homes, apartments, and condos.

➤ RESERVATION SERVICES: **Bed & Breakfast, Inc.—Reservations Service** (✉ 1021 Moss St., Box 52257, 70152, ☎ 504/488–4640 or 800/729–4640, FAX 504/488–4639, www.historiclodging.com; no credit cards). **New Orleans Bed & Breakfast and Accommodations** (✉ Box 8163, 70182, ☎ 504/838–0071 or 504/838–0072, FAX 504/838–0140, www.neworleansbandb.com).

HOME EXCHANGES

If you would like to exchange your home for someone else's, **join a home-exchange organization,** which will send you its updated listings of available exchanges for a year and will include your own listing in at least one of them. It's up to you to make specific arrangements.

➤ EXCHANGE CLUBS: **HomeLink International** (✉ Box 650, Key West, FL 33041, ☎ 305/294–7766 or 800/638–3841, FAX 305/294–1448, usa@homelink.org, www.homelink.org; $98 per year). **Intervac U.S.** (✉ Box 590504, San Francisco, CA 94159, ☎ 800/756–4663, FAX 415/435–7440, www.intervac.com; $89 per year includes two catalogues).

HOSTELS

No matter what your age, you can **save on lodging costs by staying at hostels.** In some 5,000 locations in more than 70 countries around the world, Hostelling International (HI), the umbrella group for a number of national youth-hostel associations, offers single-sex, dorm-style beds and, at many hostels, rooms for couples and family accommodations. Membership in any HI national hostel association, open to travelers of all ages, allows you to stay in HI-affiliated hostels at member rates; one-year membership is about $25 for adults (C$26.75 in Canada, £9.30 in the U.K., $30 in Australia, and $30 in New Zealand); hostels run about $10–$25 per night. Members have priority if the hostel is full; they're also eligible for discounts around the world, even on rail and bus travel in some countries.

➤ ORGANIZATIONS: **Hostelling International—American Youth Hostels** (✉ 733 15th St. NW, Suite 840, Washington, DC 20005, ☎ 202/783–6161, FAX 202/783–6171, www.hiayh.org). **Hostelling International—Canada** (✉ 400–205 Catherine St., Ottawa, Ontario K2P 1C3,

☎ 613/237–7884, FAX 613/237–7868, www.hostellingintl.ca). **Youth Hostel Association of England and Wales** (✉ Trevelyan House, 8 St. Stephen's Hill, St. Albans, Hertfordshire AL1 2DY, ☎ 01727/855215 or 01727/845047, FAX 01727/844126, www.yha.uk). **Australian Youth Hostel Association** (✉ 10 Mallett St., Camperdown, NSW 2050, ☎ 02/9565–1699, FAX 02/9565–1325, www.yha.com.au). **Youth Hostels Association of New Zealand** (✉ Box 436, Christchurch, New Zealand, ☎ 03/379–9970, FAX 03/365–4476, www.yha.org.nz).

HOTELS

All hotels listed have private bath unless otherwise noted.

➤ TOLL-FREE NUMBERS: **Best Western** (☎ 800/528–1234, www.bestwestern.com). **Choice** (☎ 800/221–2222, www.hotelchoice.com). **Clarion** (☎ 800/252–7466, www.choicehotels.com). **Colony** (☎ 800/777–1700. www.colony.com),**Comfort** (☎ 800/228–5150, www.comfortinn.com). **Days Inn** (☎ 800/325–2525. www.daysinn.com). **Doubletree and Red Lion Hotels** (☎ 800/222–8733, www.doubletreehotels.com). **Embassy Suites** (☎ 800/362–2779, www.embassysuites.com). **Fairfield Inn** (☎ 800/228–2800, www.marriott.com). **Four Seasons** (☎ 800/332–3442, www.fourseasons.com). **Hilton** (☎ 800/445–8667, www.hiltons.com). **Holiday Inn** (☎ 800/465–4329, www.holiday-inn.com). **Howard Johnson** (☎ 800/654–4656, www.hojo.com). **Hyatt Hotels & Resorts** (☎ 800/233–1234, www.hyatt.com). **Inter-Continental** (☎ 800/327–0200, www.interconti.com). **La Quinta** (☎ 800/531–5900, www.laquinta.com). **Marriott** (☎ 800/228–9290, www.marriott.com). **Le Meridien** (☎ 800/543–4300, www.lemeridien-hotels.com). **Omni** (☎ 800/843–6664, www.omnihotels.com). **Quality Inn** (☎ 800/228–5151, www.qualityinn.com). **Radisson** (☎ 800/333–3333, www.radisson.com). **Ramada** (☎ 800/228–2828. www.ramada.com), **Sheraton** (☎ 800/325–3535, www.sheraton.com).**Sleep Inn** (☎ 800/753–3746, www.sleepinn.com). **Westin Hotels & Resorts** (☎ 800/228–3000, www.starwood.com).

MAIL & SHIPPING

➤ POST OFFICES: Main post office (✉ 701 Loyola Ave.). Post office in French Quarter (✉ 1022 Iberville St.).

MEDIA

NEWSPAPERS & MAGAZINES

The local daily newspaper is the Newhouse-owned *Times-Picayune,* which has won Pulitzer Prizes in the last few years for investigative reporting and editorial cartooning. *Gambit,* a locally owned weekly paper, is free around town and covers local issues as well as theater and dining. *OffBeat* is a free monthly publication that explores the music scene in depth. *City Business* is the city's weekly publication about commerce and local economic issues. *New Orleans Magazine* is a glossy, monthly publication about local culture and attractions.

RADIO & TELEVISION

AM radio stations include WWL 870 (news, talk, country music late at night), WYLD 940 (gospel), WQUE 1280 (sports), and WSMB 1350 (talk). FM stations include WWNO 89.9 (classical, National Public Radio), WWOZ 90.7 (notable for regional music and jazz), WTUL 91.5 (Tulane University student-operated, various formats, mainly rock and new music), WKCW 92 (rock), WQUE 93.3 (contemporary), WNOE 101 (country), and WLMG 102 (easy listening).

The network television stations are WWL (4, CBS), WDSU (6, NBC), WVUE (8, Fox), WGNO (26, ABC), and WNOL (38 Warner Bros.). The public television stations are WYES (12) and WLAE (32). Channel 7 is the locally run government channel.

MONEY MATTERS

Prices throughout this guide are given for adults. Substantially reduced fees are almost always available for children, students, and senior citizens. For information on taxes, *see* Taxes, *below.*

CREDIT CARDS

Throughout this guide, the following abbreviations are used: **AE,** American

Express; **D,** Discover; **DC,** Diner's Club; **MC,** Master Card; and **V,** Visa.

➤ REPORTING LOST CARDS: To report lost or stolen credit cards, call the following toll-free numbers: **American Express** (☎ 800/327–2177); **Discover Card** (☎ 800/347–2683); **Diners Club** (☎ 800/234–6377); **Master Card** (☎ 800/307–7309); and **Visa** (☎ 800/847–2911).

PACKING

New Orleans is casual during the day, and casual to slightly dressy at night. A number of restaurants in the French Quarter require men to wear a jacket and tie. For sightseeing, pack walking shorts, sundresses, cotton slacks or jeans, T-shirts, and a light sweater. In winter, you'll want a coat or warm jacket, especially for evenings, which can be downright cold. In summer, pack for hot, sticky weather but **be prepared for air-conditioning bordering on glacial, and bring an umbrella in case of sudden thunderstorms; leave the plastic raincoats behind** (they're extremely uncomfortable in the high humidity). In addition, **pack a sun hat and sunscreen lotion,** even for strolls in the city, because the sun can be fierce. Insect repellent will also come in handy if you plan to be outdoors on a swamp cruise or in the city dining alfresco, since mosquitoes come out in full force after sunset in the hot weather.

In your carry-on luggage, **pack an extra pair of eyeglasses or contact lenses** and **enough of any medication you take** to last the entire trip. You may also ask your doctor to write a spare prescription using the drug's generic name, since brand names may vary from country to country. In luggage to be checked, **never pack prescription drugs or valuables.** To avoid customs delays, carry medications in their original packaging. And don't forget to carry with you the addresses of offices that handle refunds of lost traveler's checks.

CHECKING LUGGAGE

How many carry-on bags you can bring with you is up to the airline. Most allow two, but not always, so make sure that everything you carry aboard will fit under your seat or in the overhead bin, and get to the gate early. Note that if you have a seat at the back of the plane, you'll probably board first, while the overhead bins are still empty.

If you are flying internationally, note that baggage allowances may be determined not by piece but by weight—generally 88 pounds (40 kilograms) in first class, 66 pounds (30 kilograms) in business class, and 44 pounds (20 kilograms) in economy.

Airline liability for baggage is limited to $1,250 per person on flights within the United States. On international flights it amounts to $9.07 per pound or $20 per kilogram for checked baggage (roughly $640 per 70-pound bag) and $400 per passenger for unchecked baggage. You can buy additional coverage at check-in for about $10 per $1,000 of coverage, but it excludes a rather extensive list of items, shown on your airline ticket.

Before departure, **itemize your bags' contents** and their worth, and label the bags with your name, address, and phone number. (If you use your home address, cover it so potential thieves can't see it readily.) Inside each bag, **pack a copy of your itinerary.** At check-in, **make sure that each bag is correctly tagged** with the destination airport's three-letter code. If your bags arrive damaged or fail to arrive at all, file a written report with the airline before leaving the airport.

PASSPORTS & VISAS

➤ Contacts: **U.S. Embassy Visa Information Line** (☎ 01891/200–290; calls cost 49p per minute, 39p per minute cheap rate) for U.S. visa information. **U.S. Embassy Visa Branch** (✉ 5 Upper Grosvenor Sq., London W1A 1AE) for U.S. visa information; send a self-addressed, stamped envelope. **U.S. Consulate General** (✉ Queen's House, Queen St., Belfast BT1 6EO) if you live in Northern Ireland. **Office of Australia Affairs** (✉ 59th floor, MLC Centre, 19–29 Martin Pl., Sydney, NSW 2000) if you live in Australia. **Office of New Zealand Affairs** (✉ 29 Fitzherbert Terr., Thorndon, Wellington) if you live in New Zealand.

PASSPORT OFFICES

The best time to apply for a passport or to renew is in fall and winter. Before any trip, check your passport's expiration date, and, if necessary, renew it as soon as possible.

➤ Australian Citizens: **Australian Passport Office** (☎ 131–232, www.dfat.gov.au/passports).

➤ Canadian Citizens: **Passport Office** (☎ 819/994–3500 or 800/567–6868, www.dfait-maeci.gc.ca/passport).

➤ New Zealand Citizens: **New Zealand Passport Office** (☎ 04/494–0700, www.passports.govt.nz).

➤ U.K. Citizens: **London Passport Office** (☎ 0870/521–0410) for fees and documentation requirements and to request an emergency passport.

SAFETY

New Orleans, which has drawn attention for its crime rate in the past, has experienced a decrease in all major crimes in the past two years. Tourists are seldom the target of major crimes but can, like other citizens, be the target of pickpockets and purse-snatchers. In recent years, the New Orleans Police Department has beefed-up patrols in areas most frequented by tourists—Jackson Square, the Mississippi Riverfront and the French Quarter. Still, common sense is invaluable, so keep a couple of things in mind. Know where you're going or ask someone, preferably the concierge at your hotel. In the French Quarter, particularly, if you are on foot, stay on main streets that are heavily populated. Take a taxi late at night or when the distance is too great to walk; this is even more important if you've been drinking. Be aware of your surroundings.

SENIOR-CITIZEN TRAVEL

To qualify for age-related discounts, **mention your senior-citizen status up front** when booking hotel reservations (not when checking out) and before you're seated in restaurants (not when paying the bill). When renting a car, ask about promotional car-rental discounts, which can be cheaper than senior-citizen rates.

➤ EDUCATIONAL PROGRAMS: **Elderhostel** (✉ 75 Federal St., 3rd floor, Boston, MA 02110, ☎ 877/426–8056, FAX 877/426–2166, www.elderhostel.org). **Interhostel** (✉ University of New Hampshire, 6 Garrison Ave., Durham, NH 03824, ☎ 603/862–1147 or 800/733–9753, FAX 603/862–1113, www.learn.unh.edu).

SIGHTSEEING TOURS

ORIENTATION TOURS

Several local tour companies offer three- to four-hour city tours by bus that include the French Quarter, the Garden District, Uptown New Orleans, and the lakefront. Prices range from $20 to $30 per person. Both Gray Line and New Orleans Tours offer a longer, seven-hour city tour by bus that includes a steamboat ride on the Mississippi River. Gray Line also operates a narrated loop tour by bus with 13 drop-off and pick-up points around the city.

➤ TOUR OPERATORS: **Gray Line** (☎ 504/587–0861). **New Orleans Tours** (☎ 504/592–1991). **Tours by Isabelle** (☎ 504/391–3544). **Steppin' Out Tours** (☎ 504/246–1006).

RIVERBOAT CRUISES

Narrated riverboat cruises up and down the Mississippi and bayou cruises on authentic paddle wheelers are offered by the New Orleans Steamboat Company. Ticket sales and departures are at the Toulouse Street Wharf behind Jackson Brewery. New Orleans Paddle Wheel has a river plantation and battlefield cruise twice daily departing from the Riverwalk and also a river plantation harbor cruise and a Crown Point swamp tour. There is also an evening jazz dinner cruise from 8 to 10 (boarding at 7 PM); tickets are available for the dinner and cruise or just the cruise and live music. The ticket office is at the Poydras Street Wharf near the Riverwalk and at the Aquarium on Canal Street.

➤ CRUISE OPERATORS: **New Orleans Steamboat Company** (☎ 504/586–8777 or 800/233–2628). **New Orleans Paddle Wheel** (☎ 504/524–0814).

SPECIAL-INTEREST TOURS

Full-day plantation tours by bus from New Orleans, which include guided tours through two antebellum plantation homes along the Mississippi River and a stop for lunch in a Cajun-Creole restaurant outside the city, are offered by Gray Line and New Orleans Tours. Tours by Isabelle includes lunch in its full-day plantation package that traces the history of the Cajun people. Also available is the Grand Tour: A full-day minibus tour that includes a visit to one plantation, lunch in a Cajun restaurant, and a 1½-hour boat tour in the swamps with a Cajun trapper. American-Acadian (☞ Swamp Tours, *below*) has a six-hour tour that includes the city's Garden District plus two plantations upriver.

Other special-interests tours focus on popular activities. Nightlife tours that visit popular jazz clubs and Bourbon Street nightclubs are given by New Orleans Tours. The evening concludes at Café du Monde. You can take cooking classes or arrange a shopping tour.

A visit to either the Audubon Zoo (☞ St. Charles Avenue from the CBD to Uptown *in* Chapter 1) or the Aquarium of the Americas (☞ Foot of Canal and Algiers Point *in* Chapter 1) or both can be combined with a ride on the riverboat *John James Audubon,* a ship that can accommodate 600 passengers. The 7-mi (11-km) ride takes 30 minutes. Tickets for such package tours are available in kiosks at both the zoo and the aquarium. Prices vary depending on whether you choose only the cruise or combine it with zoo and aquarium admissions.

Exploring an exotic Louisiana swamp and traveling into Cajun country is an adventure not to be missed. Dozens of swamp tour companies are available. You can check at your hotel or visitor center for a complete listing. Many do not provide transportation from downtown hotels; those listed below do. Full-day tours often include visiting a plantation home.

For highlights of African-American history and culture, contact Le'Ob's Tours.

➤ AFRICAN-AMERICAN TOURS: **Le'Ob's Tours** (☎ 504/288–3478).

➤ COOKING CLASSES: **Cookin' Cajun** (✉ Riverwalk, ☎ 504/523–6425). **Cuisine! Cuisine! Cooking School** (☎ 504/945–0992). **New Orleans School of Cooking** (✉ Jackson Brewery, ☎ 504/525–2665). **Spice, Inc.** (✉ 1051 Annunciation St., ☎ 504/558–9993).

➤ MUSIC: **Hidden Treasures Tours** (☎ 504/529–4507) gives van tours of jazz and blues landmarks and St. Louis Cemetery #1.

➤ NIGHTLIFE: **New Orleans Tours** (☎ 504/592–1991).

➤ PERSONALIZED SHOPPING: **Macon Riddle** (☎ 504/899–3027).

➤ PLANTATIONS AND SWAMPS: **Gray Line** (☎ 504/587–0861). **New Orleans Tours** (☎ 504/592–1991). **Tours by Isabelle** (☎ 504/391–3544).

➤ SWAMP TOURS: **Cypress Swamp Tours** (☎ 504/581–4501). **Gray Line** (☎ 504/587–0861). **Chacahoula Tours** (☎ 504/436–2640). **Tours by Isabelle** (☎ 504/391–3544). **Honey Island Swamp Tours** (☎ 504/242–5877).

WALKING TOURS

Free 1½-hour general history tours of the French Quarter are given daily at 10:30 AM by rangers of the Jean Lafitte National Park. Occasionally at 11:30 AM, a daily "tour du jour" is given, which focuses on a particular historical or cultural aspect of the Quarter. Each visitor may procure tickets for either tour at the Park Service office in the French Market after 9 AM on the morning of the tour. Tickets are limited; call for details. Three-hour general history tours are given daily at 10 and 1:30 by Friends of the Cabildo. The tour price includes admission to two state museums of your choice.

Several specialized walking tours conducted by knowledgeable guides on specific aspects of the French Quarter are also available. Because some of these tours accommodate as few as two people, be sure to make advance reservations. Classic Tours is operated by a native Orleanian who loves to share her city on casual insider tours that cover art, antiques, architecture, and local lore. Heritage Tours offers a general literary tour and others focusing on either William Faulkner or Tennessee Williams. A Garden District walking tour, called "Faubourg Promenade," is given daily at 2:30 PM by Jean Lafitte National Park rangers. Mile-long walks last for 90 minutes. Reservations are required. Classic Tours also conduct tours in this historic section of New Orleans.

The cemeteries of New Orleans fascinate many people because of their unique above-ground tombs. The most famous, St. Louis Cemetery #1, is just outside the French Quarter; Magic Walking Tours, Hidden Treasures Tours, Save Our Cemeteries, and the New Orleans Historic Voodoo Museum offer guided walking tours. Reservations are generally required.

➤ FRENCH QUARTER: **Friends of the Cabildo** (☎ 504/523–3939).

➤ FRENCH QUARTER AND GARDEN DISTRICT: **Jean Lafitte National Park** (✉ 419 Decatur St., ☎ 504/589–2636). **Gray Line** (☎ 504/587–0861).

➤ GARDEN DISTRICT: **Classic Tours** (☎ 504/899–1862).

➤ LITERARY: **Heritage Tours** (☎ 504/949–9805).

➤ VOODOO, GHOSTS, VAMPIRES, AND CEMETERIES: **Haunted History Tours** (☎ 504/861–2727 or 888/644–6787). **Hauntings Today** (☎ 504/522–0045). **Historic New Orleans Walking Tours** (☎ 504/947–2120). **Magic Walking Tours** (☎ 504/588–9693). **New Orleans Historic Voodoo Museum** (☎ 504/523–7685). **New Orleans Spirit Tours** (☎ 504/566–9877). **New Orleans Tours** (☎ 504/592–1991).**Save Our Cemeteries** (☎ 504/525–3377).

OTHER TOURS

Limousine services make arrangements for personal interests and private guides; rentals vary. Southern Seaplane will fly you over the city and its surrounding areas. The Gray Line Trolley Loop Tour has vans that look like trolley cars and travel a route past major sights downtown. Passengers may get on and off at various sights for $18.

➤ BY BICYCLE: **French Louisiana Bike Tours** (☎ 800/346–7989) specializes in Cajun Country.

➤ BY LIMOUSINE: **Bonomolo Limousines** (☎ 504/523–2666 or 800/451–9258). **Carey Limousines** (☎ 504/523–5466). **A Touch of Class Limousine Service** (☎ 504/522–7565 or 800/821–6352). **New Orleans Limousine Service** (☎ 504/529–5226).

➤ BY SEAPLANE: **Southern Seaplane** (☎ 504/394–5633).

➤ BY VAN: **Gray Line Trolley Loop Tour** (☎ 504/587–0861).

STREETCARS

The Riverfront streetcar covers a 1.9-mi route along the Mississippi River, connecting major sights from the end of the French Quarter (Esplanade Avenue) to the New Orleans Convention Center (Julia Street). Eight stops en route include the French Market, Jackson Brewery, Canal Place, the World Trade Center, the Riverwalk, and the Hilton Hotel. This streetcar operates weekdays 6 AM until midnight and weekends 8 AM until midnight passing each stop every 15 minutes. One of the cars is specially equipped for elderly passengers and those with mobility impairments. The St. Charles Avenue streetcar runs the 5 mi from the CBD to Carrollton Avenue 24 hours a day, about every 10 minutes 7 AM–8 PM, every ½ hour 8 PM–midnight, and every hour midnight–7 AM. It's a great way to explore such areas as the Garden District (☞ St. Charles Avenue from the CBD to Uptown *in* Chapter 1). Work is underway to install a third streetcar line the length of Canal Street. Work on this section of the streetcar line is expected to be completed in late 2001.

FARES & SCHEDULES

One-way fare is $1.25 (exact change); one-day and three-day visitor passes are available at $5 and $12, respectively, for unlimited rides on both the St. Charles Avenue and Riverfront streetcar lines. Visitor passes apply to buses as well as streetcars. For information on schedules and visitor passes, check information centers at hotels and retail centers or call the RTA.

➤ STREETCAR INFORMATION: **RTA** (☎ 504/248–3900, 504/242–2600 for automated information).

STUDENTS IN NEW ORLEANS

➤ I.D.S & SERVICES: **Council Travel** (CIEE; ✉ 205 E. 42nd St., 14th floor, New York, NY 10017, ☎ 212/822–2700 or 888/268–6245, ℻ 212/822–2699, info@councilexchanges.org, www.councilexchanges.org) for mail orders only, in the U.S. **Travel Cuts** (✉ 187 College St., Toronto, Ontario M5T 1P7, ☎ 416/979–2406 or 800/667–2887, www.travelcuts.com) in Canada.

TAXES

The local hotel tax is 12%, which includes the local sales tax (☞ *below*). There is also an additional surcharge of $1–$3 per room, depending on the size of the hotel. There is no departure tax at the airport.

SALES TAX

A local sales tax of 10% applies to all goods and services purchased in Orleans Parish. Taxes outside Orleans Parish vary and are slightly lower than the 10% ceiling.

TAX REFUNDS

Louisiana is the only state that grants a sales-tax rebate to shoppers from other countries. Look for shops, restaurants, and hotels that display the distinctive tax-free sign and ask for a voucher for the 9% state sales tax tacked on to the price of many products and services. Present the vouchers with your plane ticket at the tax rebate office at the New Orleans International Airport and receive up to $500 in cash back. If the amount redeemable is more than $500, a check for the difference will be mailed to your home address.

TAXIS

Cabs are metered at $2.10 minimum plus 75¢ for each additional passenger and $1.10 per mile. You can either hail cabs in some of the busier areas, or call one.

➤ TAXI COMPANIES: **Checker Yellow Cabs** (☎ 504/943–2411). **Liberty Bell Cabs** (☎ 504/822–5974). **United Cabs** (☎ 504/522–9771).

TIME

New Orleans is in the Central Time Zone, the same as Chicago. It's one hour behind New York and two hours ahead of Los Angeles.

TIPPING

As everywhere else in the world, tipping should be done for good service. 15% is the standard (20% for outstanding service) for waiters. And, since New Orleans is a service-based city, keep a few dollar bills handy. They'll go a long way with bellhops, doormen, and valet parking attendants. As always, use your discretion when tipping.

If you use the services of the consierge, a tip of $5 to $10 is appropriate, iwth an additional gratuity for special services or favors.

TOURS & PACKAGES

Because everything is prearranged on a prepackaged tour or independent vacation, you'll spend less time planning—and often get it all at a good price.

BOOKING WITH AN AGENT

Travel agents are excellent resources. But it's a good idea to collect brochures from several agencies as some agents' suggestions may be influenced by relationships with tour and package firms that reward them for volume sales. If you have a special interest, **find an agent with expertise in that area**; ASTA (☞ Travel Agencies, *below*) has a database of specialists worldwide.

Make sure your travel agent knows the accommodations and other services of the place they're recommending. Ask about the hotel's location, room size, beds, and whether it has a pool, room service, or programs for children, if you care about these. Has your agent been there in person or sent others whom you can contact?

Do some homework on your own, too: local tourism boards can provide information about lesser-known and small-niche operators, some of which may sell only direct.

BUYER BEWARE

Each year consumers are stranded or lose their money when tour operators—even large ones with excellent reputations—go out of business. So **check out the operator.** Ask several travel agents about its reputation, and try to **book with a company that has a consumer-protection program.** (Look for information in the company's brochure.) In the United States, members of the National Tour Association and the United States Tour Operators Association are required to set aside funds to cover your payments and travel arrangements in the event that the company defaults. It's also a good idea to choose a company that participates in the American Society of Travel Agents' Tour Operator Program (TOP); ASTA will act as mediator in any disputes between you and your tour operator.

Remember that the more your package or tour includes the better you can predict the ultimate cost of your vacation. Make sure you know exactly what is covered, and **beware of hidden costs.** Are taxes, tips, and transfers included? Entertainment and excursions? These can add up.

➤ TOUR-OPERATOR RECOMMENDATIONS: **American Society of Travel Agents** (☞ Travel Agencies, *below*). **National Tour Association** (NTA; ✉ 546 E. Main St., Lexington, KY 40508, ☎ 606/226–4444 or 800/682–8886, www.ntaonline.com). **United States Tour Operators Association** (USTOA; ✉ 342 Madison Ave., Suite 1522, New York, NY 10173, ☎ 212/599–6599 or 800/468–7862, FAX 212/599–6744, ustoa@aol.com, www.ustoa.com).

TRAIN TRAVEL TO AND FROM NEW ORLEANS

Three major Amtrak lines arrive at and depart from New Orleans's Union Passenger Terminal. The *Crescent* makes daily runs weekly from New York to New Orleans by way of Washington, DC. The *City of New Orleans* runs daily between New Orleans and Chicago. The *Sunset Limited* makes the two-day trip between New Orleans and Los Angeles. It departs New Orleans on Monday, Wednesday, and Saturday, and leaves Los Angeles on Sunday,

Wednesday, and Friday. The same line makes the 24-hour trip to Miami three times a week, but days and departure times vary. Some routes may change with cutbacks in Amtrak funding. Trains arrive and depart from New Orleans's Union Passenger Terminal in the heart of the CBD.

➤ TRAIN INFORMATION: **Amtrak** (☎ 800/872–7245, www.amtrak.com). **Union Passenger Terminal** (1001 Loyola Ave., ☎ 504/528–1610 or 800/872–7245).

TRANSPORTATION AROUND NEW ORLEANS

New Orleans is one of the most compact cities in North America. On good days, walking is an easy way to get to and from your destination. Bicycling is also good and there are many bike shops that provide rentals. Taxis are inexpensive, with a trip across town costing less than $8. The transit system is large and efficient and includes buses (☞ Bus Travel around New Orleans, *above*) and streetcars (☞ Streetcars, *above*), which can be a great way to tour the city. If you drive, remember that New Orleans has quite a few one-way streets—so be cautious.

TRAVEL AGENCIES

A good travel agent puts your needs first. Look for an agency that has been in business at least five years, emphasizes customer service, and has someone on staff who specializes in your destination. In addition, **make sure the agency belongs to a professional trade organization.** The American Society of Travel Agents (ASTA), with 27,000 agents in some 170 countries, is the largest and most influential in the field. Operating under the motto ìIntegrity in Travel,î it maintains and enforces a strict code of ethics and will step in to help mediate any agent-client disputes if necessary. ASTA also maintains a Web site that includes a directory of agents. (If a travel agency is also acting as your tour operator, *see* Buyer Beware *in* Tours & Packages, *above*.)

➤ LOCAL AGENT REFERRALS: **American Society of Travel Agents** (ASTA; ☎ 800/965–2782 24-hr hot line, FAX 703/684–8319, www.astanet.com).

Association of British Travel Agents (✉ 68–71 Newman St., London W1P 4AH, ☎ 020/7637–2444, FAX 020/7637–0713, abta.co.uk, www.abtanet.com). **Association of Canadian Travel Agents** (✉ 1729 Bank St., Suite 201, Ottawa, Ontario K1V 7Z5, ☎ 613/521–0474, FAX 613/521–0805, acta.ntl@sympatico.ca). **Australian Federation of Travel Agents** (✉ Level 3, 309 Pitt St., Sydney 2000, ☎ 02/9264–3299, FAX 02/9264–1085, www.afta.com.au). **Travel Agents' Association of New Zealand** (✉ Box 1888, Wellington 10033, ☎ 04/499–0104, FAX 04/499–0827, taanz@tiasnet.co.nz).

VISITOR INFORMATION

For general information and brochures contact the city and state tourism bureaus below. The Greater New Orleans Black Tourism Network offers the "Soul of New Orleans," a black heritage directory, free of charge.

➤ TOURIST INFORMATION: **Greater New Orleans Black Tourism Network** (✉ 1520 Sugar Bowl Dr., 70112, ☎ 504/523–5652, FAX 504/522–0785). **Louisiana Office of Tourism** (✉ Box 94291, Baton Rouge, LA 70804–9291, ☎ 800/633–6970, FAX 504/342–8390, www.louisianatravel.com). **New Orleans and River Region Chamber of Commerce** 601 Poydras Street 70190, ☎ 504/527-6900 FAX 504/527-6970. **New Orleans Metropolitan Convention & Visitors Bureau** (✉ 1520 Sugar Bowl Dr., 70112, ☎ 504/566–5011 or 800/672–6124, FAX 504/566–5021, www.neworleanscvb.com; in the U.K., ✉ 20 Barclay Rd., Croydon, Surrey CRO 1JN, ☎ 020/8760–0377, FAX 020/8666–0365).

WEB SITES

Do **check out the World Wide Web** when you're planning. You'll find everything from current weather forecasts to virtual tours of famous cities. Fodor's Web site, www.fodors.com, is a great place to start your online travels. When you see a 🕸 in this book, go to www.fodors.com/urls for an up-to-date link to that destination's site.

➤ NEW ORLEANS WEB SITES: **www.crt.state.la.us; www.neworleansonline.com; www.**

new-orleans.la.us, the city's official site; www.nojazzfest.com, the site of the New Orleans Jazz and Heritage Festival; www.nolalive.com; www.offbeat.com, site of *OffBeat* magazine, with music coverage; and www.prcno.org, the site of the Preservation Resource Center.

WHEN TO GO

New Orleans is nothing if not festive. It's no surprise then that festivals play an important role in the city's cultural and entertainment calendars. Some of the more significant events include the Sugar Bowl on New Year's Day, Mardi Gras celebrations, and the Jazz & Heritage Festival that runs from late April to early May. Smaller festivals may not be quite as showy as Fat Tuesday, but they often give visitors a better understanding of New Orleans than the better-publicized, star-studded events. Some examples of these are the Tennessee Williams/New Orleans Literary Festival, held each March; April's Spring Fiesta; and a New Orleans Christmas, which runs throughout the month of December.

Travelers planning to participate in the larger festivals should be aware that hotel space is at a premium during those times: many people book rooms a year in advance.

FESTIVALS AND SEASONAL EVENTS

➤ JAN.: The **Sugar Bowl Classic** (✉ 1500 Sugar Bowl Dr., 70112, ☎ 504/525–8573), the city's oldest annual sporting event, includes not only one of the biggest college football games of the year but also tennis, basketball, sailing, running, and flag football championship events. Soccer, swimming, basketball, and even a regatta have been added to the festival, making the Sugar Bowl Classic one of the most extensive athletic festivals in the United States.

➤ LATE FEB. OR EARLY MAR.: **Mardi Gras** is rollicking, raucous, and ritualistic. Expect street celebrations, parades, and formal masked balls. For information, *see* "Carnival" in Chapter 8 and "Close-Up: Making the Most of Mardi Gras" in Chapter 1.

➤ EARLY MAR.: The **Black Heritage Festival** (✉ Audubon Zoo, Box 4327, 70178, ☎ 504/581–4629) includes gospel and jazz performances, art exhibits, and soul food.

➤ MID-MAR.: The **St. Patrick's Day Parade** begins at Molly's at the Market Pub (✉ 1107 Decatur St., 70116, ☎ 504/525–5169) and covers the French Quarter. Uptowners can catch it on Magazine Street, where paraders throw potatoes, carrots, and onions instead of the usual beads and trinkets. Why? So they can go home and fix themselves a mess of Irish stew, of course.

➤ LATE MAR.: **Earth Fest** (c/o the Audubon Zoo, ☎ 504/581–4629) is a fun-filled educational celebration with exhibits, shows, and nationally known entertainers, all with an eye on the environment.

➤ LATE MAR.: The **Tennessee Williams–New Orleans Literary Festival and Writer's Conference** (☎ 504/581–1144) began, as the name implies, as a forum for writers and scholars to talk about literature—particularly the work of Tennessee Williams. Over the years, the focus of the festival has steadily expanded to include a broad range of New Orleans–based authors and writings. Now, attendees of the weekend-long festival are just as likely to see stagings of Williams plays (especially his more obscure gems) as they are panel discussions of the Southern Gothic novel and lectures by notable literary figures like John Berendt, Dorothy Allison, and Felice Picano. Everyone's favorite event? The Stanley and Stella screaming match that takes place in Jackson Square. And don't miss the walking tour of the Quarter; you'll get to visit some of Williams's favorite haunts.

➤ LATE MAR. OR EARLY APR.: The **Crescent City Classic** (✉ 104 Metairie Heights, Metairie, 70001, ☎ 504/861–8686) is a very popular 10-km foot race culminating in a huge party in Audubon Park.

➤ APR.: The **French Quarter Festival** (✉ 100 Conti St., 70130, ☎ 504/522–5730) is a weekend of free music and entertainment for all ages throughout the Quarter. It includes fireworks as well as the world's largest jazz brunch.

➤ EARLY TO MID-APR.: The **Spring Fiesta** (✉ 826 St. Ann St., 70112, ☎ 504/581–1367) spotlights the French Quarter's historic homes and includes a parade and the coronation of a queen.

➤ LATE APR.–EARLY MAY: The **New Orleans Jazz & Heritage Festival** (✉ 1205 N. Rampart St., 70116, ☎ 504/522–4786) at the Fair Grounds involves more than 4,000 musicians.

➤ LATE MAY: The **Greek Festival** (✉ 1200 Robert E. Lee Blvd., 70122, ☎ 504/282–0259) fills the Hellenic Cultural Center with Greek music, food, and crafts. Ouzo and baklava are plentiful.

➤ JUNE: The **Great French Market Tomato Festival** (☎ 504/522–2621) includes cooking demonstrations and tastings at the French Market.

➤ JUNE OR JULY: **New Orleans Wine & Food Experience** (✉ Box 70514, 70172, ☎ 504/529–9463) is a weekend of tasting the products of the best local chefs and beverage managers. Held at the Ernest N. Morial Convention Center, the event features more than 350 wines and 80 restaurants.

➤ JULY 4: The Fourth of July is celebrated in grand style during **Go 4th on the River** (☎ 504/586–8777), a day-long series of music, food, and entertainment events along the riverfront and in Woldenberg Park. A spectacular fireworks display completes the day.

For the last three years, the **Essence Music Festival** (☎ 504/522–4786) has been held over the 4th of July weekend in the Louisiana Superdome. This predominately African-American music festival plans to keep coming back indefinitely.

➤ EARLY SEPT.: **Southern Decadence,** one of the city's largest gay and lesbian events, is held the Sunday of Labor Day weekend. For information, contact Ambush Magazine (✉ 828-A Bourbon St., 70116, ☎ 504/522-8047). One highlight is a parade of elaborately costumed drag queens.

➤ LATE SEPT.: **Words and Music Festival,** an annual event celebrating the birthdate of author William Faulkner, is presented by the Pirate's Alley Faulkner Society (632 Pirate's Alley, at Royal St., 70116, ☎ 504/586–1612). It includes panels, seminars, and readings by famous actors, writers, and musicians.

➤ EARLY TO MID- OCT.: **Art for Art's Sake,** produced by the Contemporary Arts Center (✉ 900 Camp St., 70115, ☎ 504/523–1216), is an upscale street art festival. At the same time galleries in the Warehouse District showcase their own artists. The **Lesbian and Gay Pride Festival** (☎ 504/949–9555), which is both educational and fun, includes lots of live entertainment, multicultural food, and crafts. **New Orleans Film and Video Festival,** hosted in mid-month by the New Orleans Film and Video Society (✉ 225 Baronne St., Suite 1712, 70112, ☎ 504/523–3818), showcases local, regional, and international films, with visits from actors, writers and other industry professionals.The **Swamp Festival** (☎ 504/861–2537) means hands-on contact with live Louisiana swamp animals, Cajun food, music, and crafts at Audubon Zoo.

➤ LATE NOV.–DEC.: From Thanksgiving through December, thousands of tree lights surround Storyland and the Carousel Gardens for the evening **Celebration in the Oaks** at City Park (✉ 1 Dreyfous Ave., 70122, ☎ 504/483–9415). For many New Orleanians, Christmas just isn't Christmas without the mandatory drive through City Park with its dazzling and dramatic assortment of lights.

➤ DEC.: **A New Orleans Christmas** (✉ French Quarter Festival, 100 Conti St., 70130, ☎ 504/522–5730), held December 5–January 5, includes tree lighting, teas, caroling, parades, and open houses. Also included are Réveillon (New Year's) celebrations at various restaurants, including Arnaud's, Begué's, and the Rib Room, which feature special fixed-price menus for the occasion. Special hotel rates are available December 5–25.

➤ DEC. 24: **Christmas Eve bonfires** are lighted on the Mississippi levees in St. James Parish. The bonfires, legend says, originally were lit by the early settlers to help Papa Noël (the Cajun Santa Claus) find his way to their new homes. Residents begin gathering wood for these huge pyres on Thanksgiving. **New Orleans Paddle Wheels** (☎ 504/529–4567) and **New Orleans Steamboat** (☎ 504/586–8777) run boats up the muddy Mississippi for this blazing festival.

➤ DEC. 31: **Countdown** is a huge, televised New Year's Eve celebration in Jackson Square that's similar to the one in New York's Times Square. This is *the place* to be to ring in the year.

WEATHER

In New Orleans, as in most of the South, May through October is hot and humid. Just mustering the energy to raise a mint julep to your lips may cause malaise. During these long, hot summers, the sun shines for as long as 11 hours each day, which may explain why things are less hurried down here—there's lots of time and it's so hard to stay cool. If you visit during these sticky months, you'll find that all hotels and restaurants are air-conditioned and hotel prices are lower.

June through November are the months to watch for heavy rains, and even occasional hurricanes. These conditions occur mainly with quick changes in temperature that accompany cold fronts.

Heavy fogs can occasionally plague the city October–March. Although winters are mild compared to those in northern climes, the high humidity can really put a chill in the air. Don't be surprised to see women wearing fur coats in many of the city's finer establishments.

Perhaps the best time to visit the city is early spring. Days are pleasant, except for seasonal cloudbursts, and nights are cool. The azaleas are in full bloom while the city bustles from one outdoor festival to the next.

The following are average daily maximum and minimum temperatures for New Orleans.

➤ FORECASTS: **Weather Channel Connection** (☎ 900/932–8437), 95¢ per minute from a Touch-Tone phone.

Jan.	62F	17C	May	83F	28C	Sept.	86F	30C
	47	8		68	20		73	23
Feb.	65F	18C	June	88F	31C	Oct.	79F	26C
	50	10		74	23		64	18
Mar.	71F	22C	July	90F	32C	Nov.	70F	21C
	55	13		76	24		55	13
Apr.	77F	25C	Aug.	90F	32C	Dec.	64F	18C
	61	16		76	24		48	9

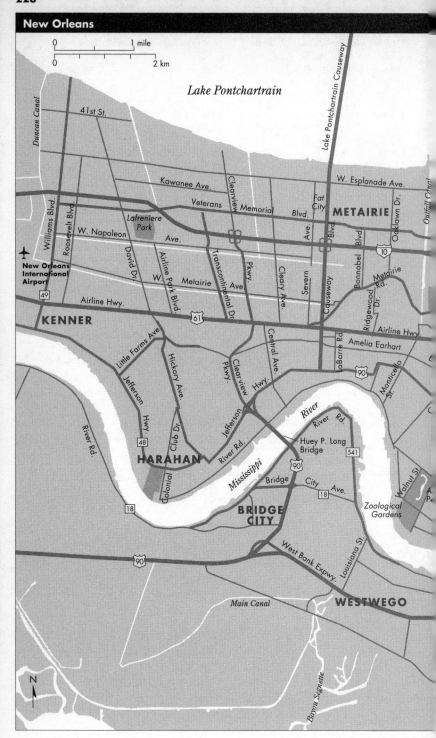

Lake Pontchartrain

41st St.

Kawanee Ave.

W. Esplanade Ave.

Veterans Memorial Blvd.

Fat City

METAIRIE

Lafreniere Park

W. Napoleon Ave.

Clearview

Cleary Ave.

Severn Ave.

Bonnabel Blvd.

Oaklawn Dr.

Outfall Canal

Williams Blvd.

Roosevelt Blvd.

David Dr.

Airline Park Blvd.

W. Metairie Ave.

Transcontinental Dr.

Pkwy.

Causeway

Ridgewood Dr.

Metairie Rd.

Duncan Canal

New Orleans International Airport

49

Airline Hwy.

KENNER

61

Little Farms Ave.

Jefferson Hwy.

Hickory Ave.

Clearview Pkwy.

Central Ave.

Hwy.

LaBarre Rd.

Airline Hwy

Amelia Earhart

90

Monticello St.

River Rd.

Colonial Club Dr.

River Rd.

Jefferson Pkwy.

Lake Pontchartrain Causeway

River

River Rd.

Huey P. Long Bridge

541

Walnut St.

48

HARAHAN

Mississippi

Bridge

City Ave.

18

Zoological Gardens

18

BRIDGE CITY

90

90

West Bank Expwy.

Louisiana St.

WESTWEGO

Main Canal

N

Bayou Segnette

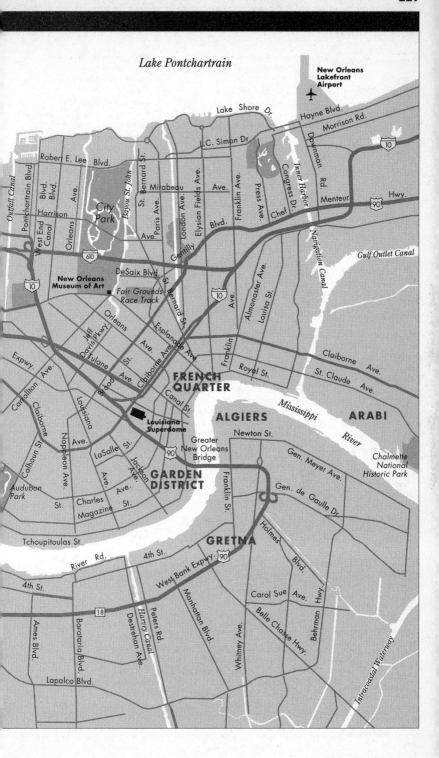

Lake Pontchartrain

New Orleans
Lakefront
Airport

Lake Shore Dr.

Hayne Blvd.

Morrison Rd.

I.C. Simon Dr

Robert E. Lee Blvd.

Outfall Canal

Pontchartrain Blvd

Blvd.

Blvd.

Ave.

City
Park

St. Bernard St.

Bayou St. John

Mirabeau

Paris Ave.

London Ave.

Elysian Fields Ave.

Ave.

Franklin Ave.

Press Ave.

Congress Dr.

Chef

Menteur

Hwy.

Dowman Rd.

Inner Harbor

Navigation Canal

Gulf Outlet Canal

Harrison

West End Canal

Orleans

Ave.

Blvd.

Gentilly

New Orleans
Museum of Art

DeSaix Blvd.

St. Bernard St.

Ave.

Almonaster Ave.

Louisa St.

Fair Grounds
Race Track

Orleans

Jeff
Davis Pkwy.

Tulane

Broad

Ave.

Ave.

St.

Esplanade Ave.

Claiborne Ave.

Franklin

Ave.

Claiborne   Ave.

St. Claude Ave.

Royal St.

**FRENCH
QUARTER**

Carrollton

Expwy.

Ave.

Claiborne St.

Louisiana

Napoleon Ave.

Canal St.

Louisiana
Superdome

ALGIERS

Mississippi

River

ARABI

Calhoun

Ave.

LaSalle St.

Jackson Ave.

St.

Greater
New Orleans
Bridge

Newton St.

Gen. Meyer Ave.

Chalmette
National
Historic Park

Audubon
Park

St.

Charles

Magazine

Ave.

St.

**GARDEN
DISTRICT**

Franklin St.

Gen. de Gaulle Dr.

Tchoupitoulas St.

GRETNA

Holmes

Blvd.

Behrman   Hwy.

River   Rd.

4th St.

West Bank Expwy.

Carol Sue Ave.

4th St.

Ames Blvd.

Barataria Blvd.

Peters Rd.

Harvey Canal

Destrehan Ave.

Manhattan Blvd.

Whitney Ave.

Belle Chasse Hwy.

Intracoastal Waterway

Lapalco Blvd.

230

INDEX

NOTES

FODOR'S NEW ORLEANS 2001

EDITOR: Linda Cabasin

Editorial Contributors: Gene Bourg, Mary Gehman, Paul A. Greenberg, Michaela Morrissey, Honey Naylor

Editorial Production: Brian Vitunic

Maps: David Lindroth Inc., *cartographer;* Rebecca Baer and Bob Blake, *map editors*

Design: Fabrizio La Rocca, *creative director;* Guido Caroti, *art director;* Jolie Novak, *picture editor;* Melanie Marin, *photo researcher*

Cover Design: Pentagram

Production/Manufacturing: Robert Shields

COPYRIGHT

SPECIAL SALES

IMPORTANT TIP

Although all prices, opening times, and other details in this book are based on information supplied to us at press time, changes occur all the time in the travel world, and Fodor's cannot accept responsibility for facts that become outdated or for inadvertent errors or omissions. So always confirm information when it matters, especially if you're making a detour to visit a specific place.

PHOTOGRAPHY

The Image Bank, *Angelo Cavalli, cover* (La Branche House in the French Quarter).

Audubon Institute: *David Bull, 15C.*

Bayona Restaurant, *9F.*

Syndey Byrd, *3 bottom left, 11D, 12B, 12C, 13A, 13B, 16.*

City Park New Orleans, *3 center.*

Owen Franken, *8C, 11E.*

Robert Holmes, *6B, 8B, 9E, 10B, 13C.*

Hotel Maison de Ville and the Audubon Cottages, *3 top right.*

The Image Bank: *Tim Bieber, 4–5. Bullaty & Lomeo, 11F. Luis Castañeda, 6C. Angelo Cavalli, 6A, 7D, 7E, 10C, 14B. Piecework Productions, 8 center right, Harald Sund, 1.*

Keating Magee, *2 top right, 8A.*

Bob Krist, *9D.*

Louisiana Office of Tourism, *2 bottom left, 2 bottom center, 2 bottom right, 3 top left, 3 bottom right, 12A, 14A.*

Louisiana State Museum, *2 top left.*

Preservation Hall, *10A.*

ABOUT OUR WRITERS

Every trip is a significant trip. Acutely aware of that fact, we've pulled out all stops in preparing *Fodor's New Orleans*. To help you zero in on what to see in New Orleans, we've gathered some great color photos. To show you how to put it all together, we've created great itineraries and neighborhood walks. And to direct you to the places that are truly worth your time and money, we've rallied the team of endearingly picky know-it-alls we're pleased to call our writers. Having seen all corners of New Orleans, they're real experts on the subjects they cover for us. If you knew them, you'd poll them for tips yourself.

After nine years as restaurant reviewer for the *Times-Picayune*, **Gene Bourg** now writes on food and travel for national and regional magazines. In 1996 he received the National Magazine Award for a feature article in *Saveur* magazine on the food and culture of Louisiana's Cajuns. He added 11 new restaurants to this year's Dining chapter.

A licensed tour guide and updater of our Exploring chapter (and of the Great Itineraries), **Mary Gehman** has lived in New Orleans for almost three decades. She enjoys sharing the fruits of her research with visitors. The author of two history books about New Orleans, she says that "history doesn't get any livelier than in this city, nor more accessible."

Paul A. Greenberg, who revised the Lodging chapter as well as Smart Travel Tips, is a New Orleans writer with 20 years' experience writing about the City That Care Forgot. His passions include spicy food, southern hospitality, and great jazz. New Orleans is the only place he has ever found that combines all three. A perfect day in his life? Breakfast at Brennan's, shopping in the French Quarter, lunch at Commander's Palace, an ice-cold martini at the Polo Lounge at the Windsor Court, dinner at Mr. B's, and a concert by the Louisiana Philharmonic.

Born under the sign of travel, New Orleans–based **Michaela Morrissey** used her experience writing reviews and reports for the hospitality industry to win her Fodor's gig, covering places old and new for the Nightlife and the Arts chapter. She also added her insights about the Great River Road and Cajun Country to the Side Trips section. A freelance writer and graphic designer, she writes and edits interviews and features for local and national publications as well as Web sites.

Honey Naylor, who has worked on the Side Trips and Shopping chapters, delights in exploring the bayous and byways of South Louisiana and discovering treasures and trifles in Crescent City stores. For this edition, she updated the Shopping and Outdoor Activities and Sports chapters.

Don't Forget to Write

We love feedback—positive and negative—and follow up on all suggestions. So contact the New Orleans editor at editors@fodors.com or c/o Fodor's, 280 Park Avenue, New York, NY 10017. Have a wonderful trip!

Karen Cure
Karen Cure
Editorial Director